Praise for *A History of Human Rights in Canada*

"With all of its plusses, this book will constitute a valuable contribution to Canadian Human Rights literature. It has the potential to become an important work in the growing field of human rights, and makes for a very good publication with cross-disciplinary appeal in areas like political science, sociology, philosophy, and history."

—THE HONOURABLE NOËL A. KINSELLA,
Speaker, Senate of Canada, Professor of Human Rights, past Director,
Atlantic Human Rights Centre, St. Thomas University

"The idea for a book on the history of Canadian human rights is a good one. There is not a similar book in existence. The academy is increasingly turning its attention to human rights. This book would fill a perceived need. The selection of materials reflects state of the art in human rights analysis today."

—CONSTANCE BACKHOUSE,
Distinguished University Professor and University Research Chair
at the Faculty of Law, University of Ottawa

"The text presents some of the important human rights issues that have evolved in Canada over the years. The book helps one appreciate the topics in a new way. This text will add to the corpus of literature on a very important and relevant subject."

—MICHAEL MCGOWAN,
Director, Atlantic Human Rights Centre,
and Professor of Human Rights, St. Thomas University

"[This volume] pulls together a number of human rights issues as they've specifically played out in Canada. The chapters cover issues that are crucial to investigating human rights in Canada."

—BILL SKIDMORE,
Academic Supervisor, Human Rights BA Program, Carleton University

"The book is timely: There is a growing literature on the history of human rights in Canada, and seemingly a great interest in the subject both inside the academy and beyond."

—CARMELA PATRIAS,
Department of History, Brock University

TABLE OF CONTENTS

PREFACE

Canadians have taken pride in the survival of the francophone identity and culture after the British Conquest of New France, the passage of the Act to Limit Slavery in Upper Canada in 1793, and the proverbial Underground Railroad that allowed African Americans to find refuge in British North America. However, the tendency to exalt such events, to contrast Canada's historical record with that of the United States, often obscures critical issues and details and leads to the portrayal of the past as devoid of discrimination and oppression, and instead characterizes it by a tradition of inclusion and tolerance. Despite the stubborn persistence of certain myths and notions, Canadians have increasingly sought to acknowledge and study the instances of injustice that ripple throughout the country's history. Undoubtedly, this is owing to the fact that discrimination and inequality are firmly recognized as matters of public concern. The principle of human rights has now become deeply embedded in our social values and expressions of national identity.

This collection stems from society's widespread interest in human rights, as reflected in popular culture, political discourse, and academia. The contributors represent a diverse array of disciplines ranging from Indigenous Studies to Sociology, and highlight not only the advantages of different perspectives, theoretical frameworks, and methodologies, but, more fundamentally, the importance of studying Canada's past through the paradigm of human rights. While literature that focuses on the working class, women, race and ethnicity, and disability have enriched our understanding of the complexities and workings of power and oppression in Canada's history, only recently has the rubric of "human rights" itself become a prominent analytical approach. The contributors to this collection are at the forefront of this trend. Their chapters serve as testaments to those who suffered discrimination, struggled against injustice, and fought for equality in manifold ways.

It is a pleasure to finally be able to publicly thank specific people who played fundamental roles in this project. First and foremost, I sincerely thank the authors of original chapters for their crucial contributions to this project. They displayed great commitment, engagement, and patience throughout the book's creation and were thoroughly enjoyable to work with from beginning to end. As well, this collection would not have been possible without the help of my colleague Robert Wright, who first approached me about putting together a collection for Canadian Scholars' Press Inc. Furthermore, I am very grateful to Megan Mueller at the press, who consistently offered invaluable insight, direction, and suggestions for improvement. Also, I would like to thank the reviewers of the manuscript: The Honourable Noël A. Kinsella, Speaker of the Senate; Professor Michael McGowan, Director, Human Rights Programme, St. Thomas University; and one anonymous referee, who provided substantive feedback in order to strengthen the book. Finally, I would like to thank the respective publishers for permission to reprint the articles by Michael D. Behiels, Ruth Frager, and Miriam Smith.

INTRODUCTION

F. R. Scott (1899–1985) was a poet, civil libertarian, social democrat, and political theoretician. Co-founder of the League for Social Reconstruction in 1931 and national chairman of the Co-operative Commonwealth Federation from 1942 to 1950, Scott was an outspoken critic of the repressive regime of Quebec's premier Maurice Duplessis and a prominent advocate of freedom of speech and religion. Described as embracing a "lifelong vision of Canada that exemplifies tolerance and social justice,"[1] Scott fought for the rights of minority groups in the courts, in published works, and on the political stage, and was deeply committed to civil liberties and equal rights. Like other activists in the twentieth century, Scott sought to make human rights a characteristic of Canadian culture and, over time, helped to dramatically redefine social attitudes and the role of the government. However, his sense of justice was not without controversy and some of the positions he took in the 1970s were criticized by other rights advocates. In particular, he supported Pierre Elliott Trudeau's implementation of the War Measures Act and suspension of civil liberties during the Front de libération du Québec crisis. Shortly thereafter, he opposed French language legislation enacted by the province of Quebec in an effort to protect the francophone identity.[2] That some of Scott's actions could be interpreted either as upholding rights and liberties or as undermining them reveals fundamental features concerning human rights in general and their specific history in Canada. The example of Scott highlights the fact that notions of human rights are culturally constructed, inextricably tied to specific historical contexts, and often the subject of both conflict and consensus. Indeed, the development of human rights in Canada has been a slow and gradual process marked not only by opposition and struggle, but, at times, unevenness and paradox.

Today many hold the protection and promotion of human rights, equality, and dignity as central to the Canadian national identity. An array of rights are now protected by government institutions, an official policy of multiculturalism, the Charter of Rights and Freedoms, provincial statutes, courts of law, and shared socio-political values and ideals. Internationally, support for human rights is widespread and enshrined in codified laws and constitutions, yet, even within this broader context, Canada is often identified as exceptional in its embrace of an extensive rights culture. According to Michael Ignatieff, "our rights culture ... is the core of what makes us distinctive as a people."[3]

Over the last few years issues and events surrounding equality and social justice have been at the forefront of public concern and political debate both in and outside of

Canada. International events—including the American invasion of Iraq, the "war on terror," and the use of torture—have fostered a growing interest in human rights and their violation, especially when instances of abuse have been sanctioned or perpetuated by democratic governments. While many events have encouraged Canadians to critically reflect upon both their own government and society, current debates and issues cannot be understood or appreciated without an awareness of their broader historical background. Consequently, this book examines many of the marginalized groups in Canadian society who were affected by discrimination and challenged oppression, and the efforts of those, such as Scott, who sought to create a more democratic and inclusive country. It is about the state's use of laws and cabinet directives to control and influence the political, economic, and social lives of Canadians and the instances in which "ordinary" people have either advocated for the expansion of civil liberties or demanded their retraction or restriction.

This book is dedicated to expanding our understanding of human rights in Canada and exploring the complexities involved in the endeavour to identify discrimination and define rights through a study of the past. In his *Human Rights: Concept and Context*, philosopher Brian Orend writes, "Human rights do not tell us who or what we are; rather, they tell us how we should treat our fellow human beings."[4] However, Canada's historical treatment of minority rights does tell us a great deal about how earlier generations sought to define themselves and the society in which they lived, while further highlighting what has both changed and remained the same over time. This history also broadens our knowledge of how different groups were affected by and fought against discriminatory laws, attitudes, and practices, and sheds light on how power historically has operated in Canada.

The articles presented here delineate forms of discrimination in times of both peace and war and deal with a variety of themes, including ethnicity, gender, sexuality, class, and disability. Tracing the constantly changing definition of human rights over time, the authors examine the violation of civil liberties in Canada's past and discriminatory attitudes in government and greater society, as well as the people who challenged injustices and struggled to create a more open and tolerant society. Three key issues are concentrated on in the book: incidents of discrimination, the efforts of human rights and civil liberties activists, and the implementation of state legislation designed to protect or enhance civil rights. The book encompasses a broad definition of human rights pertaining to inequality, injustice, and discrimination in economic, political, and socio-cultural realms, rather than limiting discussion to a minimalist definition of basic legal rights, and further deals with both individual and group rights. Each chapter focuses on a specific theme, group of people, or event. The focus is not meant to imply that these are the most vital issues in the history of human rights in Canada and no attempt has been made to provide a thorough or comprehensive overview. Rather, it is hoped that the chapters offered here will incite interest and encourage readers to pursue further study into the growing number of publications that focus on human rights.

In spite of a strong contemporary human rights culture, Canada's history is characterized by a long tradition of discrimination and a very slow evolution of commitment to protecting human rights. As Gary Kinsman, Dieter K. Buse, and Mercedes Steedman write, "The features of Canadian state formation were historically based on the subordination of indigenous peoples, Québécois, and Acadians ... The state's primary goal has never been to protect the security of Canadian working-class people, immigrants, lesbians, gay men, and women in general."[5] In contrast to the United States' Bill of Rights and constitutional guarantees of civil liberties and individual rights, the British North America Act of 1867 offered explicit protection only in regard to language rights and religion through denominational schools. British common law was assumed to provide sufficient protection for civil liberties. The term "human rights" was rarely voiced prior to the mid-twentieth century in Canada, yet today the concept is widely employed and a popular discourse of rights resonates across the country. Aside from their constitutional entrenchment within the Charter of Rights and Freedoms in 1982, principles of human rights have influenced educational policy, the criminal justice system, employment equity or affirmative action programs, social policy, and family policy.[6] Laws now provide (at least in theory) equal rights regardless of sexual orientation, gender, ethnicity, or disability. In Canada, homosexuals have the right to marry, women have the right to an abortion, overtly racist immigration laws have been abolished, and all Canadians have the right to medical care. As well, memorials and plaques have been erected to recognize the suffering experienced by some Canadians, and redress and apology have become significant elements of human rights political discourse. These gestures symbolize the importance of acknowledging instances of abuse and ensuring that they hold a place in the nation's collective memory.[7]

Historians, sociologists, political scientists, and others have been examining different dimensions of this history and have created a vibrant and growing field of academic scholarship. The contributors to this collection in many ways are at the forefront of the establishment of human rights as a critical field of scholarly analysis. They represent a broad spectrum of disciplinary backgrounds and employ a variety of methodological and theoretical approaches. Together they highlight the ways in which the historiography of human rights is not simply about documenting specific instances of injustice, but it is also about the broader implications and complexities of power, discrimination, and cultural ideas and practices. In particular, many of the authors explore the often unacknowledged efforts of historical actors who challenged discriminatory structures. Ross Lambertson, Dominique Clément, and Stephanie Bangarth focus on human rights advocates to reveal both the challenges they faced and the ways in which the human rights movement itself changed over time. In two articles, Lambertson discusses human rights activism in the pre-

1960s period and links together the different struggles for egalitarian and libertarian rights, providing an insightful analysis of the factors that compelled people to rise up and resist oppression. Also focusing on state protection of human rights and the emergence of grass roots movements, Clément compares the notoriety of the American civil rights movement with Canadians' limited familiarity with their own history. Situating Canada within the international context, he argues that the revolution in human rights has been characterized in part by limitation and examines the variables necessary for the full realization of human rights. In particular, he sees the state as critical to their enforcement and entrenchment in the public realm. Bangarth focuses on the Second World War era and specific ethnic groups, and documents the transformation of a rights discourse in Canada, which initially revolved around notions of British liberties. She delineates the convergence of minority groups (in this case, Chinese and Japanese Canadians) with white, middle-class liberals in the 1940s in an effort to redefine the Canadian socio-political landscape and initiate an early human rights community. The chapter by Ruth Frager also concentrates on ethnicity and race, but deals with the internal divisions and discriminatory attitudes labour activists confronted in attempting to improve working conditions.

The accomplishment and effects of legislative change is also a prominent theme in this book. Michael D. Behiels discusses the political factors that led to the introduction of the Charter of Rights and Freedoms and emphasizes the pivotal role played by Pierre Elliott Trudeau. Without neglecting political history, Matthew Hayday concentrates on the broader social and cultural issues connected to language legislation in Quebec. He argues that language rights did not follow a clear trajectory in Canadian history, but instead were increasingly restricted over the late nineteenth and twentieth centuries only to be significantly strengthened in the post–Second World War period, especially with the passage of the Charter. Also experiencing significant strengthening in the 1980s, gay and lesbian rights in Canada symbolize to many how much progress has been made in the contemporary period. On this topic, Miriam Smith not only addresses the legal impact of the Charter on the expansion of gay and lesbian rights, but also assesses the effects judicial empowerment had on social movement politics.

By concentrating on specific social, ethnic, or demographic populations and the construction of identities, many of the contributors investigate elements of political culture, law, and thinking in Canada. While assessing the successes and limitations of the movement in protecting children, Dominique Marshall traces international recognition of children's rights and Canada's important role in this process. Her study attests to the ways in which commitment to rights can be unpredictable and not deliberate, yet, over time, become universally supported. Also situating Canada in the international context, Barrington Walker reveals the ways in which the term "Jim Crow" can be employed to refer to a Canadian culture of jurisprudence that helped to entrench racist policies, including segregation. In doing so, he links racist ideologies in Canada with those of the

United States, thereby transcending conventional geopolitical boundaries. By unravelling the paradoxes and contradictions of nineteenth- and twentieth-century liberal ideas of "race," he reminds us that racism need not be formally embedded in legal codes to be both insipid and powerful. David T. McNab also examines race relations, but concentrates on Canada's First Peoples. Tracing the history of denial and betrayal from the early colonial period to the present time, he challenges many misconceptions and assumptions that are evident in contemporary interpretations and presents the Canadian nation-state as consistent in its efforts to deny the rights of Indigenous peoples. Jana Grekul turns our attention to another marginalized group, those labelled "mentally unfit." She highlights the ways in which a dichotomy of "fit" versus "unfit" was employed by government and medical authorities to deny individuals control over their bodies and to undermine fundamental rights and freedoms.

Although some of the articles delve into earlier periods, this collection has a strong focus on post-Confederation Canada, especially the interwar and post-Second World War era. Prior to the mid-twentieth century, prejudice permeated socio-cultural, economic, political, medical, and legal realms; racism, sexism, and other forms of discrimination were systemically and formally perpetuated by the state and informally by dominant groups in society. Discrimination was public, private, and pervasive. First Nations peoples faced a barrage of government-supported incentives designed to eliminate their cultures and traditional ways of life, policies that ranged from residential schools to removal and relocation programs. The Indian Act of 1876 and subsequent amendments to it were perhaps the greatest vestige of assimilationist policies. At various points throughout its history, the Indian Act restricted people's rights to move freely, associate with others, and practice cultural activities, and it also contained provisions designed to dissolve ethnic identity. Other ethnic groups experienced profound racism regardless of whether they were immigrants or Canadian-born. Many examples of the deep-rooted and often deadly nature of discrimination in Canada have become entrenched in popular memory, including the expulsion of the Acadians, the Chinese Head Tax in effect from 1885 to 1923, the *Komagatu Maru* in 1914, the *St. Louis* in 1939, the segregation of Black Canadians, and the internment of Japanese Canadians during the Second World War. Both political dissent and labour activism were suppressed and closely monitored by the state, and consequences for "agitators" ranged from arrest to deportation. Police surveillance was often used to try to enforce political and "moral" conformity and to intimidate Canadians into adhering to heterosexual, gendered, and capitalist mores. A fear of communism, homosexuality, and women's liberation activism led to human rights violations for decades, and ranged from Duplessis's notorious Padlock Law in 1937 to the RCMP spying on folk singer Rita MacNeil in the 1970s.

Very gradually, and often in a piecemeal fashion, Canada changed from being a racist, heterosexist society dominated by an elite that wanted to keep Canada white, British, and Christian to a society that is multi-ethnic, based on ideals of inclusive democracy, and distinguished by an array of social programs and policies aimed at protecting citizens from discrimination and ensuring a certain standard of living. What precipitated this dramatic transformation and commitment to human rights? As many of the authors in this book show, both national and international factors helped foster changes in Canada. The formation of the United Nations in 1945, the passage of the Universal Declaration of Human Rights in 1948, and a number of other important international covenants on human rights were both the cause and effect of many changes and demonstrated that a major ideological and political transformation was taking place. In addition, radical, democratic, and anti-imperialism movements appeared throughout the world, including the African American civil rights movement in the United States. Horror at the atrocities committed during the war, international pressures, and a changing socio-political climate precipitated a paradigm shift in thinking.

Factors within Canada were equally if not more important than international ones in stimulating tangible changes both in Canadian government and the greater society. In particular, waves of political, labour, and social activism rose across the country, challenging the status quo and forcing Canadians to confront antiquated conventions and rethink their perspective of the government and treatment of fellow Canadians. The efforts of activists led to a shift in morality and a change in attitudes towards racism, sexism, and other forms of discrimination, thereby inaugurating what has been identified as an age of rights. The emergence of the second-wave women's movement sought to address equality issues affecting Canadians and was especially concerned with liberation and disparate standards of living. As well, First Nations increasingly organized against assimilationist policies, demanding self-determination and protection of their cultures. Gays and lesbians, many of whom were inspired by New York's Stonewall Riots in 1969, mobilized to confront homophobia and inequality. Francophones in Quebec endeavoured to transform their society and protect their culture, in large part to overcome domination by an English-speaking minority. Religious associations, civil liberties groups, ethnic organizations, women's groups, and trade unions struggled to improve society through a range of activities including demonstrations, public meetings, boycotts, litigation, rallies, strikes, and coalition building. As the human rights movement coalesced and moved from a focus on group rights to a broader commitment to universal values,[8] activists finally found a climate receptive to their aims and visions. Economic prosperity helped facilitate changes: social welfare programs were expanded, federal and provincial governments slowly enacted laws that enshrined the country's commitment to human rights, and education levels rose across the country (albeit unevenly). Gradually, immigration policies were revised and legislation aimed at protecting the rights of minorities was enacted. What one gay activist described as "the irrepressible human desire for liberty and dignity"[9] had inspired profound sociological and political change in Canada.

Consequently, as Ross Lambertson has argued, "Canada moved from being a society drenched in prejudice and discrimination to one that was far more willing to tolerate (and even embrace) ethnic and religious diversity."[10]

These changes certainly did not represent a panacea for all Canadians and an end to discrimination. The rights revolution has not dissolved inequality nor has everyone benefited to the same degree. For example, wage disparity between men and women persists and First Nations still face profound discrimination in the courts, Parliament, and greater society. Job insecurity and inadequate access to medical care plague the lives of many, child poverty persists, and immigrant domestic or child-care workers are placed in exploitative positions by government policies[11]. Furthermore, many are skeptical of the very premise of the human rights movement. Critics question not only the effectiveness of the movement, but the fundamental issues, principles, and actions behind it. Some have charged that the Charter and ensuing dominance of court action have had a conservatizing effect on social movements; the emphasis on litigation has compelled activists to work within the conventions of pre-existing institutions, thereby hindering the possibility of progressive social change.[12] While the political left generally has been at the forefront in advocating strong civil rights protections and equality, some have criticized the rights movement as a bourgeois agenda that obfuscates endemic inequalities created by capitalism.[13] Others have interpreted the international discourse of human rights as a western attempt to impose its values and attitudes on other countries and cultures. Yet another concern highlights the tension between individual and group rights. For example, some First Nation treaty rights, such as fishing rights, have been interpreted by some as impinging on the rights of others. Similarly, some have charged that Quebec's language laws undermine the rights of individuals to choose freely the language of the workplace and of education for their children. Right-wing political parties have historically represented the most vocal adversary to human rights movements and, seeing the Charter as a threat to democracy, have argued that the courts should not be determining legal rights and public policy. Furthermore, the argument persists that rather than creating identity and serving as an instrument for nation building, human rights and related policies have fostered division and created fragmented identities.[14]

There will always be challenges to the status quo, new definitions of what constitutes discrimination will arise over time, and not all Canadians will support the broadening of either individual or group rights. Nevertheless, decades of history have shown that most want social values and political ideals like equality, non-discrimination, compassion, and communal responsibility to be a definitive part of the Canadian identity. The essays in this collection attest to the resiliency of these notions and the strength and determination of both familiar and unacknowledged Canadians who struggled to instill a sense of social justice in the Canadian consciousness.

Notes

1   Thomas R. Berger, *Fragile Freedoms: Human Rights and Dissent in Canada*, revised edition (Toronto: Irwin Publishing, 1982), 264.

2   See Allen Mills, "Of Charters and Justice: The Social Thought of F. R. Scott, 1930–1985," *Journal of Canadian Studies* 32, no. 1 (1997): 44–62.

3   Michael Ignatieff, *The Rights Revolution* (Toronto: Anansi, 2000), 13–14.

4   Brian Orend, *Human Rights: Concept and Context* (Peterborough: Broadview Press, 2002), 19.

5   Gary Kinsman, Dieter K. Buse, Mercedes Steedman, "How the Centre Holds—National Security as an Ideological Practice," in Gary Kinsman, Dieter K. Buse, Mercedes Steedman, eds., *Whose National Security? Canadian State Surveillance and the Creation of Enemies* (Toronto: Between the Lines, 2000), 281.

6   Miriam Smith, *Lesbian and Gay Rights in Canada: Social Movements and Equality-Seeking, 1971–1995* (Toronto: University of Toronto Press, 1999), 11.

7   For example, in 1988, the Mulroney government apologized to the Japanese Canadians for their internment during the Second World War and, in 2008, the Harper government apologized to First Nations peoples for residential schools.

8   On this transformation, see Ross Lambertson, *Repression and Resistance: Canadian Human Rights Activists, 1930–1960* (Toronto: University of Toronto Press, 2005).

9   Maurice Flood, "Editorial," *Gay Tide* (August 1973): 2, cited in Smith, *Lesbian and Gay Rights in Canada*, 3.

10 Lambertson, *Repression and Resistance,* 376.

11 For example, see Song Gao et al., "Access to Health Care among Status Aboriginal People with Chronic Kidney Disease," *Canadian Medical Association Journal* 179, no. 10 (2008): 1007–1012; Children's Aid Society of Toronto, "Greater Trouble in Greater Toronto: Child Poverty in the GTA" (December 2008), www.casmt.on.ca; Sedef Arat-Koç, "Importing Housewives: Non-citizen Domestic Workers and the Crisis of the Domestic Sphere in Canada," in Meg Luxton, Harriet Rosenberg, and Sedef Arat-Koç, eds., *Through the Kitchen Window: The Politics of Home and Family*, 2nd ed. (Toronto: Garamond Press, 1990).

12 Smith, *Lesbian and Gay Rights*, 18.

13 Lambertson, *Repression and Resistance*, 15.

14 For example, see Neil Bissoondath, *Selling Illusions: The Cult of Multiculturalism in Canada* (Toronto: Penguin Books, 1992).

PART I

Activism and
Human Rights Movements

DOMINATION AND DISSENT:
EQUALITY RIGHTS BEFORE WORLD WAR II

ROSS LAMBERTSON

> Power concedes nothing without a demand. It never did and it never will. Find out just what any people will quietly submit to and you have found out the exact measure of injustice and wrong which will be imposed upon them, and these will continue till they are resisted with either words or blows, or with both. The limits of tyrants are prescribed by the endurance of those whom they oppress.
>
> —FREDERICK DOUGLASS, 1849[1]

Introduction

This chapter examines conflict between human rights abusers and those who resist domination, with special reference to the history of human rights in Canada in the years prior to the Second World War. It focuses on the right of equality and touches upon the struggles of a number of minorities.

Given the predominant social values of the day, as well as the limited protections in the Constitution, people fighting for equality were often fatally handicapped. Although there were some successes, such as the granting of voting rights for women, racial and religious discrimination remained an integral part of the Canadian experience. The so-called "Rights Revolution" would not take place for years to come.

Canadian Human Rights History

Canadian human rights history can be seen as a dialectical dance between those who wished to deny others the enjoyment of human rights, and resistance on the part of those who were denied these rights.[2] The goal of the historian is therefore twofold: to understand why and how the forces of the status quo have oppressed and exploited different minorities,[3] and to understand why and how these groups have resisted—the way demands for justice arose, how they were transformed into political action, and the reasons why they either succeeded or failed.

While many Canadian historians have tackled specific examples of human rights struggles, such as the women's movement, race relations, labour history, "Queer history,"

First Nations history, etc., few generalizations link them together. A general theory about the "why" of oppression or domination might begin with the concept of self-interest, exacerbated by both egocentrism and fear. It is usually difficult for people who benefit from the economic-social-political status quo to give up their privileges, especially when this means transcending their egocentrism to recognize the legitimacy of other points of view.[4] Of course, sometimes the privileged may believe that they are acting altruistically, but often their paternalism is not in the best interests of those whom they see as "the other"—for example, Aboriginal children forced into residential schools. Moreover, when any group is viewed as a threat to core values or interests, there is likely to be severe repression. It is no accident, for example, that discrimination against Asian Canadians was strongest when they were feared both as socially inassimilable and as economic threats.

To understand repression, however, we have to examine the values of those who enjoy power and privilege. In Canadian history, this means looking at such things as the patriarchal notions of women primarily as homemakers, ideas about "racial" superiority, liberal values about the sanctity of private property, and conservative beliefs in the importance of moral regulation.[5]

As for the "how" of domination and repression, here too there is little theoretical analysis. We can say, however, that it occurs at both the governmental and non-governmental level. At the governmental level, the state can help to promote ideas and perceptions (such as racism and sexism) that inhibit attitudes about human rights.[6] It can also deny human rights explicitly, refuse to guarantee them, or support them in theory but not in practice. Yet society (as opposed to government) can also abridge human rights; Canadian history is littered with stories of non-governmental rights violations, ranging from mob violence to petty acts of individual discrimination.[7]

Some of the earliest human rights historiography tended to portray certain oppressed groups as "hapless victims" who accepted their fate.[8] However, more recent historians have focused on the resistance of particular ethnic groups. Without denying that the subjects of their studies were *victimized*, these historians have stressed their resistance to victimization. In other words, the emphasis has shifted from passivity to agency.[9]

This is closely tied to another theoretical issue: how much is the resistance of the victimized a fight against not just unjust laws and social discrimination, but against the very values of society? For example, some feminists have written of the need to free themselves from the "interior colonization" of patriarchal values, while Marxists have suggested that "false consciousness" caused by the hegemony of capitalist values stands in the way of proletarian freedom. Recently, several Canadian human rights historians have argued that early twentieth-century ideas about "race" were so all-pervasive and generally accepted that they constituted a sort of "common sense" perspective.[10]

Other thinkers, however, discount the impact of domination through ideas.

Some Critical Race Theory academics, for example, have argued that, at least when it comes to members of the Black community in North America, it is not false consciousness but rather coercion (including the racist values of others) that is the real source of repression.[11] Similarly, the American anthropologist James C. Scott has concluded, after examining both anthropological and historical literature on a wide variety of situations such as slavery, serfdom, colonialism, and even Communist societies, that people usually reject the legitimizing ideology of their oppressors, and only resist openly when it is safe. Otherwise, he argues, they dissent and resist at a more subterranean level that he calls "infrapolitics," which includes everything from illegal behaviour to evasion and foot dragging. "When the grand lord passes," he notes, quoting an Ethiopian proverb, "the wise peasant bows deeply and silently farts."[12]

Probably the truth lies somewhere in between. You can fool some of the people some of the time, P.T. Barnum is alleged to have said, but you cannot fool all of them all of the time, he also concluded. Domination is achieved through a mixture of ideas and naked force, appeals to legitimacy, and reliance on fear. Only the proportions differ from time to time and from situation to situation.

One way of persuading people that their treatment is legitimate is by appealing to principles. For example, the alleged principle of racial superiority helped to sustain the treatment of non-whites in Canada. Yet most societies are based on a variety of principles, many of which are somewhat open-ended and capable of different interpretations. This means that both oppressors and oppressed can appeal to the same principles to legitimize their very different positions. In fact, buttressing an exploitive status quo with principled arguments may create ideological leverage. The oppressed can, in effect, argue: "You say that you believe in such-and-such, but you are not living up to your principles in the way you are treating us."[13] Guilt and shame can be powerful political weapons.

Violations of Egalitarian Rights

Since 1867 Canada has been a predominantly liberal society, with two key leverage points: the principles of liberty and equality. While the exact meaning of these two terms has been, and continues to be, politically contested, people striving for "justice" have usually focused their attention on one or the other of these ideals. This chapter focuses on the latter—violations of what we can call egalitarian human rights, which resulted in demands to be treated as equals and not as second-class citizens by either the state or other members of society.[14]

In the early years of Canadian history, a period of "nation-building," the socio-political status quo in Canada was profoundly inegalitarian, favouring those members of the developing nation who were white, British, middle class, Protestant, male, heterosexual, and in moderately good health.[15] In other words, discrimination against the working class, members of certain ethnic and religious groups, women, gays or lesbians, and people with significant physical or mental disabilities was far more prevalent than today. Indeed, not just nativist racism, but also sexism, heterosexism, and other discriminatory "isms" were widely considered to be "common sense," legitimizing the position of those who benefited from the status quo.

Consequently, governments often denied equality to certain minorities. In the early years of Confederation the vote was denied to anyone without a certain amount of property, an amount that varied from province to province. (Electoral history is complicated, because at certain periods a denial of the vote at the provincial level automatically disenfranchised a person at the federal level.)[16]

Women too were denied the vote during this early period, and the law also subordinated them in other ways, including what might be called an "iron ceiling" on employment opportunities. Demands for equality, however, were seen by most men and even some women as a threat to traditional family life. For some, like Stephen Leacock (writing as a political economist, not a humourist), giving in to these demands would engender a declining birth rate, which in turn would lead to race suicide.[17]

Chinese, Japanese, and Indo-Canadians also encountered disenfranchisement and employment discrimination. For example, British Columbia and Saskatchewan barred Asians from voting, as did Ottawa in some cases. Asians were feared because they were viewed as unfair economic competitors, but also because they were considered to be incapable of assimilation; Sir John A. Macdonald remarked that persons of Chinese origin should not have the vote because they had "no British instincts or British feelings or aspirations." Consequently, they were forbidden to work in certain jobs or to practice certain middle-class professions in British Columbia, and they suffered the additional indignity of exclusionist measures designed to keep most of them out of the country at a time when Canada welcomed the "right" immigrants with open arms.[18]

Jews and "Negroes" also encountered prejudice. Neither group was ever denied the vote or prohibited by law from working in any jobs, but both were nevertheless regarded as inappropriate elements of the developing nation, and therefore were often excluded by federal immigration policies. Moreover, several provinces instituted what Canadians today like to think of as a quintessentially American institution—school segregation. Indeed, Nova Scotia retained some separate schools for Blacks until the 1960s.[19]

Most other immigrants entered the country easily and did not normally encounter governmental discrimination, although for a while Manitoba had a literacy franchise qualification clearly aimed at recent immigrants of Polish, Ukrainian, and Russian extraction. However, during the First World War the federal government disenfranchised naturalized Canadians born in an enemy country and interned a great many Ukrainian Canadians, mistakenly assuming that they were "enemy aliens" and therefore disloyal.[20]

Catholics formed another "outsider" category. Most Catholics were also French Canadian, so the issue of religious prejudice was often tied up with tensions between what was then called "the two founding races." Nativists, however, attacked Irish Catholics as readily as they opposed francophone Catholics, and several populist western provincial governments blocked the spread of Catholic denominational schools as well as placing limits on the spread of the French language outside Quebec.[21]

Three religious groups, Doukhobors, Mennonites, and Hutterites, were also the victims of state-based human rights violations. Doukhobors were disenfranchised during World War I (along with Mennonites), and again from 1934 to1955, ostensibly because they were pacifists, but partly because they were so different from mainstream Canadians. At different times all three groups resisted attempts to educate their children in public schools, fearing that this would lead to assimilation into an English-speaking secular culture.[22]

Aboriginals also suffered. Some of their resistance to Canadian domination consisted of such things as the armed resistance of the Métis under Louis Riel in 1870 and 1885, and the continued refusal of the Nisga'a of British Columbia to accept that their Aboriginal title had been shunted aside,[23] but Ottawa also denied them the vote and created a pass system to keep them on reserves and isolate them from mainstream society. Yet the government did provide for a transition from internal "foreigner" to "citizen" status. Under certain conditions assimilated Aboriginals could give up their status as native Indians in return for all the rights and privileges of "white" citizens. Moreover, the government facilitated this cultural destruction in a remarkably insensitive fashion through such policies as the banning of the potlatch and the Sun Dance,[24] as well as compulsory education in residential schools.[25]

All of these minorities encountered unofficial (non-governmental) discrimination as well. Canadians also frequently pulled back the welcome mat for those "strangers at our gates" who had squeezed through. In addition to well-publicized incidents such as the anti-Asian riots in Vancouver in 1908,[26] or the appearance of the Ku Klux Klan on more than one occasion,[27] it was acceptable to refuse service in a restaurant or hotel to someone whose presence might alienate the other customers. It was equally part of the common-sense world of Canadians to refuse employment to people who were seen as "just not fitting in." These informal barriers to the privileges and advantages of citizenship in a supposedly upwardly mobile liberal society were (and to some degree still are) primarily directed at visible minorities, especially Asians, Blacks, and Aboriginals, but there was also considerable prejudice against Jews and any non-British group obviously "just off the boat," such as Ukrainian Canadians.[28]

Of course, it was not just the First Nations peoples and certain immigrants who were denied equality by the privileged members of society. As noted earlier, the prevailing attitudes of the day accepted and normalized discrimination for a wide variety of reasons, including race, religion, sex/gender, sexual orientation, and physical or mental disabilities. For example, the notion that the natural order of things involved a bread-winning male in the workplace and wife/mother at home led to wide acceptance of gender-based employment discrimination. It was also common and acceptable in those days for males to exclude women from their clubs and associations.[29] Discrimination against other groups in the workplace, public services and recreation, housing, and so forth, was so common as to go almost unremarked—and certainly unopposed—by most mainstream members of Canadian society.

Resistance to Discrimination

Yet repression frequently engendered resistance. There are many examples of courageous individuals refusing to accept discrimination at both the state and non-state levels. For example, in the 1880s the city of Victoria passed a bylaw that discriminated against Chinese laundry owners. A resident of Victoria named Mee Wah challenged the legality of this bylaw and won his case.[30] A few years later, in the 1890s, an Ontario law school informed a young woman named Clara Brett Martin that she and other females were ineligible for admission. She fought successfully to gain entry, then pursued her studies in the face of "taunting, hissing, vicious classroom sexual harassment, and unprecedented media attention."[31]

Success, however, usually came more easily if one was part of an organization. As a result, the story of human rights in Canada is less the histories of individual resistance than narratives about the struggles of groups, especially what political scientists call "advocacy groups,"[32] and a look at the literature on the political resistance of ethnic, religious, and women's groups reveals a number of patterns. For example, most political resistance to inequality (aside from labour and socialist resistance to capitalist inequities) falls roughly into two categories: litigation and lobbying.[33] Both these options were possible, and to some extent effective, because Canada was a liberal society and Canadians were not *in principle* opposed to equality. What different groups had to do was convince either a court or a legislature (sometimes Ottawa, sometimes the provinces) that the principle of equality should be interpreted favourably.

When it came to litigation, the potential leverage came primarily from the constitution, but since Canada did not have an American-style bill of rights, most litigation was doomed to fail. True, the British North America Act did contain a few explicit protections of what we today would call human rights: francophone rights in the federal Parliament and courts, anglophone rights in the Quebec National Assembly and courts, and the right of Protestants and Catholics to any separate denominational schools that had existed at the time of Confederation. However, although Catholic (francophone) minorities tried to use the latter protection on several occasions, they were largely unsuccessful, as anglophone Protestants, including the nativist and inaptly named Equal Rights Association, did their best in the nineteenth century to make Canada outside Quebec as "British" as possible.[34]

The BNA Act also incorporated certain British constitutional principles, one of which was the "Rule of Law" (usually written in adulatory capital letters). This concept, which means in part that neither the government nor any person in government is above the law, put limits on the powers of both Ottawa and the provinces.[35] (Of course, governments can change the law, but only according to the Constitution, itself a form of law.) For example, in 1921 Eliza Sero, a member of the Mohawk Nation in Ontario, asked the courts for damages because a fishery inspector had seized and confiscated her seine net. The government claimed that she was illegally fishing without a licence, but Sero, supported by the Six Nations of Grand River, claimed that the seizure was illegal because provincial laws did not apply to Mohawks living within Mohawk territory. This was therefore an egalitarian rights case in the sense that the Mohawks consider themselves a collective group equal to the Canadian state. Unfortunately for Sero, this argument was not acceptable to the judge hearing the case, who quickly dismissed notions of treaty rights and Aboriginal sovereignty. This and other cases made it clear that the legal leverage of the Canadian legal system was limited indeed for Indigenous people. Just in case, however, in 1927 the federal government amended the Indian Act, making it illegal to raise money for claims to Aboriginal title. This flagrant violation of fundamental legal rights remained until 1951.[36]

The rule of law also means that all people are to be considered equal before the law. Not surprisingly then when immigrant Chinese (such as the previously mentioned Mee Wah) encountered governmental discrimination in nineteenth-century British Columbia, they frequently took to the courts for redress. But the precise meaning of the rule of law depended upon the values of those who interpreted it. Although the earlier BC judges were predisposed towards formal equality for Asians, by the twentieth century it was clear that governmental discrimination would not be struck down by the judiciary who now breathed the same racist "common sense" air as did the politicians and voters. [37]

The rule of law provides extra leverage when it is yoked to a written constitution, as is the case with Canada, for the legislatures can discriminate only if, and to the extent that, the Constitution permits them to do so. The federal-provincial division of powers in the BNA Act therefore provides possible leverage points. Yet when Tomekichi Homma, acting on behalf of the local Japanese-Canadian community, went to court to challenge a BC law that denied him the vote, the law was determined to be constitutional. Similarly, when Quong Wing challenged a Saskatchewan law prohibiting Chinese people from employing "white" women in restaurants and laundries (ostensibly to protect them from sexual exploitation), it also turned out to be constitutional. It was clear by the early twentieth century that further litigation would be fruitless.[38]

When it came to discrimination by private citizens rather than governments, the resisters relied on provincial law. For example, in 1898 a concert hall in Montreal refused to let Frederick Johnson sit in the orchestra section because he was Black. He sued for breach of contract on the grounds that his ticket was an agreement to admit him to the performance. He was successful, but it became clear in a later case that Blacks had little to gain from litigation. When Fred Christie was refused admission to the tavern at the Montreal Forum, he argued that the establishment had a legal obligation to serve him, and with the support of an ad hoc organization called The Fred Christie Defence Committee, he took his case all the way to the Supreme Court of Canada. In 1939, however, the judges dismissed his claim, ruling that freedom of commerce was a more important legal principle than racial equality.[39]

The years leading up to World War II, therefore, were years of trial and error, with ethnic groups gradually realizing that any further progress towards equality would probably not proceed through litigation. Yet lobbying was a sort of political roulette, with the odds clearly stacked in favour of the "house."

Perhaps the most successful struggles were those of the suffragists. In 1877 they began lobbying for equality by founding the innocuously named Toronto Women's Literary Society,[40] and by the end of the First World War they had almost completely succeeded in achieving votes for "white" women.[41] In addition, women won a landmark struggle through litigation. In the 1929 *Persons* case, five well-known and determined feminists persuaded what was then Canada's highest court, the Judicial Committee of the Privy Council, to interpret the BNA Act in such a way as to permit women to be appointed to the Senate.

But ethnic groups won few equality rights concessions in the pre-war era. In 1922, the Chinese community in Victoria managed to prevent the city from segregating its school system, but on the larger issue of immigration restrictions the Chinese were unsuccessful. Beginning in 1886, Ottawa imposed a "head tax" on Chinese immigrants, and then in 1923 barred the gates almost completely. The Chinese Benevolent Association lobbied Ottawa for an amendment to the Chinese Immigration Act, but the barriers remained until after the Second World War.[42]

The Japanese-Canadian community had somewhat better luck with immigration law; Ottawa also restricted their entry, but in a way that was less severe and somewhat less insulting.[43] Yet they were totally unsuccessful when, in 1936, a delegation from the Japanese Canadian Citizens League addressed a House of Commons committee, arguing that they were entitled to all the rights of Canadian citizens. The reactions of the MPs were not encouraging. One patronizing committee member commended the second-generation delegates on their "splendid command of the English language," and another influential MP believed that intermarriage between Asians and Whites would usually produce "a mongrel wastrel with the worst qualities of both races."[44] It was clear that progress was unlikely until there was a shift in the attitudes of those leading the two governing parties, the Liberals and the Conservatives.

True, political pressure can sometimes lead to value shifts and policy changes, but minority ethnic groups wielded little clout during this period. They were often fragmented by class, regional, religious, or even generational divisions. Moreover, most recent immigrants, especially Asians in British Columbia who were excluded from middle-class professions, may have had trouble financing political struggles. Finally, Canada was largely "a multiplicity of ethnic solitudes."[45] In the face of white supremacist pressures, one might have expected a coalescing of ethnic minority groups, but such was not normally the case. For example, discrimination against Blacks does not appear to have been regarded as a human rights issue of interest to other minority groups, nor did discrimination against Asians elicit much reaction from Blacks or Jews.

This was partly caused by external forces. Chinese and Japanese Canadians, for example, were at odds when Japanese troops invaded Manchuria in the 1930s. At other times, however, ethnic divisions seem to have been intensified by the competition inherent in Canada's vertical mosaic; groups that were not entirely "respectable" could often take comfort in the fact that they were, at least, not as "disreputable" as other groups lower down the scale, and consequently they strove to maintain their relatively superior positions. While these groups refused to accept the subordinate status imposed on them by the racism of the day, they usually swallowed the rest of the "common sense" ideology.[46]

Other potential allies also found it difficult to transcend these racial divisions.

Women's groups, frequently imbued with the moral purity perspective, often embraced a genteel but toxic middle-class nativist bias.[47] Moreover, labour organizations were often among the strongest supporters of ethnic discrimination, engendered or exacerbated by an economic system largely unbuffered by legal protections from cutthroat competition. Without minimum wage laws, for example, Asians could undercut the bargaining power of "white" workers, who therefore often demanded legislation to keep them out of certain jobs.[48]

Admittedly, there were a few exceptions to this rule of subcultural isolationism. For example, in the early part of the twentieth century the plight of Aboriginal peoples led an Anglican missionary, Arthur O'Meara, to create an egalitarian rights group called the Society of Friends of the Indians of British Columbia. For a while this organization educated the public and helped to raise money in support of First Nations' land claims.[49] Also, the Sikhs' Khalsa Diwan society acted on behalf of all South Asians in Canada in the early part of the century, and there was some Black-Jewish cooperation in fighting the Ku Klux Klan in the 1930s.[50] At about the same time, a number of "establishment" Gentile organizations (but no minority ethnic groups) joined forces with the Jewish community to create the Canadian National Committee on Refugees and Victims of Political Persecution. Lobbying the Canadian government to admit Jewish refugees fleeing Nazi Germany, the CNCR also took a stand against Canadian anti-Semitism in general.[51]

In addition, the principle of the brotherhood of workers and the pragmatic need for class solidarity sometimes trumped nativist prejudices. For example, in 1914 the Social Democratic Party in Ontario attempted to elect a candidate to municipal office in Toronto by appealing to "Jew and Gentile, British and Foreign Born." Similarly, the Independent

Labour Party (ILP), which elected eleven members of the Ontario legislature in 1919 and one member of Parliament in 1921, championed "equal rights of citizenship irrespective of sex, class, origin, religion or property qualification," while the Communist Party often reached out to ethnic "underdogs." For example, in the late 1930s it appointed "Negro" organizers in a number of Ontario communities in order to fight against racial discrimination against Blacks. In addition, the social democratic Co-operative Commonwealth Federation (CCF), which later became the New Democratic Party (NDP), demanded in its Regina Manifesto of 1933 the "equal treatment before the law of all residents of Canada irrespective of race, nationality or religious or political beliefs."[52]

Nevertheless, these were exceptions to the dominant perspective of racial privilege and discrimination, and most demands for racial and ethnic equality were defeated by the smugly satisfied dominant groups. It would still be years to come before it was a matter of "common sense" that all people should be given equal treatment as a basic human right.

Conclusions

Although Canadians often like to think that their history has been for the most part "nice" or even boring, the human rights history of this country reveals many struggles between those who wished to maintain their dominant social, economic, and political positions and those who dissented by challenging the status quo. Resistance to repression seems to be an almost universal phenomenon, and the Canadian story is no exception.

This chapter has briefly examined some ideas about social and political resistance to domination, and then looked at how, in the years prior to the Second World War, some members of Canadian society tried to maintain their privileges while others attempted to achieve equality rights. It has touched upon struggles over women's rights, workers' rights, the rights of Aboriginals, French language rights, the rights of certain religious minorities, and the rights of ethnic minorities, especially Chinese Canadians, Japanese Canadians, Indo-Canadians, and Blacks.

A number of conclusions emerge when one examines these diverse struggles for equality. First, while in some cases courageous individuals did their best to protest what they considered to be injustice, the most effective form of dissent and resistance was usually achieved through group activity. Second, different groups remained relatively weak partly because they were isolated. They needed to work together for something broader than their own particular interests, but the ethnic-religious pecking order often served to divide the weak and permit the established groups to conquer. Finally, although some resisters made limited gains by pressing on the lever of equality, the ambiguous nature of this term as well as competing values of British nationalism, racial purity, and freedom of commerce, all in the context of a constitution with limited rights protections, made it extremely difficult for minorities to gain much egalitarian traction either through litigation or lobbying.

In 1939, therefore, just before war broke out, there was little reason to believe that Canada would ever become a far less sexist and racist society. For this to take place it would take a radical transformation in the values and laws of the country. But before this could happen, the nation was faced with a major challenge—the Second World War, which paradoxically would both undermine and foster the development of egalitarian values in Canada. But this is the topic of another chapter.

Notes

1 Frederick Douglass [1857], "The Significance of Emancipation in the West Indies," in John W. Blassingame, ed., *The Frederick Douglass Papers*, Series One: Speeches, Debates, and Interviews, vol. 3, 1855–63, (New Haven: Yale University Press, 1985), 204.

2 The scope of the term "human rights" is immense, open to debate, and changing over time. I have briefly discussed Canadian human rights history and historiography in "The Black, Brown, White and Red Blues: The Beating of Clarence Clemons," *Canadian Historical Review* 85 (December 2004). See also Timothy J. Stanley, "Why I Killed Canadian History: Towards an Anti-Racist History in Canada," *Histoire sociale/Social History* 33 (May 2000): 79–103, at 91-3, 99-100. For wider discussions, see Kenneth Cmiel, "The Recent History of Human Rights," *American Historical Review* 109 (February 2004): 117-135, and Micheline R. Ishay, *The History of Human Rights: From Ancient Times to the Globalization Era* (Berkeley: University of California Press, 2004).

3 In assuming the self-evident existence of domination, oppression, and exploitation, this paper skates over the ontological thin ice of postmodern critiques.

4 Charles Taylor maintains that minority group demands for justice or an end to discrimination are really calls for "recognition," which he defines as "a demand that such people be acknowledged and valued for what they are." See "The Politics of Recognition," in Charles Taylor (ed. Guy Laforest), *Reconciling the Solitudes: Essays on Canadian Federalism and Nationalism* (Montreal and Kingston: McGill-Queen's, 1993), 192.

5 See Carolyn Strange and Tina Loo, *Making Good: Law and Moral Regulation in Canada, 1867–1939* (Toronto: University of Toronto Press, 1997).

6 See, for example, chapters 1 and 2 of Kay J. Anderson, *Vancouver's Chinatown: Racial Discourse in Canada, 1875–1980* (Montreal and Kingston: McGill-Queen's University Press, 1991).

7 For examples of racist violence, see: Timothy J. Stanley, "White Supremacy, Chinese Schooling and School Segregation in Victoria: The Case of the Chinese Students' Strike, 1922–1923," *Historical Studies in Education/Revue d'histoire de l'éducation* 2 (Autumn 1990): 287–305, at 298.

8 For criticism of the "hapless victims" approach to historiography, see Wing Chung Ng, *The Chinese in Vancouver, 1945–80: The Pursuit of Identity and Power* (Vancouver: UBC Press, 1999), 6.

9 Constance Backhouse, *Colour-Coded: A Legal History of Racism in Canada, 1900–1950* (Toronto: The Osgoode Society, 1999), 11; James W. St. G. Walker, "Allegories and Orientations in the African-Canadian Historiography: The Spirit of Africville," *Dalhousie Review* 77 (Summer 1997): 155–177.

10 See chapter 1 of James W. St. G. Walker, "Race," Rights and the Law in the Supreme Court of Canada: Historical Case Studies (Waterloo: Wilfrid Laurier Press 1997). See also Patricia E. Roy, *The Oriental Question: Consolidating a White Man's Province, 1914–41* (Vancouver: UBC Press, 2003), 7–11.

11 See chapter 1 of Carol A. Aylward, *Canadian Critical Race Theory: Racism and the Law* (Halifax: Fernwood Publishing, 1999).

12 James C. Scott, *Weapons of the Weak: Everyday Forms of Peasant Resistance* (New Haven: Yale University Press, 1985); *Domination and the Arts of Resistance: Hidden Transcripts* (New Haven: Yale University Press, 1990), 198-9.

13 I am indebted to Scott for his arguments about how the legitimizing arguments of the oppressors provide some leverage for the oppressed. See, for example, *Domination*, 18, 77; *Weapons*, 317, 336, 338–99.

14 The next chapter of this book looks at violations of libertarian rights (such as the right to free speech, or religious freedom), and people's responses to this form of oppression.

15 Vic Satzewich, "Whiteness Limited: Racialization and the Social Construction of 'Peripheral Europeans'," *Histoire sociale/Social History* 33 (November 2000): 271–289; Mariana Valverde, *The Age of Light, Soap, and Water: Moral Reform in English Canada, 1885–1925* (Toronto: McClelland and Stewart, 1991).

16 Only by about the end of the nineteenth century did all white male Canadians have the legal right to vote, although there were still a few limitations in some provinces. See *A History of the Vote in Canada* (Ottawa: Ministry of Public Works, 1997).

17 Carol Lee Bacchi, *Liberation Deferred? The Ideas of the English-Canadian Suffragists, 1877–1918* (Toronto: University of Toronto Press, 1983), 48. See also Catherine L. Cleverdon, *The Woman Suffrage Movement in Canada*, 2nd ed. (Toronto: University of Toronto Press, 1975); Linda Kealey, ed., *A Not Unreasonable Claim: Women and Reform in Canada, 1880s–1920s* (Toronto: Women's Press, 1979). For a discussion of how women were subordinated in a number of other ways, such as the law on seduction, rape, divorce and separation, etc., see Constance Backhouse, *Petticoats and Prejudice: Women and Law in Nineteenth Century Canada* (Toronto: The Osgoode Society, 1991).

18 For Asians, see chapter 2 of Walker, "Race," Rights and the Law; Patricia E. Roy, A White Man's Province: British Columbia Politicians and Chinese and Japanese Immigrants, 1858–1914 (Vancouver: UBC Press, 1989), and The Oriental Question; Constance Backhouse, "Legal Discrimination Against the Chinese in Canada: The Historical Framework," in David Dyzenhaus and Mayo Moran, eds., Calling Power to Account: Law, Reparations, and The Chinese Canadian Head Tax Case (Toronto: University of Toronto Press, 2005), 24–59. The quotation from Macdonald is from Patricia E. Roy, "Citizens without Votes: East Asians in British Columbia, 1872–1947," in Jorgen Dahlie and Tissa Fernando, eds., *Ethnicity, Power and Politics* (Agincourt, Ontario: Methuen, 1981), 151–171, at 152.

19 For Blacks/Afro-Canadians, see Robin W. Winks, *The Blacks in Canada: A History* (New Haven: Yale University Press, 1971), at 386 for Nova Scotia's segregated schools; Walker, *"Race," Rights and the Law*, chapter 3. For Jews, see chapter 4 of Walker; Irving Abella and Harold Troper, *None is Too Many: Canada and the Jews of Europe 1933–1948* (Toronto: Lester & Orpen Dennys, 1983); Alan Davies, ed., *Antisemitism in Canada: History and Interpretation* (Waterloo: Wilfrid Laurier University Press, 1992).

20 Frances Swyripa and John Herd Thompson, eds., *Loyalties in Conflict: Ukrainians in Canada During the Great War* (Edmonton: Canadian Institute of Ukrainian Studies, 1983); Lubomyr Y. Luciuk, *In Fear of the Barbed Wire Fence: Canada's First National Internment Operations and the Ukranian Canadians, 1914–1920* (Kashtan Press, 2001).

21 J. R. Miller, "Anti-Catholic Thought in Victorian Canada," *Canadian Historical Review* 66 (1985): 474–94; Scott W. See, "The Orange Order and Social Violence in Mid-Nineteenth Century Saint John," in P. M. Toner, ed., *New Ireland Remembered: Historical Essays on the Irish in New Brunswick* (Fredericton: New Ireland Press, 1988), 71–89. See also Howard Palmer, *Patterns of Prejudice: A History of Nativism in Alberta* (Toronto: McClelland and Stewart, 1982).

22 William Janzen, *Limits on Liberty: The Experience of Mennonite, Hutterite, and Doukhobor Communities in Canada* (Toronto: University of Toronto Press, 1990).

23 Thomas Berger, *Fragile Freedoms: Human Rights and Dissent in Canada* (Toronto: Irwin Press, 1981), chapters 2 and 8.

24 Potlatches were (and still are) ceremonial community gatherings of members of different tribes of the Pacific Northwest Coast in which a host would lavishly distribute wealth to the guests. The Sun Dance was a key part of the culture of many prairie Aboriginals, involving dancing, praying, fasting, and in some cases a ritual whereby young men attached by slits in their skin to a central pole would have to break loose, tearing the skin.

25 On Aboriginals and Aboriginal rights, in addition to chapters in Backhouse's *Colour-Coded*, see J. R. Miller, *Skyscrapers Hide the Heavens: A History of Indian-White Relations in Canada* (Toronto: University of Toronto Press, 1989); Paul Tennant, *Aboriginal Peoples and Politics: The Indian Land Question in British Columbia, 1949–1989* (Vancouver: UBC Press, 1990); Alan D. McMillan and Eldon Yellowhorn, *First Peoples in Canada* (Vancouver/ Toronto: Douglas & McIntyre, 2004).

26 Peter Ward, *White Canada Forever: Popular Attitudes and Public Policy Toward Orientals in British Columbia*, 2nd ed. (Montreal and Kingston: McGill-Queen's University Press, 1990), chapter 4.

27 Martin Robin, *Shades of Right: Nativist and Fascist Politics in Canada, 1920–1940* (Toronto: University of Toronto Press, 1992); Julian Sher, *White Hoods, Canada's Ku Klux Klan* (Vancouver: New Star, 1983); Backhouse, *Colour-Coded*, chapter 6.

28 Davies, ed., *Antisemitism in Canada*; Satzewich, "Whiteness Limited," 283 [on Ukrainian Canadians]; Franca Iacovetta, *Such Hardworking People: Italian Immigrants in Postwar Toronto* (Montreal and Kingston: McGill-Queen's University Press, 1992), 107–8.

29 See: Alison Prentice et al., *Canadian Women: A History*, 2nd ed. (Toronto: Harcourt Brace, 1996).

30 John P.S. McLaren, "The Early British Columbia Supreme Court and the 'Chinese Question': Echoes of the rule of Law," *Manitoba Law Journal* 20 (1991): 107–47.

31 Constance Backhouse, "Clara Brett Martin: Canadian Heroine or Not?" *Canadian Journal of Women and the Law* 5, no. 2 (1992): 265–79, at 263.

32 Lisa Young and Joanna Everitt define an advocacy group as "any organization that seeks to influence government policy, but not to govern." *Advocacy Groups* (Vancouver: UBC Press, 2004), 5.

33 My definition of "lobbying" includes not just direct pressure on legislators, but also indirect pressure through public demonstrations, marches, letters to the editor, etc. There are, of course, other political options. Japanese Canadians, for example, used force to counter mob violence during the Vancouver anti-Asian riots of 1907, and the Chinese responded with a temporary economic boycott of services. The use of the boycott was also employed by Chinese Canadians in Victoria in 1922, successfully protesting against school segregation.

34 Berger, *Fragile Freedoms*, chapter 3.

35 The rule of law is implied by the preamble of the BNA Act, which says that Canada is to have "a constitution similar in principle to that of the United Kingdom." Traditional "legal liberalism" sees the rule of law as the jewel in the crown of the legal system, while Critical Legal Studies theorists consider it largely a myth that obscures the fundamental inequalities of society and legitimizes the status quo. See Andrew Altman, *Critical Legal Studies: A Liberal Critique* (Princeton, N.J.: Princeton University Press, 1990). My position is that the rule of law has helped to legitimize some capitalist inequalities, but has sometimes been a useful "lever" for oppressed groups seeking protection.

36 Backhouse, *Colour-Coded*, chapter 4; Berger, *Fragile Freedoms*, 235. On Aboriginal people's resistance, see also McMillan and Yellowhorn, *First Peoples in Canada*, 333, and Robin Jarvis Brownlie, "'A better citizen than lots of white men': First Nations Enfranchisement—an Ontario Case Study, 1918–1940," *Canadian Historical Review* 87 (March 2006): 29–52, at 31.

37 McLaren, "The Early British Columbia Supreme Court," 107–47.

38 For *Cunningham v. Tomey Homma* [1903] A.C. 151, see Andrea Geiger-Adams, "Pioneer Issei: Tomekichi Homma's Fight for the Franchise," *Nikkei Images* 8, no. 1 (Spring 2003): 1–6; Ross Lambertson, "After *Union Colliery*: Law, Race, and Class in the Coal Mines of British Columbia," in Hamar Foster and John McLaren, eds., *Essays in the History of Canadian Law: British Columbia and the Yukon* (Toronto: University of Toronto Press, 1995). For *Quong Wing v. The King* [1914] 49 S.C.R. 440, see chapter 3 of Walker, *"Race," Rights and the Law* and chapter 5 of Backhouse, *Colour-Coded*.

39 For a discussion of *Christie v. The York Corporation* [1940] S.C.R. 139, see Walker, *"Race," Rights and the Law*, chapter 3.

40 Sylvia B. Bashevkin, "Independence versus Partisanship: Dilemmas in the Political History of Women In English Canada," in Veronica Strong-Boag and Anita Clair Fellman, eds., *Rethinking Canada: The Promise of Women's History*, 2nd ed. (Toronto: Copp Clarke, 1991), 415–445, at 418.

41 All "white" women were able to vote in the 1921 federal election, but women were not able to vote in Quebec elections until 1940. For the most part, the "first wave" of feminist resistance was over by the 1920s, although there were still some female political activists, such as Agnes Macphail and Thérèse Casgrain, as well as lesser-known women in a variety of organizations, such as the National Council of Women or the Women's Labour League of the Communist Party. See Ruth Roach Pierson, "Introduction," and 343–354 of Beth Light and Ruth Roach Pierson, *No Easy Road: Women in Canada, 1920s to 1960s* (Toronto: New Hogtown Press, 1990).

42 Roy, *The Oriental Question*, 75, 236; Anderson, *Vancouver's Chinatown*.

43 A "Gentleman's Agreement" between the Canadian and Japanese governments restricted the number of people emigrating from Japan to Canada. Ottawa accepted this primarily because of the Imperial preference for good relations between Japan and Britain. Indo-Canadians were excluded by a rule that one could only come to Canada by a boat that had made a non-stop journey. See Hugh Johnston, *The Voyage of the Komagata Maru: The Sikh Challenge to Canada's Colour Bar* (Vancouver: UBC Press, 1979).

44 Ken Adachi, *The Enemy that Never Was* (Toronto: McClelland and Stewart, 1976), 160–3; Roy, *The Oriental Question*, 159–60.

45 Ross Lambertson, *Repression and Resistance: Canadian Human Rights Activists, 1930–1960* (Toronto: University of Toronto Press, 2005), 375.

46 Ruth A. Frager and Carmela Patrias, *Discounted Labour: Women Workers in Canada, 1870–1939* (Toronto: University of Toronto Press, 2005), 13.

47 Bacchi, *Liberation Deferred?*, 5, 53, 55, 123, 140, 149; Backhouse, *Colour-Coded*, 155–6.

48 Roy, *A White Man's Province*; Lambertson, "After Union Colliery."

49 Tennant, *Aboriginal Peoples and Politics*, 82–8, 111.

50 Norman Buchignani and Doreen Indra, "The Political Organization of South Asians in Canada, 1904–1920," in Dahlie and Fernando, eds., *Ethnicity, Power and Politics in Canada*, 202–232; Backhouse, *Colour-Coded*, 213.

51 Abella and Troper, *None is Too Many*, chapter 2.

52 James Naylor, *The New Democracy: Challenging the Social Order in Industrial Ontario, 1914–1925* (Toronto: University of Toronto Press, 1991), 107, 249; Ivan Avakumovic, *Socialism in Canada: A Study of the CCF-NDP in Federal and Provincial Politics* (Toronto: McLelland and Stewart, 1978), 37, 40; Gregory S. Kealey and Reg Whitaker, eds., *R.C.M.P. Security Bulletins: The Depression Years, Part III, 1936* (St. John's: Committee on Canadian Labour History, 1996), 233, 346–7, and *Security Bulletins: The Depression Years, Part IV, 1937*, 92, 94; Keith Henry, *Black Politics in Toronto since World War I* (Toronto: The Multicultural History Society of Ontario, 1981), 30; Peter Hunter, *Which Side Are You On, Boys. Canadian Life on the Left* (Toronto: Lugus Productions, 1988), 68; Kenneth McNaught, *A Prophet in Politics: A Biography of J.S. Woodsworth* (Toronto: University of Toronto Press, 1959), 147–153.

See also Carmela Patrias "Relief Strike: Immigrant Workers and the Great Depression in Crowland, Ontario, 1930–1935," in Franca Iacovetta, ed., *A Nation of Immigrants: Women, Workers, and Communities in Canadian History, 1940s–1960s* (Toronto: University of Toronto Press, 1998), 322–358. Note, however, that the CCF demonstrated a pragmatically weakened commitment to equal rights for Asians, committing to their enfranchisement only in 1938. See Roy, *The Oriental Question*, 155–6, 161, 202, 215.

Glossary

British North America Act (BNA Act), 1867. This was the constitutional document that created Canada in 1867 and set out the powers of both Ottawa and the provinces. It also contained some limited protection for what today we would call human rights: limited protections of francophone rights in the federal Parliament and courts, anglophone rights in the Quebec National Assembly and courts, and the right of Protestants and Catholics to continue the separate denominational schools that existed at the time of Confederation.

Denominational schools. These are government-funded religious schools or school systems. The BNA Act guarantees denominational schools for any religious minority that enjoyed separate schools at the time their province entered Confederation. In practice, this meant Protestant denominational schools in Quebec and Catholic schools in several other provinces.

Egalitarian rights. These rights, which are rooted in liberalism, are supposed to ensure that people will be treated as equals and not as second-class citizens by either the state or other members of society. This includes the right not to suffer discrimination because of one's sex or gender, race, religion, etc.

Federal-provincial division of powers. This it is set out in the BNA Act so that Ottawa can only pass laws in certain areas and provinces can only pass laws in other areas. Consequently, sometimes people were able to argue that a federal or provincial law that violated their rights should be struck down by the courts because it was unconstitutional for violating this division of powers.

Liberalism. A belief system or ideology that emphasizes individual freedom as well as equality before the law. This has always been the dominant ideology in Canada, although over time it was supplement by ideas about democracy.

Nativism. This is an attitude or point of view that includes both prejudice against members of other races and prejudice against members of other religions. It is therefore broader than the term "racism." In Canada, nativists were usually people who were prejudiced against such "visible minority" immigrant groups as Asians and Blacks, as well as Aboriginal peoples (who of course were the real natives), but they also were often prejudiced against Jews and Catholics (especially if they were French Canadians).

Parliamentary supremacy. The British principle that no law should limit the sovereignty of the legislature. This principle is implicit in the BNA Act and therefore permitted a legislature to override a fundamental human right at any time, as long as it was acting within the federal-provincial division of powers set out in the BNA Act.

Further Reading

Backhouse, Constance. *Colour-Coded: A Legal History of Racism in Canada, 1900–1950.* Toronto: The Osgoode Society, 1999.

Written by a legal historian, this discusses the history of racism in Canada and examines in detail a number of legal cases dealing with discrimination against Aboriginals (including the Inuit), Chinese, and Blacks.

Berger, Thomas. *Fragile Freedoms: Human Rights and Dissent in Canada.* Toronto: Irwin Press, 1981.

This is a non-academic history of human rights in Canada. It looks at pre–World War II issues such as the expulsion of the Acadians, the resistance of Louis Riel, the separate schools issue of the 1890s, the treatment of Japanese Canadians, limitations on the rights of Communists, the struggle of the Jehovah's Witnesses for religious freedom, and the struggle of the Nisga'a for Aboriginal title. Some chapters contain material on the war and post-war periods.

Ishay, Micheline R. *The History of Human Rights: From Ancient Times to the Globalization Era.* Berkeley: University of California Press, 2004.

Although this says very little about Canada, it is an excellent introduction to the topic of human rights in general, including the evolution of the idea of human rights.

Prentice, Alison, et al. *Canadian Women: A History*, 2nd ed. Toronto: Harcourt Brace, 1996.

An overview of the history of Canadian women, this has many references to their struggles for equality, and also contains a useful bibliography.

Walker, James W. St. G. *"Race," Rights and the Law in the Supreme Court of Canada: Historical Case Studies.* Waterloo: Wilfrid Laurier Press 1997.

This discusses the history of racism in Canada, and examines in detail a number of legal cases dealing with discrimination against Chinese, Jews, Blacks, and Indo-Canadians.

Relevant Websites

Canada's Rights Movement: A History
www.historyofrights.com
This covers the period from the 1930s to the 1980s and "provides a history of the human rights movement in Canada. Although the site has sections on various aspects of the 'rights revolution', it is primarily designed to highlight the activities of social movement organizations (non-governmental organizations—NGOs)."

Celebrating Women's Achievements

www.collectionscanada.gc.ca/women/002026-800-e.html

www.collectionscanada.gc.ca/women/002026-309-e.html

The first part of this website, "Canadian Women in Government," contains a short history of women fighting for the right to vote and participating in politics. It contains a list of key reference sources. The second part, "Changing Women, Changing History: Canadian Women Activists," is a short discussion of the *Persons* case, with biographies of the "Famous Five" who launched the case along with biographies of other famous Canadian women activists.

CHAPTER 2

SUPPRESSION AND SUBVERSION:
LIBERTARIAN AND EGALITARIAN RIGHTS UP TO 1960

Ross Lambertson

Few men are aroused by injustice when they are sure of not being its victims.

—Pierre Elliot Trudeau[1]

Introduction

The previous chapter focused on the history of egalitarian rights in Canada. It ended with an overview of the years up until the Second World War, concluding that at that time little progress seemed possible without a major shift in societal values.

This chapter turns to the early history of libertarian rights in Canada—liberal rights emphasizing individual freedom, such as free speech, free association, freedom of religion, etc., as well as certain procedural rights, such as the right to habeas corpus, the right to be presumed innocent until proven guilty, and the right to an impartial judge.[2] The chapter begins with a look at the Constitution, including the inherited concept of British "civil liberties," and then examines a number of early struggles for libertarian rights. It then focuses on a societal value shift towards human rights in the 1940s, and examines how this affected both egalitarian and libertarian rights in Canada. By 1960, Canada was a much more liberal society, well on its way to what has been called its "rights revolution."

Early Civil Liberties Struggles

Although the 1867 British North America Act did not specifically guarantee civil liberties (or "British liberties," as they were often called), they were implicit in its guarantee that Canadians were to have a "Constitution similar in principle to that of the United Kingdom." This provided some measure of protection for basic liberal freedoms, and as Walter Tarnopolsky has argued, "The [Canadian] statesmen of 1867 would probably have defined their civil liberties as including the freedoms of speech, press, religion, assembly, and association, the rights to habeas corpus, to a fair and public trial, and perhaps also such freedoms as freedom of contract and such rights as that to property."[3] To be sure, the constitutional principle of parliamentary supremacy meant that these rights were not absolute and could be eliminated by an act of Parliament, but both the politicians and the courts usually tried to respect them, especially when they were exercised by "respectable" middle-class citizens of British or French extraction.

Canadian historians have not specifically examined libertarian rights struggles in the late nineteenth century,[4] but secondary sources reveal a number of issues, such as the demands of so-called "free thinkers" for the right to free speech,[5] conflicts over the right to demonstrate in front of legislative assemblies, and struggles over the rights of both Catholics and Orangemen to hold public processions.[6]

Many conflicts were the by-product of struggles for a more equitable economic system. It was illegal until 1872 to form a trade union or to go out on strike for better working conditions (such as a working day no longer than nine hours), and workers fighting for these "rights and liberties of men" opposed governmental limitations on their rights of public protest.[7]

By the early twentieth century, governments also began to suppress left-wing radicals. For example, many cities tried to limit public meetings by the anarcho-syndicalist Industrial Workers of the World (IWW), and the "Wobblies" resisted with a series of "free speech fights" throughout Western Canada.[8] Then, during the First World War, Parliament created the War Measures Act, which gave the Cabinet almost unlimited power to create any orders-in-council it might "deem necessary or advisable for the security, defence, peace, order and welfare of Canada ..." Not only did the government intern a large number of Ukrainian Canadians who were incorrectly suspected of harbouring enemy sympathies,[9] it also banned a number of radical left-wing organizations and newspapers, especially those in foreign languages. This produced a civil libertarian backlash, including the creation of a Workers' Political Defense League.[10]

Governmental fears continued into peacetime. In 1919, in response to a general strike in Winnipeg, Ottawa charged a number of radicals with sedition and passed new legislation aimed at political subversives. Section 41 of the Immigration Act permitted the deportation of anyone not born in Canada—British-born or otherwise—who sought to overthrow the government by violence, who destroyed property unlawfully, or who "by word or act create[d] or attempt[ed] to create riot or public disorder in Canada." Section 98 of the Criminal Code prohibited, among other things, "any association whose purpose it is to bring about any governmental, industrial or economic change in Canada by force or violence, or which teaches or defends such uses of violence." As usual, repression led to resistance. A Winnipeg Defence Committee was created in 1919 to fight the sedition trials, and both social democrats and Communists worked to obtain the repeal of these laws.[11]

The 1920s were a period of relative political and labour peace, but the Communist Party of Canada was founded in 1922, and in response to the arrests of striking miners in Drumheller three years later, the party founded the Canadian Labor Defence League to protect anyone persecuted for supporting "the class interests of the industrial and agricultural workers." At one point the CLDL claimed a membership of about 20,000 individuals, fighting for the rights of free speech and free association in a number of legal cases, as well as lobbying for the deletion of section 98 of the Criminal Code and section 41 of the Immigration Act.[12]

At the end of the decade municipal authorities began to crack down on political dissent. Foreigners and radicals were considered to be virtually synonymous, and therefore in 1928 the Toronto Board of Police Commissioners posted the following in all public halls: "You are hereby notified that if any Communistic ... meetings held in a public hall, theatre, music hall ... are carried on in a foreign language ... the licence for such public hall etc. shall be immediately thereafter cancelled." The Toronto police also prohibited left-wing political rallies in city parks, resorting to violence whenever necessary, and used section 98 of the Criminal Code as a tenuous legal justification for this suppression.[13]

Although Karl Marx referred to liberal rights as "bourgeois claptrap," the Communist Party as well as other Canadian socialists—the Socialist Party of Canada, the Independent Labour Party (ILP), and the Cooperative Commonwealth Federation (CCF)—became staunch defenders of the right to speak freely and to hold demonstrations. Without these rights they had little chance of persuading workers to support the deeper struggle for economic and social justice.[14]

One of the best-known cases taken on by the CLDL was the 1931 trial of Tim Buck, leader of the Communist Party, and eight other members of his party who were charged with membership in an illegal organization and participation in a seditious conspiracy, contrary to section 98 of the Criminal Code. All were found guilty and sent to prison, with a recommendation that those who were foreign-born be deported. The judge was not swayed by their defence that they and their party had simply predicted, but never advocated, the violent overthrow of the capitalist system.[15]

Because of the suppression of left-wing and trade union political dissent throughout Canada, in the early 1930s the Communists also sponsored a Canadian League against War and Fascism to oppose section 98 and other repressive "fascist" measures.[16] Although the Communists had previously distanced themselves from moderates on the left, they now maintained that all "progressives" should unite in response to the dangers of the far right, and did their best to make CLAWF attractive to social democrats.

Nevertheless, the spectre of Communist affiliation was unappealing to many CCF members. Moreover, neither the CLDL nor CLAWF were true civil liberties organizations. Unlike the American Civil Liberties Union or the British National Council for Civil Liberties, they were committed to protecting only the rights of the "right" kind of people—those on the left. In short, they were pragmatic rather than principled organizations.

Early Civil Liberties Groups

Consequently, in 1937 a few left-liberals and social democrats created the Canadian Civil Liberties Union. Formed largely in reaction to the authoritarian Premier of Quebec,

Maurice Duplessis, this was Canada's first national civil liberties organization, although it consisted only of a few autonomous branches in Montreal, Toronto, Vancouver, and Ottawa, and never achieved the degree of national representation and coordination that its founders had envisaged.[17]

The Montreal branch of the Canadian Civil Liberties Union (MCLU) was the most active of the groups, primarily because of its fight against Duplessis' Padlock Law, which permitted the police to lock up, and prevent the use of, any premises being used for spreading Communist propaganda.[18] An organization dominated by anglophones, aided by a smattering of francophone liberals, the MCLU lobbied Ottawa to disallow the law, whipped up nationwide public indignation, and launched several legal cases challenging its constitutionality. However, the civil libertarians failed to persuade either Ottawa or the courts that the legislation should be struck down. They were considering an appeal to the Supreme Court of Canada when the Second World War broke out and the Padlock Law suddenly became a dead issue.

Indeed, by 1939 the major threat to civil liberties was Ottawa, not Quebec. Using the War Measures Act, Ottawa created the Defence of Canada Regulations (DOCR) to take draconian steps: imposing harsh limits on freedom of speech; forcing Japanese Canadians to leave the West Coast and also interning a number of German and Italian Canadians erroneously suspected of being disloyal; and outlawing several organizations, including the Communist Party, the Jehovah's Witnesses, and even the innocuous and insignificant Technocracy Association.[19]

The paradox of civil liberties organizations is that they tend to wither during good times and prosper during bad times. Within a few years new civil liberties groups popped up in Montreal, Toronto, Winnipeg, and Vancouver. The major activists were almost entirely "white," Anglo-Celtic, and male. They were also middle class except for the occasional high-ranking labour leader, and predominantly liberal or social democratic, although a few were professed or suspected Communists. Most importantly, they were usually prominent members of the academic, legal, journalistic, religious, and (very occasionally) business elite. This gave them considerable political clout.

They were, however, weakened by their voluntary nature, as well as by their regional isolation. None, not even the branches of the CLU, worked closely with one another. They constituted a small archipelago of dissent and criticism, each group lobbying independently.

Their effectiveness was also diminished by the schism between Communists and non-Communists. At the beginning of the war the Communists followed (as usual) the Soviet party line, which built upon the recent non-aggression pact between Stalin and Hitler; therefore, they opposed the war effort. When the Communist Party of Canada was declared an illegal organization, Communists within the different civil liberties groups became passionate defenders of free speech and the rule of law. Yet when Nazi Germany

invaded the Soviet Union in 1941, the radicals suddenly turned into enthusiastic warmon-
gers and lukewarm civil libertarians. Indeed, the Communist-infiltrated Montreal branch
of the Canadian Civil Liberties Union folded completely.

Towards the end of the war, as the government loosened its restrictions on civil
liberties, the remaining groups began to pay attention to egalitarian rights. The Toronto
Civil Liberties Association in particular seems to have refocused. Without dropping its
traditional libertarian emphasis, it connected with Blacks, Jews, and Japanese Canadians
who were seeking equal treatment.

This shift was facilitated by distaste for the Nazi values of racial discrimination, augmented
by a corresponding international embracing of human rights. Allied governments had justified the war as a Manichean conflict between the forces of democracy and the totalitarian
Axis powers, and in August 1941 Roosevelt and Churchill prefaced their Atlantic Charter
with a statement that victory was "essential to decent life, liberty, independence and religious freedom, and to preserve human rights and justice…." Then, in 1945, the United
Nations enshrined the notion of "fundamental human rights" in its founding Charter, and
in 1948 produced the Universal Declaration of Human Rights. Such references to human
rights became increasingly common over time, and in Canada they began to replace the
language of "British liberties" and "British justice."[20] The entire world, including Canada,
was beginning to accept that some rights belong to all human beings, not just to certain
preferred members of particular states. This was the beginning of what some scholars have
referred to as "The Age of Rights" or the era of "The Rights Revolution."[21]

Meanwhile, some Canadian minority groups were realizing the truth of the adage,
"Either we hang together, or we hang separately." Jews and Blacks, for example, together
successfully opposed a wartime federal employment program that turned a blind eye to
racial discrimination, and Japanese Canadians allied themselves with what might be called
"righteous gaijin"—progressive-minded Canadians who abhorred any racist policies that
smacked of Nazi-style discrimination.

For example, when in 1944 Ottawa decided to disenfranchise Japanese Canadians
who were now living outside British Columbia, opposition was spearheaded by the
Cooperative Committee on Japanese Canadians with support from the Civil Liberties
Association of Toronto. The CCJC included several Japanese Canadians, but it was
primarily a "white" organization of altruistic human rights activists, many of whom
were church-affiliated and committed to Social Gospel principles.[22] It was, at its peak, a
coalition of ethnic, church, labour, civil libertarian, and women's organizations, many of
which joined when, at the end of the war, the federal government attempted to deport
several thousand Japanese Canadians. A campaign against this policy slowed down the
government's efforts and by 1947 persuaded it to drop its plans altogether.[23]

This was arguably the first major human rights battle in Canadian history. It brought
together a wide spectrum of organizations and ethnic groups (although Blacks, Chinese,

Indo-Canadians, and Native peoples were absent), and also employed the relatively new language of human rights, asking Ottawa to respect the UN founding Charter and calling the deportation policy a violation of human rights, a sort of "Nazi treatment of an innocent and highly reputable minority." [24]

Meanwhile, another issue was troubling civil libertarians. Igor Gouzenko, a clerk in Ottawa's Soviet Embassy, informed Canadian authorities about a Russian espionage network in Canada. In early 1946, the RCMP began to round up suspects, holding them (at first) without charge and without access to their lawyers under the authority of a legal but morally dodgy secret order-in-council passed the previous year.

Civil libertarians protested, but could neither alter government policy nor provide much help for the alleged spies, not all of whom were found guilty.[25] In addition, the Gouzenko Affair helped split radical left-wing civil libertarians from moderate activists, for some members of the Toronto group, complaining that it had not taken a strong enough stance on this issue, formed an Emergency Committee on Civil Rights. This organization then morphed into a Toronto-based group called the Civil Rights Union, which formed the core of a national organization, the League for Democratic Rights.

The LDR claimed, by 1953, to have "branches, committees, or affiliates in 31 centres across the country." It was primarily committed to freedom of speech and association, but it occasionally spoke out on egalitarian rights issues. For the most part, it defended radical leftists who were frequently harassed during the Cold War "red scare" of the late 1940s and early 1950s. In fact, it was a Communist-front organization funded by Communist-infiltrated ethnic organizations and trade unions and led by a mixture of Communists and "fellow-travellers."[26]

The civil liberties movement remained ideologically divided throughout the 1940s and 1950s. Perhaps the only successful joining of forces occurred when a social democratic civil libertarian, Frank Scott, worked with the LDR-affiliated Montreal Civil Liberties Union in 1957 to persuade the Supreme Court that the Padlock Law, resuscitated by Premier Duplessis after the war, was an unconstitutional violation of the federal-provincial division of powers in the BNA Act.[27]

The non-Communist civil liberties groups were also divided by geography and Canadian federalism. The Toronto organization, for example, which in 1949 reorganized and changed its name to the Association for Civil Liberties, often acted like a national organization, but had little contact with the civil liberties groups in Vancouver and Manitoba, or the short-lived Ottawa and Montreal Civil Liberties Associations. As a result, there were few clear-cut triumphs. When it came to fighting against censorship or defending citizens against the red scare, Canada's civil liberties organizations were too often either pusillanimous or ineffective. They perhaps had some impact on the government's state-security amendments to the Criminal Code in the early 1950s, but there were few major successes.[28]

The Jehovah's Witnesses and the Triumvirate

There was, however, one group that remained aloof from both the civil liberties organizations of the left and right, but nevertheless significantly bolstered the legal protections of
Canadians. The Jehovah's Witnesses, an activist minority religious sect, had a long history
of being harassed—in Quebec because of their zealous proselytizing, in Ontario because
their children refused to salute the flag, and, as mentioned earlier, during the Second
World War because of their pacifist beliefs.[29] After the war, Quebec Premier Duplessis
declared a "war without mercy" against the Jehovah's Witnesses, and the authorities began
to crack down on their activities, using the sedition provisions of the Criminal Code as
well as a number of recently passed municipal bylaws that prohibited the distribution
of literature without a licence. In addition, the Premier cancelled the liquor licence of a
prominent Jehovah's Witness, Frank Roncarelli, because he had annoyed the Premier by
arranging bail for church members arrested for handing out religious pamphlets.

As William Kaplan puts it, "The Jehovah's Witnesses did not respond to what they
believed was another satanic attack on God's work by turning the other cheek. Instead,
they entered the lion's den."[30] Their resistance proceeded on three different fronts. First,
they printed and distributed pamphlets attacking not only the government and the judges
in Quebec, but also the Roman Catholic Church, which they claimed was behind their
persecution. Second, they frequently went to court, often all the way to the Supreme
Court of Canada. Third, they lobbied for a national bill of rights that would provide
better protection for minorities.[31]

In retrospect, their pamphlets probably did little to help their cause, especially when
they referred to the Catholic Church as the "whore of Babylon." Moreover, demands for a
national Bill of Rights in the late 1940s were regarded by most people as inconsistent with
the inherited British constitutional principle of parliamentary supremacy. Neither the passage
of a Saskatchewan Bill of Rights in 1947 nor a national Bill of Rights in 1960 was more
than tangentially affected by the campaigns of this "outsider" organization. Yet the litigation
did have considerable impact. Most of the major Supreme Court civil liberties cases of the
1950s involved the Jehovah's Witnesses, and the *Roncarelli* decision is still regarded today as
an important statement of the rule of law principle. The Supreme Court ruled that Premier
Duplessis could not do as he wanted simply because he was the Premier; he had to pay
damages because there was no specific law giving him the power to cancel the liquor licence
of the troublesome restaurateur who had arranged bail for his church members.[32]

Perhaps the most important early post-war rights group was a triumvirate consisting of
the Toronto Association for Civil Liberties (ACL), the Canadian Jewish Congress (CJC),
and the Jewish Labour Committee (JLC).[33] Each organization brought certain strengths
to the coalition. For example, the ACL was eminently respectable, with leaders such as
B. K. Sandwell, editor of the influential journal *Saturday Night*, and Reginald Seeley,
Provost and Vice-Chancellor of Trinity College at the University of Toronto. Arising

from the ashes of internecine squabbling between Communist and non-Communist civil libertarians in the earlier Toronto-based organization (the CLAT), it was adamantly anti-Communist and attracted, as is usually the case with civil liberties groups, liberal and social democratic academics, lawyers, and religious figures.

While the ACL provided a respectable front for lobbying a nation that was frequently anti-Semitic, much of the organizational and financial power of the triumvirate came from the two Jewish organizations. The Canadian Jewish Congress was the official voice of Canadian Jews and was largely middle class. The Jewish Labour Committee, by contrast, was working class and social democratic. Despite these differences, and the occasional turf wars that simmered beneath the surface, the CJC and the JLC were united in their fear of anti-Semitism and their awareness that Canadian Jews were a very small (and unpopular) minority group that badly needed allies such as the ACL.

Yet it was clear that a campaign against anti-Semitism would often fall upon deaf ears. It made more sense to promote the nascent principle of "human rights," focusing upon the dangers of discrimination in general. To achieve this, the CJC and the JLC set up and jointly funded a number of egalitarian rights organizations in different Canadian cities. These were labour committees representing the major trade union umbrella groups, and they provided much of the "muscle" for subsequent human rights campaigns. Because the law now protected workers who wanted to form unions, go on strike, and bargain collectively, trade unions were much more secure and able to engage in social union-ism, including anti-discrimination work. Consequently, the trade union human rights committees did much more than educate workers about how prejudice could split and weaken the workforce. They also educated the general public and built coalitions to lobby governments for legislative change.[34]

These campaigns were facilitated by important developments in the later 1940s. Chinese, Japanese, and Indo-Canadian communities had successfully pressured both Ottawa and the province of BC to give them the franchise and remove restrictions on their right to employment.[35] In addition, an inter-ethnic coalition called the Committee for the Repeal of the Chinese Immigration Act partially levered open the immigration gates.[36] The major goal of equality-seeking groups was therefore no longer an end to state discrimination, but instead an end to private discrimination.[37]

However, any law prohibiting businesses from discriminating on the basis of race or religion contravened the principle of freedom of commerce. To coin a phrase, classical liberals believed that the state had no business in the boardrooms of the nation. Also, as noted in the previous chapter, many organizations promoted the interests of their own members rather than focusing on the bigger picture. For example, Chinese Canadians were not involved in the campaign against Ottawa's plan to deport Japanese Canadians after the war, nor did Japanese Canadians support Chinese Canadians in their campaign to remove barriers to their immigration. The emerging concept of human rights was only slowly catching on. "Common sense" ideas about a racist pecking order died slowly, and economic competition could still produce an "us first" attitude. For example, the Native Brotherhood of British Columbia protested the government's decision to give Japanese Canadians the vote in 1949, fearing that this might eventually lead to renewed competition from Japanese fisherman.[38]

Nevertheless, shifting attitudes began to open up new possibilities. In addition to the new human rights discourse, and unprecedented post-war economic growth that diminished the threat of workers losing jobs to "foreigners" working for low wages, Canada was becoming a welfare state. Reform liberalism, with its acceptance of state intervention in people's lives, was rapidly replacing classical liberalism. By the early 1950s, even the influential civil libertarian B. K. Sandwell, an avowed disciple of laissez-faire, had come to the conclusion that anti-discrimination legislation might not be a bad idea after all.[39]

Consequently, the triumvirate and its allies, which included a wide spectrum of organizations—ethnic, religious,[40] labour, women's, and other groups—demanded and achieved one law after another. They managed to create the basis for today's regime of federal and provincial human rights codes, laws which today supplement the Charter in the protection of human rights.

To appreciate the impact of such statutes, consider the case of Viola Desmond, a young Black woman arrested in 1946 for sitting in the "Whites only" section of a Nova Scotia movie theatre. From her perspective she was simply asserting her right to racial equality, but no law in the province guaranteed this and she was fined for attempting to evade the local entertainment tax.[41]

Consider also a newspaper story from 1955, noting that "Chief Mungo Martin, famous totem pole carver at Thunderbird Park [in Victoria] said today he has been refused a suite of rooms in Victoria for himself and his wife because he is 'an Indian.' The kindly, 76-year-old Indian was deeply hurt, although not bitter over the incident.... The Attorney-General's department reported it had been informed of the incident and had tried to assist in the matter. 'But we could find no regulations which oblige a man to rent his rooms,' said an official."[42]

Protection against such forms of discrimination was pioneered by Ontario, which passed a series of statutes in the early 1950s prohibiting racial and religious discrimination in employment, and then in services available to the public, as well as a rather weak guarantee of gender equality in employment, but it was not until 1962 that such laws were consolidated into a modern human rights code.[43]

Nevertheless, even the early legislation had an impact. For example, several establishments in the town of Dresden, Ontario, discriminated against its substantial Black population. A Black carpenter named Hugh Burnette objected and, with the help of the Ontario triumvirate, used the recently passed Fair Accommodation Practices Act and the courts to force an end to this discrimination.[44]

Most of these human rights organizations also campaigned for a federal bill of rights. Many people believed that the authoritarian wartime track record of the Liberal government, as well as its Japanese deportation policy and the Gouzenko Affair, demonstrated the need to put constitutional shackles on the iron fist of government. In 1960, the Conservative Prime Minister John Diefenbaker created the Canadian Bill of Rights, intended to provide some protection from both discrimination and political oppression by the federal government. This was the last major human rights campaign of the 1950s.[45]

This chapter has focused primarily on major human rights stories, but there were many other injustices. Some of them, such as the treatment of Aboriginals, the Sons of Freedom Doukhobor controversy,[46] or women's equality rights,[47] were occasionally touched on by libertarian and egalitarian groups, but they were largely peripheral concerns. Others, such as the treatment of gays and lesbians,[48] or the physically and mentally disabled, [49] involved manifest injustices but resistance was largely infrapolitical, beneath the radar screens of government and the press. Changes in these areas were contingent upon even further shifts in Canadian social values.

Conclusions

This chapter has charted the early libertarian rights issues in Canadian history, as well as the rise of the first rights groups in the 1930s. It has shown that in the late wartime period civil liberties groups began to turn their attention to egalitarian rights, and after the war there emerged a number of civil libertarians and equality-seeking groups. Although the Cold War and other factors limited the effectiveness of the former, the latter were relatively successful in their quest for anti-discrimination legislation. Moreover, these groups demonstrated that not all Canadians acted out of self-interest; there were many who were "aroused by injustice" and altruistically protested violations of other people's rights.

Why was there so much more human rights activism during the post-war period as opposed to earlier times? Resistance to oppression is almost always present in any society, but it is translated into political activism only under certain circumstances. In Canada, these facilitating circumstances included, first, the worldwide "rights revolution" that began during the Second World War, including a discourse shift from "British liberties" to human rights. Also, high levels of economic growth and employment in the 1940s and 1950s provided considerable security. This in turn facilitated the growth of altruism, including liberal and socialist attitudes of ethnic toleration, as well as government awareness that discrimination might discourage the much-needed flow of immigrants into the overheated workforce.[50] True, for a while fear of communism undermined libertarian principles, but it also fostered liberal egalitarian policies; the protection of human rights in Canada was to some degree a Cold War soft-power weapon aimed at the self-proclaimed non-racist Soviet Union.[51]

In addition, activist success at one level encouraged campaigns at other levels. Workers who were now protected by minimum wage laws, and who had also won the right to collective bargaining, turned their attention to anti-discrimination legislation. Asian Canadians who had won the right to vote now addressed the problems of non-governmental discrimination. Then, success in lobbying for limited protection in Ontario in the early 1950s encouraged groups to ask for better protection in both Ontario and other jurisdictions. A revolution was taking place, but it was a revolution of incremental steps.

By the early 1960s most of the pressing battles of this period had been won. At the egalitarian rights level, most jurisdictions prohibited some forms of racial and religious discrimination.[52] As for libertarian rights, the fears of the Cold War were subsiding, the economy continued to grow, and there was more tolerance for radical political ideas. Moreover, the Bill of Rights had not yet turned out to be little more than a wet cardboard shield.[53] Consequently, many of the original rights groups were either becoming moribund or had disappeared. It was, in retrospect, the end of the first phase of the human rights movement in Canada.[54]

Notes

[1] Quoted in Thomas Berger's *Fragile Freedoms: Human Rights and Dissent in Canada* (Toronto: Irwin Press, 1981), 210 [originally in *Vrai*, 1958].

[2] There are different ways to categorize rights. Walter Tarnopolsky, for example, distinguished between egalitarian, political, legal, and economic civil liberties. Walter Surma Tarnopolsky, *The Canadian Bill of Rights* (Toronto: Carswell, 1966). See also Peter Hogg, *Constitutional Law of Canada*, Student edition (Toronto: Carswell, 2005), 695.

[3] W. S. Tarnopolsky, "Discrimination in Canada: Our History and Our Legacy" (Canadian Institute of Administration of Justice, 1989), 11, accessed at http://www.ciaj-icaj.ca/english/publications/TARNOPOL.pdf. See also his *Discrimination and the Law in Canada* (Toronto: Richard De Boo, 1982). The BNA Act specifically allocated "property and civil rights" to the provinces, but this provided no special protection for the civil liberties of Canadians. The term "property and civil rights" in the Canadian constitutional sense was intended to be "a compendious description of the entire body of private law which governs the relationships between subject and subject, as opposed to the law which governs the relationships between the subject and the institutions of government ... [so as to] comprise primarily proprietary, contractual, or tortious rights." Hogg, *Constitutional Law of Canada*, 526–528.

[4] See, however, the legal history of D. A. Schmeiser, *Civil Liberties in Canada* (London: Oxford University Press, 1964).

[5] Ramsay Cook, *The Regenerators: Social Criticism in Late Victorian English Canada*, (Toronto: University of Toronto Press, 1985), 48–9.

[6] Gregory S. Kealey, *Toronto Workers Respond to Industrial Capitalism, 1867–1892* (Toronto: University of Toronto Press, 1980), 119–23, 402 n. 24.

[7] Programme of the Labor Day Celebration, 1882, quoted in Bryan Palmer, *A Culture in Conflict: Skilled Workers and Industrial Capitalism in Hamilton, Ontario, 1860–1914* (Montreal: McGill-Queen's University Press, 1979), at 60. See also Gregory S. Kealey and Bryan D. Palmer, *Dreaming of What Might Be: The Knights of Labor in Ontario, 1880–1900* (Toronto: New Hogtown Press, 1987), 116–126; Kealey, *Toronto Workers Respond*, 70, 133–153, 205. There were also struggles for a more democratic system well into the early twentieth century; see James Naylor, *The New Democracy: Challenging the Social Order in Industrial Ontario, 1914–1925* (Toronto: University of Toronto Press, 1991).

[8] Mark Leier, "Solidarity on Occasion: The Vancouver Free Speech Fights of 1909 and 1912," *Labour/Le Travail* 23 (Spring 1989): 39–66. The government also used deportation as a way of suppressing the IWW and other groups; see Barbara Roberts, *Whence They Came: Deportation from Canada 1900–1935* (Ottawa: University of Ottawa, 1988), 89–97.

[9] Frances Swyripa and John Herd Thompson, eds., *Loyalties in Conflict: Ukrainians in Canada During the Great War* (Edmonton: Canadian Institute of Ukrainian Studies, 1983); Lubomyr Y. Luciuk, *In Fear of the Barbed Wire Fence: Canada's First National Internment Operations and the Ukranian Canadians, 1914–1920* (Kashtan Press, 2001).

[10] Gregory S. Kealey, "State Repression of Labour and the Left in Canada, 1914–20: The Impact of the First World War," *Canadian Historical Review* 73 (1992): 281–314; Craig Heron and Meyer Siemiatycki, "The Great War, the State, and Working-Class Canada," in Craig Heron, ed., *The Workers' Revolt in Canada, 1917–1925*, (Toronto: University of Toronto Press, 1998).

[11] Ross Lambertson, *Repression and Resistance: Canadian Human Rights Activists, 1930–1960* (Toronto: University of Toronto Press, 2005); Tom Mitchell, "'Repressive Measures': A.J. Andrews, the Committee of 1000 and the Campaign against Radicalism after the Winnipeg General Strike," *left history* 3.2 & 4.2 (Fall 1995–Spring 1996): 133–67.

[12] J. Petryshyn, "Class Conflict and Civil Liberties: The Origins and Activities of the Canadian Labour Defense League, 1925–1940," *Labour/Le Travail* 10 (Autumn 1982): 39–63, and "R.B. Bennett and the Communists: 1930–1935," *Journal of Canadian Studies* IX:4 (November 1974): 43–55; Lita-Rose Betcherman, *The Little Band: The Clashes Between the Communists and the Canadian Establishment 1928–1932* (Ottawa: Deneau, 1982).

[13] Betcherman, *The Little Band*; Suzanne Skebo, "Liberty and Authority: Civil Liberties in Toronto, 1929–1935," M.A. thesis (University of British Columbia, 1968).

[14] Kenneth McNaught, *A Prophet in Politics: A Biography of J.S. Woodsworth* (Toronto: University of Toronto Press, 1959); Walter Young, *The Anatomy of a Party: The National CCF 1932–61* (Toronto: University of Toronto Press, 1969). An example of the connection between the rights of free speech and association is the 1935 cross-country protest of the unemployed, known as the On-to-Ottawa trek, stopped by the police in the "Regina Riot" and subsequent laying of charges using section 98. Lorne Brown, *When Freedom Was Lost: The Unemployed, the Agitator, and the State* (Montreal: Black Rose Books, 1987), 194, 203.

[15] Betcherman, *The Little Band*, chapters xvi and xvii.

[16] The CLAWF was actually founded in 1934, but a few years later changed its name to the Canadian League for Peace and Democracy. See Lambertson, *Repression and Resistance*, 37. On the rise of fascism, see Lita-Rose Betcherman, *The Swastika and the Maple Leaf: Fascist Movements in Canada in the Thirties* (Don Mills: Fitzhenry and Whiteside, 1975).

[17] Lambertson, *Repression and Resistance*, chapter 1. The first real civil liberties group, the Canadian Civil Liberties Protective Association, founded in Edmonton in 1932, soon withered away.

[18] In 1936, the Liberal government in Ottawa repealed section 98 of the Criminal Code. The Quebec government responded by passing the Padlock Law.

[19] On civil liberties and civil liberties groups in World War II, see Lambertson, *Repression and Resistance*, chapter 2; Berger, *Fragile Freedoms*, chapter 3; Ramsay Cook, "Canadian Freedom in Wartime 1939–1945," in W. H. Heick and Roger Graham, eds., *His Own Man: Essays in Honour of Arthur Reginald Marsden Lower* (Montreal: McGill-Queen's University Press, 1974); Larry Hannant, *The Infernal Machine: Investigating the Loyalty of Canada's Citizens* (Toronto: University of Toronto Press, 1995); Norman Hillmer, Bohdan Kordan, and Lubomyr Luciuk, eds., *On Guard for Thee: War, Ethnicity, and the Canadian State, 1939–1945* (Ottawa: Ministry of Supply and Services, 1988); William and Kathleen M. Repka, *Dangerous Patriots: Canada's Unknown Prisoners of War* (Vancouver: New Star Books, 1982); Daniel Robinson, "Planning for 'The Most Serious Contingency': Alien Internment, Arbitrary Detention, and the Canadian State 1938–39," *Journal of Canadian Studies* 28: 2 (Summer 1993): 5–20; Patricia E. Roy, *The Triumph of Citizenship: The Japanese and Chinese in Canada, 1941–67* (Vancouver: UBC Press, 2007); Ann Gomer Sunahara, *The Politics of Racism: The Uprooting of Japanese Canadians During the Second World War* (Toronto: James Lorimer, 1981); Reg Whitaker, "Official Repression of Communism During World War II," *Labour/Le Travail* 17 (Spring 1986): 135–166; Franca Iacovetta, Roberto Perin, and Angelo Principe, *Enemies Within: Italian and Other Internees in Canada and Abroad* (Toronto: University of Toronto Press, 2000).

[20] Using the *Globe and Mail*'s digitalized newspaper archival system, a search for the phrase "human rights" in the editorials revealed no "hits" from 1900 to 1935, 8 hits from 1935 to 1940, 22 hits from 1940 to 1945, and 60 hits for the period from 1945 to 1950. During the period between 1950 and 1955 the number went down to 26, but from 1955 to 1960 the score went up to 68, from 1960 to 1965 it was 210, and it leaped to 320 for the period from 1965 to 1970.

[21] Lambertson, *Repression and Resistance*, 5, 107, 376; Louis Henkin, *The Age of Rights* (New York: Columbia University Press, 1990); Michael Ignatieff, *The Rights Revolution* (Toronto: Anansi, 2000).

[22] The Social Gospel was a Christian perspective emphasizing the brotherhood of mankind and the necessity of social action (as opposed to simple prayer and individual rectitude). There were liberal, social democratic, and even some communist followers of the Social Gospel movement.

[23] Lambertson, *Repression and Resistance*, chapter 3; Stephanie D. Bangarth, *Voices Raised in Protest: Defending North American Citizens of Japanese Ancestry, 1942–1949* (Vancouver: UBC Press, 2007).

[24] Lambertson, *Repression and Resistance*, 119.

25 For a specific look at the civil liberties implications of the Gouzenko Affair, see Lambertson, *Repression and Resistance*, chapter 4, as well as Dominique Thomas Clément, "The Royal Commission on Espionage and the Spy Trials of 1946–9: A Case Study in Parliamentary Supremacy," *Journal of the Canadian Historical Association* 11 (2000): 151–171. Recent books on Gouzenko include: Mark Kristmanson, *Plateaus of Freedom: Nationality, Culture and State Security in Canada, 1940–1960* (Don Mills, Ont.: Oxford University Press, 2003); Amy Knight, *How the Cold War Began: The Gouzenko Affair and the Hunt for Soviet Spies* (Toronto: McClelland and Stewart, 2005).

26 Lambertson, *Repression and Resistance*, 257ff. More detailed works on the Cold War suppression of civil liberties include: Merrily Weisbord, *The Strangest Dream: Canadian Communists, The Spy Trials, and the Cold War* (Toronto: Lester & Orpen Dennys, 1983); Reg Whitaker and Gary Marcuse, *Cold War Canada: The Making of a National Insecurity State, 1945–1957* (Toronto: University of Toronto Press, 1994); Frank K. Clarke, "'Keep Communism out of our Schools': Cold War Anti-Communism at the Toronto Board of Education, 1948–1951," *Labour/Le Travail* (Spring 2002): 93–119. See also portions of Michiel Horn, *Academic Freedom in Canada: A History* (Toronto: University of Toronto Press, 1999), and Berger, *Fragile Freedoms*, chapter 4.

27 The case is *Switzman v. Elbling and AG Quebec* [1957] S.C.R. 285. For a discussion of the politics of this case, see Lambertson, *Repression and Resistance*, 273–8.

28 Lambertson, *Repression and Resistance*, chapter 6 and "Conclusion." On the other hand, any resistance can be empowering, even if there are no obvious external gains.

29 W. Glen How, "The Case for a Canadian Bill of Rights," *Canadian Bar Review* 26 (May 1948): 759–796; James M. Penton, *Jehovah's Witnesses in Canada* (Toronto: Macmillan, 1976); William Kaplan, *State and Salvation: The Jehovah's Witnesses and Their Fight for Civil Rights* (Toronto: University of Toronto Press, 1989); Lambertson, *Repression and Resistance*, 338–9; Berger, *Fragile Freedoms*, chapter 6.

30 Kaplan, *State and Salvation*, 233.

31 The important 1950 civil liberties cases involving Jehovah's Witnesses were: *Boucher v. The King, Saumur v. Quebec, Chaput v. Romain, Roncarelli v. Duplessis,* and *Lamb v. Benoit.*

32 The case was *Roncarelli v. Duplessis* [1959] S.C.R. 121. See Lambertson, *Repression and Resistance*, 339. On the Saskatchewan Bill of Rights, see Schmeiser, *Civil Liberties in Canada*, 73–4, and Carmela Patrias, "Socialists, Jews, and the 1947 Saskatchewan Bill of Rights," *Canadian Historical Review* 87 (June 2006): 265–92. On *Roncarelli*, see Kaplan, *State and Salvation*, 245–62.

33 The term "triumvirate" comes from Herbert Sohn, "Human Rights Policy in Ontario: A Case Study," Ph.D. diss. (University of Toronto, 1975), 277. Much of what follows on anti-discrimination activism is taken from chapters 5, 7, and 8 of Lambertson, *Repression and Resistance*. See also Irving Abella, "Jews, Human Rights, and the Making of a New Canada," *Journal of the Canadian Historical Association* 11 (2000): 3–14; Carmela Patrias and Ruth A. Frager, "'This Is Our Country, These Are Our Rights': Minorities and the Origins of Ontario's Human Rights Campaigns," *Canadian Historical Review* 82 (March 2001): 1–35; James Walker, "The 'Jewish Phase' in the Movement for Racial Equality in Canada," *Canadian Journal of Ethnic Studies* 34:1 (2002): 1–29.

34 There were also a few legal cases, especially two involving discriminatory restrictive covenants, which were agreements that the purchaser of a property would not resell it to someone of a particular ethnic or religious group: *Drummond Wren* and *Noble and Wolf.* See James W. St. G. Walker, *"Race," Rights and the Law in the Supreme Court of Canada: Historical Case Studies* (Waterloo: Wilfrid Laurier Press, 1997), chapter 4; Lambertson, *Repression and Resistance*, chapters 5 and 7.

35 Carol Lee, "The Road to Enfranchisement: Chinese and Japanese in British Columbia," *BC Studies* 30 (Summer 1976): 44–76. Some First Nations opposed enfranchisement as a Trojan horse that would carry them along the road to assimilation. See Paul Tennant, *Aboriginal Peoples and Politics: The Indian Land Question in British Columbia, 1949–1989* (Vancouver: UBC Press, 1990), 121. Nevertheless, at the provincial level they received the vote in different provinces from the late 1940s to the late 1960s, and nationally in 1960. See Backhouse, *Colour-Coded*, 129.

36 Stephanie Bangarth, "'We are not asking you to open wide the gates for Chinese immigration': the Committee for the Repeal of the Chinese Immigration Act and early human rights activism in Canada," *Canadian Historical Review* 84 (September 2003): 395–422. Some racist immigration restrictions, however, remained until the 1960s.

37 Because of the case *Christie v. York*, discussed in the previous chapter, it was unlikely that litigation would put an end to private discrimination. Note that there continued, and in some cases increased, governmental discrimination against certain minority religious communities. In addition to the Doukhobor troubles (discussed below), Alberta, Manitoba, and Saskatchewan all limited the amount of land that could be purchased by Hutterite colonies. See William Janzen, *Limits on Liberty: The Experience of Mennonite, Hutterite, and Doukhobor Communities in Canada* (Toronto: University of Toronto Press, 1990), 64–73.

38 Lee, "The Road to Enfranchisement," 72–3.

39 Lambertson, *Repression and Resistance*, 76, 239, 381–2.

40 For a discussion of the role of religion in this period, see George Egerton, "Entering the Age of Human Rights: Religion, Politics, and Canadian Liberalism, 1945–50," *Canadian Historical Review* 85:3 (September 2004): 451–79.

41   Constance Backhouse, *Colour-Coded: A Legal History of Racism in Canada, 1900–1950* (Toronto: The Osgoode Society, 1999), chapter 7.

42   "Chief refused rooms because 'he's Indian'," *Victoria Daily Times*, 11 August 1955.

43   Tarnopolsky, "Discrimination in Canada," 12–14, and *Discrimination and the Law in Canada*; Shirley Tillotson, "Human Rights Law as Prism: Women's Organizations, Unions, and Ontario's Female Employees Fair Remuneration Act, 1951," *Canadian Historical Review* 72 (1991): 532–57.

44   See Ross Lambertson, "'The Dresden Story': Racism, Human Rights, and the Jewish Labour Committee of Canada," *Labour/Le Travail* 47 (Spring 2001): 43–82. See also Lambertson, *Repression and Resistance*, chapter 7.

45   Christopher MacLennan, *Toward the Charter: Canadians and the Demand for a National Bill of Rights, 1929–1960* (Montreal and Kingston: McGill-Queen's University Press, 2003); Lambertson, *Repression and Resistance*, chapter 8.

46   Tensions between these anti-state religious zealots and Canadian governments unwilling to make many concessions to their demands to be left alone produced a spate of Freedomite protests in the late 1940s and 1950s, including house burnings, nude marches, and the bombing of public facilities. This led to one of the most unsavoury rights violations in Canadian history—a decision by government to take children away from their Freedomite parents and resocialize them into mainstream Canadian society. See Janzen, *Limits on Liberty*; John McLaren, "The State, Child Snatching, and the Law: The Seizure and Indoctrination of Sons of Freedom Children in British Columbia, 1950–60," in John McLaren, Robert Menzies, and Dorothy E. Chunn, eds., *Regulating Lives: Historical Essays on the State, Society, the Individual, and the Law* (Vancouver: UBC Press, 2003): 259–93.

47   This was not a period in which "women's issues" were front and centre. However, there was some political pressure for legislation to prohibit gender discrimination in employment. See, for example, Tillotson, "Human Rights Law as Prism"; Ruth A. Frager and Carmela Patrias, *Discounted Labour: Women Workers in Canada, 1870–1939* (Toronto: University of Toronto Press, 2005), 154–5; Joan Sangster, *Dreams of Equality: Women on the Canadian Left* (Toronto: McClelland & Stewart, 1989).

48   For example, see Mary Louise Adams, *The Trouble with Normal: Postwar Youth and the Making of Heterosexuality* (Toronto: University of Toronto Press, 1977); Gary Kinsman, "'Character Weaknesses' and 'Fruit Machines': Towards an Analysis of the Anti-Homosexual Security Campaign in the Canadian Civil Service," *Labour/Le Travail* 35 (Spring 1995): 133–161, and *The Regulation of Desire: Homo and Hetero Sexualities*, 2nd ed. (Montreal: Black Rose, 1996); Becki Ross, "A Lesbian Politics of Erotic Decolonization," in Veronica Strong-Boag, Sherrill Grace, Avigail Eisenberg, and Joan Anderson, eds., *Painting the Maple: Essays on Race, Gender, and the Construction of Canada* (Vancouver: UBC Press, 1998): 187–214.

49   For example, see Ruth Marina McDonald, "A Policy of Privilege: The Alberta Sexual Sterilization Program 1928–1972," M.A. thesis (University of Victoria, 1996).

50   Lambertson, *Repression and Resistance*, 219, 233.

51   There was, of course, a huge gap between Soviet propaganda and reality.

52   I am not suggesting that prejudice and discrimination had been eliminated, or even that it is absent in Canada today. But some of the worst forms of discrimination had been made illegal and curtailed.

53   See, for example Tarnopolsky, *The Canadian Bill of Rights*. By the time of the revised second edition of the book (Toronto: McLelland and Stewart, 1975), the author was far more pessimistic about the Bill of Rights, primarily because of a leading case called *Attorney General for Canada v. Lavell, Isaac et al. v. Bedard* [1973] 38 D.L.R. (3d) 481.

54   Dominique Clément has distinguished between the "first generation" of rights organizations in the era ending in the early 1960s and the "second generation" groups that emerged later. See his "Rights in the Age of Protest: A History of the Human Rights and Civil Liberties Movement in Canada, 1962–1983," Ph.D. diss. (Memorial University, Newfoundland, 2005).

Glossary

Egalitarian rights. These rights, which are rooted in liberalism, are supposed to ensure that people will be treated as equals and not as second-class citizens by either the state or other members of society. This includes the right not to suffer discrimination because of one's sex or gender, race, religion, etc.

Federal-provincial division of powers. The British North America Act permits Ottawa to pass laws only on certain matters and the provinces to pass laws only on other matters.

The courts can sometimes protect a right by holding that an unjust law (either federal or provincial) is unconstitutional because it violates this division of powers.

Libertarian rights. These rights, which are rooted in liberalism, are supposed to ensure that people will enjoy free speech, free association, freedom of religion, etc., as well as certain procedural rights, such as the right to habeas corpus, the right to be presumed innocent until proven guilty, and the right to an impartial judge.

Parliamentary supremacy. The British principle that laws made by Parliament are supreme over all other laws. This principle is implicit in the BNA Act, and it permits either Ottawa or a province to override human rights, as long as the legislature is not violating the federal-provincial division of powers set out in the BNA Act. The 1982 Charter of Rights and Freedoms places limits on the principle of parliamentary supremacy.

Sedition. Essentially, attempting to overthrow the state or government by means of violence. However, in the past this was vaguely defined and could encompass even such things as causing social unrest or engaging in harsh criticism of the government or the courts.

Social unionism. Trade union activity that goes beyond simply campaigning for rights such as the right to form a trade union, to go on strike, or to picket. This activity includes campaigns for worker education and other programs involving social welfare and human rights work.

Further Reading

Berger, Thomas. *Fragile Freedoms: Human Rights and Dissent in Canada.* Toronto: Irwin Press, 1981.

This is a popular history of human rights in Canada. It looks at a number of issues during World War II and afterwards: the treatment of Japanese Canadians, limitations on the rights of Communists, the struggle of Jehovah's Witnesses for religious freedom, and the struggle of the Nisga'a for Aboriginal title.

Kaplan, William. *State and Salvation: The Jehovah's Witnesses and Their Fight for Civil Rights.* Toronto: University of Toronto Press, 1989.

This explains how and why the Jehovah's Witnesses were considered to be subversive, and how they resisted their suppression.

Lambertson, Ross. *Repression and Resistance: Canadian Human Rights Activists, 1930–1960.* Toronto: University of Toronto Press, 2005, 375.

This looks at both libertarian and egalitarian rights issues, especially the Padlock Law, civil liberties problems during World War Two, the attempted deportation of Japanese Canadians at the end of the war, the Gouzenko crisis, the suppression of communism, the struggle for anti-discrimination legislation, and campaigns for a Canadian Bill of Rights.

Schmeiser, D. A. *Civil Liberties in Canada.* London: Oxford University Press, 1964.

This is a law professor's discussion of civil liberties cases from Confederation until the early 1960s.

Whitaker, Reg, and Gary Marcuse, *Cold War Canada: The Making of a National Insecurity State, 1945–1957.* Toronto: University of Toronto Press, 1994.

This is the most comprehensive discussion of the post-war "red scare" era in Canada, when governments and others tried to suppress communism.

Relevant Websites

Canada in the Making

www.canadiana.org/citm/specifique/asian_e.html

www.canadiana.org/citm/specifique/abagitation_e.html

This site contains specific events and topics in Canadian human rights history. The first part of this website, "Asian Immigration," contains a brief historical overview of Asians in Canada, from the very beginning (1788) to the 1990s. It touches upon most of the ways Asian immigrants suffered discrimination. The second part, "Aboriginal Political Agitation," touches upon the many grievances of First Nations peoples, as well as their resistance to injustice. It contains a good link to the topic of treaties and relations.

Canadian Black Heritage in the Third Millennium

fcis.oise.utoronto.ca/~gpieters/blklinks.html

This is "an online resource for educators, researchers, writers, students and people researching Black History from a Canadian Perspective." It also contains a number of useful Internet links.

CHAPTER 3

"RIGHTS WITHOUT THE SWORD ARE BUT MERE WORDS":

THE LIMITS OF CANADA'S RIGHTS REVOLUTION

Dominique Clément

Introduction

Is pornography free speech? Are housewives entitled to any assets if they seek a divorce? Is equality about treating people the same or providing everyone with the same opportunities? The following article provides a brief overview of some of the core themes of Canada's rights revolution, defined herein as the creation of a state apparatus for protecting human rights and the emergence of a grass roots human rights movement. Human rights are, by their very nature, statist. This does not mean that human rights are derived from the state. In fact, human rights claims have a powerful *moral* force in our community. Nonetheless, human rights are not fully realized until they are recognized and enforced by the state. Thus, to play on Hobbes' famous phrase, rights without the sword are but mere words. In the following article we explore the origins of the modern human rights state in Canada in an international context, and consider the obstacles and limits to a statist conception of human rights.

In 1960, four Black freshmen from the Agricultural and Technical College in Greensboro, North Carolina, sat down at a Whites-only lunch counter in Woolworths and refused to move until they were served. Their singular act of defiance against a culture of oppression inspired thousands across the United States, and a wave of sit-ins soon swept across the South. Over time, the American Civil Rights Movement of the fifties and sixties has become the stuff of legend. Most Canadians today would undoubtedly recognize references to Martin Luther King, *Brown v. Board of Education*, or the National Association for the Advancement of Colored People. But who would be as familiar with Frank Scott, *Switzman v. Elbling*, or the Jewish Labour Committee? Unbeknownst to many Canadians today, a similar rights revolution took place in Canada, often led by the same minorities who felt the sting of discrimination. In small-town Dresden, Ontario, one of the most segregated communities in Canada in the fifties, African Canadians fought for the right to be served at Morley McKay's diner, which, until 1956, only served Whites. At one point, a Black man was seriously concerned that he might be attacked by the restaurant owner, who was wielding a large meat cleaver and appeared to be having trouble controlling his notorious temper.[1] Only after a protracted struggle would African Canadians in Dresden eventually secure the right to eat anywhere, irrespective of their skin colour.

Mobilizing the state to act as guarantor of human rights is one of the central themes in the history of the Canadian human rights movement. A powerful grass roots movement, often led by the same people who were targets of violence and discrimination, was ultimately successful in securing numerous state human rights polices and laws. Yet, despite the incredible achievements of the past three generations, the rights revolution was no panacea. Many leading human rights advocates have historically proffered a limited conception of rights by either being blind to discrimination against other people in their community, or focusing on civil and political rights to the detriment of social rights. Moreover, while the value of early human rights legislation should not be overlooked, it is critical to appreciate the limits of these reforms in both their content and application. The history of the rights revolution in Canada is in many ways a testament to the limits of human rights activism and human rights law.

What Is a Human Right?

"The language of rights is used in so many circumstances, to defend so many lines of argument, that it is now a debased form of rhetoric."[2] As Beth Gaze and Melinda Jones have suggested, we lack a clear understanding of human rights. It has evolved into a vague discourse that is used to defend everything from free speech to making war on oppressive regimes.

Within the vast international literature on human rights, scholars generally place human rights claims into two distinct categories.[3] *Civil* and *political rights* refer to those rights necessary to the functioning of a liberal capitalist democratic state, including private property, due process (e.g., fair trial), speech, religion, association, assembly, and free press. *Economic, social,* and *cultural rights* (referred to hereafter as social rights) are primarily associated with the modern welfare state. Health care, education, and abortion, for example, are considered by many people today as human rights. These conceptual divisions have been an integral part of contemporary debates over human rights. In 1948, the United Nations' General Assembly (with the Soviet bloc, South Africa, and Saudi Arabia abstaining) passed the Universal Declaration of Human Rights (UDHR). The UDHR, however, was little more than a statement of vague principles. When the time came to create a treaty to bind states to a series of human rights principles, the United Nations was forced to create two distinct covenants.[4]

Defining and applying human rights norms is a difficult process. Despite being quick to blame other countries for their poor human rights record, the United States did not ratify the 1966 International Covenant on Civil and Political Rights until 1992 (and only with numerous reservations attached). The United States has yet to ratify its sister document, the International Covenant on Economic, Social and Cultural Rights. Canada ratified both covenants in 1976, but the Charter of Rights and Freedoms, an American-style Bill of Rights that was added to the Canadian Constitution in 1982 and has since become an

• icon of Canada's human rights system, is almost silent with regards to social rights. If Canada could be said to have a rights culture, it is arguably limited by a conception of rights as liberal, individualistic, and favouring civil and political rights over social rights.[5]

The most common argument against social rights is that the right to vote or to due process does not require positive state action, whereas it would be unrealistic to bind the state to provide, for example, all of its citizens with adequate housing. Social rights require the state to actively distribute resources in order for people to participate equally in their community. Yet, as Isaiah Berlin, one of the most famous liberal thinkers of the twentieth century, once suggested: "To offer political rights, or safeguards against intervention by the state, to men who are half-naked, illiterate, underfed, and diseased is to mock their condition; they need medical help or education before they can understand, or make use of, an increase in their freedom."[6] It is not impractical to impose economic obligations on the state; after all, consider the huge costs involved in maintaining a justice system. We choose not to provide adequate housing to all Canadians, not because we lack the resources, but for political and economic reasons.

Historical studies in Canada on the human rights movement often assume that human rights activism is inherently progressive. But the devil is in the details, and the application of human rights norms should be examined critically. For instance, human rights claims often come into conflict. In theory, free speech is a noble ideal, but it must be applied in a particular cultural context to have meaning. Does a commitment to gender equality require us to censor pornography, or is this a violation of free speech? These debates often pit honest defenders of human rights against each other. John Dixon, a former president of the British Columbia Civil Liberties Association (a group dedicated to defending free speech), once quipped about his organization's relationship with the women's movement: "It was very soon the case that we got to be called unconscious exploiters only on our luckiest days."[7] Rights discourse also encourages activists to conceive of social change as legal change. As Michael Mandel suggests, the courts have historically been a poor forum for promoting systemic social change, and tend to be anti-statist, right wing, and pro-business.[8] Human rights activism can be also be elitist. Rainer Knopff and F. L. Morton have argued that the courts can be hijacked to promote the interests of a well-trained, educated minority who pursue social change through the courts because they are incapable of mobilizing enough support to promote change through the political process.[9] Clearly, human rights discourse should not be embraced uncritically, but should be appreciated for the obstacles and limits to equality inherent in their application.

Early Human Rights Campaigns

One of the most blatant violations of individual rights in Canadian history unfolded in the nation's capital in 1946. A young Russian cipher clerk from the Soviet embassy in

Ottawa, armed with evidence of a spy ring operating in Canada, decided to try his luck as a defector. Based on Igor Gouzenko's accusations, the federal government responded by invoking the draconian War Measures Act to detain dozens of *suspected* spies. Most historians and the popular media refer to the October Crisis of 1970 as the only time war powers have been used in peacetime in Canada; in fact, it was the second. The War Measures Act, a statute barely two pages long passed in 1914, provides the federal government, and by extension the cabinet, with dictatorial-like powers. A few cabinet members authorized the Royal Canadian Mounted Police (RCMP) to hold a group of people incommunicado, with no access to family or lawyers, trapped in tiny cells with little lighting and under suicide watch by an RCMP guard at all times. The suspects were vigorously interrogated, some for up to five weeks, and then brought before a royal commission, which had been implemented specifically for the purpose of circumventing the judicial system. Their testimony was later used against them and others in court. One of the detainees, Emma Woikin, was so traumatized by her incarceration that, when she was finally brought before a judge, all she could do was repeat over and over again, in a flat and unnatural tone, "I did it ."[10]

As late as the 1940s, the term "human rights" had yet to gain popular currency in Canada. Instead, Canadians were possessed of civil liberties, those fundamental rights gained on the battlefield of Runnymede and with the death of kings who denied their people the right to practice their own religion or arbitrarily imprisoned their subjects. In the United States, the Supreme Court has historically been responsible for protecting individual rights from the state by invalidating government legislation that offends the Bill of Rights. In contrast, the Canadian Constitution of 1867 did not contain a declaration of rights. Parliament, not the courts, would be the ultimate guarantor of people's rights.[11] Thus, in 1946 the Minister of Justice, J. L. Ilsley, could justify his government's decision to suspend the rights of suspected spies by appealing to the principle of parliamentary supremacy. Fundamental freedoms were "privileges which can be and which unfortunately sometimes have to be interfered with by the actions of Parliament or actions under the authority of Parliament."[12] By the 1940s, however, many Canadians reacted to appeals to parliamentary supremacy with increasing skepticism.

The Gouzenko Affair and similar examples of gross violations of civil liberties by the state prompted people to fight back. Human rights laws simply did not exist by the 1940s. It was a fact of daily life in Canada that everyone did not enjoy the same rights. While the federal government laid the groundwork for detaining suspected spies in 1946, thousands of Canadian citizens of Japanese descent were deported to Japan in the aftermath of the Second World War (WWII).[13] Immigration policies were explicitly racist until 1962 and restrictive covenants (restrictions on the ethnic, racial, or religious mix in a neighbourhood) were common. During WWII, Canada was among the world's least hospitable destinations for Jewish refugees, allowing barely 5,000 to enter during the course of the war. Blacks and many other minorities who sought to enlist were rejected by recruiting centres. Women did not get the vote in Quebec until 1940, and several minority groups, including Aboriginals, were denied the right to vote until well after the war. Without the franchise, individuals could not hold public office or serve on a jury. Minorities were regularly denied licences to operate businesses. Anti-semitism, segregation amongst Blacks and Whites in Nova Scotia and Southern Ontario schools, limited economic opportunities for women, and widespread discrimination against Aborignals was a basic reality of life in Canada.

Early human rights campaigns were undertaken by many of the same people who experienced discrimination. Jews, in particular, were at the forefront of leading many of the early human rights campaigns. The Jewish Labour Committee (JLC), formed in 1936, established offices across Canada and worked alongside organized labour to promote tolerance towards all minorities.[14] By the 1940s, the labour movement had become one of the leading forces in the human rights movement, a position that represented a significant shift in its attitudes towards racial minorities. For most of the first half of the twentieth century, labour had been a strong proponent of closed borders. Labour leaders portrayed immigrants and racial/ethnic minorities, most notably the Chinese in British Columbia, as low wage strike-breakers who threatened the power of organized labour.[15] Changes within the labour force and the realization that racism was a significant obstacle to working class unity had a profound impact on the labour movement (over two million immigrants entered the country between 1946 and 1961, many of whom filled the ranks of unions).[16] Racial minorities were also active agents in challenging their own marginalization. In 1946, for instance, a group of Chinese Canadians formed the Committee for the Repeal of the Chinese Immigration Act to lobby for the removal of a ban on Chinese immigration to Canada.[17] Racial and religious minorities found allies among the country's white, Anglo-Saxon elite. A collection of civil liberties associations, the first in Canadian history, emerged in the 1930s and by the 1940s played a key role in campaigning for the implementation of human rights legislation.[18]

Many of the early campaigns centred around two objectives: a Bill of Rights entrenched in the constitution, and anti-discrimination legislation for employment, services, and housing. A breakthrough occurred in Saskatchewan in 1947 when the Co-Operative Commonwealth Federation, led by Tommy Douglas, passed the country's first Bill of Rights (as a statute applicable only in that province). In Ontario, the JLC and the Civil Liberties Association of Toronto successfully mobilized dozens of organizations to lobby for legislation banning discrimination. Their efforts bore some fruit in 1951 when the Conservative government of Leslie Frost passed the country's first Fair Employment Practices legislation, followed soon after by a Female Employees Fair Remuneration Act and a Fair Accommodation Practices Act. Within five years similar laws were enacted in five other provinces.[19] Another landmark achievement of the early human rights movement was the enactment of a federal Bill of Rights in 1960 under the Conservative government of John Diefenbaker. The Bill of Rights, which purported to empower judges to veto legislation that violated fundamental freedoms such as free speech or due process, was a radical departure from a political tradition in which the courts did not challenge legislation passed by Parliament unless it was beyond the government's jurisdiction.

Canada's early human rights campaigns paralleled similar developments on the international scene. The Charter of the United Nations included a mandate to promote human rights and the United Nations General Assembly had passed the UDHR in 1948. Within a generation the United Nations had established a human rights commission to monitor various human rights treaties developed in the wake of the UDHR. Canada's human rights movement predated international developments, but the international community provided domestic activists with greater ammunition for making human rights claims at home. Activists could exploit Canada's international commitments to pressure the state to implement human rights policies.

At first glance, these achievements appear to have placed important limits on the state. In theory, the courts were now in a position to act as a check on the actions of both the state and private citizens who violated individual rights. Certainly no one would dispute that human rights activists had achieved a significant victory with the creation of laws clearly delineating people's rights. More importantly, a new culture of rights was emerging. As James Walker notes, rights discourse and the role of the state had traditionally favoured the discriminator; the rights to freedom of speech or association were interpreted to mean the right to refuse service to certain peoples or to express prejudicial ideas. In contrast, anti-discrimination legislation "represented a fundamental shift, a reversal, of the traditional notion of citizens' rights to enroll the state as the protector of the right of the victim to freedom from discrimination. It was, in fact, a revolutionary change in the definition of individual freedom."[20] Racial hierarchies were challenged as immoral, women demanded equal pay, and religious minorities spoke out against state repression.

The reality, however, was that these were baby steps. Anti-discrimination legislation went largely unused; a decade after their implementation in Ontario only two complaints had been sustained.[21] Early anti-discrimination legislation signalled a new era of state intervention to protect minorities; yet it was weakly enforced and many people hesitated to embrace this new role for the state, which they saw as legislating morality. After the passing of the Ontario Racial Discrimination Act in 1944, which prohibited the display of discriminatory signs, Ontario Premier George Drew emphasized that "the best way to avoid racial and religious strife is not by imposing a method of thinking, but by teaching our children that we are all members of a great human family."[22] Judges, who found it difficult to conceive of discrimination as a criminal act, were reluctant to convict. Fines did not help victims find new jobs and most minorities were unaware of the existence of the legislation.[23] Perhaps the most damning indictment of early human rights legislation, however, was the lack of any recognition of discrimination faced by women. None of the early anti-discrimination laws, and even the Ontario Human Rights Code of 1962, did not include sex discrimination. Early human rights campaigns simply did not prioritize gender discrimination and male activists were often blind to discrimination against women.

As for the federal Bill of Rights, with the exception of a single case in the late 1960s, it was never used to invalidate government legislation. It was a vague and limited statute that contained only the most elementary civil and political rights. Frank Scott, perhaps the country's most notable constitutional scholar in this period, disdained the law: "That pretentious piece of legislation has proven as ineffective as many of us predicted."[24]

In many ways, the achievements of early human rights activists highlighted the weaknesses of the country's early human rights regime. Frank Scott, for instance, defended the rights of two popular targets of repression (Communists and Jehovah's Witnesses) in a series of famous civil liberties cases in the 1950s. Maurice Duplessis, the autocratic Premier of Quebec who claimed that the Bible was sufficient protection for human rights, waged a virtual war against unpopular minorities. Communists were easy targets in the heydays of the Cold War, and Jehovah's Witnesses, whose religion led them to viciously attack the Roman Catholic Church (often on people's doorsteps), were hardly popular in a vastly Catholic province. In *Switzman v. Elbling* (1957), Scott convinced the Supreme Court of Canada to invalidate a Quebec law that allowed the province to padlock any premises suspected of promoting communism (without warrant or the need for any evidence). The law, passed in the 1930s, had long been considered one of the most offensive violations of civil liberties in a generation; it was so vague that it was used against unionists, Jews, Jehovah's Witnesses, Communists, and people on the political left in general. Victims could only appeal to the Attorney General who, conveniently, was Duplessis (he was both Attorney General and the Premier). Scott was involved in two other important civil liberties cases: *Saumur v. City of Quebec and Attorney-General* (1953) and *Roncarelli v. Duplessis* (1959). In both cases, the court provided redress to Jehovah's Witnesses who were targets of repression and abuse in Quebec.

Still, as with the groundbreaking legislation of the fifties, these victories had limits. Although several judges referred to the sanctity of freedom of speech and religion, in the end their decisions had little to do with civil liberties. Instead, in *Switzman* and *Saumur*, the court ruled that the province had exceeded its jurisdiction under the constitution. The Bill of Rights was little help. In *Attorney General of Canada v. Lavell* (1974), the court refused to accept that a section of the Indian Act, which required women (but not men) to surrender their Indian status if they married a non-Indian, was a violation of the Bill of Rights' guarantee of equality under the law. The court essentially claimed that the government could discriminate against Aboriginal women as long as it discriminated against all Aboriginal women equally. A year later, in *Murdoch v. Murdoch*, the court once again demonstrated the limits of these early achievements. After having worked most of her life on a farm, an abused farm wife claimed that she was entitled to half of her husband's assets after their divorce. The court disagreed. With a lone dissent by Bora Laskin, the judges concluded that her labour constituted the expected obligations of a farm wife and that she was entitled to nothing.

The Age of Rights:
Activism and the Human Rights State

The creation of the welfare state was a milestone in the evolving role of the state in Canada. True, social rights were not entrenched to the same degree as civil and political rights. Ontario's anti-discrimination legislation banned employers from refusing jobs to African Canadians, but it did nothing to alleviate the poverty facing racial minorities or recognize employment as a human right. Nevertheless, such welfare state programs as unemployment and health insurance protected citizens from fluctuations in the market economy. The expansion of the welfare state represented a challenge to traditional conceptions of rights as civil and political rights.

A cultural shift was underway by the sixties. James Walker, for example, has identified three stages in the movement for racial equality. The first phase, "equal citizenship," sought to end legal distinctions among citizens in areas such as immigration and the franchise; the second phase involved demands for "protective shields," which led to anti-discrimination legislation; and the third phase, "remedial sword," involved state policies designed to "correct systemic conditions that produce discriminatory results even in the apparent absence of overt prejudicial acts."[25] Each phase was informed by changing common sense notions about race and the nature of prejudice. Anti-discrimination legislation campaigns were guided by a belief that discriminatory acts were the result of individual aberrant behaviour, or psychological problems attributed to pathological individuals. These individuals influenced popular notions of what was right and moral (like a contagious disease). The solution, therefore, was to stop the disease at its source, and mobilize the state to prevent individual acts of discrimination.

In the sixties and seventies, the move towards "remedial sword" policies in the form of proactive human rights commissions or funding for education programs paralleled another shift in ideas about the nature of prejudice. Instead of focusing on the threat of pathologically prejudiced individuals, human rights activists increasingly raised concerns about systemic racism. In Toronto, for instance, although the Canadian Civil Liberties Association (CCLA) refused to support employment quotas (requiring employers to hire a minimum number of minorities or women), it recognized that two decades after the passing of the Fair Employment Practices Act, certain professions remained bastions of white male Christians. Firemen were a perfect example. Toronto's fire department in the mid-seventies employed only two non-whites, less than 0.2% of the workforce. As a solution, the CCLA called on the city to implement new hiring practices, such as recruiting in minority areas and advertising in the ethnic press, or requesting non-white leaders to recruit candidates.[26] Meanwhile, feminists spoke about the "glass ceiling," the disabled demanded a rethinking of "normal" or ableness, and gay liberationists challenged ideas about sexuality and the family. These developments were informed by a belief that prejudice could be unspoken and systemic, rather than simply the overt act of individuals.

The rights revolution entered a new phase in the sixties with the rise of a powerful grassroots human rights movement. It is fair to say that by this time Canadians participated in social movements to a degree never before seen in history. Social movement activism defined the sixties and seventies. Civil disobedience, mass demonstrations, and the emergence of new collective identities were only some of the many forms of collective behaviour and contentious actions that characterized the social movement activism of the boomer generation.

At the same time, people began to *organize* in unprecedented levels. New student groups exploded on to the scene, led by the Combined University Campaign for Nuclear Disarmament, the Student Union for Peace Action, the Union général des étudiants québécois, and the Company of Young Canadians. Women's organizations proliferated. In British Columbia alone, women established more than a hundred advocacy groups (there were only 2 in 1969), 46 women's centres, 15 transition houses, and 12 rape crisis centres in the 1970s. The country's first organizations representing homosexuals appeared in Vancouver in 1964 (Association for Social Knowledge) and Toronto in 1969 (University of Toronto Homophile Association). Aboriginals were also highly active in mobilizing locally and at the national level. Between 1960 and 1969 four national Aboriginal associations and 33 separate provincial organizations were born. By the mid-1980s, the federal Secretary of State was providing funding to 3,500 community groups across the country.[27] Prisoners' rights groups became increasingly vocal and well organized; the Quebec Prisoners' Rights Committee, one of the most prominent in the country, sought the abolition of all prisons. Greenpeace was founded in Vancouver in 1971. Perhaps the only thread linking all of these disparate movements was a discourse of rights. Canada's rights revolution had finally come of age.

Once again, developments at home mirrored international trends. By 1996, there were no less than 295 registered human rights groups worldwide, almost half of which were formed since the seventies. Amnesty International was founded in 1961 and was awarded the Nobel Peace Prize in 1977. Human Rights Watch began to monitor compliance with the Helsinki Accords in 1978, a landmark achievement in which the Soviet Union, for the first time in history, agreed to a series of human rights principles in a treaty. The United Nations human rights regime also matured. The United Nations' Human Rights Committee and the Committee on the Elimination of Racial Discrimination came into being to enforce the covenant on civil and political rights and the International

Convention on the Elimination of All Forms of Racial Discrimination. An Inter-American Commission and Court of Human Rights were instituted following the ratification in 1978 of the American Convention on Human Rights (representing South, Central, and North America). The European Convention of Human Rights came into effect in 1953, but it was not until the early 1970s that the institutions it created, particularly the court, began to play an important role in the implementation of the Convention.

Federal and provincial legislation to protect human rights was implemented in Canada. Privacy Acts were passed in most jurisdictions by the 1980s; they protected individuals from such actions as unnecessary police wiretaps or insurance companies disclosing information about their clients. British Columbia became the first province to prohibit sex discrimination in 1969 and, in the same year, linguistic rights were reaffirmed with the passage of the federal Official Languages Act. Children were recognized as having their own rights as well. Quebec's Youth Protection Act of 1977, for instance, guaranteed youths the right to be consulted about switching foster care parents and to consult a lawyer before judicial proceedings, while the Ontario Child Welfare Act of 1978 protected the privacy of adopted children. Restrictions on women serving on juries were removed by the 1980s, as were requirements for women to leave the civil service after they were married. Mental patients also became rights-bearing citizens; in some jurisdictions, they were included in minimum wage laws and greater restrictions were placed on forcible confinement. The first major land-claims treaty was signed in 1975 between the Quebec government and the James Bay Cree to develop hydro power, and revisions to the Indian Act placed First Nations on more equal footing with other Canadians. Female Aboriginals, for instance, could now retain their status after marrying non-Aboriginals. Prisoners were granted the vote for the first time in Quebec in 1979.

Meanwhile, human rights activists, including the Jewish Labour Committee, sought improvements to the anti-discrimination laws passed in the fifties. Ontario introduced the first Human Rights Code in Canada in 1962 (by 1977, every jurisdiction in the country had introduced a Code). Unlike previous anti-discrimination laws, human rights codes were far more expansive; they consolidated all existing human rights legislation into one statute, which dealt with discrimination in employment, services, and housing. Whereas the fair practices legislation of the fifties mainly focused on racial, ethnic, and religious discrimination, human rights codes included a host of new categories such as gender and political opinion (an innovation introduced by Newfoundland in 1969). One of the most frustrating aspects of the early anti-discrimination laws was the lack of an effective enforcement mechanism; the Minister of Labour had to agree to create an ad hoc commission to investigate a complaint. In contrast, human rights codes were enforced by standing commissions with full-time government staff who educated the public and helped victims of discrimination advance their claims. Human rights violators could, among other options, be forced to pay a fine, provide a service, apologize to an employee, or re-hire someone. Human rights commissions remain a mainstay of the state's human rights program today, although in 1984 British Columbia enjoyed the dubious distinction of being the first province to disband its human rights commission (it was re-established in 1994 only to be disbanded, again, in 2002).

These developments set the stage for the ultimate manifestation of the human rights state: the Charter of Rights and Freedoms passed in 1982. The Charter did more than create a legal framework for defending human rights; it represented a significant cultural shift. Common sense notions about racial hierarchies, gender roles, and the role of the state had to change before the Charter could be embraced by Canadians. Parliamentary supremacy was all but abandoned. As early as 1970, a Special Committee on the Constitution concluded that "parliamentary sovereignty is no more sacrosanct a principle than is the respect for human liberty which is reflected in a Bill of Rights."[28] Granted, section 33 of the new constitution allowed governments to immunize laws from legislative review, a remnant of a political tradition in which the legislature was supreme. Yet, certain parts of the Charter were protected from section 33 (specifically, democratic rights such as the right to vote and hold office, as well as mobility and language rights), and it quickly became apparent that political leaders would only employ the controversial section to their peril (section 33 has only been used once outside Quebec).

Canada's rights culture, however, still had limits. Social rights had been realized through a variety of state policies, from health care to labour legislation. Yet, social rights lacked the status of civil and political rights. The protections contained in the Charter, for instance, were primarily civil and political rights. With the exception of language rights, clauses that could be characterized as "social rights," such as multiculturalism, have proven to be weak and ineffective. Unlike countries such as South Africa, Canada's constitution continues to offer no clear commitment to social rights.

Social rights advocates have enjoyed their own victories over time. Through the Charter, for example, people who are deaf have successfully fought for the right to have sign-language interpreters in hospitals. The experience of the labour movement, however, is one example of how social rights are not easily enforced in Canada. The Supreme Court of Canada has been hostile to any suggestion that the Charter's guarantee of freedom of association includes the right to strike or collective bargaining. The court ruled in 1987 against organized labour in a series of challenges to provincial and federal wage controls and prohibitions on strikes. Although Chief Justice Brian Dickson acknowledged that the "role of association has always been vital as a means of protecting the essential needs and interests of working people," the court did not accept that freedom of association meant the right to strike.[29] This did not prevent the court from extending freedom of association to the right to advertise and the right of two companies to merge. In fact, only a year earlier, an Ontario judge ruled that a union could not use its members' dues to support a political party even though such a restriction would not apply to a professional organization or a corporation (the Supreme Court of Canada overruled the decision in 1991). Given the labour movement's dismal experience with the Charter, legal historian Michael Mandel concluded that "the whole idea of the Charter can be seen as a legitimation of the basic inequalities of Canadian society, of which the subordination of labour to business is one of the most basic."[30]

The Charter is only one of many examples of how various institutions in Canada promote a limited conception of rights. Non-governmental organizations (NGOs) are often guilty of focusing too much on civil and political rights, and fail to take into consideration the underlying socio–economic factors that lead to rights violations.[31] Irwin Cotler, a future federal Minister of Justice, suggested in the early 1990s that at the time "a disproportionate number of NGOs deal with matters pertaining to political and civil rights, while the cause of economic, social and cultural rights appears to be under-represented among the NGOs."[32]

Take, for instance, one of the largest and most influential human rights organizations in the country: the Canadian Civil Liberties Association (CCLA). With more than 5,000 members in the early 1980s, the Toronto-based CCLA (which was founded in 1964) had evolved into one of the largest and most established advocacy groups in the country. By the turn of the twenty-first century, the CCLA has intervened in the Supreme Court of Canada more times than any other organization in the country, except for the Women's Legal Education and Action Fund. Throughout its entire history, the CCLA and other like-minded organizations have promoted a limited conception of human rights. No issue best exemplifies the association's rights philosophy than Ontario's infamous "man in the house" rule.

Jennifer Smith was a thirty-year-old single mother trying to raise four children in Toronto after having been deserted by her husband.[33] She was taking courses to complete her high school degree and had been on welfare since the mid-1960s. Smith received an unexpected letter in 1970 informing her that her welfare was being cut off because she was no longer living as a single person.[34] Single women suspected of having a male in the house were routinely denied access to welfare. The government simply assumed that men, as breadwinners, would provide for women. The "man in the house" rule clearly discriminated against women, assuming a sexual relationship implied a financial one, and the abruptness with which recipients could be denied welfare raised the potential for numerous procedural abuses. There were also serious concerns about the tactics employed by the welfare office in determining whether women were living as single persons. During some surprise visits, inspectors would demand to know about the most intimate aspects of a recipient's relationships and in some cases drew conclusions based on such flimsy evidence as the presence of open beer cans or a raised toilet seat.[35]

Smith was typical of single mothers in the seventies and eighties who were victims of a welfare system eager to cut costs. Recipients lived well below the poverty line, receiving an estimated 60 percent of the basic amount required to lead a healthy and functional lifestyle.[36] As one CCLA study suggested, a "person accused of the most heinous crimes enjoys more discernible protection of his domestic privacy than does an innocent recipient of public welfare."[37]

The CCLA helped Smith secure her benefits. Unfortunately, the "man in the house" rule was more resilient and lasted until 1986 when the Ontario government, concerned that the regulation violated the newly entrenched Charter of Rights and Freedoms, decided to eliminate the regulation.[38] What is significant, however, is that in all its years of advocacy on behalf of welfare recipients, at no time did the CCLA suggest that welfare recipients had a right to better benefits. The amount of welfare individuals received was never an issue; the group was solely concerned with the procedures for distributing benefits. In other words, the CCLA was only concerned with the *administration* of welfare and the equitable treatment of welfare recipients, not the amount or the nature of state support.

Such a conception of rights is inherently limited, if not outright contradictory. In many ways, negative rights (civil and political rights) *derive* from positive (social) rights, and to deny the latter is to undermine the former:

> Rules, regulations, laws, and other forms of coercion, manipulation, and threat are all limitations upon one's negative freedom—some justified, some not. These are familiar restrictions. Lack of training, accommodation of needs, or realistic opportunities are also restrictions; they are limitations upon one's positive freedom, one's capacity to exercise one's freedom to do or become what one wishes. Both kinds of freedom open the door to options and choices, but only positive freedom captures the actual capability to achieve or bring about what one chooses. Since the importance of negative freedom presumes one's abilities to do or become something, if one so chooses, the value of negative freedom must be derivative from positive freedom.[39]

The idea of social rights has had many advocates. Anti-poverty groups and disability rights activists, for instance, have long demanded that that state recognize their social rights. In the sixties and seventies, however, when the key building blocks of the modern human rights state were established, the state did not embrace the notion of social rights. Human rights codes were a significant breakthrough but, despite their broad mandate, human rights commissions dealt almost exclusively with employment discrimination (86% of the Ontario commission's case load involved employment in 1979–80).[40] Moreover, human rights commissions had a mandate to promote awareness but they were not proactive: commissions had to wait for individuals to file complaints. Thus, although the staff of the Ontario Human Rights Commission may have sympathized with the lack of ethnic minorities in the Toronto fire department, they could do nothing unless someone could prove that individuals had been victims of discrimination. But there are few things more difficult to prove than discrimination in hiring, since most employers do not inform applicants that they were denied a job because of their race or gender. Human rights codes conceived of human rights in terms of individual rights, and there were no provisions for collective remedies. Most human rights codes, for instance, did not allow for class action lawsuits on behalf of aggrieved minorities.

Human rights codes were never designed to deal with systemic inequalities. With the exception of Quebec and Alberta, human rights codes did not take primacy over other pieces of legislation. Quebec's Charter of Human Rights and Freedoms, in fact, stands out in many other ways from other human rights codes. When it was passed in 1975, the Quebec Charter included several progressive sections dealing with the needs of the elderly and children. But, as always, this innovation had limits. Despite repeated attempts by the Ligue des droits de l'homme, the government refused to recognize the right for elderly people to have affordable medication or the rights of prisoners to have healthy food. Many of the people intimately involved with human rights commissions have recognized these limitations. According to a 1975 report commissioned by the Ontario Human Rights Commission, the oldest and largest commission in the country:

> The most pervasive discrimination today often results from unconscious and seemingly neutral practices which may, none the less, be as detrimental to human rights as the more overt and intentional kind of discrimination. These practices perpetuate the discriminatory effects of past discrimination, even when overt acts of discrimination have ceased. Unfortunately, the Commission does not have the power, under the present Code to deal effectively with such practices despite their clearly discriminatory consequences.[41]

Canada's rights revolution, for all its impressive achievements, faced immense obstacles. The achievements of the human rights movement were ultimately overshadowed by a culture of rights that was individualistic, liberal, and concerned primarily with civil and political rights.[42]

Conclusions

Canada's rights revolution should be seen as the beginning, not the end, of the campaign for liberty and equality. There has often been a significant gap between the rhetoric of human rights and the implementation of human rights policies. This is not to deny the remarkable achievements of the twentieth century. In a generation, human rights activists helped transform the role of the state from an active agent of oppression into a tool for combating discrimination. Parliamentary supremacy no longer informs most of the political debates surrounding human rights, and an impressive state system for defending human rights was created. Today, it is illegal, and for most people morally repugnant, to deny Aboriginals work or services on the basis of their race. And yet, does the right to free speech, assembly, or to vote apply equally when Aboriginals are represented disproportionately among prisoners, the unemployed, and people who commit suicide? The history of human rights activism is as much about the limits of rights discourse as it is about the potential for human rights to promote equality and tolerance.

Acknowledgements

I would like to extend special thanks to Eric Sager (University of Victoria) for his feedback on an early draft of this article.

Notes

1   Ross Lambertson, "The Dresden Story: Racism, Human Rights, and the Jewish Labour Committee of Canada," *Labour/Le Travail* 47 (Spring 2001): 75.

2   Beth Gaze and Melinda Jones, *Law, Liberty and Australian Democracy* (Sydney: The Law Book Company Ltd., 1990), 9.

3   It is also common to see references to a third "generation" of rights in the human rights literature, specifically collective or developmental rights.

4   There are several useful introductory texts on the debates over the nature of human rights and civil liberties, including: Maurice Cranston, *What is a Human Right?* (New York: Basic Books, 1973); Jerome Shestack, "The Philosophic Foundations of Human Rights," *Human Rights Quarterly* 20:2 (1998); Michael Ignatieff, *The Rights Revolution* (Toronto: House of Anansi Press Ltd., 2000); Brian Orend, *Human Rights: Concept and Context* (Peterborough: Broadview Press, 2002); Jack Donnelly, *Universal Human Rights in Theory & Practice* (New York: Cornell University Press, 2003).

5   Gary Teeple provides a useful overview of the historical evolution of human rights and how rights entrench class inequalities. Gary Teeple, *The Riddle of Human Rights* (New York: Humanity Books, 2005).

6   Isaiah Berlin, *Four Essays on Liberty* (London: Oxford University Press, 1969), 124.

7   John Dixon, "The Porn Wars," in John Russell, ed., *Liberties* (Vancouver: New Star Books, 1989), 26.

8   Michael Mandel, *The Charter of Rights and the Legislation of Politics in Canada* (Toronto: Thompson Educational Publishing, 1994).

9   Rainer Knopff and F. L. Morton, *The Charter Revolution and the Court Party* (Peterborough: Broadview Press, 2000).

10   Dominique Clément, "The Royal Commission on Espionage and the Spy Trials of 1946–9: A Case Study in Parliamentary Supremacy," *Journal of the Canadian Historical Association* 11 (2000); Dominique Clément, "Spies, Lies and a Commission, 1946–8: A Case Study in the Mobilization of the Canadian Civil Liberties Movement," *Left History* 7, 2 (2001).

11   Although there is no reference to civil liberties or human rights in the British North America Act, section 92 refers to property and civil rights (section 92 delineates the jurisdiction of the provinces). However, the courts interpreted "civil rights" narrowly and limited the provinces' responsibilities under this section to contract and property law. Unlike the United States, therefore, the term "civil rights" has different connotations north of the border. It is more common to use the term "civil liberties" when discussing free speech or freedom of association.

12   NAC, John Diefenbaker Papers, series 3, v. 82, p. 65434, copy of St. Laurent speech before the House of Commons, 1947.

13   Technically, Canadian citizenship did not exist before 1947 and people in Canada held British citizenship. Nonetheless, the federal government's decision to deport its own citizens was virtually unheard of and was vigorously challenged in the courts, although in the end the Judicial Committee of the Privy Council in England supported the government's actions with only minor reservations.

14   For a history of the Jewish Labour Committee and the role of minorities in securing anti-discrimination legislation, refer to Ruth Frager and Carmela Patrias, "'This Is Our Country, These Are Our Rights': Minorities and the Origins of Ontario's Human Rights Campaigns," *The Canadian Historical Review* 82, 1 (March 2001).

[15] Bryan Palmer, *Working Class Experience: Rethinking the History of Canadian Labour, 1800–1991* (Toronto: McClelland & Stewart Inc., 1992), 266.

[16] Lambertson, "The Dresden Story," 48–9.

[17] Stephanie D. Bangarth, "'We are not asking you to open wide the gates for Chinese immigration': The Committee for the Repeal of the Chinese Immigration Act and Early Human Rights Activism in Canada," *Canadian Historical Review* 84, 3 (2003).

[18] Ross Lambertson, *Repression and Resistance: Canadian Human Rights Activists, 1930–1960* (Toronto: University of Toronto Press, 2005).

[19] Manitoba (1953), Nova Scotia (1955), New Brunswick (1956), British Columbia (1956), Saskatchewan (1956), and Quebec (1964). The first Fair Accommodation Practices Act was passed in Ontario in 1954, with Saskatchewan (1956), New Brunswick (1959), Nova Scotia (1959), Manitoba (1960), and British Columbia (1961) passing similar legislation. British Columbia enacted a more restricted statute in 1961 while Quebec avoided passing fair accommodation practices legislation entirely, but the government of Quebec did add a section to the Hotels Act to forbid discrimination in hotels, restaurants, and camping grounds. Walter Surma Tarnopolsky, *Discrimination and the Law in Canada* (Toronto: De Boo, 1982), 27–8.

[20] James Walker, "The 'Jewish Phase' in the Movement for Racial Equality in Canada," *Canadian Ethnic Studies* 34:1 (2002).

[21] *Toronto Star*, 3 August 1961.

[22] Quote in Walker, "The 'Jewish Phase' in the Movement for Racial Equality in Canada."

[23] Walter Tarnopolsky examines the history of early anti-discrimination legislation in Tarnopolsky, *Discrimination and the Law in Canada*.

[24] Frank Scott to Gordon Dowding, 20 September 1964, vol. 47, NAC, Frank Scott Papers, MG30, D211.

[25] Walker, "The 'Jewish Phase' in the Movement for Racial Equality in Canada," 1.

[26] Library and Archives of Canada (LAC), Canadian Civil Liberties Association Papers (CCLA), R9833, f. 14, v. 10, Submission to Ontario Human Rights Commission Re. Review of Ontario Human Rights Code, January 1977.

[27] For further information on the Secretary of State's funding programs, refer to Dominique Clément, *Canada's Rights Revolution: Social Movements and Social Change, 1937–1982* (Vancouver: UBC Press, 2008).

[28] Canada, 1972. *Special Joint Committee of the Senate and House of Commons on the Constitution of Canada—First Report*, 18–19.

[29] Reference Re. *Public Service Employee Relations Act* (Alta.), [1987] 1 S.C.R. 313.

[30] Mandel, *The Charter of Rights and the Legislation of Politics in Canada*, 260.

[31] For a sample of critiques raised about the activities of human rights NGOs, refer to Makau Mutua, *Human Rights: A Political and Cultural Critique* (Philadelphia: University of Pennsylvania Press, 2002); James Ron, Howard Ramos, and Kathleen Rodgers, "Transnational Information Politics: NGO Human Rights Reporting, 1986–2000," *International Studies Quarterly* 49, (2005); Teeple, *The Riddle of Human Rights*.

[32] Irwin Cotler, "Human Rights as the Modern Tool of Revolution," Kathleen E. Mahoney and Paul Mahoney, eds., *Human Rights in the Twenty-first Century: A Global Challenge* (London: Martinus Nijhoff Publishers, 1993), 19.

[33] Due to access-to-information regulations, Jennifer Smith's real name has been concealed.

[34] Alan Borovoy to John Yaremko, 4 January 1971, LAC, CCLA, R9833, vol. 15, f. 2.

[35] NAC, June Callwood Papers, MG31 K24, vol. 18, f. 6, extracts from a letter from the CCLA to John Yaremko, Minister of Social and Family Services, 15 June 1970.

[36] The Toronto Social Planning Council estimated that the average family of four required $3,000 annually to meet basic needs, but only received 60 percent of this amount, even after increases through General Welfare Assistance (Ontario) in 1967. Canadian Civil Liberties Association, *Welfare Practices and Civil Liberties—A Canadian Survey* (Toronto: Canadian Civil Liberties Education Trust, 1975).

[37] There were several reasons, practical and psychological, why women with an illegitimate child did not want to name the father. For instance, in several cases the women in question had married or moved in with another man and did not want to involve the father of one of her children in her life. In the study conducted by the CCLA, 37 women stated they were told to name the father and 32 did so. Canadian Civil Liberties Association, *Welfare Practices and Civil Liberties— A Canadian Survey* (Toronto: Canadian Civil Liberties Education Trust, 1975).

[38] *Globe and Mail*, 19 September 1986.

[39] Jerome Bickenback, *Physical Disability and Social Policy* (Toronto: University of Toronto Press, 1993), 37.

[40] Daiva Kristina Stasiulis, "Race, Ethnicity and the State: The Political Structuring of South Asian and West Indian Communal Action in Combating Racism," Ph.D. diss. (University of Toronto, 1982), 267.

[41] Ontario Human Rights Commission, *Life Together: A Report on Human Rights in Ontario*, July 1977, 33.

[42] Makau Wa Mutua examines the link between liberalism and the evolutions of "universal" human rights ideas in Makau Wa Mutua, "The Ideology of Human Rights," *Virginia Journal of International Law* 36 (1995–6): 591.

Glossary

Civil liberties (civil and political rights). Civil and political rights are those rights necessary to the functioning of a liberal capitalist democratic state, including private property, due process (e.g., fair trial), speech, religion, association, assembly, and free press.

Human rights (social, economic, and cultural rights). Economic, social, and cultural rights are primarily associated with the modern welfare state and include such rights as health care, education, and multiculturalism.

Human Rights Code. First implemented in Ontario in 1962, human rights codes prohibit discrimination in employment, services, and accommodation on the basis of numerous groups including, but not limited to, race, gender, religion, and age. Human rights commissions, composed of full-time salaried government employees, enforce the legislation.

Indian status. Aboriginals who are covered under the federal Indian Act are considered to have "Indian status." Indian status provides Aboriginals with a unique legal status in Canada.

Parliamentary supremacy. According to the famed British legal philosopher A.V. Dicey, the "principle of Parliamentary sovereignty means neither more nor less than this, namely, that Parliament thus defined has, under the English Constitution, the right to make or unmake any law whatever; and, further, that no person or body is recognised by the law of England as having a right to override or set aside the legislation of Parliament."

Further Reading

Bangarth, Stephanie. *Voices Raised in Protest: Defending North American Citizens of Japanese Ancestry, 1942–49.* Vancouver: UBC Press, 2007.

This book examines the removal and deportation of persons of Japanese ancestry during the Second World War by highlighting how its meaning and impact diverged in Canada and the United States.

Clément, Dominique. *Canada's Rights Revolution: Social Movements and Social Change, 1937–1982.* Vancouver: UBC Press, 2008.

In the first major study of post-war social movement organizations in Canada, Dominique Clément provides a history of the human rights movement as seen through the eyes of two generations of activists.

Clément, Dominique. "The October Crisis of 1970: Human Rights Abuses under the War Measures Act." *Journal of Canadian Studies* 42:2 (Spring 2008).

An important article on the human rights abuses that took place under the War Measures Act.

Lambertson, Ross. *Repression and Resistance: Canadian Human Rights Activists, 1930–1960.* Toronto: University of Toronto Press, 2005.

A significant publication that looks at human rights activists in Canada from 1930 to 1960.

MacLennan, Christopher. *Toward the Charter: Canadians and the Demand for a National Bill of Rights, 1929–1960*. Montreal: McGill-Queen's University Press, 2003, 1996.

In *Toward the Charter,* author Christopher MacLennan explores the origins of this dramatic revolution in Canadian human rights, from its beginnings in the Great Depression to the critical developments of the 1960s.

Tarnopolsky, Walter Surma. *Discrimination and the Law in Canada*. Toronto: De Boo, 1982.

A seminal work by Mr. Justice Walter Surma Tarnopolsky, a leading jurist, human rights activist, and internationally respected constitutional expert.

Walker, James. "The 'Jewish Phase' in the Movement for Racial Equality in Canada." *Canadian Ethnic Studies* 34, no. 1 (2002): 1–23.

An important article by a leading Canadian historian who specializes in human rights inquiries.

Relevant Websites

Canada's Rights Revolution: A History
www.HistoryofRights.com

A teaching and research portal on human rights and social movements in Canada. The site includes primary documents, narrative overviews, lists of key events and individuals, further reading, and key links.

Censorship in British Columbia
www.bclibrary.ca/bcla/ifc/censorshipbc/intro.html

This website contains a list of books, magazines, newspapers, and some music materials that have been subject to censorship challenges in British Columbia, including materials that have been banned nationwide by the government of Canada.

Supreme Court of Canada
www.scc-csc.ca

Recent cases are available on-line, as well as biographical data on all Supreme Court of Canada justices, past and present.

United Nations Human Rights Treaties
www.bayefsky.com

Bayefsky.com was designed for the purpose of enhancing the implementation of the human rights legal standards of the United Nations. Accessibility to UN human rights norms by individuals everywhere is fundamental to their successful realization. The information provided herein encompasses a range of data concerning the application of the UN human rights treaty system by its monitoring treaty bodies since their inauguration in the 1970s.

CHAPTER 4

THE SECOND WORLD WAR AND CANADA'S EARLY HUMAN RIGHTS MOVEMENT:
THE ASIAN CANADIAN EXPERIENCE

STEPHANIE BANGARTH

Introduction

In the famous Wilcoxon speech, the Vicar in the British Second World War film, *Mrs. Miniver*, proclaimed, "… this is not only a war of soldiers in uniform. It is a war of the people, of all the people, and it must be fought not only on the battlefield, but in the cities and in the villages, in the factories and on the farms, in the home, and in the heart of every man, woman, and child who loves freedom!"[1] The powerful "national experience" that war elicited from its participating nations resulted in significant changes, both positive and negative, to the economic, social, cultural, and political spheres in Canada. Specifically, the World War II period heralded the start of a concerted battle at home to end racial persecution and to recognize the human rights of all citizens of Canada. While the battle for rights certainly did not involve "every man, woman, and child," groups of Canadians roused the ire of their fellow citizens and confronted various levels of government to initiate the policy changes that many Canadians demanded. The nature of these demands was based on a number of important shifts taking place at the time.

One of the most significant transformations to occur over the course of World War II was that Canadians became more rights conscious. Civil liberties groups expanded their areas of concern from libertarian rights (i.e., the right to free speech, to legal counsel, to property ownership) to include concern for violations of egalitarian rights (the right to equal protection under the law). In terms of discourse, the language of rights shifted from an emphasis on "British liberties" to a focus on "human rights."

Two cases aptly demonstrate the growing concern of Canadians about racism, rights, and equality during the World War II and immediate post-war period: the campaign by the Co-operative Committee on Japanese Canadians (CCJC) to prevent the expatriation of thousands of Canadians of Japanese ancestry, and the efforts of the Committee for the Repeal of the Chinese Immigration Act (CRCIA) to have the discriminatory 1923 Chinese Immigration Act repealed. Both campaigns appealed to the emerging discourse of human rights and were notable for the participation of Japanese Canadians and Chinese Canadians in leadership roles. While their practical mandates were limited, the activities of the CCJC and the CRCIA demonstrate how a number of organizations, including the major church denominations of the day and trade unions, politicians and political parties, certain liberal newspapers and periodicals, as well as prominent individuals and members of the affected communities could transcend politics and coalesce to advance the human rights of a particular minority ethnic group. Most notably, some Japanese Canadians and Chinese Canadians did not passively accept their "fate" and submit to racist and oppressive government policies; they were active in their own defence, thus heralding the increasing politicization of minority groups in the post-war period. In eschewing the view of Japanese and Chinese Canadians as victims of government policy, this study prefers to focus on "what people did rather than what was done to them."[2] The CCJC, and later the CRCIA, united these disparate groups and their efforts can be viewed as a progression of the achievement of short-term goals pursued by select Canadians collectively functioning as members of an early human rights community.

The Japanese Canadian Experience

Recent scholarship points to the federal government's policies of incarceration and expatriation of Japanese Canadians as having an impact on the "surge of egalitarian idealism" that took place in post-war Canada.[3] Indeed, the campaign to obtain justice for persons of Japanese ancestry, especially with respect to the expatriation, represents Canada's earliest and most significant involvement with the discourse of human rights. The attention of advocates and their lobbying strategies moved beyond civil liberties and the call to respect "traditional British liberties" to a rhetoric that included the newly articulated ideals of human rights as expressed in the Atlantic Charter and later in the Charter of the United Nations. While the lack of an American-style Bill of Rights compelled Canadian advocates to look to the international charters to give their arguments meaning and substance, it does not suggest, however, that the Canadian experience heralded something more laudable; indeed, Canadians made a virtue out of necessity.

The contrasting implications of "race" and ethnicity and World War II were nowhere more clearly revealed than in the case of a group that fit both categories: persons of Japanese ancestry resident in Canada. Despite the various restrictions targeting many minority groups, it was the wartime plight of the Japanese Canadians that piqued the interest of advocates. Canadians of Japanese ancestry, both native-born and naturalized, suffered a multitude of injustices based on "race" since their arrival in the late nineteenth century. The policies enacted during the Second World War, however, were extreme and seriously challenged many Canadians' views about their democratic institutions.

Evidence then and now indicates that there was no military need for the relocation policy. Canadian military officials and the RCMP disagreed strongly with King's government that removal was necessary. In the end, over 21,000 persons of Japanese ancestry, representing more than 90% of the entire Japanese population in Canada, were exiled from their homes. Of those, almost 4,000 would be "repatriated" to Japan, or more accurately in the case of Canadian citizens of Japanese ancestry, expatriated. Of the remaining

17,000, only about 4,000 returned to the West Coast, while the remainder resettled east of the Rockies.

Today it is conventional wisdom that the incarceration policy was a violation of democratic values, but virtually all liberals in 1942 saw it as a necessary evil, justifiable in terms of national security as well as a defence against the possibility of anti-Japanese mob violence. Those members of the early human rights community who might under different conditions have protested government policy were instead supportive. But in February of 1945, the federal government provided more details in orders-in-council PC 7355, 7356, and 7357 about the future of Japanese Canadians. Unlike the American government, which had recently removed all controls on Japanese Americans, it announced a "voluntary repatriation" program whereby Japanese Canadians could opt either to move east of the Rocky Mountains or be deported/expatriated to Japan. By May, over 6,000 repatriation forms had been signed, on behalf of over 10,000 men, women, and children, most of them Canadian citizens, and representing over 40% of the Japanese Canadian population.

It was at this point that the Co-operative Committee on Japanese Canadians played a prominent national role. It began as a purely philanthropic organization for Japanese Canadian relocates to Toronto, with no political intentions, in 1943. But by 1946, the CCJC was sufficiently organized to launch a vigorous protest of the government's deportation policy when Andrew Brewin was retained as counsel for the Committee. This change in focus was due to the decision by the Liberal government of Mackenzie King to deport all persons of Japanese ancestry who wished for "repatriation" to Japan, or for those who did not desire relocation to eastern Canadian provinces. The CCJC thus launched a legal challenge that was eventually heard by the Supreme Court of Canada and then, on appeal, by the Privy Council.

The chair of this new body was Rev. James Finlay, an outspoken and controversial United Church minister with a strong pacifist background and a long commitment to the cause of the Japanese Canadians. What other sorts made up the CCJC? Members of other minority groups, especially from the Japanese Canadian community, as well as the Jewish community, represented by the Canadian Jewish Congress (CJC), could be found among its ranks. It is also important to recognize that "white liberals" were not exclusively involved in an advocacy role. Persons of Japanese descent were active in defending their own rights and worked very closely with the CCJC. As the CCJC transformed itself from a welcoming committee to one concerned with civil liberties, its membership began to reflect this change. The CCJC letterhead grew to include some fifty-six names, many of whom can be traced to Canada's academic, libertarian, and literary elite. Members of various trade unions, ironically some of the very same trade unions that argued against Japanese immigration in the early twentieth century, could also claim members in the CCJC, as could some women's organizations. But by and large the membership was mainly that from religious institutions, namely the Anglican and United churches, who saw their role as advocates to be an extension of the home and abroad missionary work among "Oriental" peoples that had been carried out since the mid-1800s. The CCJC also changed in a structural sense, in that local groups across Canada, such as in London, Ontario, Winnipeg, Manitoba, and throughout Alberta, were formed to localize the efforts of the national group based in Toronto.

Already by 1944, however, the leadership of the Canadian Christian churches began to have their doubts about the direction of the federal government's plans with respect to Japanese Canadians. While dispersal (especially voluntary dispersal) was widely acceptable, disfranchisement and wholesale expatriation were not, and some Christian church leaders publicly voiced their opposition. Their increasing activism corresponded with Canadian public opinion in general. According to a Canadian Institute of Public Opinion poll issued in February of 1944, only 33% of Canadians supported the idea of deportation. Those results were in stark contrast to a poll commissioned in December 1943 that indicated that slightly over 50% of Canadians, including a significant majority of British Columbians, were in favour of deportation.[4]

In May of 1944, the Vancouver Consultative Committee (VCC) added its voice to the growing opposition to any proposal for deportation. The group eventually became a significant civil liberties organization in the fight against deportation/expatriation. In many respects the VCC was the western wing of the CCJC, keeping those in Toronto informed of movements afoot on the West Coast. The VCC urged the federal government to enact policies that would quell anti-Asian sentiment. In his letter to the Prime Minister, Dr. Norman F. Black, president of the VCC, wrote:

> The proposal that all persons of Japanese stock should be forcibly expelled from this Dominion seems to us wicked and preposterous. We have difficulty in understanding how anyone can champion such a suggestion unless, consciously or unconsciously, he had surrendered to the characteristic racial attitude of Nazism.... [W]e feel that talk about "repatriation" is an abuse of language, and that the forcible exile of these 16,261 Canadian citizens would be an act of indefensible tyranny and folly.... Finally ... the proposed expulsion would do violence to the conscience of a large section of the Canadian people.[5]

Surely the "conscience" to which the VCC referred in its letter to Prime Minister King was the growing acceptance of the concept of "human rights" that was gaining recognition internationally and in Canada. This letter was also signed by leaders of the Anglican, United, Baptist, and Roman Catholic denominations in Vancouver.

The Christian churches committed large sums of money to financing the test case, and the Student Christian Movement issued an impassioned plea that was sent to all Christian youth groups, in which members were asked to "[S]top and think what this [deportation] means in terms of the failure of Canadian democracy, the impotence of the Christian

Church, the degradation of Canada's position among the nations, the seeds of World War III, and the cost in human suffering to thousands of fellow Canadian citizens.... This is a challenge to the conscience of the Christian community to act in defence of *fundamental human rights* [emphasis mine]."[6]

Political parties, the media, and government moderates were also influential in advocating for the rights of Japanese Canadians. The Co-operative Commonwealth Federation (CCF), for example, was the only political party to denounce openly in the House of Commons the deportation policies from their inception. Liberal MP David Croll never broke ranks with the government in the House of Commons, but in a speech at a CCJC forum at the University of Toronto in February 1946, he argued that the government's policy violated the principles of the UN Charter. Croll also accompanied CCJC members and their supporters to their audience with the Prime Minister. Senators Arthur Roebuck and Cairine Wilson were also supporters of the actions of the CCJC, speaking with force against the deportation policy at a mass meeting partly organized by the CCJC in early January 1946.[7]

Long-time advocates of persons of Japanese ancestry in Canada, Angus MacInnis, CCF MP for Vancouver East, and his wife Grace, BC CCF MLA, wrote frequently on issues of equal rights. Certainly, both did not deviate from the liberal view that held resettlement in eastern Canada as a beneficial outcome of the incarceration. However, an article that Angus MacInnis contributed to a 1943 edition of *Maclean's* is interesting for its inchoative awareness of the concepts of human rights and of Canadian citizenship. His summation, in particular, hinted at egalitarian principles:

> To conclude, I advocate granting to those of Japanese origin in Canada all the rights and privileges that I have, on the sole basis that they are human beings. To deny them one iota of the rights and privileges enjoyed by … individuals of the race to which I belong would be a denial of the brotherhood of man; a denial to fellow humans of rights and privileges which I enjoy for no better reason than that my race was here first.[8]

While the media in general were unanimous in their support for relocation at the outbreak of war, as allied victories in the Far East were more numerous, this unanimity began to unravel. It began with traditionally liberal newspapers such as the *Winnipeg Free Press* and the *Toronto Star*, as well as the weekly newsmagazine, *Saturday Night*. Gradually, letters to the editor and editorials opposing the deportation of Canadian citizens of Japanese descent were found in other newspapers across the country. In addition to the pamphleteering, the day-to-day ministering to the Japanese Canadians, and the numerous petition campaigns undertaken by religious organizations, the response of the media represented an effective opposition to the rigid anti-Japanese racism of the day.

While advocates for persons of Japanese ancestry were, for the most part, of a certain "type," that is, usually white, male, religious and/or professional, many Japanese Canadians carried their own momentum in the movement to advocate for their rights. Indeed, Japanese Canadians contributed to the discourse of human rights as it was articulated in the immediate post-war period. In the early days of the Co-operative Committee, its Japanese Canadian members were instrumental in providing direction for its advocacy activities, and in educating the broader CCJC membership about the hardships specific to the Japanese Canadian community. Members of the Nisei Men's and Women's Sub-Committees of the CCJC felt, however, that action beyond the very practical objectives of housing and employment was needed. Many were looking to become politically organized, and so in 1944 created the Japanese Canadian Committee on Democracy (JCCD). Its creation coincided with the decision of CCJC members to become more politically active on behalf of the welfare of Japanese Canadians. When the House of Commons passed Bill 135, which would effectively extend provincial disfranchisement as it existed in British Columbia entirely on racial grounds to the federal level, the CCJC and the JCCD saw this as an opportunity to demonstrate newfound political ambitions. Representatives of the JCCD travelled to Ottawa to present a brief to the government, noting its opposition to the bill on seven positions, which included the point that the proposed amendment was "an unwarranted deprivation of the rights of Canadian citizens ... and ... is contrary to British justice, and contrary to the expressed war aims of the United Nations."[9]

In its explanation, the JCCD noted that it was only arguing on behalf of "naturalized and native-born Canadians," and not for the rights of enemy aliens, a stance in line with that of the CCJC and other advocacy groups in Canada. The brief also noted that the position of the Canadian government on the issue of the franchise was out-of-step with American policy, where Japanese Americans were guaranteed the right to vote and were even allowed to serve in the Armed Forces. Few Japanese Canadians were in the Canadian military, as many volunteers were rejected on grounds of "race." The JCCD brief also reflected the attitudes of the emerging human rights discourse when it noted that it was "commonplace to speak of broad general principles of justice and fair play which must win the peace after the war," and subsequently followed with the warning that echoed the sentiments of other advocates that, "in fighting oppression abroad we must also guard against injustice at home."[10]

Eventually, the battle for equality would appear in Canada's highest courts. The Canadian case was produced from a collective decision among both Japanese Canadians and non-Japanese Canadians. It did not involve an individual plaintiff; rather, it represented the desires of a group of people who wanted Japanese Canadians to share equally in all rights and duties, and that no distinctions should be made between Canadians on racial grounds. In January 1946, when the Supreme Court of Canada heard the *Japanese Canadian Reference Case*, a number of positions were presented. The crux of the argument was whether or not the federal government had virtually unlimited powers under the "Peace, Order and Good Government" clause of the BNA Act and the War Measures

Act. Note that at the same time the Gallup Poll organization announced that 62% of Canadians now believed that those Japanese Canadians who were also citizens should be allowed to stay. And the government had become swamped by thousands of letters and telegrams protesting the deportation policy. Additionally, the deportation orders seemed at odds with the principles of Bill 20, the soon-to-be Canadian Citizenship Act, introduced in Parliament on October 22, 1946. This Act expressed the growing belief that legal distinctions among Canadians on racial or any other grounds were very "un-Canadian." In introducing the bill, however, Secretary of State Paul Martin assured Parliament that its passage would not stand in the way of the deportation of Japanese Canadians.[11]

In February 1946, the court handed down a decision that was decidedly mixed. The court held that the federal government had the power to deport any adult male Japanese Canadians who had asked for "repatriation" but not rescinded their requests prior to the end of the war. However, a majority of the court also found that there was insufficient justification for the deportation of wives and children.[12]

The CCJC appealed to the Judicial Committee of the Privy Council in London, England. Brewin laid out the main arguments of the CCJC against the deportation policy, some of which were legal, but most rested on moral grounds: the policy disparaged Canadian citizenship, it was racially discriminatory, and it was unjust and inhumane. In conjunction with these efforts, the CCJC sent a memorandum to all members of Parliament and the Senate that accused the government of employing the "methods of Nazism" and challenged parliamentarians and senators to consider carefully the ramifications of carrying out deportation, which it noted "on racial grounds has been defined as a crime against humanity, and the war criminals of Germany and Japan are being tried precisely for this offence." Even in American newspapers, the Canadian government's policy was attracting unfavourable attention. In a *Washington Post* editorial, for example, the policy was referred to as "an odious manifestation of Canadian racialism."[13]

On December 2, 1946, the Privy Council ruled entirely in favour of Ottawa, holding that it had the power to deport even the Canadian-born wives and children of the Japanese Canadians. This was unwelcome news for the CCJC, but not unexpected. They already intended to immediately ask the federal government to abandon its plans in case they lost the case. Condemned by the media and thousands of Canadians across the country, on January 24, 1947 the government stated that its deportation policy was "*no longer necessary*," although it maintained that the success of the resettlement program in Canada necessitated the continuation of restrictions on travel and West Coast fishing licences.[14] The CCJC continued to battle for the end of these restrictions, as well as for a just settlement of Japanese Canadian property claims. However, these issues did not have the immediacy that could generate public opinion in the way that deportation could, and so the CCJC began to lose its position as the central player within the nascent Canadian human rights community. It diminished in size from a large coalition protecting civil liberties to a small committee focusing entirely on property restrictions. By the early 1950s most of these issues had been resolved, and the CCJC wound up its affairs.

The Chinese Canadian Experience

As the CCJC campaign moved towards virtual completion by early 1947, the Committee for the Repeal of the Chinese Immigration Act (CRCIA) was in the midst of an impressive advocacy movement working towards the elimination of the 1923 Chinese Immigration Act (known colloquially as the Exclusion Act). Here too, as in the CCJC campaign, the wartime discourse of rights had an impact. The CRCIA and its efforts to promote a more judicious handling of Chinese immigration policy provide another illustration of coalition-building in the early human rights movement in Canada.

Long-time anti-Asian sentiment that had been building since the late nineteenth century culminated in 1923 with the passage of the most explicitly racist piece of legislation to date: the Chinese Immigration Act. It replaced the ineffective (but lucrative) Head Tax, once seen as a way to curb Chinese immigration. The law prohibited Chinese immigration to Canada, with the exception of diplomats, Canadian-born returnees, students, and merchants. The day the Act officially took effect, July 1, 1923, became known as "Humiliation Day" to the Chinese in Canada. Between 1923 and 1946, only eight immigrants from China were admitted, so stringent were its measures.[15]

Certainly from the perspective of public policy, the Act was effective. But it also served to demonstrate how pervasive the ideology of "race" was by the early twentieth century. In singling out the Chinese, the federal Liberal government under William Lyon Mackenzie King endorsed the idea of superior and inferior races. Far beyond economic or moral distinctions was the notion that a person's race was indelible, permanent, and if the "superior races" were not protected, the "inferior races" would, through immigration and miscegenation, weaken the superior strain. As such, the federal Liberal government again targeted the Chinese population in Canada for discriminatory treatment in public policy with the passage of more restrictive legislation designed to close all loopholes enabling Chinese to immigrate to Canada and gain membership in its society. PC 2115, passed in 1930, allowed Asians who were citizens to bring members of their immediate families to Canada, provided that they were not part of any group whose immigration was regulated by a special act. Under the terms of the 1923 Act, the Chinese were the only such group. Thus, the Chinese community in Canada leading up to the Second World War was essentially a community where many men were without their families and were unable to participate fully in Canadian life, as the barriers to citizenship meant barriers to the franchise and to certain professions, among other issues.

While it has already been noted that the Second World War period helped to precipitate a change in rights discourse, it also marked a change in the way Canadians perceived those of Chinese ancestry living among them. As war ravaged China, Canadians' sympathy for the Chinese grew. Beginning in the 1930s with the Sino-Japanese War and later with the bombing of Pearl Harbor in December 1941, the Chinese were viewed in a much more positive light when set against their Japanese aggressors. Newspaper reports stressed the positive character of the Chinese—virtuous, heroic, dignified, and patient—in contrast to the Japanese, who were considered proud and arrogant. "It is a well known fact," declared BC Liberal Thomas Reid, "that when you speak to anyone ... and ask them which of the two races they preferred, the Chinese or the Japanese, they will answer, 'I will take the Chinaman any time against the Japanese.'"[16]

By the end of World War II, many Canadians began to view the 1923 Chinese Immigration Act as an embarrassment to Canada. Within the context of the 1940s, it certainly was a humiliation. China emerged as one of the allied victors of the Second World War; how could a government justify a discriminatory immigration policy towards the citizens of an allied country? Chinese Canadians also contributed significantly to the war effort, donating $10 million to the Victory Loan Drive, more, per capita, than any other group in Canada, in addition to participating in the Red Cross and other service work. Six hundred Chinese Canadian men served in Canada's war effort and were lauded for their heroism. It is notable that the Chinese community contributed more manpower than any other ethnic group to the war effort.[17]

To add further evidence of Canadian straggling on the issue of immigration policy reform, the American government repealed its Chinese Exclusion Act in 1943 and replaced it with an annual quota of 105 spaces for Chinese immigrants. This and other significant developments did not go unnoticed by Canadian government officials. By July 1943, even Mackenzie King admitted in the House of Commons that the Chinese Immigration Act was a "mistake" that needed to be corrected. Moreover, by 1946 his government enacted the Canadian Citizenship Act, which only served to highlight the contradictions in the status of Asians in Canada.[18]

After a series of informal meetings, the Committee for the Repeal of the Chinese Immigration Act was formed in Toronto in November 1946. It brought together seventy-nine prominent Canadians, including several Chinese Canadians, notably Dr. S. K. Ngai, a Toronto surgeon, Chong Ying of the *Shing Wah Daily News*, Wong Yick, editor of another Chinese-language publication, Professor C. C. Shih of the University of Toronto, and K. Dock Yip, the first Chinese Canadian called to the bar. Like the CCJC before it, the CRCIA established regional branches of the committee in Ottawa, London, Kingston, Montreal, Halifax, Winnipeg, Calgary, Victoria, and Vancouver. In an organization that was comprised mainly of non-Chinese, leadership of the four co-executive positions was shared between Chinese and non-Chinese members, an important example of interracial cooperation (albeit limited) in this early period of engagement with human rights discourse and the associated movement.

The CRCIA counted among its membership individuals and organizations that lent support to the CCJC. From its inception, these included support from the leaders and laity of religious organizations—the United, Roman Catholic, Presbyterian, and Anglican churches of Canada. Representatives of the media also supported the CRCIA, including B. K. Sandwell of *Saturday Night*. Other notables included Toronto Jewish lawyer Irving Himel who, in addition to acting as frequent spokesperson and legal adviser for the group, was also the executive secretary of the Association for Civil Liberties (ACL) and a former classmate with Yip at Osgoode Hall Law School.

Some trade union members formally supported the CRCIA, such as Murray Cotterill, president of the Toronto Labour Council, publicity director of the Steelworkers' Union and, from 1947 on, executive member of the Toronto Joint Labour Committee to Combat Racial Intolerance. The Canadian Congress of Labour and the Toronto Trades and Labour Councils—the same organizations that once recommended restrictions on Chinese immigration—now called for repeal of the law. The support of trade unions was reflective of what scholars have termed the emerging "social unionism" of the post-war period in which unions undertook social welfare work in an effort to improve the place of trade unions within the larger society. The fight against discrimination and prejudice was an extension of this goal.[19]

Ben Kayfetz, secretary of the Joint Public Relations Committee (JPRC), a Jewish organization formed in 1938 by the combined efforts of the B'nai Brith and the Canadian Jewish Congress, and Rabbi Abraham Feinberg of Holy Blossom Temple in Toronto represented an example of the participation of the Jewish community in the CRCIA. These Jewish activists, among others, recognized that by participating in organizations such as the CCJC and the CRCIA, and in obtaining change by promoting the rights of other groups, the rights of Jews could be promoted by avoiding the perception as "pushy" Jews pursuing their own self-interests.[20]

By December 1946, the CRCIA grew to include eighty-seven names on its letterhead and received support from some very "respectable" elements in Canadian society. Several members of Parliament, the federal CCF and Conservative parties, and the Council of Women all expressed support for the repeal of the Chinese Immigration Act. In addition to the various organized interests that participated in and supported the CRCIA were a number of individuals with no ties to either religious or secular institutions. They were mainly social democrats and reform liberals, academics, and professionals, whose paths connected through professional and volunteer ties. Primarily white, well-educated, upper- or middle-class anglophone males, and generally supporters of the Liberal or CCF parties, these men (and a few women) believed that the state could be an agent of positive social change, and that it was the responsibility of intellectuals and other prominent members of society to facilitate such change through their professional and volunteer activities.[21]

That the Chinese community did not accept the established doctrine of inferiority and resisted the assumed permanence of the law is demonstrated in the numerous letters received by Mackenzie King and his government from various Chinese community organizations such as the Vancouver Hoysun Ningyung Benevolent Association, the Chinese Community Centres of Ontario, the Chinese Nationalist League of Canada, and through the formation of pressure groups and the implementation of education campaigns through church congregations and union locals. Their written entreaties for repeal of the Chinese Immigration Act echoed many of the sentiments expressed in the numerous briefs from the CRCIA to the federal government. Just as Japanese Canadians played a major role in the cooperative efforts to seek justice, so too did Chinese Canadians in the active campaign for equal treatment in immigration legislation.[22]

By the mid-1940s, newspapers began to appear at the forefront of demands for equal treatment for the Chinese in Canada. Both national and regional newspapers figured prominently. The *Ottawa Citizen* and the *Toronto Star* published several articles written by Irving Himel, including one titled "Chinese Rights in Canada," which read like a manifesto, urging all Canadians to take an active interest in the campaign for repeal. The *Winnipeg Free Press* was the most active of all.

Over the course of the latter part of 1946 and in early 1947, the CRCIA sent delegations to Ottawa to meet with government ministers and mandarins, sent briefs to members of the federal government, and wrote numerous letters to leaders of Chinese and non-Chinese organizations. Letters were also directed to Canadian immigration officials in China. In a brief sent to J. A. Glen, the Minister of Mines and Resources (the governmental body with jurisdiction over immigration matters), the committee gave nine reasons for repeal, some of which reflected the internal and external influences that bore upon the emergent human rights discourse: the Act was in conflict with the UN Charter of which Canada was a signatory; it was the "greatest single" cause of disturbance of the friendly relations between Canada and China; it was a "major barrier" to the development of trade between the two nations; it was against "all principles of humanity, morality and social welfare" by preventing normal family life for the majority of Chinese in Canada, as they were not allowed to bring in spouses or children; it was contrary to the principles of Canadian democracy; it ran counter to the recommendations of the Senate Standing Committee on Immigration and Labour contained in its report of August 13, 1946; Canada was the only remaining North American nation with a special Chinese Immigration Act; both the CCF and the Progressive Conservatives supported repeal; and, finally, the CRCIA statement pointed out that Prime Minister King already admitted in October 1943 that the Act was a mistake.[23]

On January 24, 1947, the representation by the CRCIA was followed by a strongly worded brief to Mackenzie King, which denounced outright the Chinese Immigration Act as a racist law. In appealing to the UN Charter, the brief stated that Canada's actions were especially hypocritical given Canada's recent condemnation of South Africa at the UN Assembly for its treatment of its Indian minority.[24] More significantly, the brief is illustrative of the shift in discourse and in argument from "British liberties" to the human rights approach. As the CRCIA focused more specifically on the removal of all discriminatory anti-Chinese laws and policies, its campaign exemplified the growing recognition in the immediate post-war period of the right not to suffer state discrimination.

Confronted by growing public opposition and a well-organized advocacy group in the CRCIA, the federal government began to focus on post-repeal public policy. Various government documents reveal that by December 10, 1946, the Cabinet already agreed on a policy towards the Chinese. Debates in the House of Commons over repeal, however, revealed the difficulties in arriving at the complete equality of treatment advocated by the CRCIA. Politicians of all stripes from BC feared the usual chimera of the inundation of dependants of the Chinese already resident in the province. Even Angus MacInnis of the CCF, a party that had long stood on the side of the Chinese, stressed that while his party did not advocate flooding the country with Chinese immigrants, it did maintain equal treatment "for every person in this country, regardless of race, creed, colour or any other consideration."[25] According to the CRCIA and its supporters, the only way to end Canada's humiliating and discriminatory policy on Chinese immigration, especially in the face of the UN Charter, was to put Chinese immigration on the same basis as that from all other countries—under PC 695. Passed in 1931, PC 695 covered the question of immigrants' dependants. According to its terms, any immigrant resident in Canada for five years could bring over members of the immediate family. To members of the CRCIA and their supporters, while it seemed only logical in light of Canada's newly signed commitments to human rights that the Chinese be treated equally alongside European immigrants to Canada, the practical reality was that the Mackenzie King government held a slim majority in the House of Commons and some elements of Canadian society held fast to the notion of the inassimilable Asian.

On May 1, 1947, King announced to the country that the government intended to repeal the Chinese Immigration Act and order-in-council PC 1378. He explained that "the effect of repeal will be to remove all discrimination against the Chinese on account of race," but noted in his speech that "there will, I am sure, be general agreement with the view that the people of Canada do not wish, as a result of mass immigration, to make a fundamental alteration in the character of our population. Large-scale immigration from the Orient would change that fundamental composition of the Canadian population." Later that same day, King expressed his pleasure in his diary over coming to such a pragmatic solution. The 1923 Chinese Immigration Act was officially repealed on May 14th, but the Chinese were still, along with other Asians, subject to restrictive and racist immigration barriers.[26] Order-in-council PC 2115, which limited sponsorship of wives and children under the age of eighteen to Chinese who were Canadian citizens, would govern Canadian immigration policy with respect to Asians from 1947 to the 1960s. It underscored the federal government's determination to maintain the racial character of Canadian society. For many Chinese Canadians, the repeal of the Act seemed a mockery of official Canadian expressions of commitment to human rights, as such rules did not apply to European immigrants.

Since the repeal represented only a partial victory, the CRCIA continued its efforts to seek justice for Chinese Canadians and their family members in China. A CRCIA delegation that appeared before the Standing Committee on Immigration and Labour of the Senate of Canada urged the repeal of PC 2115 on the basis that discrimination on racial grounds should be avoided in immigration law. It was careful to point out that the request was only for modest change: "We are not asking you to open wide the gates for Chinese immigration. We are only asking you to allow the wives and children of Chinese residents of Canada to come here, giving them the same privileges as we do Europeans and South Americans."[27]

The members of the Senate Standing Committee, including its chair, Senator Cairine Wilson, were impressed with the arguments of the delegation, but inasmuch as Senator Wilson and her colleagues were sympathetic, the barriers to Chinese immigration and family reunification remained intact. The CRCIA and Chinese community organizations continued their lobbying efforts. They achieved a small victory in late 1950 when regulations with respect to the age of admissible dependent children were changed to age twenty-one (up from age eighteen). But the basic operation of PC 2115 remained unchanged, and it was not until 1956 that the order-in-council was finally abandoned. Thus, with the major battle fought and only a few minor issues left to resolve, none of which would capture the public's attention as did the repeal of the Chinese Immigration Act, the activities of the CRCIA petered out by 1951.

Conclusions

Few in Canada before the war viewed Japanese Canadians and Chinese Canadians as citizens. But the decade of the 1940s precipitated a fundamental re-evaluation of the rights of the Japanese and the Chinese and their place in Canadian society. Similarly, these groups would reconsider their place amongst their fellow Canadians.

The relocation, deportation, and immigration exclusion issues enabled minority groups in Canada to realize that the problems faced by one group, especially with regard to racial prejudice, would have implications for other minorities. As World War II was nearing its end, marked by allied victories, public opposition to such racially based policies as relocation, expatriation, and exclusion became more pronounced. As a result, a more accommodating atmosphere for dissent developed, including dissent from minority representative organizations. When groups such as the Canadian Jewish Congress, for example, joined other organizations in decrying the treatment of the Japanese Canadians and Chinese Canadians, it marked a significant step towards greater post-war cooperation on other matters of mutual interest.

The Canadian struggle to overcome racial disadvantage required a cooperative effort of minorities and non-minorities. Thus, when the CJC requested the support of the National Japanese Canadian Citizens Association (NJCCA) to push the enactment of Fair Employment Practices legislation, the NJCCA readily agreed, in the words of its President, George Tanaka, "because we know what it is like to be discriminated against."[28] Indeed, shortly before the NJCCA was formed, Kinzie Tanaka in his role as chairman of *Nisei Affairs*, a Japanese Canadian newspaper, was among the first to exhort the Japanese Canadian community to work towards the "common good," noting that "we shall not attain *our* ends until we have fought unselfishly for *the other's* struggle for some basic human right [emphasis mine]." Author Muriel Kitagawa, writing in *Nisei Affairs* under the pen name Sue Sada, published a critique of government policy on the continuation of post-war restrictions against Japanese Canadians that was conspicuously titled, "Today the Japanese— Tomorrow?"[29] Not surprisingly then, the National JCCA would also support the demand of Canadians for a bill of rights and for fair employment practices (FEP) legislation.

It is also significant that persons of Japanese and Chinese ancestry were active in their own defence, and participated in the articulation of human rights as an important concept. Despite community pressures to abide by government policy, some Japanese Canadians and Chinese Canadians initiated much of the early protests of the discriminatory policies directed against them. Indeed, many even took leadership roles within the CCJC and the CRCIA. In Canada, the two dynamics—that of the minority group and the non-minority group movements—had to come together to be effective, heralding the cooperative nature of the developing Canadian human rights community. Furthermore, the decision of minority-based organizations to cooperate fully with the other advocacy groups in Canada, particularly with the CCJC and the CRCIA, and the evidence that persons of Japanese and Chinese ancestry were welcomed into these groups as relatively equal participants both symbolize the nature of the emerging human rights movement in post-war Canada. Long before multiculturalism was a state-sanctioned policy in Canada, certain members of the Japanese Canadian and Chinese Canadian communities were among the first to champion the full participation of racial and ethnic minorities in Canadian democracy, alongside their Anglo-Canadian comrades.

A shift both in language and in focus from a concern for the erosion of British liberties to an interest in human rights emerged slowly in 1940s Canada. Racial discrimination received a greater degree of attention than was the case before the Second World War. Groups such as the CCJC and the CRCIA, although notable for their aims, did not act as champions of rights for all in Canada; citizenship was an important determining factor in their level of support. These were private interest groups that addressed single-issue matters of public policy. The absence of a system of protecting human rights was not challenged; that work would remain for future campaigns by members of Canada's human rights community.

Notes

1   *Mrs. Miniver* (1942).
2   Roger Daniels, *Asian America: Chinese and Japanese in the United States since 1850* (Seattle: University of Washington Press, 1989), 4.
3   Note that this author uses the term "incarceration" instead of "internment" to describe the wartime treatment of Japanese Canadians. In fact, only 750 Japanese Canadians and Japanese nationals were interned in the legal sense of the word at a camp near Angler, Ontario. For more on the debate on terminology, see Roger Daniels, "Words Do Matter: A Note on Inappropriate Terminology and the Incarceration of the Japanese Americans," in Louis Fiset and Gail M. Nomura, eds., *Nikkei in the Pacific Northwest: Japanese Americans and Japanese Canadians in the Twentieth Century* (Seattle and London: University of Washington Press, 2005), chapter 9. On the "surge of egalitarian idealism," see, for example, Ruth Frager and Carmela Patrias, "'This Is Our Country, These Are Our Rights': Minorities and the Origins of Ontario's Human Rights Campaigns," *Canadian Historical Review* 82, no. 1, (March 2001): 2; James W. St. G. Walker, *"Race," Rights and the Law in the Supreme Court of Canada: Historical Case Studies* (Waterloo and Toronto: The Osgoode Society for Canadian Legal History and Wilfrid Laurier University Press, 1997), 31; Ross Lambertson, *Repression and Resistance: Canadian Human Rights Activists 1930–1980* (Toronto: University of Toronto Press, 2005), chapter 3.
4   "Slim Majority of Canadians Favour 'Repatriation' Says Poll," and "Public Opinion on 'Repatriation'," *The New Canadian*, 8 January 1944; "Cross-country Poll Against Deportation of Citizens," *The New Canadian*, 26 February 1944.
5   Library and Archives Canada (LAC), RG 25, vol. 2798, file 773-B-1-40, part 3, letter, Black to King, 29 May 1944.
6   McMaster University Archives, Cooperative Committee on Japanese Canadians papers (hereafter CCJC-MAC), fldr #20, "Emergency Bulletin of Japanese-Canadians," special bulletin to all youth Christian groups from the Student Christian Movement of Canada, 15 October 1945.
7   CCJC-MAC, file #12, Edith Fowke, *They Made Democracy Work: The Story of the Co-operative Committee on Japanese Canadians* (Toronto: n.p., 1951), 22.
8   Grace MacInnis, "Wanted: A Country," Canadian Forum, June 1942; Grace and Angus MacInnis, "Oriental Canadians—Outcasts or Citizens?"; Angus MacInnis, "Should We Send the Japs Back?—No," *Maclean's*, 1 December 1943, 12, 37–38; Werner Cohn, "The Persecution of Japanese Canadians and the Political Left in British Columbia, December 1941–March 1942, *BC Studies*, no. 68 (Winter 1985–86): 3–22.
9   NAC, MG 28 V7, vol. 1, file #23, JCCD Brief in the matter of the War Services Elector's Bill (#135 of 1944), Section 5 Regarding Certain Amendment to Section 14, ss. 2 of the Dominion Elections Act, 1938 and in the matter of the Proposed Disfranchisement of British Subjects and Canadian Citizens in Canada, 24 June 1944, 2.
10 Ibid., 6–10.
11 For numerous letters and petitions protesting the actions of the government, see LAC, RG 2, ser. G-2, vol. 3554, file 773-B-1-40, pt. 4. On Bill 20, see Canada, House of Commons, Debates, 22 October 1945, 1335 (first reading). Martin's comments were made during the second reading of the Bill, on 6 April 1946. The Canadian Citizenship Act was passed in 1946 and took effect on 1 January 1947. Prime Minister William Lyon Mackenzie King has the distinction of being Canada's first citizen.
12 In the Matter of a Reference as to the Validity of Orders in Council of the 15th Day of December, 1945 (P.C. 7355, 7356 and 7357), in Relation to Persons of the Japanese Race, (1946) Supreme Court Reports 248.
13 LAC, MG 28, vol. 1, file 1, minutes, 22 January and 22 March 1946, and CCJC news bulletin 7 and 14 September 1946; LAC, MG 32 C26, vol. 3, file 3-3, Brief, "To the honourable Members of Senate and the House of Commons," 1946; editorial, "Halt Exile of Japs, US advice to Canada," *Washington Post*, 11 June 1945.
14 Fowke, They Made Democracy Work, 23. The official titles of the Privy Council appeal is Co-operative Committee on Japanese Canadians v. A.G. Canada (1947) A.C. 87, 1 DLR 577.
15 The 1923 law is found at Canada, Statutes, 1923, c. 38. Studies of the Chinese in Canada are numerous. Some examples are: W. Peter Ward, *White Canada Forever: Popular Attitudes and Public Policy Toward Orientals in British Columbia* (Montreal and Kingston: McGill-Queen's University Press, 1978); Patricia E. Roy, *The Oriental Question: Consolidating a White Man's Province, 1914–1941* (Vancouver: UBC Press, 2003).

[16] Carol F. Lee, "The Road to Enfranchisement: Chinese and Japanese in British Columbia," *BC Studies* 30 (1976): 45–47; House of Commons, Debates, 11 February 1947, 318.

[17] Jin Tan and Patricia E. Roy, *The Chinese in Canada*, Canadian Historical Association Booklet #9 (Ottawa: 1985), 12–13.

[18] United States, Congressional Record—House, 10 June 1943, 5716 –21. The repeal of Chinese exclusion legislation in the United States certainly concerned Canadian officials, who feared that Canada, by continuing discriminatory legislation, would "be more open to criticism by contrast." LAC, RG 76, vol. 122, file 23635, pt. 7, Robertson to Jolliffe, 22 March 1944; Crerar to Jolliffe, 24 March 1944; Crerar to Adamson, MP, 27 March 1947; House of Commons, Debates, 12 July 1943, 4682 –4683. For the Citizenship Act, see Canada, Statutes, 1946, c. 15.

[19] Richard Allen, *The Social Passion: Religion and Social Reform in Canada, 1914–1928* (Toronto: University of Toronto Press, 1971), 16–17; Lambertson, *Repression and Resistance*, chapter 1.

[20] Lambertson, *Repression and Resistance*, chapters 5 and 7; James W. St. G. Walker, "The 'Jewish Phase' in the Movement for Racial Equality in Canada," *Canadian Ethnic Studies*, vol. 34, no. 1, (2004): 3 –4.

[21] For more on Canada's "reform elite" see: Doug Owram, *The Government Generation* (Toronto: University of Toronto Press, 1998), chapter 6.

[22] LAC, MG 26, J1, vol. 422: Philip Chan, Hoysun Ningyung Benevolent Association to King, 18 February 1947; Frank Chow, Moose Jaw Chinese Association to King, 16 February 1947; Lee Wi, Halifax Chinese Community Centre to King, 18 February 1947; RG 76, vol. 589, file 827821, pt. 13: Chong Ying, Chinese Canadian Community Centres of Ontario to King, 5 July 1946; Shih Ken, Chinese Nationalist League of Canada to King, 15 July 1946; Dong Wong Jung and Foon Sien, Hoysun Ningyung Benevolent Association to King, 5 December 1946.

[23] *Ottawa Citizen*, 6 December 1946.

[24] LAC, MG 26, J1, King Papers, Primary Correspondence, vol. 420, Armstrong and Ngai to King, 24 January 1947. The contents of the brief and the meeting were described in several newspapers: *Halifax Mail*, 23 & 27 January 1947, *Vancouver Sun*, 23 January 1947, *Victoria Times*, 28 January 1947, and the *Regina Leader-Post*, 29 January 1947.

[25] Canada, House of Commons, Debates, 11 February 1947: 307–47 [MacInnis quote at 337]; *Winnipeg Free Press*, 8 February 1947; *Edmonton Bulletin*, 12 February 1947.

[26] Canada, House of Commons, Debates, 1 May 1947, 2644–2646. LAC, MG 26 J13, 1 & 2 May 1947.

[27] Ibid., 98–99.

[28] LAC, MG 31 F8, Minoru Takada Papers, "Report of 2nd National JCCA Conference."

[29] Muriel Kitagawa, *This is My Own: Letters to Wes and Other Writings on Japanese Canadians, 1941–1948* (Vancouver: Talonbooks, 1985), 236–241.

Glossary

Nikkei. Refers collectively to citizens of Japanese ancestry in North America, including both immigrant and successive generations.

Nisei. Second generation Japanese Americans and Canadians.

Orders-in-council. In Canada, an order-in-council is a notice of an administrative decision issued by the Governor General of Canada. In reality, orders-in-council originate with the federal cabinet and are approved by the Governor General.

Pearl Harbor. The bombing of an American naval base at Pearl Harbor, on December 7, 1941, by Japan, which brought the United States into World War II.

War Measures Act. Adopted in 1914, it gave emergency powers to the federal government when it detected "a war, invasion, or uprising, real or suspected."

Further Reading

Adachi, Ken. *The Enemy That Never Was: A History of the Japanese Canadians.* Revised ed. Toronto: McClelland and Stewart, 1991.

The classic account of the incarceration of the Japanese Canadians during World War II.

Bangarth, Stephanie. *Voices Raised in Protest: Defending North American Citizens of Japanese Ancestry, 1942–49.* Vancouver: UBC Press, 2008.

A comparative study of the campaigns to protect the citizenship rights of Japanese Americans and Japanese Canadians amid their wartime exclusion and confinement.

Bangarth, Stephanie. "'We Are Not Asking You to Open Wide the Gates for Chinese Immigration': The Committee for the Repeal of the Chinese Immigration Act and Early Human Rights Activism in Canada." *Canadian Historical Review* 84, 3 (September 2003): 395–422.

An in-depth account of the efforts of the CRCIA and the campaign to repeal the 1923 Chinese Immigration Act.

Roy, Patricia E. *The Triumph of Citizenship: The Japanese and Chinese in Canada, 1941–67.* Vancouver: UBC Press, 2007.

This study explores the campaigns for the full citizenship of the Chinese and the Japanese in Canada.

Ward, Peter W. *White Canada Forever: Popular Attitudes and Public Policy Toward Orientals in British Columbia,* 2nd ed. Montreal, Quebec: McGill-Queen's University Press, 1990.

A comprehensive study of anti-Asian attitudes and public policies in British Columbia between the mid-nineteenth and mid-twentieth centuries.

Relevant Websites

CBC Digital Archives, Chinese Immigration to Canada: A Tale of Perseverance
archives.cbc.ca/society/immigration/topics/1433/

Several television and radio clips detail the history of Chinese immigration and its restriction.

CBC Digital Archives, Relocation to Redress: The Internment of Japanese Canadians
archives.cbc.ca/war_conflict/second_world_war/topics/568/

A multimedia site with interviews, radio clips, photographs, and links to related topics.

Chinese Immigration Act 1923, 1314 George V., c. 38.
www.asian.ca/law/cia1923.htm
The complete text of this historic Act.

National Association of Japanese Canadians
www.najc.ca/
Offers both historical and contemporary information about Japanese Canadians, with links to other resources and blogs of interest.

The Politics of Racism
www.japanesecanadianhistory.ca/
Ann Gomer Sunahara's comprehensive published account of the internment is available as a free download or viewable via HTML files.

PART II

Denying, Defining, and Demanding Rights in Social, Political, and Economic Context

CHAPTER 5

FINDING JIM CROW IN CANADA, 1789–1967

BARRINGTON WALKER

Introduction

This chapter has two major overlapping themes. The first is an exploration of dominant ideas of "race" in Canada and how, as a consequence of the influence of intellectual currents sweeping the British Empire, in the late eighteenth and early nineteenth centuries, a liberal ideology towards race and racial differences—a "liberal racial order"—developed here, resulting in a noticeable absence of laws that racially codified white supremacy. Nonetheless, the constant presence and power of illiberal views of racial difference meant that the law in Canada did support racial discrimination in Canada—but passively so—upholding the individual's right to discriminatory treatment against minorities. Thus, the second major theme of this chapter explores the concept of "Jim Crow"—a term that originates out of the African American experience of discrimination both legally codified and supported by social custom—and suggests that Jim Crow has also existed in Canada. Despite the lack of legally codified Jim Crow laws in Canada, social customs and court rulings that allowed individuals the freedom to act in a racially biased manner led many Black Canadians to identify Jim Crow as a continental rather than exclusively US phenomenon.

A few years ago, a prestigious research centre at one of Canada's premier research universities invited me to present a paper on the history of African Canadians' struggle for civil rights during the era which I, perhaps a little too unreflectively, called "the age of Jim Crow." After I presented my paper, a member of the audience asked me whether it was a mistake to take a term like "Jim Crow" out of its "proper" Southern US context and uncritically and inelegantly apply it to the study of Canadian history. My colleague reminded me that many of the struggles that Blacks faced in Canada were mirrored in the British Caribbean, and yet no one would dare use a term like "Jim Crow" in that context. In a final volley she reminded me that the British Caribbean, a region that shared a colonial tie with Canada, was arguably a more solid basis for comparison with Canada than the United States. "I was wondering what you think of that?" she asked. At a loss for words, I handled her (probably rhetorical) question badly. This led me to ponder a question as I headed back to Kingston, Ontario: by applying a term like Jim Crow to analyze African Canadian history, was I merely playing with words or, even worse, just writing bad history?

This is a difficult issue and there is some justification for simply saying "no" to the question of whether one can speak of Jim Crow in Canada. Jim Crow was a term that was coined in the postbellum American South, a more distinct cultural and social landscape than that which took root north of the 49th parallel. While I, like others, may have been a little careless at times in using this term whilst doing race work in Canada, Jim Crow is, nonetheless, a useful analytical lens for looking at race relations and anti-racist struggle in Canada. In Canada, discriminatory practices were levelled against Black Canadians in many areas of their lives. However, the major difference between the two countries is that segregation and other forms of racial discrimination in the United States were legally codified while in Canada such practices were legally supported though rarely enshrined in positive law. The pattern in Canada was legal support for racial discrimination and White supremacy rather than legal codification with, perhaps, the startling exception of our country's immigration laws.[1] This was a subtle yet important distinction in the relationship between race and the law on either side of the 49th parallel.

Scholars have argued for the existence of a Canadian version of Jim Crow by identifying myriad areas where Blacks in Canada, similar to the United States, faced social ostracism, economic deprivations, and political marginality. Saje Mathieu and James W. St. G. Walker have perhaps made the best case for using the language of Jim Crow in the Canadian context.[2] I want to push the existing literature further in this short piece. Identifying racial discrimination as a fact of life on the North American continent is vitally important work, but merely identifying simple points of comparison between patterns of discrimination in the US and Canada doesn't quite go far enough. It does not tell us *why* or *how* this sad state of affairs came to be. Given that Jim Crow South and pre- and post-Confederation Canada had quite different ways of legally supporting White supremacy, what exactly were the ideological currents that meshed the sad fact of racism on both sides of the border so seamlessly that a few elite Blacks and Whites in Canada pointed to the existence of Jim Crow in Canada? One way to get at this question is to think carefully about ideas that linked racial thought on both sides of the border: the legacy of biologically driven ideas and assumptions about the immutability of Black racial inferiority, its fixity in nature, the blood, and the body.

Both countries share a nasty history of slavery and a rather profound legacy of biological racism, but over time each country developed divergent ways of constituting the relationship between race and the law. Canada's legal culture, particularly where it concerned questions of "race," was forged within a context that bore the heavy imprint of the British Empire. In broad strokes, racial thought at the turn of the eighteenth-century British Empire was guided by a more culturally driven and historicist notion of race, the idea that racial characteristics were not immutable but subject to change—indeed progress—over time. Canadians inherited these ideas, which they argued were more "progressive" than racial attitudes in the United States.[3] They strengthened their "progressive" racial attitudes through an ethos of colourblindness and, as Constance Backhouse has so eloquently put it, racelessness.[4] Unlike its Southern US counterpart, Jim Crow in Canada was by no means a totalizing system of legal racial governance, but frequent breaks or ruptures in the liberal veneer of racial thought. When contemporary African Canadians spoke of "Jim Crow," they were explaining when and how biologically driven racial discourse in Canada frequently managed to pierce through the fragile tapestry of racial thought and feeling in Canada.

In this chapter I want to suggest that Canada's racial order was characterized by overt and often violent racism in the context of a broader legal and British colonial (racial) liberalism.[5] In other words, ideas about the biological fixity of "race" were always teeming just beneath the surface of "liberal" racial attitudes and practices in the British Empire, particularly from the late eighteenth century until the late 1860s. British colonial rule was ostensibly governed by an ethos of justice and fair play, civility, colourblindness, and legal neutrality during this era. It is also true that over time and in various British colonial contexts these liberal ideas of colonial and racial governance certainly did not go uncontested.[6] The ugly histories of race and racial discrimination in Canada must be examined in the light of a British imperial and colonial context, and as a contest between competing visions of racial differences as fixed versus historically determined. There was, however, always a fair amount of slippage between these two ways of thinking about race in Canada. Keeping this in mind gives us the tools to avoid the crude positions that either Canada was free of racial discrimination or, conversely, that racism in Canada was essentially no different from the *de jure* racism that shaped much of the US. Neither position is accurate.

Regimes of Racial Governance: Naturalism and Historicism

In *The Racial State*, David Theo Goldberg argues that historically there have been two dominant modes of state racial governance in the Western tradition: racial naturalism and historicism.[7] Goldberg locates the origins of racial naturalism in the work of Thomas Hobbes and his racialized concept of the "state of nature" that fixed the bodies of the Indian and the Hottentot in a permanent state of nature in the transition to the modern state.[8] A countervailing tradition, says Goldberg, emerged out of the intellectual tradition of John Locke. Lockean racial thought ran in contrast to the idea that "Natives" had a fixed essence, that they were prehistorically and naturally incapable of development and historical progress.[9] Locke's view:

> ... explicitly and self-consciously historicizes racial characterization, elevates Europeans and their (postcolonial) progeny over primitive and undeveloped Others as a victory of History, of historical progress even as it leaves open the possibility of those racial Others to historical development....[10]

Over time, Locke's view came to characterize the colonial governance in the British Empire. The debates over the end of slavery that took place in the late eighteenth century and early part of the nineteenth century in the British Empire is one subject that can shed light on this issue. During this period, abolitionists and their opponents argued about the desirability of doing away with slavery. There was a marked difference between the slavery debates in the British Empire and those that would follow in the United States when it faced its own emancipation question.[11] In Britain, Seymour Drescher argues, the discussions that took place on the issue of the slave trade and slavery "tended to marginalize racial analysis, insofar as it tended to imply inherent and inherited differences in potential and behaviour."[12] Morever, says Drescher, the parliamentary record shows that "reference to the disabling characteristics of blacks as natural or inherent was preemptively dismissed out of hand."[13]

This is not to suggest, however, that the British regarded Blacks as equals. On the contrary, what the emancipation debates tell us is that biological or naturalist assumptions about Black racial inferiority, save from a few violent critics of the anti-slavery movement, had little saliency in Britain.[14] That Blacks were inferior to White Europeans was never in doubt within Britain's learned circles. Many believed that Blacks' inferiority was not rooted in biology but in their lack of historical development. Proponents of abolitionism tended to frame their arguments in precisely these terms. They tended to see human history in terms of stages of civilization and Africans simply had not achieved the pinnacle of civilization that had been reached by Europeans. "Civilization implied a broad front of economic, civil, and cultural improvement. Each socio-economic stage was perceived as a socio-educational experimental process, in which each stage was more efficient, more rational, and more humane than its predecessor."[15] The end of slavery in the British Empire in 1833 was regarded as an "unprecedented experiment in human development" by British lawmakers.[16] Abolitionism then went hand in hand with the civilizing process—indeed it was inextricably bound to it—a triumph of historical progress over biological determinism. The emancipation debates in Britain and the racial historicist assumptions that structured them had resonance across the Atlantic in British North America where the slavery question was front and centre between 1783 and 1865.

Racial Naturalism and the Origins of Jim Crow

In contrast, racial segregation in the United States, and the American South in particular, was an exemplary example of a prevalently naturalist racial order, commonly referred to as "Jim Crow." The term Jim Crow first emerged in the US in 1832 when a future White minstrel performer by the name of Thomas D. Rice "discovered" and popularized a song and dance routine that came to be known as "Jim Crow."[17] Legend has it that one day as Rice "sauntered along one of the main thoroughfares in Cincinnati," he heard a voice "carrying clear above the street noise." Rice soon came upon the source of the voice, a Black male street performer named Cuff. Rice's encounter with Cuff was to shape American popular culture in rather profound ways. Rice looked on while a dancing Cuff sang "Turn about an' wheel about and do jis so. An ebery time I turn around I jump Jim Crow." In an act of the kind of cultural borrowing, appropriation, and commodification that continues to underwrite the racial scripts of American popular culture, Rice "purchased" the song and dance from Cuff for a small fee, thereby "elevating" it from mere street culture to the new American minstrel stage.[18]

According to historian C. Vann Woodward, by 1838 the term Jim Crow had leapt from the minstrel stage into the broader realm of America's racial order; it became an adjective used to describe a regime of discriminatory laws coined the "Jim Crow Laws."[19] In 1877, the withdrawal of Northern troops, the end of the Second Reconstruction, and the Redemption of White Southerners set the context for the emergence of Jim Crow in both its legal and extra-legal manifestations. Jim Crow came to dominate almost every sphere of Southern life. In all Southern states Blacks were also disenfranchised, most commonly through devices such as "grandfather clauses" and literacy tests. Residential segregation and so-called "sundown laws" (laws requiring Blacks to be off the streets by a certain time) were also common. Segregation of public facilities was also a ubiquitous feature of life in the postbellum Southern racial order. Blacks were also subject to extra-legal terrors represented in the Ku Klux Klan, lynching, and other forms of mob violence. They were also routinely forced to face a constant barrage of "Negro atrocity" stories in newspapers throughout the South.[20]

While the society that emerged in the post-1877 Southern US is widely regarded as the paradigmatic example of Jim Crowism, the fact is that when Jim Crow ventured beyond the minstrel stage, his first stop was in the antebellum North, not the postbellum South.[21] To put it simply, the antebellum South had no need for legal and extra-legal mechanisms to regulate contact between Blacks and Whites. That had already existed: slavery. By contrast, in the antebellum North, slavery was all but dead by the 1830s. Hence, northern Whites, who found it desirous and necessary to withhold full civic equality from Blacks, were the original architects of the system that would later become synonymous with the American South. Blacks in the antebellum North, though free from the bonds of slavery, were not full participants in civil society.

In the antebellum North White supremacy was legally sanctioned in myriad areas. Leon Litwack tells us that many Northern states were willing to create state laws to ensure the second class citizenship status of Blacks where there were no federal laws on the books. Many states implemented laws against the immigration of Negroes, and in the mid-nineteenth century the newer states of "Illinois, Indiana, and Oregon ... incorporated anti-immigration provisions into their constitutions."[22] While increasing numbers of white men were granted the franchise in the nineteenth century, many Northern states passed laws denying those same rights to Black men.[23] In the courts, Blacks also found their testimony limited or subject to strict limitations. Blacks also had to contend with Jim Crowed public conveyances, and in many Northern states intermarriage with White women was illegal.

Jim Crow's reach extended beyond the reach of the law, however. Tocqueville observed that where there were no legal statutes to enforce the separation of Blacks and Whites in the US, "custom and popular prejudices exerted a decisive influence." In the criminal justice systems across the North, the "absence of Negro jurors, judges and witnesses when added to the general economic degradation of the coloured people largely explains the disproportionate number of Negroes in northern jails, prisons and penitentiaries."[24] Churches, the bedrock of the spiritual and political life of northern antebellum Black communities, were also separate.[25] Schools too were segregated in the antebellum North. Blacks were kept out of public schools with the use of social custom and legal statute. In a pattern that was remarkably similar to the story of Black education in Ontario and the Maritimes, Pennsylvania and Ohio "required district school directors to establish separate facilities for Negro students whenever twenty or more could be accommodated."[26] Throughout the North, says Litwack,

> In an era of expanding opportunities and social mobility, northern Negroes faced economic discrimination and exploitation. For the greater portion of the black labour force, racial prejudice meant much more than restrictions at the polls, in the theatres or on public conveyances; it manifested itself in the daily struggle for existence, in the problems of subsistence living, employment in the lowest-paid unskilled jobs, hostile native and immigrant white workers, exclusionist trade unions, and deplorable housing in the "Negro section" of town.[27]

The socio-economic marginalization of Black Americans in the antebellum North, then, was ubiquitous, powerful, and also formally outside the realm of legal discrimination (though certainly buttressed by it).

It is here, in areas like religion, social attitudes, and socio-economic status and the forms of racial violence most commonly associated with the South—the realms of "custom" and "popular prejudice"—that the continental dimensions of Jim Crow get thrown into sharp relief. The similarities between *de facto* extra-legal manifestations of Jim Crow in the US and Jim Crow in Canada are a result of the naturalist racial presumptions that structure them. As Goldberg argues, mob violence in the American South—typified in the alarming number of lynchings that took place between the 1880s and 1920s—was racial naturalism's reassertion in the face of challenges posed by the rule of law.[28] The opposite was true in Canada where vigilante justice was a naturalist challenge to the dominant historicist legalism that simply was too inadequate to police the colour line or, more pointedly, interracial sex. Mob violence in Canada was an expression of racists' frustration at the law's inability to maintain a proper natural racial hierarchy.

A Liberal Racial Order?

In one of the most influential articles ever published in Canadian historiography, Ian McKay makes the argument for a "liberal order framework" for understanding Canadian history. Canada, says McKay, should be rethought as a "historically specific project of rule"—a liberal order—"a belief in the epistemological and ontological primacy of the category 'individual.'"[29] McKay asks us to think about Canadian history as a "process of liberal rule" mapped through sites of power like schools and penitentiaries.[30] How might McKay's schema shed light on race and racial governance in Canada? McKay argues that as a rule,.Canada's liberal order framework excluded the racially subaltern from its conception of the subject, as these individuals were deemed too deficient to be worthy of full citizenship rights including the franchise.[31] Colonial and provincial governments denied the Chinese and South Asians the vote in British Columbia in the nineteenth and early twentieth centuries (which, in turn, prevented them from voting in federal elections), and Aboriginals were constituted as non-citizens. For Aboriginal people, enfranchisement meant relinquishing their Indian status.[32] It is certainly true that the Canadian state's project of building a modern Canada based upon liberal principles often placed the racial Other outside of its purview, deeming them objects rather than subjects. However, in his desire to answer critics who might blanch at the notion that a liberal order framework might "stand in for other subaltern histories," McKay has perhaps been too hasty in placing the racially subaltern outside of the reach of liberal order governance.[33] Rather, racialized peoples' relationship to Canada's liberal order was uneven and often ambivalent. The laws of Canada constituted unassimilated Aboriginal peoples as non-citizens and even non-persons until the mid-twentieth century. Nonetheless, the state was willing to grant the assimilated Indian—who was, of course, the opposite of the figure excluded from McKay's liberal order schema—the fruits of full citizenship, albeit at the high cost of his or her Indian status. Goldberg argues that colonial policies of assimilation were quintessentially historicist. "Colonial assimilationists were confident of their possession of universally just laws, building the policy on the assumption that natives should become civilized through their acquisition of the rule of law and the custom of the colonizers, by ceasing, that is, to be native."[34]

Like Aboriginal peoples, Black Canadians were by no means fully outside of the purview of Canada's liberal order framework. This had much to do with the dominance of a historicist attitude towards race in the British Empire, particularly with the dawn of the Age of Reform from the late eighteenth century to the early nineteenth century.[35] The end of slavery in British North America began in Upper Canada in 1793 when

Governor John Graves Simcoe—who many scholars argue was affronted by the violent spectacle of the sale and forced removal of a female slave named Chloe Coolie in Upper Canada—engineered slavery's gradual demise and was complete with the Imperial Act of 1833, which abolished slavery across the British Empire.[36] The abolition of slavery in the British Empire created a frontier of legal freedom for Blacks in Britain's North American possessions. The British were also willing to flex the muscle of the lion's paw to provide legal protections for runaway US slaves who were threatened with extradition to the United States between the 1820s and the American Civil War. During this period, US officials made several attempts to criminally extradite runaway slaves and, in the vast majority of cases, Canadian officials refused to grant these requests. Their actions were informed by a British colonial policy and an international treaty hammered out with the United States (the Webster-Ashburton Treaty). British Canadian authorities held firm in their conviction that only slaves who had committed offences deemed crimes on both sides of the border were candidates for extradition. Therefore, the US slave owners charge of "theft of a slave" fell upon deaf ears in British North America, where slavery had been abolished. Moreover, the colonial and imperial governments north of the 49th parallel also refused to extradite slaves for crimes such as horse theft, which were used to aid their transit to freedom.[37]

Colonization experiments in the late eighteenth and nineteenth centuries are also evidence of the British Empire's prevalently historicist conception of race and blackness, as it was also evidence of Blacks' desire, freedom and coveted land in the context of the British Empire. The founding and settlement of Sierra Leone on the West Coast of Africa was an opportunity for Black Nova Scotians who were bitterly disappointed by the province's unfulfilled promise of social and economic equality.[38] Many of slavery's opponents looked at Sierra Leone, a company/colony charted by the British government as an "experiment in social change" in the all-important transition from slavery to freedom.[39] By the early twentieth century, on the other side of the Atlantic, a number of all-Black settlements were founded in Upper Canada and Canada West. These settlements, which bore names like Oro, Wilberforce, Dawn, the Refugee Home Society, and Elgin/Buxton Mission, were also conceived of as sites where Blacks could overcome their backward historical development and gain the necessary social, cultural, and economic tools to make the transition to freedom.[40]

Finding Jim Crow in a Liberal Racial Order

Jim Crow in Canada must be considered within the broader context of a British Empire that was generally committed to a brand of White supremacy in support of evolutionary and historicist racial ideas (though not racial equality) and a Canadian state which, in stark contrast to the United States, granted Black citizens the franchise and "full legal protections."[41] These legal protections did not reflect the reality of the lowly social and economic status of Black Canadians.[42] The term Jim Crow was often invoked by African Canadians and sympathetic Whites to describe attitudes, values and outlooks, and social practices in Canada that strongly resembled the racial cultures of the US's Jim Crow regime. In Canada, Jim Crow frequently reared its ugly head when the liberal racial order could not seamlessly accommodate the powerful biologist assumptions about Blacks' racial inferiority.

Allen P. Stouffer has written that after the end of the American Civil War many Ontario newspapers looked on and commented on the freed slave's bleak prospects for making the transition to a post-emancipation society. Stouffer tells us that one editorial stated:

> [Blacks] are savage by nature, and utterly incapable of self-sustained civilization. Four thou-sand years ago, they lived side by side with Egyptian and Arab civilization, and were just as savage then in Africa as they are now. More pains have been taken, more money and labour extended to civilize the Negro than any other race. Yet, in his native wilds, he is still a savage, and is reverting rapidly to the savage state wherever relieved from slavery and left to cultivate a civilization of his own. There was never found a nation, tribe, or society, however small, of white savages. The civilization of whites is indigenous—part of their natures congenial with their race. The savage is natural to the savage state is natural to the Negro. He never was found with an indigenous civilization, nor any civilization at all, after he had lived in a society composed on Negroes for five generations.[43]

These kinds of biologically driven explanations of Black racial inferiority and a rejec-tion of evolutionary or historicist explanations for Blacks' low status were quite common in Canada and they tell us a lot about the power of the naturalist racial commitment in Canada, even if it wasn't constituted through positive law as it was elsewhere.

The spectre of interracial rape also reflected naturalist racial anxieties. In a 1920s rape case in which an itinerant Black Canadian labourer was found guilty of the horrible assault of an eighty-year-old White woman, the presiding judge congratulated the jurors for respecting the law, maintaining their faith in British justice, and resisting the urge to lynch the accused. In another case, the defence counsel of a Black man charged with raping a White farmwoman contended that the victim died "of shock" rather than physi-cal violence. Crown counsel argued that the shock produced by merely seeing a Negro was enough to kill the victim.[44]

In the 1920s, in Saint John New Brunswick a Black man named John Paris was accused of the sex-murder of an eight-year-old white girl. They key eyewitness was the little girl's companion, who could only say that the man who had abducted her friend wore a hat similar to Paris's. Blacks from Truro, Nova Scotia, Paris's home town, travelled en masse to Saint John to testify on Paris's behalf. Several witnesses maintained that Paris was seen in and around Saint John on the day that he was alleged to have committed the murder. The Crown tried Paris a total of five times. The first trial resulted in a hung jury. In the second trial, the Attorney General of the Province of New Brunswick personally took over the case; he won a decision against Paris (which included a mandatory sentence of death), but the decision was overturned on appeal. The third, fourth, and fifth trials all ended in the same result as the first. During his last trial Paris was finally released, but only on the condition that a recognizance was placed on him in case the court found any more evidence against him for a sixth trial. The John Paris case stands as one of the least known and most unsettling events in the history of Canadian jurisprudence.[45]

The control of Canada's borders is the most significant area where White supremacy was positively expressed in and through the law. The history of Canadian immigration is long and complex, but some general patterns in its evolution are clear. In the colonial era, immigration policy was in essence a recruitment and settlement policy designed to fill the empty lands that had been surrendered by First Nations people who had now fallen from being allies of the Crown to Crown wards. The era of "coercive tutelage," which was tied to the drive to create and entrench white settler colonies in British North America, quickly followed.[46] The Immigration Acts that were passed in 1906 and 1910 created a framework for immigration policy based on "the principle that the absolute right of the state [was] to admit and exclude new members...."[47] In the early twentieth century, Canadian immigration policy was characterized by a dialectic of inclusion and exclusion that was based on explicit racial hierarchies. Citizens of the British Isles were preferred over Central Europeans who were in turn favoured over those from Southern Europe. Asians, Africans, and South Asians were either barred outright or kept out of the country through a range of ingenious devices, such as the continuous journey immigration requirements that were passed in 1910.[48] However, exceptions were made when cheap, exploitable labour of racialized Others was required to build the nation.

It is in this historical context that African Canadians and others began to defiantly make a case for the existence of Jim Crow in Canada—even in the face of a largely "race-less" legal order—a Canadian manifestation of dominant British colonial articulations of race. Carrie Best, a Black Nova Scotian and editor in the 1940s of a newspaper called the *Clarion*, frequently argued for the existence of Jim Crow in Nova Scotia. In 1942, Best wrote a letter to the owner of a New Glasgow, Nova Scotia, movie house called the Roseland Theatre expressing her dismay and outrage at its policy of racial segregation:

> ... I have spent the entire afternoon conducting a personal Gallup poll to see if this rule is
> the carry over from the faraway days of slavery or if this is the rule of the Board of Directors
> and Shareholders of the Roseland Theatre Company.... Scores of respected citizens were
> amazed to believe that such Jim-crow tactics are practiced on such law abiding citizens and
> when the time comes have said they will not hesitate to speak against it.[49]

Through the *Clarion's* editorial pages, Best declared New Glasgow, Nova Scotia, "the centre of Jim Crowism in Canada." New Glasgow, said Best, "stands for Jim Crowism, at its basest, over the entire globe"[50]

A few years later when Viola Desmond, at times referred to as the "Rosa Parks of Canada," appeared before a judge to combat discriminatory treatment in the very same movie theatre, one judge wondered aloud whether "a surreptitious endeavour to enforce Jim Crow by misuse of a public statute" had occurred.[51] In 1960s Nova Scotia, the Black freedom struggle was waged in the crucible of Jim Crow. In the late 1960s, essayist Nancy Lubka wrote a short piece for the *Queen's Quarterly* comparing aspects of Nova Scotian society and culture to the American South:

> Last October the whole nation read about the burial incident, when a Negro child was refused burial in the cemetery.... It was a sort of anachronism, a slipping of yesterday into the present. In days gone by there were many such barriers, echoing the traditions of Jim Crow in the U.S. In nearly every sizable town in Nova Scotia black people live, and in most of these places there were colour bars.[52]

This "echoing of the traditions of Jim Crow" haunts the memories of Black Canadians whose bodies undermine the narration of a White Canada. Black Canadians and their allies had no difficulty pointing out similarities between patterns of racial discrimination in Canada and the Southern United States. But these observable patterns were the result of the terrible legacy of racial naturalism on both sides of the border. Blacks fought hard against these discriminatory practices; their struggle for civil rights in Canada, from the mid-nineteenth century until the late 1960s, was primarily waged in the courts.

Fighting Jim Crow in a Liberal Racial Order

Throughout the nineteenth and twentieth centuries, Black Canadians turned to the courts to combat racism. The central irony of Canada's civil rights struggle, one that plagues the anti-racist struggle in Canada to this day, is that the liberal racial order that characterized Canada often made racism quite difficult to fight in the courts. Canada's liberal racial order meant that, particularly early on, the strategy met with a modicum of success. After enduring three trials in 1855, a Black Canadian man won damages against the school board trustees in Simcoe for their refusal to allow his child to attend school through the gerrymandering of the school district. Unfortunately, this turned out to be a pyrrhic victory as he had to sell his own farm to cover the court costs (the defendant had no such assets).[53] The prohibition of gerrymandering of school districts to exclude African Canadian children was a welcomed development for Blacks and their supporters, but ultimately it proved insufficient to stem the tide of racist feeling in Canada West.

By 1859, separate schools were given formal status through an Act which "provided that twelve or more heads of families, could open their own institutions and receive appointments from the common school funds." Canada West's Superintendent of Education, Egerton Ryerson, advised that where there was strong opposition to the Negroes, separate schools should be created. As a result, they were often imposed by racist whites.[54]

Through the courts, Black Canadians fought unequal access to theatres in 1899 and 1914. Evocative of the earlier pattern in education, both cases resulted in victories.[55] In the long run, however, these cases turned out to be aberrant rather than typical. In 1924, for example, in the case of *Franklin v. Evans,* a Black Canadian man was denied service in a restaurant on the basis that the establishment did not serve "coloured people."[56] Later at trial Justice Lennox decried the restaurateurs for behaving in a manner that was "unpardonably offensive." He was moved by the plaintiff's appeal for "recognition as a human being, of common origin with ourselves." Nonetheless, the court found in favour of the defendant. Viola Desmond and Fred Christie witnessed similar defeats in the 1930s and 1940s when they tried to fight the colour bar in a New Glasgow, Nova Scotia, movie theatre and a Montreal tavern, respectively.[57]

Ultimately, African Canadians would have much more success in combating discriminatory treatment in public accommodations via the legislative route, and it would be done through forming alliances with labour unions and ethnic leaders outside of the Black community. Robin Winks argues that a change in racial attitudes "was punctuated, and perhaps hastened, by World War II."[58] James Walker, who wrote after Winks, presents a more nuanced argument, agreeing that there might have been a change in racial sensibilities, but cautioning against assuming that a complete paradigm shift took place in the aftermath of the war.[59]

The Jewish community in particular, which long felt the sting of virulent anti-Semitism, took an active leadership role in shaping the human rights agenda in Canada. In cities like Toronto, Calgary, Oshawa, and Dresden, social activists demanded that municipal governments take action against racial discrimination.[60] Dresden, popularly known as the Alabama of the North, had a large Black population that was subject to virulent racism. A local organization called the National Unity Association focused attention on restaurants and barbershops that discriminated against Blacks, launching a public awareness campaign that received a lot of attention (much of it negative) in the press. In 1944, Ontario passed the Racial Discrimination Act, and the Fair Accommodations Practices Act was passed in 1954, forbidding racial discrimination in public places. In 1963 Quebec, a similar Hotel Act was passed. In 1962, the Ontario Human Rights Commission was created.[61] The struggles waged by Christie and Desmond were vindicated in the long run and perhaps indirectly they had a role in shaping public consciousness.

The struggle for civil rights that took place in the realm of immigration policy was an extension of the human rights gains in the other areas mentioned above. Sheldon Taylor, in both his doctoral dissertation and his co-authored memoirs of Bromley L. Armstrong, has skillfully studied these themes in some detail.[62] In the 1950s, the Negro Citizenship Committee, later renamed the Negro Citizenship Association, lobbied the Canadian government to "enlarge the section of the Immigration Act, in order to permit freer entry of Negroes into the Dominion of Canada." Though a new Immigration Act was passed in 1952, it did not address this issue. The government obstinately refused to allow sizeable numbers of Black immigrants into the country. However, under pressure from the NCA and Caribbean governments, by 1955 the Canadian government agreed to allow a limited number of domestics into the country from Jamaica and Barbados. A few years prior to this, in 1950, a small number of Black Caribbean nurses of "exceptional merit were granted entry into Canada." By 1962, an amendment to the Immigration Act dropped all overt references to racial preference. By 1967, the points system was implemented, ostensibly affirming the government's commitment to a colourblind admissions policy on immigration. This did not trumpet the emergence of a new social order devoid of white supremacy; we must be wary of rushing to embrace a liberal-triumphalist narrative of this struggle. For, as Theo Goldberg argues, the "raceless" states that emerged in the late twentieth century are nonetheless characterized by racist practices. As we have seen, this racelessness in Canada was not a "colourblinding," but it was in fact "the raceless absorption and transmogrification of the racially differentiated into a state of values and rationality defined by white standards and norms, ways of knowing, thinking and doing."[63]

Conclusions

As more historians begin to write on the nature of the relationship between race and the law in Canada, we will have more evidence about what Jim Crow means in a Canadian context. It cannot begin to be fully resolved in a preliminary piece such as this one. This research will be done in a context in which some Canadian historians' aversion to exploring racial themes and the imposition of a term like Jim Crow on "our" history is palpable, and in some respects perhaps reasonable. We must always be vigilant to make sure that the tools of analysis we employ are suitable for the times and places we wish to study. We have always had to be careful about developing infatuations with US historical and historiographical paradigms and inelegantly imposing them upon Canada. Canadian political historians, labour historians, scholars of native-newcomer relations, and feminist scholars all struggle with this; it is not unique to African Canadian historiography or the growing literature on race and human rights in Canada. Yet, our aversion to a term like Jim Crow in Canada has much more to do with how it assaults traditional Canadian notions of self. The unpleasant reality that Blacks in early twentieth-century Truro, Nova Scotia, called the city "Little Mississippi", or that Dresden, Ontario, in the 1940s and 1950s was routinely referred to as "Canada's Alabama,"[64] does not fit many conventional understandings of Canadian history or even many non-conventional conceptions of Canada's past. Employing the language of Jim Crow in Canada is no mere rhetorical device, nor is it a misguided attempt to impose an Americanism upon cherished Canadian historiographical traditions. Rather, it is an important conceptual orientation that deserves honest attention—a counter-narrative that demands a re-orientation of Canadian historiography—while we come to grips with the history of the continental reach of legally sanctioned White supremacy. From the perspective of Black Canadians, Jim Crow in Canada makes perfect sense.

Acknowledgements

I would like to thank Georgina Riel, Karen Dubinsky, and Rebecca Manley for their suggestions on earlier versions of this article. I would like to thank Murray Wicket and Rick Halpern for giving me opportunities to present this work in public forums where I benefited from insightful feedback.

Notes

1 James W. St. G. Walker, *"Race," Rights and the Law in the Supreme Court of Canada: Historical Case Studies* (Waterloo: Wilfred Laurier Press and Osgoode Legal Society, 1997). Saje Mathieu has also written about "Jim Crow" in Canada. In her well-received and oft-cited article, "North of the Colour Line: Sleeping Car Porters and the Battle Against Jim Crow on Canadian Rails, 1880–1920," Mathieu argues that discriminatory occupational practices which began in the United States were imported into Canada. Jim Crow, says Mathieu, "was institutionalized as an ideal rationale for labour-management relations in the Canadian railway industry." Indeed, I would add that the fact that the railway was a continental system that routinely crossed the 49th parallel highlights the folly in trying to argue that Jim Crow was only a US phenomenon. The boldest claim for a Canadian history of Jim Crow is also the most recent, a website titled "The Many Faces of Jim Crow: Stories of Racial Discrimination in 20th Century Canada, A Documentary and Oral History Project." See Saje Mathieu, "North of the Colour Line: Sleeping Car Porters and the Battle Against Jim Crow and Canadian Rails, 1880–1920," *Labour/Le Travail,* 47 (Spring 2001): 9–41.

2 Ibid., p. 124; see also James W. St. G. Walker, *Racial Discrimination in Canada: The Black Experience,* (Ottawa, 1985: The Canadian Historical Association Historical Booklet No. 41).

3 I don't mean to suggest that Canada was free from racism, but rather that we need to pay attention to Ann Laura Stoler's claim that racism and racist practices can be produced within progressive or liberal social formations as well as conservative ones. See Ann Laura Stoler, "Racial Histories and Their Regimes of Truth," in Philomena Essed and David Theo Goldberg, eds., *Race Critical Theories* (Blackwell, 2002), 333–337.

4 Constance Backhouse, *Colour-Coded: A Legal History of Racism in Canada 1900–1950* (Toronto: University of Toronto Press, 1998), 13.

5 David Sealy was the first to make these observations in his work on Black Nova Scotians. See David Sealy, "Africville: From Savages to Welfare Recipients," unpublished paper, 2005.

6 David Theo Goldberg, *The Racial State* (London: Blackwell Publishers, 2002), 162. Catherine Hall's work superbly recounts how the ascendancy of liberalism in the late eighteenth century shaped British colonialism until the mid-nineteenth century. After anti-colonial rebellions in India, New Zealand, and Jamaica in the period after 1850, the idea that there were fixed racial differences began to gain increased currency in the British Empire. Those who believed in the "civilizing mission" were increasingly marginalized. However, post-colonial literary theorist Anindyo Roy's work shows that in the nineteenth and early twentieth centuries British Colonization of India was a project of "liberal" colonial governance that was often expressed in the language and rhetoric of "civility" and its link to ideas of citizenship in the British Empire. Roy's sophisticated work engages with the

liberalism of J. S. Mill (who developed many of his ideas while working in the colonial office of Britain's East India Company), Foucauldian concepts of "discipline," "normativity," and genealogy, as well as Homi Bhabha's work on·the ambivalent desires of the colonial project. Roy demonstrates that civility was an uneven, fractured and flexible, and contradictory discourse. In the metropole, civility was intricately linked with the idea of Britain's state modernity and modern citizenship. Civility, defined as "fair and democratic 'public discussion'" was unattainable in a colonial setting marked by the repression that was necessary to colonialism, and this was true in the colonial context despite the antagonistic relationship between the ideal of civility and the reality of despotism. See Catherine Hall, *Civilizing Subjects: Metropole and Colony in the English Imagination 1830–1867* (Chicago: The University of Chicago Press, 2002), 12, and Anindyo Roy, *Civility and Empire: Literature and Culture in British India, 1822–1922* (New York: Routledge, 2005), 10–11, 16.

7   Ibid., chapter 2.

8   Ibid., 42.

9   Ibid., 43.

10 Ibid.

11 Seymour Drescher, *The Mighty Experiment: Free Labour versus Slavery in British Emancipation* (New York: Oxford University Press, 2002), 81.

12 Ibid.

13 Ibid.

14 Jamaican planter Edward Long's *The History of Jamaica*, says Drescher, was the most virulently biologist enunciation of the pro-slavery position during this era. Long argued that Blacks occupied a position below Europeans and above the "Orang-outans." Ibid., 75.

15 Ibid., 85.

16 Ibid., 7.

17 C. Vann Woodward, *The Strange Career of Jim Crow: Third Revised Edition* (New York: Oxford University Press, 1974), 7n.

18 Eric Lott, *Love and Theft: Blackface Minstrelsy and the American Working Class* (New York: Oxford University Press, 1995), 18, 56.

19 C. Vann Woodward, *The Strange Career of Jim Crow.*

20 Woodward, 83–102; A useful account of the history of the Ku Klux Klan is Chester L. Charles, *The Ku Klux Klan and Related American Racialist and Antisemetic Organizations: A History and Analysis* (Jefferson, N.C.: McFarland, 1999). A Canadian example is William Peter Baergen, *The Ku Klux Klan in Central Alberta* (Red Deer, Alta.: Central Historical Society, 2000). The literature lynching in the American South is too voluminous to mention in its entirety. Two recent works that have been most influential in shaping my thinking on these matters are Jacquelyn Dowd Hall, *Revolt Against Chivalry: Jessie Daniel Ames and the Women' s Campaign Against Lynching* (New York: Columbia University Press, 1974), and Hall, "The Mind That Burns in Each Body: Women, Rape and Racial Violence," in Ann Snow et al., eds., *Powers of Desire: The Politics of Sexuality* (New York: Monthly Review Press, 1983), 328–49. David Marriot, *On Black Men* (New York: Columbia University Press, 2000); Grace Hale, *Making Whiteness: The Culture of Segregation in the South, 1890–1940* (New York: Vintage Books, 1999).

21 Woodward, 17.

22 Leon Litwack, *North of Slavery: The Negro in the Free States, 1790–1860* (Chicago: Chicago University Press, 1961), 70.

23 Ibid., 74–93.

24 Ibid., 94–95.

25 Ibid, chapter 6.

26 Ibid., 114.

27 Ibid., 153.

28 Goldberg, 147.

29 Ian McKay, "The Liberal Order Framework: A Prospectus for a Reconnaissance of Canadian History," *Canadian Historical Review* 81:4 (2000): 620, 623.

30 Ibid., 622.

31 Ibid., 625.

32 The British colonial government passed laws in the mid-nineteenth century to assist Aboriginal peoples in making their transition to "civilization": the Act for the Gradual Civilization of the Indian Tribes. Among its stipulations was the "gradual removal of all legal distinctions" between Indians and whites and to encourage Indians' acquisition of property. The Act spelled out the conditions under which Aboriginal peoples could become citizens and drop their Indian status (enfranchised), such as acquiring education, Christian habits, and evidence of high moral character. Enfranchisement was again enshrined as a legal principle in the 1867 Indian Act, sections 86 to 94. See J. R. Miller, *Skyscrapers Hide the Heavens: A History of Indian-White Relations in Canada Third Edition* (Toronto:

University of Toronto Press, 2000), 139–147.

[33] McKay, "The Liberal Order Framework," 637.

[34] Goldberg, "The Racial State," 82. For an example of French colonial Amerindian policy in New France and the links between racial ideas and assimilation, see Sahila Belmissous, "Assimilation and Racialism in Seventeenth and Eighteenth-Century French Colonial Policy," *American Historical Review* 110:2 (April 2004).

[35] I am well aware that sex between white men and black women as a means to assimilate Blacks was never seriously considered by Whites in the pre- or post-Confederation periods in Canada despite the widespread phenomenon of Blacks "passing" for Whites throughout North American history. In this way, the experiences of Blacks and Aboriginals are quite distinct. For a discussion of the Age of Reform in the British Empire, see Jane Sampson, ed., *The British Empire* (Oxford: Oxford University Press, 2001), 121–138.

[36] Maureen Elgersman, *Unyielding Spirits: Black Women and Slavery in Early Canada and Jamaica* (New York: Garland Publishing, 1999).

[37] See Robin Winks, *The Blacks in Canada* (Kingston and Montreal: McGill-Queen's Press, 1997), 168–177.

[38] The seminal text on this history is of course James W. St. G. Walker's *The Black Loyalists: The Search For a Promised Land in Nova Scotia and Sierra Leone 1776–1893* (Toronto: University of Toronto Press, 1992).

[39] Drescher, *The Mighty Experiment,* chapter 6.

[40] See, for example, Winks, *The Blacks in Canada,* chapter 7, and William and Jane Pease, *Black Utopia: Negro Communal Experiments In America* (Madison: State Historical Society of Wisconsin, 1963).

[41] Winks, *The Blacks in Canada,* 251–252.

[42] Ibid.

[43] Allen P. Stouffer, "A Restless Child of Change and Accident: The Black Image in Nineteenth Century Ontario," *Ontario Historical Society* 76 (2) (1984): 128–150.

[44] See Barrington Walker, *The Gavel and the Veil: Blackness in Ontario's Criminal Courts, 1858–1958,* chapter 5, Ph.D. diss. (University of Toronto, 2003).

[45] See Barrington Walker, "John Paris' Journey: A Scottsboro Trial in 1920s Canada?", unpublished manuscript.

[46] See J. R. Miller, *Skyscrapers,* chapter 5.

[47] Ninette Kelley and Michael Trebilcock, *The Making of the Mosaic: A History of Canadian Immigration Policy* (Toronto: University of Toronto Press, 2000), 113.

[48] As a result of orders-in-council passed by the federal government that year, South Asians who journeyed to Canada could only do so "by continuous journey from the country of which they are natives or citizens, and upon through tickets purchased in that country or prepaid in Canada." See Walker, *"Race," Rights and the Law,* 257.

[49] Constance Backhouse, "I Was Unable to Identify with Topsy: Carry M. Best's Struggle Against Racial Segregation in Nova Scotia, 1942," *Atlantis,* 22:2 (Spring/Summer 1998): 18.

[50] Backhouse, *Colour-Coded: A Legal History of Racism in Canada* (Toronto: University of Toronto Press, 1999), 248.

[51] Backhouse, 266.

[52] Nancy Lubka, "Ferment in Nova Scotia," *Queen's Quarterly* LXXVI (1969): 213–228

[53] Winks, *The Blacks in Canada,* 369.

[54] Ibid., 370.

[55] Backhouse, *Colour-Coded,* 253–254.

[56] Walter S. Tarnopolsky, *Discrimination and the Law in Canada* (Toronto: Richard De Boo Ltd., 1982), 20–21.

[57] See Backhouse *Colour-Coded,* chapter 7, and Walker, *"Race," Rights and the Law,* chapter 3.

[58] Winks, *The Blacks in Canada,* 420.

[59] Walker, 309.

[60] Ibid.,173; Sheldon Taylor and Bromley Armstrong, *Bromley: Tireless Champion for Just Causes* (Pickering: Vitablu Publications, 2000), chapter 4.

[61] Walker, 173.

[62] Sheldon Taylor, "Darkening the Complexion of Canadian Society: Black Activism, Policy-making and Black Immigration from the Caribbean to Canada, 1940s–1960s," Ph.D. diss. (University of Toronto, 1994).

[63] Goldberg, *The Racial State,* 206.

[64] Taylor and Bromley, 81.

Glossary

De facto. Latin term meaning "of the fact" or a matter of practice, as opposed to that which is *de jure* or enshrined in law.

Lynching. A form of mob violence involving the hanging and/or dismemberment of the mob's victim. Over 3,000 black men were victimized by lynch mobs in the US South between the post-Reconstruction era (see below) years and the end of the First World War.

Racial historicism. The idea that racial attributes are a function of historical forces. Most significantly, adherents of this idea believed that "lesser races" could, with time and tutelage, achieve the same level of civilization as those races in a higher phase of historical development.

Racial naturalism. The idea that racial attributes are a function of biology or nature. Adherents of this idea believed that racial types or essences were fixed and not subject to historical forces or environmental factors.

Reconstruction. The Reconstruction Era took place in the United States in the years between 1863 and 1877. Most historians agree that the most "radical" phase took place in the years between 1865 and 1877. Some of the prominent historical developments that marked this era were the abolition of slavery and the end of the Civil War, the extension of full citizenship rights and the franchise to former slaves, and various constitutional amendments to set the conditions through which secessionist states would regain their autonomy and hold congressional seats. The era came to a close with the "compromise" of 1877, which witnessed the departure of Northern troops from the South and the end of Republican state governments.

Further Reading

Backhouse, Constance. *Colour-Coded: A Legal History of Racism in Canada, 1900–1950.* Toronto: University of Toronto Press, 1999.

Based on case studies of African Canadians, Aboriginals, and Chinese Canadians, this book details the history of legal racism in Canada from 1900 to 1950.

Drescher, Semour. *The Mighty Experiment: Free Labour versus Slavery in British Emancipation.* New York: Oxford University Press, 2002.

This book explores the role of political scientists in setting the parameters of emancipation debates in the eighteenth- and nineteenth-century Atlantic world.

Golberg, David Theo. *The Racial State.* Malden Mass: Blackwell Publishers, 2002.

This interdisciplinary book deals with theories of the state and race, and how the two have intersected over time in various national contexts, drawing transnational contrasts and comparisons.

Lambertson, Ross. *Repression and Resistance: Canadian Human Rights Activists 1930–1960.* Toronto: University of Toronto Press, 2005.

Lambertson's work highlights the struggles of individual actors and their fight for human rights in Canada from the 1930s to the 1960s. In so doing he traces the evolution of rights discourse dominated by civil libertarianism to the early Cold War period to a focus on egalitarian group rights in the late 1950s and 1960s.

Walker, James W. St. G. *"Race," Rights and the Law in the Supreme Court of Canada: Historical Case Studies.* Waterloo: Wilfred Laurier Press, 1998.

This book surveys four historical case studies between the years of 1914 to 1955, highlighting the histories of race and racialization in Canada and the Supreme Court of Canada's role in adjudicating the rights of visible minorities.

Relevant Websites

Blacks in Canada: A Long History

www.statcan.ca/english/studies/11-008/feature/11-008-XIE20030046802.pdf

Written by Ann Milan and Kelly Tran, this website examines the history of the Black community in Canada.

Canada's Rights Movement: A History

www.historyofrights.com/introduction.html

This website provides a history of the human rights movement in Canada. Although the site has sections on various aspects of the "rights revolution," it is primarily designed to highlight the activities of social movement organizations (non-governmental organizations—NGOs).

The History of Jim Crow

www.jimcrowhistory.org/geography/geography.htm

Jimcrowhistory.org is an educator's site that presents teachers with new historical resources and teaching ideas on one of the most shameful periods in American history.

A Webography: The History of Racism in Canada

www.hopesite.ca/remember/history/racism_canada_1.html

This website looks at the history of racism in Canada and profiles the experiences of many groups: Native, Black, Jewish, Chinese, and Japanese.

CHAPTER 6

A BRIEF HISTORY OF THE DENIAL
OF INDIGENOUS RIGHTS IN CANADA

DAVID T. MCNAB

Introduction

The federal government has been entirely consistent in its treatment of Indigenous rights both within the nation-state of Canada and in the international realm. It has always denied these rights both in an international context and within the Canadian nation-state. It is highly ironic that the denial of such rights is in spite of the fact that such rights are part and parcel of Canada's Constitution (1982), especially section 35, which states unequivocally that Aboriginal people are recognized as "Indian, Inuit and Métis" and their Aboriginal land and treaty rights are reaffirmed (see glossary of terms at the end of the chapter). At the same time, federal legislation is still on the books—the Indian Act (since 1876)—which is both racist and colonial and takes away the rights of those Indigenous and Canadian citizens for whom the nation-state recognizes the same rights. The federal government is able to consistently deny Indigenous rights in Canada as a result of Aboriginal policies and practices that are basically unformulated and stated to be a process of relationships between First Nations and the federal government. The latter effectively rules the lives of Aboriginal people under the assumptions of the Indian Act, namely, that Aboriginal people are second-class citizens of Canada and, in practice, have no rights. All of this history is in spite of the many initiatives, and resistance, taken by Indigenous peoples in Canada to change the policies and processes of the federal government, as well as to resist their implementation on a day-to-day basis.[1] In short, this is a story of the betrayal of Indigenous people in Canada.

The issue is a fundamental one, that of Indigenous sovereignty. The same is true on the international stage. The federal government has usually denied Indigenous rights in Canada. Recently, on June 30th, 2006, the United Nations (UN) Human Rights Council endorsed a widespread extension of the rights of the world's Indigenous people. Canada was one of only four nations in the world who opposed this international declaration. This declaration "calls on nations with Aboriginal peoples to give them more control over their lands and resources." This document "is not binding but calls on governments to introduce laws to underpin its provisions." Subsequently, it was reported that a "Canadian delegate has told the council it will have 'no legal effect in his country'" and that "several of the articles would violate the national constitution or even prevent the country's armed forces from taking measures necessary for its defense." However, "Indigenous coalition representatives say they believe the big power opposition was largely driven by concern over the potential loss of state control over how natural resources, like oil, gas and timber, are exploited."[2] Nor should this denial of Aboriginal rights be at all surprising given the policies initiated within the place known as Canada since the early seventeenth century by European empires—the French (to 1763), the British (to 1867), and then the Canadian (since 1867).

On April 8, 2008, however, it was reported (by the American *Indian Country Today*, but not in any Canadian newspapers) that the House of Commons "passed a resolution to endorse the declaration as adopted by the U.N. General Assembly and called on the government of Canada to 'fully implement the standards contained therein.'" Mary Simon, currently President of the Inuit Tapiriit Kanatami stated that "The U.N. Declaration on the Rights of Indigenous Peoples provides a road map for the reconciliation of indigenous and non-indigenous peoples in Canada and around the world." The House voted 148-113 with the Liberals, NDP, and Bloc Québécois voting in favour as a direct response to requests made to them by national Aboriginal organizations. The federal Conservatives continued with their opposition to this declaration: "This government's latest arguments against the declaration show just how ridiculous their position has become," said Chief Wilton Littlechild, international chief for Treaty Six, in a press release. "The U.N. declaration explicitly states that treaties and other agreements with indigenous peoples are to be honored and respected." Tellingly, this report states that "The Harper government's arguments are belied by briefing notes from legal advisers to the departments of Foreign Affairs, Indian Affairs and National Defense to government ministers," and even the federal government's "legal advisers had recommended that Canada endorse the U.N. declaration and support its adoption."[3] This human rights issue is now joined in Canada both at the international and the domestic levels. And it has always been so in Canada's history.

Indigenous Peoples' Initiatives on Indigenous Rights and the Historical Development of Canadian Aboriginal Policies

Policy is multi-dimensional and multi-faceted, as J. W. Cell has noted. It is "something rather less fixed, something rather more historical," and at any moment in time there is "not so much policy as policy formation, an unsettled and changing set of responses by government to the continual interaction among men [and women], forces, ideas, and institutions."[4] As such, the Indigenous policies of Canada promulgated by the nation-state have their origins in the history of Aboriginal land rights and in the treaty-making process of Canada. Canadian policies owe their development to the many misrepresentations of Aboriginal peoples, including First Nations, Métis, and Inuit peoples, by Europeans. However, First Nations have no need for such policies.[5] Creations of the nation-state of

Canada, these policies are an aberration of the Covenant Chain of Silver and especially the Two Row Wampum. The latter represented the relationship between the Dutch, English, and French imperial governments and the Aboriginal nations; namely, peace, mutual respect, and trust. Initially given by the English to the Haudenosaunee to cement the treaty entered into at Albany in 1664, its components were known at least as early as the early seventeenth century when the very first treaties of peace and friendship were entered into between the French and the Mi'kmaq Nations in Acadia, present-day Atlantic Canada. The Covenant Chain literally means "to link one's arms together" and signifies a nation-to-nation relationship.[6]

The significance of the Covenant Chain of Silver as a basis for the treaty-making process and Indian policies cannot be underestimated in terms of land and sovereignty. Sir William Johnson, the English Crown's imperial appointee to the Indian Department in 1755, highlighted its magnitude in 1764 when he wrote that: "Tis [It is] true that when a Nation find themselves pushed, their Alliances broken, and themselves tired of a War, they are verry [very] apt to say many civil things, and make any Submissions which are not agreable [agreeable] to their intentions, but are said meerly [merely] to please those with whom they transact Affairs as they know they cannot enforce the observance of them. But you may be assured that none of the Six nations, Western Nations [including the Western Confederacy] &ca. ever declared themselves to be Subjects, or will ever consider themselves in that light whilst they have any Men, or an Open Country to retire to, the very Idea of subjection would fill them with horror."[7] This statement by Johnson links the basis of this process with one of the early views also integral to Canada's Indian policies—the notion that Aboriginal peoples were subject to an empire or a nation-state. Now, this notion of subjects rather than First Nations was a direct result of the ideology of European empires, notably the French and British empires, which sought to control and dominate the natural world of North America and the peoples who resided there. Initially outnumbered and without sufficient technology (the canoe was one of the primary modes of resistance) to dominate Aboriginal peoples, the French and then the British empires recognizing Aboriginal peoples as nations sought out and entered into treaties of peace and friendship.[8]

The Royal Proclamation of 1763

One of the first unilateral statements of British imperial policy towards the First Nations was the promulgation of the Royal Proclamation of 1763, which was partly a response to the Anishinabe and Seneca resistance movements earlier that year. Owing much to the treaty-making process, the Royal Proclamation was an English imperial document, among other things, that recognized and reaffirmed the "Indian territory" to be their "absolute property." It established English imperial rules regarding the treaty-making process under the Covenant Chain, as well as recognized the significance of the sovereignty of Aboriginal trade and trading.[9] It would be reaffirmed one year later in a Grand Council of Nations at Niagara in 1764, and in subsequent treaties. The following is a contemporary First Nations' perspective on it: "While the treaties are like stones marking a spot in time, the relationship between the Nations is like two equals, respecting each of their differences but supporting each other for a common position on peace, order and justice for all. The brotherhood created by the Twenty Four Nations Belt represents a relationship of both sharing and respect. The sharing is reciprocal: as the First Nations shared land and the knowledge in the past, now that situation is reversed, the generosity of spirit and action is expected to continue. The respect is also reciprocal: respect for each other's rights, existence, laws and vision of the future."[10] Aboriginal people do not forget their histories or the promises made to them about Indigenous rights.

By the late eighteenth century, the balance of military power was beginning to shift and increasingly the treaties came to be seen by European settlers as land surrenders with the Aboriginal peoples as subjects of the imperial crowns. These promises were not inconsequential at a time when the English imperial foothold on the North American continent was at best precarious. Sir William Johnson died in 1774 and after that things began to fall apart. The solemn promises of the Crown were forgotten by the Indian Department by the 1790s.

English Imperial Aboriginal Policies in the 18th and 19th Centuries

After the disaster for Indigenous people wrought by the American War of Independence (1775–1783), the new colony of Upper Canada became of enormous significance to the English imperial government. It was important for its strategic military advantage to protect the English colony from the United States by creating a sovereign Aboriginal buffer state, effectively a military zone between the new American republic and Upper Canada. The land was also seen to be, in the long term, of great value as a place for the second English empire to promote commercial agricultural settlement for English settlement and colonization. Lieutenant John Graves Simcoe's plan for Upper Canada (1791) outlined this plan: "There are but a very few Indians who inhabit within it, the greater part of the soil has been purchased & the whole ought to be before it will become of value, as the Indians will not want for suggestions to inhance [enhance] its price. I consider the Country to be of immense value, whether it be regarded to its immediate advantages, the future prospect of Advantage, or the probable grounds for supposing it will remain the most important foreign possession of Great Britain."[11] Based on the Royal Proclamation of 1763 and a misconstruction of the treaty-making process, and Simcoe's land policy, a number of land surrenders occurred in Upper Canada from the 1790s to

Confederation (1867), and in the numbered treaties thereafter in the Canadian west and north. These treaties were not entered into without resistance by First Nations' citizens. The embodiment of the Two Row Wampum and the ostensible promise of protection of subject peoples soon became a land grab filled with corruption and land speculation, as was the case in the United States.

The War of 1812 (to 1814) was a "turntable" for Canadian Indigenous policies. Although fighting for the British in that war, after the war First Nations were no longer needed militarily. The result was that a boundary was agreed upon by the United States and Britain which split First Nations' territories, literally carved it up by the survey of the international boundary and, more seriously, effectively took away jurisdiction and governance (but not sovereignty) from First Nations.[12]

Relocation and attempted extinguishment of Aboriginal title and reserve lands in Upper Canada occurred after the War of 1812. Gradually, a full-blown English imperial policy of civilization was established by the 1820s. Many more requests came for land surrenders from the English Crown, but the land policies were not followed. Most of the monies were not deposited into trust fund accounts, and more lands were taken than outlined in the written treaty documents. Even without the overt use of force, the imperial government sometimes used another process, a process based on non-consultation and non-consent in violation of the spirit and intent of the Royal Proclamation and the treaties to achieve the same end of extinguishment. Beginning in the 1820s, with increasing British emigration, agricultural settlement by white settlers began on a large scale. Requests came for more land surrenders. In the 1820s, the imperial government embarked on its policy of "civilization" in Upper Canada because it had already been deemed a success by imperial officials in Lower Canada. While this policy was primarily designed with a hard edge to purposefully assimilate Aboriginal people, it also promised monies for education and training and economic opportunities; for example, commercial agricultural opportunities for the citizens of the First Nations. Another less desirable approach of the policy was a conscious plan of removal, developed by the Lieutenant Governor Sir Francis Bond Head in the mid-1830s. The idea was to remove and to centralize Aboriginal people into two geographical areas, Manitoulin Island and Walpole Island. According to the government, once centralized on islands they could better be "civilized" and then assimilated. This was strenuously resisted by the First Nations as threatening to their Indigenous rights as a sovereign people. The only group that became enfranchised as "white people" under this policy by the 1880s were the Wyandot of Anderdon.

This so-called civilization policy was not predicated on the surrender of Indian lands, at least initially, to pay for the policy. Rather, the monies for it would come from a general parliamentary grant from the Crown. Subsequently, the policy became one of assimilation, which was financed crudely by selling Indian lands and using the funds raised to pay for their own assimilation. This policy was anathema to First Nations. By 1840, this policy had already failed at Coldwater and other places. Yet, the Indian Department, confronted by wholesale squatting and trespass on First Nation lands, continued to implement it by taking land surrenders. This policy was codified in the late 1850s in the first Indian Act of 1857. The import of this new approach to civilization was not lost on the First Nations' leadership, who rejected it and bluntly stated that it was an attempt "to break them to pieces." It led directly to their loss of citizenship within the empire.

Partially responding to the attempted encroachments and the alienation of the "Indian territory," the English imperial government took action, flowing from the Royal Proclamation, ostensibly to protect parts of the "Indian territory." In 1839 it passed legislation to protect Crown lands, especially the Indian territory, which had been the subject of considerable concern because of trespass, squatting by non-Aboriginal people, illegal land use (e.g., taking timber from Indian lands), and outright fraud. However, this legislation proved not to be strong enough in the decade following its passage, and the illegal taking of, or other depredations on, Aboriginal lands continued. On August 10, 1850, the government of the province of Canada passed further legislation, an Act for the "protection" of the "property occupied or enjoyed" by Aboriginal people in Upper Canada "from trespass and injury." This legislation strengthened the provisions of the 1839 Act, but the legislation still appears not to have been effective since squatting and the process of dispossession continued unabated. However, Aboriginal people did not become citizens of Canada (notwithstanding Canada's first Citizenship Act of 1947) until John Diefenbaker's first Canadian Bill of Rights was established in 1960.[13]

In 1861, Herman Merivale (1806–1874), an astute English commentator and a consummate imperial bureaucrat, observed that imperial Aboriginal policy had been a failure. His commentary could well be a description of Canada's Aboriginal policy almost one hundred and fifty years later: "The subject, in short, is one which has been dealt with by perpetual compromises between principle and immediate exigency. Such compromises are incidental to constitutional government. We are accustomed to them: there is something in them congenial to our national character, as well as accommodated to our institutions; and on the whole, we may reasonably doubt whether the world is not better managed by means of them than through the severe application of principles. But, unfortunately, in the special subject before us, the uncertainty created by such compromises is a greater evil than errors of principle."[14] Merivale's description of the vacillation of Canada's Aboriginal policies between "perpetual compromises between principle and immediate exigency" is a significant observation about the failure of Canada's Indigenous policies. These policies have created great uncertainty and extreme frustration with the failure of the Crown to uphold the Covenant Chain of Silver and the concomitant solemn treaty promises. This situation goes far to explain its failure.

The Confederation of Canada

One of the primary events that eroded Indigenous rights was the Confederation of Canada in 1867. In that year, the British North America Act was passed by the imperial government and First Nations effectively lost recognition and respect for their rights of citizenship and sovereignty over their governance and over their lands and waters. The new federal government assumed responsibility for "Indians, and Lands reserved for the Indians" under section 91(24), subject to any liabilities, which the government of the province of Canada had, to First Nations. This legislation allowed the federal government to pass the first consolidated Indian Act, thereby establishing a colonial relationship of the federal government to First Nations. It also stated that the provinces had control over all other lands within the boundaries of each province (section 109). Although this imperial statute was subject to any outstanding interests, including Reserve lands as well as the Aboriginal territory, much of which was still unceded, neither the interests nor the lands were specified. If the lands were not referred to, then it was subsequently assumed that First Nations' land rights did not exist. Originally, the Confederation of Canada was conceived of and was supposed to have been a treaty among the founding nations of Canada, including all of the First Nations based on the Two Row Wampum. But it soon became a means of carrying forward the policy of extinguishment, including the surrender or relinquishment of the Indian territory, as well as the beginnings of the implementation in the late nineteenth century of the residential school system, along with its horrific cultural and sexual abuses that lasted well into the 1980s. The federal government issued a public apology only in June 2008.

The Numbered Treaties

Conflict, rooted in imperial and colonial aspirations as well as cultural disparateness, grew apace as Canadian Aboriginal policies continued to develop within regional frameworks. There were treaties of peace and friendship in Atlantic Canada, no treaties in Quebec, and land loss treaties in Upper Canada, which became a model of the subsequent numbered treaties (1871–1930) in Canada's west and north. The ostensible principle of protection gave way to assimilation, and with it came European scientific racism as part and parcel of Canada's Indigenous policies beginning in the late nineteenth century.

The dichotomy and the discrepancies over the negotiation of the so-called numbered treaties in the late nineteenth century was a clear example of the divergence not only of the treaty-making process in the 1870s, but also the weaknesses of Canada's regional policies at that time and thereafter. Mawedopenais, a Mide Chief of the Ojibwa, spoke to the Crown's commissioner and chief negotiator, Alexander Morris (1826–1889), at the Treaty #3 negotiations in October of 1873. As a spokesperson for the Rainy Lake and Rainy River people in this treaty-making process, he was clear on the position of Aboriginal nations and the title to their lands: "I lay before you our opinions. Our hands are poor but our heads are rich, and it is riches that we ask so that we may be able to support our families as long as the sun rises and the water runs." Morris replied, disingenuously, indicating that he did not understand what Aboriginal title and the treaty-making process meant for the Aboriginal nations: "I am very sorry; you know it takes two to make a bargain; you are agreed on the one side, and I for the Queen's Government on the other. I have to go away and report that I have to go without making terms with you. I doubt if the Commissioners will be sent again to assemble this nation." This threat, implying the government approach of "divide and conquer," was not, as may be expected, well received by the Anishnabek Nation. Treaty #3 was eventually negotiated and signed, but not on the basis of the treaty document or as understood by Alexander Morris. He did not believe, as many people do to this day, that the Aboriginal nations were ready to share in the treaty-making process with the riches in their heads. There was no balance in the "bargain" before or after the treaty was signed. Morris and the federal government took too much away from the life of the Ojibwa.[15] It has continued to do so here and elsewhere in Canada. From this unequal perspective, the negotiations were not successful. It was not the only treaty that could be characterized in this fashion. Yet, the treaty issues do not die; they live within a circle of time for later generations. Aboriginal people in Canada resist any changes to their land rights under the numbered treaties, or otherwise, and they never forget.

The Indian Act (1876) and Its Successors

This non-consultative late nineteenth-century treaty-making approach became central and pivotal to the development of the top-down policy approach of the federal government inherent in the Indian Act of 1876 and its successors. Moreover, except for one substantial revision to that legislation in 1951, the Indian Act essentially still remains a cornerstone of Canada's Aboriginal policies. The federal government still today decides who is or who is not an Aboriginal person under the registration process of the Indian Act (which is still based on blood quantum)—non-status and Métis persons are not and cannot be registered under it, notwithstanding that they are recognized in Canada's Constitution as Aboriginal peoples. In fact, it was not until the 1930s that the Inuit of Canada's north were recognized through a court ruling as having equal status as "Indians." Yet there is no Inuit Act today.

More than one hundred years later there is still a wide cultural gulf in the treaty-making process, which has intensified and has led to the abrogation of Aboriginal title and treaty rights and to the events of the summer of 1990. But the events at Oka were broader than the events at Kahnesatake and Kahnawake. Similar situations also occurred in northern Ontario and in British Columbia. In 1995, the denial of Indigenous rights led to the death of Dudley George, caused by an OPP officer, at Ipperwash.[16] Such events are now occurring in Ontario at Caledonia. In each instance, Indigenous rights were denied by the Canadian nation-state and at Oka the Canadian Armed Forces went in to enforce the denial of Indigenous rights.

What accounts for these differences in Canadian Indian policies and the reality of Indian existence in Canada? The answer lies in the disparate histories of Aboriginal and non-Aboriginal people in Canada. The primary objective of Aboriginal people is spiritual—one of peace and to protect the land—Mother Earth—and the waters of Turtle Island. This is a sacred trust, a trust to protect the land. The continuity and integrity of their lands are important to their survival as an Indigenous people. Generations of First Nation members have used the land and have shared in its bounty and its uses. Moreover, they will continue to use this land and teach their children about the Creator and the land. So this relationship is all-important; they owe their very survival to it. It is both simple and profound. The events of the summer of 1990 at Oka and elsewhere across Canada occurred at the initiative of Aboriginal people to protect their lands and waters. To do this, they had no choice but to resist those who wished to destroy them and their land. Not to do this would mean their own destruction, as well as the destruction of their children and grandchildren. It would have meant the end of their cultures and survival as Aboriginal people. They will continue to protect their lands and waters.

Canada's Aboriginal Policies in the Early Twenty-First Century

In the early twenty-first century we are witnessing profound structural changes in the history of the world. The world of nineteenth-century and twentieth-century European/American imperialism is beginning to come to an end. Decolonization is continuing apace. This process has been characterized both by forces of construction and destruction. In Canada, to provide but one example, Aboriginal peoples are again reaffirming their inherent right to governance through diverse approaches and a variety of means. Their lands are ever so slowly being recovered, if not always respected. Aboriginal title is beginning to be understood and recognized. One watershed in the twentieth century was the *Calder* case of 1973. This Supreme Court of Canada decision found that Aboriginal title and rights did exist in the white justice system of Canada. It opened the legal door for the prosecution of Aboriginal title and rights cases in Canada. *Calder* was followed by many constructive Supreme Court of Canada decisions that reaffirmed Aboriginal title and land rights and treaties, including *Guerin, Simon, Sioui, Sparrow, Delgamuukw* (1997), and *Marshall* (1999), to name a few.[17] *Calder* also opened the door to new land claims policies of the federal government in 1974, which has operated to undermine Canada's historic Indian policies and replace them with various forms of Aboriginal governance, which led to the creation of the territory of Nunavut in 1999 and then the first modern treaty—the Nishga Treaty—in British Columbia in 2003.

What is the basis of this new Indigenous policy embodied in the land claims processes? There are no Aboriginal land "claims," as defined by the federal government, only First Nations Aboriginal title and land rights. There are only Aboriginal title and treaty rights to the land and these must be protected. Highlighted are land grievances flowing from the treaty-making process. These areas are not restricted to Reserves, places seen to be of special and specific protection. As strategic areas of land for Aboriginal resource use, they were a major consideration for both the Crown and Aboriginal people. But, they formed antithetical concepts that still intensify conflicts over treaty areas and Reserves.

Current Land Rights Processes

The answer to the resolution of Indigenous land and resource issues lies also changes to the land rights process. Filing a claim with the federal Department of Indian Affairs is an administrative procedure. It is like filing one's income tax return, a ritual Canadians hate to complete every spring. Imagine if you had to file and you were to get back a tidy sum of a few thousand dollars. Instead of receiving a cheque in the mail after a wait of about one or two months, you received a form letter produced by a computer stating that under a new policy you did not exist, and until you could prove your existence you would not get any money. After repeatedly and vainly attempting to show on paper that you did in fact exist, you had to wait at least ten or twenty years for your cheque to come. This situation is not an exaggeration. The people of the Bkejwanong First Nation submitted a small land claim regarding 300 acres to the Specific Claims Branch of Indian Affairs in 1977, now more than thirty years ago. After years of review and analysis it was rejected in 1986, and now its rejection is being reviewed by the Indian Specific Claims Commission that was established by the Mulroney Tories as a partial response to Oka in 1991. Hearings on the rejection of this claim took place in 1994, seventeen years after the claim was submitted. To date, only a partial settlement agreement has occurred. The federal claims policy exhibits too much bureaucratic and legal process, very little substance, and too few settlements. This fact was recognized by the federal government, which passed legislation in the summer of 2008 to create an independent Specific Claims Tribunal to address such issues.[18]

The Indian Claims Commission, established after the events at Oka and elsewhere, can only recommend and publish its findings and recommendations to the federal Cabinet. But the government does not have to implement its recommendations. The Commission has continued to date. A non-Aboriginal person would feel frustrated, angry, and very, very bitter if confronted by such a process. We have seen this reaction by non-Indigenous people in the community of Caledonia in the last few years.[19] This is what Aboriginal people go through with their claims, which number more than a thousand in Ontario alone. This is felt right across Canada.

What is a land claim? It is a statement of the land rights of an Aboriginal nation that contains reference to a specific geographical area. It is a claim based on whether the Aboriginal resource users of the land in question have ever decided to enter into a treaty for it under the rules set out in the Royal Proclamation of 1763. A claim is not a court action; it is not litigation. It is a policy (actually two—one for comprehensive claims and the other for specific ones) and a program of the federal government administered by the Department of Indian and Northern Affairs. The government's purpose is to extinguish "claims" and thus effectively deny Indigenous rights. The process within government is restricted and, insofar as a claimant decides on litigation, the file wends its way through the federal bureaucracy to the Department of Justice, and the claimant is seen from the policy and program point of view to have withdrawn the claim. The bureaucrats then arbitrarily close the claim and place it on a dusty shelf along with others like a mere curio, or a collector's item, on a Victorian knick-knack shelf. It is literally another form of "captured heritage." In the late 1980s, one senior federal bureaucrat even used this very image of Victorian curios to arrogantly describe this situation with paternalistic condescension.[20]

Land rights are significant if they can, through substantive settlement agreements, add to the land and the economic base of First Nation communities. Reserves were initially strategic economic areas that were excepted from the treaty-making process. Later they were transformed and designed by English imperial policy-makers as special areas of "civilization" with the specific objective of assimilating First Nations. Soon they became mere "halfway houses," which were to be appropriated whenever they were needed for the purposes of the Crown or for non-Aboriginal uses. Thus, a form of imperial trusteeship gave way en route to a path leading to gradual and then, it was hoped, complete assimilation. This was (is) a vestige of a pure colonial relationship. Even this misguided sense of Aboriginal "claims," distorted by twenty-first-century lenses, has been rendered illegitimate over time by the alienation of land and labour of Aboriginal people. Land surrenders as well as the loss of the commons for natural resource usage by governments and by private interests assisted the process. What was seen to be legitimate was rendered both unlawful and unfair from an Aboriginal perspective. And this has not been confined to a distant past and is therefore scarcely known or seen. What cannot be seen by governments cannot be destroyed. The Temagami case, in particular the building of the Red Squirrel Road extension in 1988–1989, is a prime but not solitary illustration.[21]

Constitutional Recognition of Indigenous Rights

The repatriation of Canada's Constitution in 1982, single-handedly initiated by Prime Minister Pierre Elliott Trudeau,[22] was a watershed of Indigenous rights in Canada. The

Constitution was critical in recognizing Indigenous rights in what became a legal context. As a result of many years of Aboriginal resistance movements, the Ontario provincial government, on October 2, 1990, recognized the inherent right of Aboriginal govern-ance. The federal government followed suit a few years later, but it remains outside of the Canadian Constitution in 2006. A quarter of a century of constitution-making since 1982 has collapsed into disunity, separatism, and regional antagonisms for the white visitors to Canada. The Meech Lake Accord, the epitome of the old imperial centralist model of Confederation, stylishly referred to as "executive federalism," was defeated in 1990. This was a clear constitutional victory by Aboriginal people; they are in the Canadian Constitution. Although the Charlottetown Accord of 1992 was also a failure, the inherent right of Aboriginal people to Aboriginal governance, as well as their Aboriginal title and land rights, has since been recognized and reaffirmed.

This reversal of imperial policy was altered in 1982 when Canada's Constitution was patriated and "existing Aboriginal and treaty rights" were admitted as part of it, but not Aboriginal governance or sovereignty. Today the larger business of the Constitution and the treaty-making process through various land and natural resources rights (and policies based on them) still remains incomplete and unfulfilled. It is currently being defined by Canada's Constitution on an issue-by-issue basis by the Supreme Court of Canada.

This concept of Aboriginal history and oral traditions was reaffirmed by the Royal Commission on Aboriginal Peoples (1996) and also by the Supreme Court of Canada in 1997 in its ruling in the case of *Delgamuukw v. British Columbia*, also identified as the Gitksan and Wet'suwet'en comprehensive "claim." That legal ruling stated that oral traditions are "not simply a detached recounting of factual events but, rather, are 'facts enmeshed in the stories of a lifetime.'" Moreover, they are "rooted in particular loca-tions, making reference to particular families and communities." As a result, oral history is in fact "many histories, each characterized in part by how a people see themselves, how they define their identity in relation to their environment, and how they express their uniqueness as a people." The Supreme Court stated that the "laws of evidence" in the Canadian justice system must accommodate Aboriginal oral history and traditions such that it "be placed on an equal footing with the types of historical evidence that courts are familiar with, which largely consists of historical documents. This is a long-standing practice in the interpretation of treaties between the Crown and Aboriginal peoples." To not recognize and accept this history as an equally valid way of viewing the past is to deny Aboriginal people and their land rights. This approach was denied, among others, in the trial of this case and in the Temagami ruling by the trial judge, Mr. Justice Donald Steele.[23]

Much of Canada's modern Aboriginal land policies are still viewed one-dimension-ally as primarily assimilative, as a form of directed cultural change. This has been seen as originating in the nineteenth century and culminating in the federal government's

White Paper of 1969. Canadian historians have concentrated more on the origins and development of that policy and less on the resistance to it by First Nations, especially on aspects of it in the twentieth century. Aboriginal policies must also be viewed from the perspective of First Nations' citizens and their governments.

Canada's Aboriginal policies have developed gradually with two primary components. These are diametrically opposed to each other. They become built-in obstacles. The first component is that the federal government has been largely indifferent to Aboriginal title and land rights, taking a legalistic approach overall, only acting when it is forced to do so by Canada's courts. The second component is that the provinces continue to use their hegemony, through legislation and regulations, over lands and natural resources in self-serving ways. Canada's Aboriginal policies since 1867 have been an artificial creation, both negative and destructive, for Aboriginal people and their relationship to the rest of the country. Federal policies have always been driven by other more prominent national agenda items—western settlement, protective tariffs, free trade, and the Constitution. Consider, for example, the failure of the Meech Lake and Charlottetown Accords in the early 1990s.[24]

Conclusions

This story of betrayal of the human rights of Canada's Indigenous people has no conclusion or end. Aboriginal policies, through a long process of denial, have created institutional racism and corresponding resistance movements that culminated in violence and death. The events of the summer of 1990 at Oka have not been forgotten or erased. Initiatives for change in Aboriginal history have always come from the First Nations. Federal and provincial government policies have always been characterized by reaction, crisis management, and denial. Encountering policy words with no substance and a benign, passive policy, First Nations have always chosen to act; they had no choice but to act—to resist these polices—if they wished to survive. Aboriginal people will continue to resist and survive. In the early twenty-first century, the prominent issues for Canada's Aboriginal policies remain outstanding and unresolved. In this sense, Canada's Aboriginal policies have been a wholesale failure in the face of resistance to them by Aboriginal citizens. And, they have led directly to the consistent denial by the federal government of Indigenous rights in Canada and on the international stage.

Notes

[1]   For the significance of examples of resistance see Ute Lischke and David T. McNab, "Actions of Peace: Introduction," in *Blockades and Resistance: Studies in Actions of Peace and the Temagami Blockades of 1988–89*, co-ed. with Bruce W. Hodgins (Waterloo: WLU Press, 2003), 1–9; in the Ontario context see my *Circles of Time: Aboriginal Land Rights and Resistance in Ontario* (Waterloo: Wilfrid Laurier University Press, 1999).

2 *UN council approves indigenous rights treaty.* ABC News Online, Friday, June 30, 2006; "UN council approves indigenous rights treaty," Richard Reynolds in Toronto and wires. See also http://www.un.org/esa/socdev/unpfii/.

3 David T. McNab, "'We are sorry'?" in Olive Patricia Dickason and David T. McNab, *Canada's First Nations*, 4th ed. (Toronto: Oxford University Press, 2009), 427–457.

4 J. W. Cell, *British Colonial Administration in the Mid-Nineteenth Century* (New Haven: Yale University Press, 1970), especially see his "Introduction."

5 Ute Lischke and David T. McNab, eds., *Walking a Tightrope: Aboriginal People and their Representations* (Waterloo: Wilfrid Laurier University Press, 2005). See also in an Ontario context my *Circles of Time: Aboriginal Land Rights and Resistance in Ontario* (Waterloo: Wilfrid Laurier University Press, 1999).

6 David T. McNab (edited for Nin.Da.Waab.Jig.), *Earth, Water, Air and Fire: Studies in Canadian Ethnohistory* (Waterloo: Wilfrid Laurier University Press, 1998), 41–44.

7 Milton W. Hamilton, ed., *The Papers of Sir William Johnson*, Vol. XI (Albany: The University of the State of New York, 1953), 395–396.

8 David T. McNab, with Bruce Hodgins and S. Dale Standen, "'Black with Canoes': Aboriginal Resistance and the Canoe: Diplomacy, Trade and Warfare in the Meeting Grounds of Northeastern North America, 1600–1820," in George Raudzens, ed., *Technology, Disease and Colonial Conquests, Sixteenth to Eighteenth Centuries. Essays Reappraising the Guns and Germs Theories* (Amsterdam: Brill International, 2001), 237–92; Bruce W. Hodgins, Ute Lischke, and David T. McNab, eds., *Blockades and Resistance: Studies in Actions of Peace and the Temagami Blockades of 1988–89* (Waterloo: Wilfried Laurier University Press, 2003).

9 "October 7, 1763, Royal Proclamation of 1763," in Ian A. L. Getty and Antoine S. Lussier, eds., *As Long as the Sun Shines and the Water Flows, A Reader in Canadian Native Studies* (Vancouver: University of British Columbia Press, 1983), 29–37.

10 Nin.Da.Waab.Jig. Files, Walpole Island (Bkejwanong) First Nation.

11 E. A. Cruikshank, ed., *The Peter Russell Papers*, Vol. II, 1798–1799 (Toronto: [Ontario Historical] Society, 1933), October 22, 1798, 42–3, 53, 290–1.

12 Dickason and McNab, *Canada's First Nations*, 4th ed., 192–201.

13 James W. St. G. Walker, *"Race," Rights and the Law in the Supreme Court of Canada, Historical Case Studies* (Waterloo: The Osgoode Society for Legal History and Wilfrid Laurier University Press, 1997), 326.

14 David T. McNab, "Herman Merivale and Colonial Office Indian Policy in the Mid-Nineteenth Century," *Canadian Journal of Native Studies* 1, no. 2 (1981): 277–302. Reprinted in Ian A. L. Getty and Antoine S. Lussier, eds., *As Long as the Sun Shines and Water Flows: a Reader in Canadian Native Studies* (Vancouver, University of British Columbia Press, 1983), 85–103.

15 David T. McNab, "The Administration of Treaty #3: The Location of the Boundaries of Treaty #3 Indian Reserves in Ontario, 1873–1915," in Getty and Lussier, eds., *As Long as the Sun Shines and Water Flows*, 145–57.

16 See the Ipperwash Inquiry at www.ipperwashinquiry.ca, September 11, 2006.

17 David T. McNab, "The Spirit of Delgamuukw and Aboriginal Oral Traditions in Ontario," in Owen Lippert, ed., *Beyond the Nass Valley: National Implications of the Supreme Court's Delgamuukw Decision* (Vancouver: The Fraser Institute, 2000), 273–83.

18 The Specific Claims Tribunal Act was passed and received royal assent in June of 2008. See http://www.ainc-inac.gc.ca/ps/clm/fct3-eng.asp, accessed at September 15th, 2008. See also McNab, "'We are sorry'?", 427–457.

19 See also my section on Caledonia in "'We are sorry'?", 427–457.

20 An application for a claim must be accompanied by a statement of facts, which will include a summary statement of the historical research findings on the Aboriginal people and their lands. It includes events that have been recorded either by oral tradition or by written record since time immemorial. Legal argument and conclusions are often present, as well. Lastly, copies of the historical documents are shared.

    The government, or more correctly governments, soon to be more prevalent as the claims process leaves the North, begins to assess the claim based on its perception of its validity, its (often limited) understanding of the interpretation of the history of the Aboriginal people, and purely political considerations. The actions of previous governments are also taken into account from the time of the British Empire in the eighteenth century through to the successive colonial governments, the provinces, and Ottawa. Also significant in any bureaucratic and political judgment is the role of legal and legislative precedents with similar claims. For example, a positive response in a claimant's favour of a Supreme Court of Canada decision has an enormous impact on a claim with a similar fact situation. These will likely have the same legal issues at stake. The difficulty is that there are still, more than a quarter of a century after the Nishga decision, relatively few legal precedents. Thus, decisions on validity are often determined by the Department of Justice's lawyers whose job is in a conflict-of-interest situation: how can they judge the validity of the claim fairly while they are paid to protect the government? This system of deciding the claims by having the federal lawyers as the judge, jury, and hangman is not at all fair, and moreover it has failed.

Only a truly independent claims commission, for example an independent tribunal, can now protect the claims process and the federal government from disrepute.

[21] See my "Remembering an Intellectual Wilderness: A Captivity Narrative at Queen's Park in 1988–89," in *Blockades and Resistance: Studies in Actions of Peace and the Temagami Blockades of 1988–89* (Waterloo: Wilfrid Laurier University Press, 2003), 31–53; "No Place for Fairness: Stories and Reflections of Bear Island" (McGill-Queen's University Press, forthcoming 2009).

[22] Trudeau was an Indigenous person himself; see my book manuscript "Visitors to Turtle Island: The Impact of Aboriginal People and Places on the European Newcomers," manuscript in process.

[23] See my "No Place for Fairness: Stories and Reflections of Bear Island" (McGill-Queen's University Press, forthcoming 2009).

[24] McNab, *Circles of Time,* 187–202.

Glossary

Constitution. Defined as the "mode in which a state has been constituted or governed." In this sense, Canada's Constitution is a product of the treaty-making process, both Aboriginal and non-Aboriginal, in which the Canadian state has been constituted arising through a series of council meetings, at least since the seventeenth century if not well before that time.

Extinguishment. The "putting a total end to, or blotting out of existence." The federal policy of "extinguishment" of Aboriginal title and rights is an attempt to put an end to Aboriginal people and their way of life. A "specific" claim is part of the designation of a policy used by the federal government to mean that the grievance of a claim arises from the non-fulfillment or maladministration of a treaty. In the same context, a "comprehensive" claim is a claim by an Aboriginal group for lands and waters for which no treaty covers the geographical area in question.

Reserve or **Reservation.** An area usually designated by a treaty to be excepted or reserved from the treaty lands that have been identified by the parties to the treaty. The Reserve lands continue to remain after the treaty as the exclusive lands and waters of the Aboriginal people. "Treaty lands" are those lands designated by the parties to a treaty that in the future they wish to share in common and in the mutual interests of both of the parties to the treaty.

Title or **Aboriginal title.** Defined as "that which justifies or substantiates a claim; a ground of right; hence an alleged or recognized right." In English law it means the "legal right to the possession of property." Aboriginal title is the legal possession by First Nations or an Aboriginal group to an area of lands and waters identified by the latter. "Time immemorial" is the concept that the First Nations have held Aboriginal title and land rights to their territories at least since the first contacts or record of them by the European visitors. Effectively, this phrase means that Aboriginal title and rights have existed well before the sixteenth century.

Treaty. Defined as the "treating of matters with a view to settlement; discussion of terms, conference, negotiation." The treaty-making process in the Aboriginal context is the series of conferences held under the Covenant Chain of Silver, which has continued to be the fundamental relationship or framework between Aboriginal and non-Aboriginal people that metaphorically binds or covenants them together. The Covenant Chain is an Aboriginal concept of diplomacy and trade. The Chain, which was adopted by the Dutch, the French, and then the English, was originally in iron and then in silver. It was a metaphor for the partnership, or covenant, meaning a sacred agreement, between the Aboriginal and the European nations in all matters regarding their mutual relationship. Today, the Covenant Chain may be likened to a large diplomatic or military alliance among many nations, for example, NATO. It dates, at least in the written record, to an agreement between the English and the Aboriginal nations at Albany in 1664. References to the Covenant Chain can also be found in the oral traditions of First Nations and wampum belts, among other places. The Covenant Chain of Silver has been continued to the present day, acting as an overarching framework for the treaty-making process. In this process matters have been treated with a view towards the settlement of them in conferences and negotiations. In this view, the document itself is not the treaty; it is the conference or council meeting in which a solemn and binding agreement is reached. An "adhesion" to a treaty is the council meeting at which an Aboriginal group has become formally attached, or adhered to, a treaty.

Further Readings

Cell, J. W. *British Colonial Administration in the Mid-Nineteenth Century*. New Haven: Yale University Press, 1970.

Although published almost 40 years ago, this pioneering scholarship is still the definitive work on nineteenth-century British administration of its colonies, including Canada.

Dickason, Olive Patricia, and David T. McNab. *Canada's First Nations, A History of Founding Peoples from Earliest Times*, 4th ed. Oxford University Press, forthcoming October 2008.

The first history of Canada's Aboriginal peoples written by Métis authors and is still today the most comprehensive work on this subject.

Getty, Ian A. L., and Antoine S. Lussier, eds. *As Long as the Sun Shines and Water Flows: a Reader in Canadian Native Studies*. Vancouver, University of British Columbia Press, 1983.

This landmark Reader marks one of the first attempts by Canadian scholars to address Aboriginal and treaty rights in the Canadian context.

Hodgins, Bruce W., Ute Lischke, and David T. McNab, eds. *Blockades and Resistance: Studies in Actions of Peace and the Temagami Blockades of 1988–89*. Waterloo: Wilfrid Laurier University Press, 2003.

This collection analyzes both the Temagami Blockades of 1988–89 and the concepts of resistance from Indigenous and non-Indigenous perspectives in Canada and the United States.

Lischke, Ute, and David T. McNab, eds. *Walking a Tightrope: Aboriginal People and their Representations*. Waterloo: Wilfrid Laurier University Press, 2005.

Walking a Tightrope is the first scholarly study by Indigenous people of how they have been represented and misrepresented by non-Indigenous people.

McNab, David T. *Circles of Time: Aboriginal Land Rights and Resistance in Ontario*. Waterloo: Wilfrid Laurier University Press, 1999.

The first scholarly analysis of resistance movements in Ontario in the late twentieth century.

McNab, David T. (edited for Nin.Da.Waab.Jig.). *Earth, Water, Air and Fire: Studies in Canadian Ethnohistory.* Waterloo: Wilfrid Laurier University Press, 1998.

Provides a scholarly framework from a holistic, interdisciplinary perspective for the study of Indigenous people in Canada

Raudzens, George, ed. *Technology, Disease and Colonial Conquests, Sixteenth to Eighteenth Centuries. Essays Reappraising the Guns and Germs Theories.* Amsterdam: Brill International, 2001.

This study reappraises the guns and germs theories related to the impact of Europeans worldwide on Indigenous peoples.

Walker, James W. St. G. *"Race," Rights and the Law in the Supreme Court of Canada, Historical Case Studies.* Waterloo: The Osgoode Society for Legal History and Wilfrid Laurier University Press, 1997.

Walker explores the concept of race and human rights as the law has been applied historically by the Supreme Court of Canada.

Relevant Websites

Federal Department of Indian Affairs
www.ainc-inac.gc.ca
This is the homepage for the Federal Department of Indian Affairs in Ottawa.

The Ipperwash Inquiry and its Final Report, May 31, 2007
www.attorneygeneral.jus.gov.on.ca/inquiries/ipperwash/index.html
This is the homepage for the Ipperwash Inquiry.

United Nations Permanent Forum on Indigenous Issues
www.un.org/esa/socdev/unpfii/
This is the homepage for the UN Forum on Indigenous issues, an excellent resource.

CHAPTER 7

"MIXING WITH PEOPLE ON SPADINA":
THE TENSE RELATIONS BETWEEN NON-JEWISH WORKERS AND JEWISH WORKERS

RUTH A. FRAGER

God Protect Us from Gentile Hands and Jewish Wits.

—Yiddish folk saying[1]

Armed with knuckledusters, two unemployed Toronto ILGWU members assaulted two of the Union's leaders in October 1936, beating them badly. The victims were both Jews, the assailants were not. "The attackers, in a statement to the police, which the press featured, attempted to create anti-semitic feeling, by the contention that they were being discriminated against, because of being Gentiles," reported another local Jewish union leader. "This is without foundation, of course," the official declared, explaining that "we countered with a statement in the press by the Gentile Local repudiating this, stating that discrimination does not exist in our Union." He was so concerned about the incident that he immediately called the union members together in a mass meeting and also made a point of visiting each shop "to pull out as much poison as possible." Although he believed the base instincts of some elements among the membership have been put to flight," he felt that "generally speaking the incident was rather injurious [to the union]."[2] When David Dubinsky, president of the ILGWU, learned "the startling news," he, too, stressed that this was an explosive issue, adding: "This, in my judgment, is the effect of the propaganda being disseminated by Father Coughlin and other groups, who are interested in stirring up racial prejudice."[3]

This assault was only one of the more dramatic manifestations of the serious divisions between Jewish workers and non-Jewish workers in Toronto's needle trades. Although, initially, the vast majority of the city's garment workers were Anglo-Celtic, the proportion of Jews in this sector had increased to slightly less than half by 1931. Among the male garment workers in particular, the proportion of Jews had risen to a little under two-thirds by that year.[4]

The language barrier was only one of the many ways in which Jewish workers stood apart from their non-Jewish counterparts, but the language problem itself was no minor matter. Yiddish-speaking immigrants had seldom learned any English before emigrating, and, once here, they found that learning English involved mastering a whole new alphabet as well as the different syntax and vocabulary. Beyond the language issue, the separateness of Jewish workers reflected, in part, the legacy of relative isolation Jews had experienced for centuries in Eastern Europe in the context of vicious anti-Semitism. Even though prejudice

against Jews was less severe in Toronto, the city's immigrant Jews still experienced significant discrimination. Contrary to a common present-day misconception, anti-Semitism in
Toronto (as well as in Canada as a whole) constituted a serious problem not only during
the rise of Fascism in the 1930s but during the preceding three decades as well. Jewish
experiences of persecution in Eastern Europe, combined with the very real presence of
anti-Semitism in Canada, made Jewish workers wary of their non-Jewish co-workers.[5]

★★★★★

The leaders of the needle trades unions did, however, try to overcome the relative separateness of the two groups of workers by appealing to the ideal of working-class solidarity.
The need for class solidarity was, of course, very real, particularly since Jews and non-
Jews often toiled beside each other on the shop floor in this sector. Within a particular
union, separate locals may have eliminated some problems, but representatives from each
local had to work together on their union's joint board. More broadly, of course, union
members needed to function smoothly together at many levels.

In some cases, there were leftist political links between some of the Jews and some of
the non-Jews, who might have been connected through the CCF, the Communist party,
the Socialist party, the Social Democratic party, the Trotskyist movement, or the Anarchist
movement. Partly because there were relatively few non-Jewish garment workers involved
in these political groups, however, ethnic divisions among the city's needle trades workers
were difficult to bridge.[6]

★★★★★

The friction between Jewish workers and non-Jewish workers was, in part, related to issues
arising out of the differences in the skills involved in their work. In Toronto, such issues
became particularly important for male workers in the men's clothing industry in the 1910s.
In this particular period, the conflict between Jews and non-Jews was also heightened by
interunion rivalry in this section of the industry. A detailed examination of the development of the Amalgamated Clothing Workers highlights not only the conflicts of the 1910s
but demonstrates also the problems of ethnic conflict that continued into the 1920s and
1930s, resulting in further interunion rivalry in the midst of the Great Depression.

In the 1910s the three rival unions were the Journeymen Tailors' Union of America
(JTUA), the United Garment Workers (UGW), and the Amalgamated Clothing Workers
(ACW). The JTUA had been established for those involved in custom tailoring (a process
whereby clothing was made up according to the specifications of the individual customer).
The other two unions competed sharply in the ready-made branch of the men's clothing
industry, for the ACW had been formed by a group of secessionists from the UGW in 1914.

In Toronto, as in many of the other clothing centres in Canada and the United States, the ACW was composed mostly of Jews from the beginning of its formation. In contrast, the members of the JTUA tended to be non-immigrants, as did the members of the UGW.[7]

Shortly after the formation of the ACW, the JTUA worked out an agreement with it, merging the two organizations into one industrial union. This merger led, in fact, to a lot of friction between the two groups, both in Toronto and elsewhere. As a result, the merger was liquidated not long after it had been established. During the period of the merger, the Toronto members of the JTUA had been involved in attempts to organize the ready-made men's clothing workers, together with the ACW.

Much of the friction between the two groups stemmed from the ways in which employers used the Jewish immigrants as part of the deskilling process in this period. The traditional custom tailor was highly skilled and made the whole garment either by himself or with the help of an apprentice. This craft was being seriously undermined, however, by the increasing popularity of ready-made clothing as well as by the dramatic increases in the division of labour in the remaining custom tailoring establishments. Many of the skilled custom tailors resented those workers who made clothing according to these newer—and cheaper—systems of production. The custom tailors looked down on those whom they viewed as far less skilled than themselves, and they saw these newcomers as a threat to their own positions. In Toronto, as elsewhere, many of the workers who did these less skilled jobs were Jewish immigrants. Ironically, a considerable number of these Jews were themselves victims of deskilling, for they had done skilled tailoring before emigration and then found themselves relegated to less skilled roles in the newer production processes on this side of the ocean.[8]

★★★★★

In Toronto, James Watt, a key JTUA official, experienced serious difficulties during the brief JTUA–ACW merger, when he tried to help his organization unionize the less skilled men's clothing workers. "The section worker [the person who puts together only one section of the garment] finds it as difficult to understand the journeyman tailor as it is for the journeyman tailor to understand the section worker," declared the frustrated Watt in 1915.[9] The difficulties were compounded by the fact that Toronto's journeymen tailors were usually Anglo-Celtic, while many of the section workers were Jewish.[10] Ethnic tensions were directly related to the specific role many Jewish workers played in the labour process.

★★★★★

In the meantime, both during and after the short-lived merger with the JTUA, Toronto's Amalgamated Clothing Workers concentrated on recruiting all the ready-made clothing workers in the city's men's clothing industry. This involved trying to persuade workers they were better off in the ACW than in the United Garment Workers. At the international level, the founders of the ACW had seceded from the UGW largely because of the anti-immigrant attitudes of the UGW's head office.[11] Indeed, Jewish readers of the UGW's newspaper might well have been offended by the occasional anti-Semitic jokes it contained.[12]

In Toronto, as well, there is evidence of the UGW's insensitivity to the Jewish garment workers. Sam Landers, the union's organizer for Toronto and its most important Canadian organizer in this period, was hardly in a position to inspire confidence in Jewish workers. Originally a Jew, Landers had joined the Salvation Army, and he publicly referred to Jews as "Kikes" in the pages of the UGW's newspaper. Other indications of the UGW's insensitivity include the fact that, in 1915, the Toronto branch of the UGW held an important organizing meeting at the same time that the city's Jews had scheduled a mass meeting to organize relief for their persecuted co-religionists in Poland.[13]

In the contest between the ACW and the UGW in Toronto, ethnic differences were sometimes reinforced by skill differences. In 1917, at a time when the city's ACW had seven hundred dues-paying members, not even one cutter had joined this union. The ACW's organizer reported that the cutters had their own UGW local and that it would be a "mighty hard job" to organize the members of this highly skilled occupation into the ACW. In this branch of the city's needle trades, almost all of the cutters were non-Jews. Thus the ACW organizer suggested that the union renew its efforts to organize them by hiring a local non-Jew, someone who would be "well known amongst the Gentile element in Toronto" and well known among the cutters in particular.[14]

Although some of the cutters had joined the ACW by the following year, there was friction between them and the other ACW members. More broadly, it was still difficult for the ACW to "make any progress at all among the English speaking element." The union strove to remedy the situation by setting up a separate office for the non-Jews.[15]

In addition to the cutters, other non-Jews eventually began to join Toronto's ACW, partly to work in the shops where the employers had signed contracts with this union. This ethnic mix led to further tensions within the union itself. In 1920, for example, certain English-speaking union members reportedly had a constant "feeling of irritation" that they did not yet have their own separate local. These anglophones had temporarily been placed in a sublocal of the Jewish coatmakers' local, and their Jewish co-workers did not object to their request for their own local. When the manager of Toronto's ACW wrote to the union's head office to emphasize the need for a separate local, he explained that the new local's "designation cannot be properly placed for any particular branch of the industry, and the only distinction seemingly can be made that they cannot under any circumstances meet with the Jewish Speaking element; to them it's a matter of a moral prestige."[16]

Several years later, after the new English-speaking local had been established, the anglophone members of Toronto's ACW continued to press for more separation from the Jewish ACW members. The executive board of this English-speaking local, together with the executive board of the English-speaking cutters' local, protested to the ACW's Toronto Joint Board "against the disorderly conduct of some members at the mass meeting in the Standard Theatre. [They] recommend[ed] that in the future separate meetings shall be arranged for the Jewish and English speaking members."[17] Although the union's records do not indicate the nature of this "disorderly conduct," the non-Jews' call for separate meetings highlights the serious ethnic tensions within the union.

Relations between these two groups of ACW workers remained strained. In the context of a 1927 joint board decision to ensure that all union members were up-to-date with their dues payments, for example, the ACW's English-speaking local pointedly asked the board "why the English membership is being checked up more on the dues than the others." Although the board replied there was no evidence of discrimination, the anglophones clearly felt they were being discriminated against.[18] Another incident in the same year illustrates that Jews, too, were concerned they were being discriminated against within the union. In this case, "Brother Beckerman," an executive member of local 233, expressly asked the joint board to clarify whether this particular local was "a Gentile Local or an English-speaking Local." Beckerman decided to push for this clarification after attending one of the local's executive meetings where "an English-speaking woman who was Jewish by nationality applied for membership [in local 233] and some of the members of [the local's] Executive tried to refer her to the Jewish Locals." When he objected to her treatment, "stating that every English-speaking person has a right to belong to the Local," "he was denounced, even by Brother Tovey," the union's anglophone business agent. "By what right did Brother Tovey tell him that he would expel him from the Organization?" Beckerman indignantly inquired.[19]

Further problems developed. Several years later, for example, an ACW official reported that, in Toronto, "an attempt has been made to disrupt loyalty [to the union] by bringing in the element of antisemitism." "That is being checked, however," he optimistically declared.[20]

While Toronto's ILGWU experienced its own difficulties with "the Jew Gentile problem,"[21] tensions between Jews and non-Jews in the men's clothing industry continued to plague the ACW, leading directly to the establishment of the rival National Clothing Workers of Canada (NCWC). The NCWC was the product of the All-Canadian Congress of Labour (ACCL), a central labour body founded in 1927 in explicit opposition to the international unions that were based in the United States and included Canadian locals. While advocates of the ACCL maintained they were fighting to free the Canadian labour movement from American domination, much of the motivation for the formation of the NCWC was far less noble.[22]

Although the ACCL had made some efforts to organize Toronto garment workers in 1931, it did not gain a significant foothold in this sector until the NCWC was launched in early 1934, arising out of a struggle with the ACW at Ontario Boys' Wear. This struggle began in late 1933 when more than one hundred workers struck this Toronto shop for recognition of the Amalgamated Clothing Workers and for a substantial wage increase. After the strike had dragged on for several months, the employer turned around and signed a closed-shop agreement with the ACCL's newly formed National Clothing Workers of Canada. The NCWC supplied the firm with workers, while the ACW continued to picket for a time.[23]

The owner of Ontario Boys' Wear himself had been a key initiator of the formation of the NCWC at this shop. In the midst of the strike, Mezza Finch (soon to become president of the NCWC) contacted the ACCL's head office to explore the possibility of forming an ACCL affiliate at this firm. She explained that "the firm [is] determined against the amalgamated [the ACW] and ap[p]ealed to me as a worker against them."[24] Since Finch was already associated with the ACCL at this time, the employer was apparently turning to her in the hopes that an ACCL local could be formed in his shop to enable him to avoid having to settle with the ACW.

The collusion between management and the pro-ACCL workers at this shop was based on ethnic prejudice. The ACCL's newspaper pointedly asserted that Ontario Boys' Wear was "almost the only non-Hebrew shop in Toronto."[25] In the letter to the ACCL's head office in which Finch first explored the possibility of forming an ACCL affiliate at this firm, Finch explained that "the employees [of Ontario Boys' Wear] are all gentiles and they are a gentile firm." "The firm," she continued, "does not wish to employ any but gentiles."[26] Neither Finch nor her correspondent, the secretary-treasurer of the ACCL, objected to management's plans for continued discrimination. This employer apparently preferred the ACCL over the ACW partly because the ACCL was liable to go along with his discrimination against Jewish workers.[27] The ACCL's NCWC was formed out of this collusion.

This incident raises crucial questions about the nature of the Canadian nationalism of the ACCL. Finch, who became a member of the national executive board of the ACCL, saw herself as British and appears to have been highly ethnocentric. Her brand of Canadian nationalism was not a multicultural brand, and her belief in Canadian unionism seems to have been rooted in a more xenophobic form of nationalism. Finch's opposition to what she saw as the foreign domination of Canadian labour implied not only opposition to American control but also opposition to control by immigrants inside Canada—and Jews were considered to be foreigners by definition.[28] Moreover, Finch was not the only such nationalist labour leader opposed to Jews. Ernest Smith was another nationalist who played a leading role in the ACCL's work in the Toronto needle trades. In an attempt to discredit the ACW, Smith wrote to Ontario's attorney-general, describing the ACW as "an American union controlled by Russian Jews."[29]

The NCWC's ethnically based collusion with the boss at Ontario Boys' Wear led to significant collusion around low wages as well, for the NCWC attempted to block government officials from investigating low pay at the firm. In the late 1930s these government officials were attempting to ascertain whether this shop was violating the legal minimum wage rates, but the NCWC, which still had a closed-shop agreement with Ontario Boys' Wear, refused to allow the officials to question union members. Finch, leader of the NCWC, believed that the ACW was determined to put both Ontario Boys' Wear and the NCWC itself out of business. She apparently feared this could be done by forcing the firm to increase wages to meet the minimum wage rates stipulated in the Industrial Standards Act. Thus she wound up fighting the act as well as the ACW.[30] Meanwhile, it was the boss himself who had profited from exploiting the divisions between Jewish and non-Jewish workers in Toronto's needle trades.

Tensions between these two groups of Toronto garment workers were pronounced not only among the men's clothing workers but also among the furriers. A detailed examination of the development of the city's International Fur Workers' Union (IFWU) further illuminates the nature and sources of these inter-ethnic tensions from the 1910s through the 1930s. In the early years the IFWU was weak, consisting of only a handful of non-Jewish cutters in local 35 and a handful of Jewish operators in local 40. As a result, Toronto's IFWU leader suggested to the head office in 1915 that they dissolve local 40 "until times improve" and that the Jews from that local join local 35.[31] He soon realized, however, that the non-Jews found this unacceptable. He wrote to the head office: "I am given to understand that local #35 does not want Jews as members, and that bringing them in would most likely cause a decrease in the already small membership of local 35. Local 35 committees have [repeatedly] declined to invite Jews [in] local #40 to partake in the social gatherings of local 35. Hence I don't believe local 35 will accept them. Further local #40 prefers its own Charter [and] Union."[32]

By the late 1920s there were three IFWU locals, all of which were in the fur-coat branch of the industry. Local 40 was a Yiddish-speaking local for all the Jewish workers, regardless of skill and gender. Local 35 was for the non-Jewish cutters mainly, although it also included some non-Jewish men who were blockers and operators. There was also local 65, which was mainly for non-Jewish women. Ed Hammerstein, an IFWU activist, recalled there was a great deal of tension between the non-Jewish locals and the Jewish local: "The Joint Board consisted of the three locals, and, as you can well see, that [the Jewish] local 40 was a ... minority group. And there were some very heated arguments and battles that took place at [the Joint Board] meetings, so much so that the Labour Council of Toronto had to appoint a person to act as chairman, to sort of mediate between these groups. Otherwise, they would've never been able to come to any [agreement]." Hammerstein explained: "The decision there arrived at was that, in order to bring some equality and balance, [they should] organize the [fur] collar and cuff workers. So, aside from it being an organizing drive to help workers who were terribly exploited, it also served sort of a political purpose insofar as the union was concerned in order to equalize the strength of the two [groups]." The union succeeded in organizing the collar and cuff trade and set up local 100 for these workers, who were mostly Jewish men. However, according to Hammerstein, "the problem wasn't resolved when local 100 was formed because then you had a balance. And because you had that balance, they could very seldom come to terms on issues." As a result, the IFWU again turned to the Toronto Labour Council, which assigned a person to chair the IFWU joint board meetings "so this sort of broke the constant tie votes that took place."[33]

By 1931 "the difficulties and misunderstandings" between the Jews and non-Jews had assumed such a "serious character" that the local IFWU leaders were appealing to the union's president to come to Toronto to help them straighten out the situation. As the IFWU minutes reveal, the local officials warned the union's head office that the two non-Jewish locals were "threatening to engage their own business agent and also to hire an office for themselves."[34]

The tensions between the Jewish and non-Jewish members of Toronto's IFWU exploded a year later during a general strike in the city's fur industry. As the union prepared for the strike, some of the bosses succeeded in influencing around two dozen members of the non-Jewish local 35, the cutters' local, to break away from the IFWU and form their own union. A key Jewish IFWU leader denounced this breakaway union as a tool of the manufacturers and declared it was being used against the other workers.[35]

The *Yiddisher Zhurnal* was nonetheless optimistic about developments in the IFWU. A week before the strike began, the newspaper reported that the union's head office had succeeded in uniting the four Toronto IFWU locals under one joint board that would take over negotiations with the manufacturers. Locals 35 and 65 had apparently agreed to give up their own office and work closely with the two Jewish locals, but it soon became clear that the non-Jews were not honouring this agreement. At that point, the leaders of the two Jewish locals announced that if the manufacturers signed a contract with locals 35 and 65, the Jewish locals would not honour it. The Jewish unionists felt that a strike was becoming necessary not only to win better wages but also to force the manufacturers to recognize the joint board, of locals 40 and 100.[36]

When the 1932 general strike began in Toronto's fur industry, hundreds of Jews walked off the job while most of the non-Jewish workers refused to join the strike. The local Jewish IFWU leaders enlisted the support of the union's head office to try to solve the problem of "the two locals which didn't join the strike and [which], with their deeds, hindered the organization of the fur workers."[37] The local IFWU strike leaders had even tried, to no apparent avail, to appeal to the Trades and Labour Council of Toronto to pressure the strike-breakers into cooperating. Although the Jewish workers eventually won the month-long strike anyway, this general strike provides one of the most graphic examples of the conflict between Jewish workers and non-Jewish workers in Toronto's garment industry.[38]

Recalling the clashes between these two groups in Toronto's IFWU, Ed Hammerstein indicated that the hostility stemmed from the fact that "the Jews who were coming into the industry were, in the eyes of the Gentiles, threatening their position." He felt that much of the friction arose because the non-Jewish fur workers were less militant than the Jews.

★ ★ ★ ★ ★

Employed in the better section of the industry and "secure in their jobs," the non-Jews "didn't cotton to this militancy that was developing" among the Jews.

When Hammerstein was asked if he had experienced anti-Semitism within the union, his reply emphasized the way in which ethnic differences were reinforced by skill differences (at least as far as the male workers were concerned): "You'd find there might be some latent, incipient type of anti-Semitism on the part of individual fellow workers."

★ ★ ★ ★ ★

As Hammerstein explained, the Jewish workers and the non-Jewish workers had two very different conceptions of trade unionism. The Jewish IFWU leaders, who were themselves divided into rival Communist and CCF camps in the 1930s, felt that unions should be seriously involved in progressive political action. In contrast, the non-Jewish members, who, in any case, often voted Liberal or Conservative, did not think the union should be involved in any political activity. The fact that the non-Jewish IFWU leaders were generally opposed to socialism added to the friction between them and their Jewish counterparts.[39]

Jacob Black, another Jewish activist in the furriers' union, similarly emphasized that the non-Jewish IFWU leaders were less militant than the Jewish leaders.

★ ★ ★ ★ ★

Differences between Jewish furriers and non-Jewish furriers were also heightened by the fact that Jacob Black, along with many of the other Jewish IFWU leaders, worked to involve the union in political actions that had special significance for Jews. The non-Jews, for example, tended to be relatively indifferent to the fight against world Fascism, whereas the Jews were highly concerned about this issue. Some of the Jewish IFWU leaders were also involved in support work for the Jewish labour movement in Palestine, which did not generally interest non-Jewish workers.[40]

In the context of ethnic tensions within the various needle trades unions, many of Toronto's garment manufacturers employed a "divide and conquer" strategy, attempting to pit non-Jewish workers and Jewish workers against each other, particularly during strikes. In so doing, these garment manufacturers were acting like many other employers in Canadian industry who strove to manipulate ethnic divisions within the workforce to their own advantage. Indeed, early twentieth-century Canadian immigration policy had been strongly shaped by key Canadian entrepreneurs whose insistence on the open-door policy stemmed partly from their plans to benefit from an ethnically diverse labour force. Within Toronto's garment industry, even some of the Jewish manufacturers tried to capitalize on ethnic divisions on the shop floor. Many of the non-Jewish employers, in particular, did not hesitate to try to discredit the Jewish unions through appeals to anti-Semitism.[41]

★★★★★

Toronto's garment manufacturers used various tactics to inflame ethnic divisions in the workforce. During a shop strike in 1920, for example, one of the bosses apparently reported to the police and the magistrate that the strike was caused by the strikers' refusal to work with Christian workers. The unionists denied this was the case, and the *Zhurnal* interpreted this charge as yet another slur against Jewish workers. "Racial denunciations have already been dragged in," explained the *Zhurnal*, because "the bosses realized that they cannot fight the workers with the usual [economic] methods."[42]

"The bosses have plainly become anti-Semites," reported a Toronto ILGWU official a few years later. "They incite the English workers against the Jewish workers using such expressions as 'we want to get rid of the damned Jews.'"[43] As the employers continued to stir up racial hatred among the garment workers, Toronto's ILGWU prepared for a cloakmakers' general strike, appealing in the *Zhurnal* to the Jewish cloakmakers to support the union. This appeal explained: "At each strike … such ugly deeds of the bosses are noted, when they try, through racial hatred between Jews and non-Jews, to incite one against the other. On you, union members, lies the obligation to enlighten the non-Jewish workers that a fight for the union means only an economic, not a racial fight.… Explain to [the non-Jewish workers] also the significance of strike-breakers [and the importance of unity]."[44] Toronto's garment manufacturers also sometimes threatened Jewish union members that if any of them protested too much, they would replace them with non-Jewish women.[45]

The manufacturers' attempts to exploit ethnic divisions were particularly apparent during the 1934 strike in a dress department of Eaton's garment factory. The employees of this department were non-Jews, and several of the women strikers testified that when they became interested in the ILGWU, "[management] would try to bring in [the] racial question, about the Jewish people, telling us we should not belong to the union at all that was controlled by Jews."[46] The women were allegedly "out of [their] class" because, in seeking the help of ILGWU officials, "they were mixing with people on Spadina."[47]

The manufacturers' interest in trying to keep the non-Jewish workers from "mixing with people on Spadina" stemmed partly from the fact that, by the interwar period, Toronto's Jewish garment workers were generally more militant than the others. In the earlier years, however, the pattern of militancy was more complex. In the early to mid-1910s, in particular, the JTUA found it difficult to organize Jews, while Jewish unions such as the ILGWU found it difficult to organize the non-Jews in Toronto's needle trades. More specifically, although there was not a simple pattern of non-Jewish strikers pitted against Jewish strike-breakers during the JTUA's large, lengthy strike in 1912, some of the strike-breakers were drawn from "the scab Jewish element."[48]

Jewish garment workers tended to be less militant in the early part of the twentieth century than they were to become in the interwar years. Indeed, this increase in Jewish militancy took place despite the fact that the proportion of clothing manufacturers who were Jews was significantly higher in the interwar period. In the earlier period, when the percentage of Jews in Toronto was much smaller, Jewish working-class culture was just beginning to put down roots in this city. By the 1920s, as organizations such as the Arbeiter Ring became more firmly established, Jewish militancy was strengthened by a more solid cultural base. As Jewish workers increased in numbers and became organized in unions that were predominantly Jewish, their union activities tended to increase.

Yet even in the early 1910s there were situations where Jewish workers—mobilized by the Jewish unions—were significantly more militant than their non-Jewish counterparts. Not only the Eaton's strike of 1912 but also the Puritan strike of 1911 presented a pronounced pattern of Jewish strikers and non-Jewish strike-breakers. The strike of cloakmakers and skirtmakers at the Puritan factory began when forty-five males and females walked out in protest against wage cuts and the employer's discrimination against ILGWU members. "Who takes the place of the workers in this factory?" asked *Cotton's Weekly*, the newspaper of the Social Democratic Party of Canada. Dramatically, the newspaper exclaimed:

> In British Columbia, when miners rise up in rebellion against the shameful conditions, Chinese are brought into the mines. In this and other Western provinces, Japs, Hindoos, and Indians fill the places of the white toilers because they live on cheaper food and under such intolerable conditions no white people can stand it. Half-castes, ignorant, poverty-stricken and oppressed, slave in Southern mill-yards, plantation fields and swamps.
>
> No nation is supposed to be so advanced as the British nation, no race so progressive as the white. but here in toronto no chinese, no hindoos, no japs, no indians, no blacks, no foreigners need be imported, white girls and men of british birth break the strikes. Capitalists need not take the trouble to send to other lands for scabs. we have them always ready in toronto. loyal, patriotic canadians, anxious to keep their jobs, refuse to go out with strikers who are brave enough to struggle for human treatment. canadian girls are handed work that jewish girls refuse to do.[49]

Puritan's non-Jewish cutters apparently refused to join this strike, and *Cotton's Weekly* concluded that "Craft Unionism was shown up as selfish and incompetent, for men of other unions refused to even attempt persuading the English speaking cutters to go out, when asked to do so by the Jewish, who cannot speak English very well."[50]

This newspaper's account of the strike focused particularly on the non-Jewish women who were doing work that formerly had been done by the Jewish strikers. According to this account, "this union realizes that as they are Jewish, racial and religious prejudices are animating the girls to take their places and to decline to go out on strike with Jews."[51]

★★★★★

"In every strike it is the same," declared *Cotton's Weekly*. "Gentile girls break them. English speaking workers are unwilling to struggle for better conditions, shorter hours or higher pay for fear of losing 'my job.'"[52]

Here, ethnic and gender concerns intertwined significantly: the newspaper's indignation against the female strike-breakers was heightened by "the injustice of [the girls'] act in taking the places of these family men who cannot live on ten dollars per week, a wage that is considered exceptionally good by a single girl." "OH TORONTO WORKING WOMEN, WHY BE SO BLIND, SO SELFISH SO HEARTLESS? SHAME ON THE VAUNTED WARMTH OF WOMANLY HEARTS IF JEWISH WORKINGMEN CAN BE REPLACED BY CHEAP FEMALE LABOR!" exclaimed *Cotton's Weekly*.[53]

ILGWU activists continued to find that Toronto's non-Jewish garment workers tended to respond less favourably to their appeals than did the Jews. In 1916, for example, the *Industrial Banner*, an Ontario labour newspaper, reported that this union had experienced difficulties in trying to capture the interests of the non-Jewish workers. Although the newspaper optimistically declared that the ILGWU's new Gentile organizer was stimulating the non-Jews to become enthusiastic about the union,[54] the problem was by no means solved. In 1917 Toronto's ILGWU was carrying out an ambitious organizing campaign, when some of the employers, including Eaton's, responded by making concessions to try to keep the workers away from the union. Eaton's reduced the work week, increased wages, and instructed its supervisors to be more polite. According to the ILGWU's newspaper, "these concessions, instead of keeping the Jewish workers away from joining the union, enthused them all the more, but [the concessions] influenced a certain number of the gentile women workers in the trade, mainly in the T. Eaton shops." In response, the ILGWU's leaders were relying on the aid of two new non-Jewish organizers, one female and one male, to try to recruit more of Toronto's non-Jewish garment workers.[55] However, these workers remained a problem for the ILGWU.[56]

Toronto's Amalgamated Clothing Workers experienced similar difficulties. In 1918, for example, the *Yiddisher Zhurnal* reported that the city's ACW was hiring non-Jewish organizers "for the non-Jewish [workers] in the trade, whom no one had ever been able to organize."[57] A while later, the ACW and the manufacturers' association signed a new contract that stipulated non-union workers in the association's shops had to join the union. The signing of this agreement "brought into the ranks of the Amalgamated about 1000 members English speaking, the majority of whom had never previously belonged to a trade union." The ACW was faced with the need for a massive internal educational campaign. Although the ACW's anglophone business agent felt that the union was succeeding in instilling "the principles for which we are organised into [the] hearts and minds" of these non-Jewish workers,[58] the non-Jews continued to lag behind.

★★★★★

The Jewish needle trades unions continued to experience these kinds of difficulties in the 1930s as well. During the ILGWU's 1931 general strike in Toronto's dress trade, for example, the *Canadian Forum* reported that "the shops employing mostly gentile help" did not join the strike.[59] Non-Jewish workers apparently also posed a problem for the Communist union that was organizing Toronto's dressmakers. In 1935, for example, at a time when the Industrial Union of Needle Trades Workers had contracts with most of the city's dress shops, "nearly everyone of the workers employed in [the] open shops are Anglo-Saxon."[60]

The Jewish unions' difficulties with the non-Jewish garment workers thus took a number of different forms. In some cases, particularly in the early period when these unions were weaker, many of the non-Jews stayed away from the Jewish unions altogether. In other cases, these workers were members of the unions but were significantly less active than their Jewish counterparts. At certain times, such as during the Eaton's strike of 1912 and the ILGWU's dress strike of 1931, non-Jewish workers even served as strike-breakers while Jews went out on strike. The deep divisions between the two groups emerged particularly sharply during the large 1932 fur strike, when non-Jews acted as strike-breakers against their Jewish fellow unionists.

Although Jews still constituted less than half of Toronto's garment workers in 1931, they clearly predominated in the labour movement in the city's needle trades in the inter-war years. The non-Jewish garment unions, particularly the JTUA and the UGW, were dwarfed by the Jewish unions in this period. Jewish workers tended to be more militant than non-Jews, partly because the activism of the Jewish workers was deeply rooted in a vibrant Jewish working-class culture. The Jewish workers' loyalty to their unions was further reinforced by the ways in which the Jewish unions served a number of special functions for them, over and above the function of collective bargaining. These unions addressed specifically Jewish concerns, such as relief work for Jewish refugees in Eastern Europe and protests against the rise of world Fascism. The unions also served as social and cultural centres for the Jewish immigrants in the strange New World.

While these factors bound the Jewish workers more closely to their unions, however, they probably alienated the non-Jewish workers to a certain extent, thereby deepening the rift between the two groups. The more the unions addressed specifically Jewish concerns, the more the non-Jewish union members may have felt themselves to be outsiders. As a consequence, the non-Jews tended to be less active in the Jewish unions.

The lower level of militancy of the non-Jewish garment workers was also partly a product of language problems. In the 1920s and 1930s, many of the Jewish workers could speak Yiddish in the shop and at the meetings of their locals. In contrast, most of the various non-Jewish, non-English-speaking workers were lumped together in a local that conducted its business in English. Since their command of English was often not good, members of these different ethnic groups had trouble understanding what was going on at union meetings. It is not surprising that this kind of a miscellaneous local, within both the ACW and the ILGWU, had a reputation for being weak.[61] Although most of the non-Jewish garment workers were Anglo-Celtic, this particular aspect of the language problem was significant.

The leaders of Toronto's Jewish unions made some efforts to eliminate the friction between the Jewish and non-Jewish garment workers. These efforts included carefully recruiting non-Jewish organizers and business agents, appealing to union members for understanding, and sometimes even entreating officers of the Toronto Trades and Labour Council to help mediate. However, the Toronto leaders of these garment unions did not make the kinds of major efforts that historian Steven Fraser claims to have found in his study of Jewish-Italian relations in the ACW's major centres. Fraser argues that the ACW leaders worked hard to reconcile Jews and Italians in the men's clothing centres of North America, contending that these efforts were critical because of the predominance of these two ethnic groups in this branch of the needle trades. Even if he were right about the extent—and success—of the ACW's efforts to unite these particular ethnic groups in New York City (and he would need more evidence to prove his case), clearly these extensive efforts were not being made in Toronto.

This was perhaps partly due to limited local resources and perhaps also to the different ethnic composition of the workforce in Toronto's men's clothing industry, where Italians were a small minority. It may have been an easier task to bring Jewish and Italian immigrants together in early twentieth-century polyglot New York than to unite Jewish and Anglo-Celtic workers in the predominantly Anglo-Celtic city of Toronto. Particularly important is the absence of strong, class-conscious anglophone leadership within the Toronto branches of the "Jewish unions." Although there was an assortment of Anglo-Celtic organizers, business agents, and members of the various unions' joint boards, the Toronto branches of these unions lacked strong, dynamic non-Jewish leaders who might have made major efforts to bring the non-Jews and the Jews closer together.[62]

Throughout the period under consideration, Jewish workers and non-Jewish workers in Toronto's needle trades continued to constitute two fairly separate groups, customarily speaking different languages and organized in separate union locals. Despite the ideal of—and the real need for—working-class solidarity, serious ethnic tensions persisted within the garment unions and often emerged as key factors in the rivalries between particular unions in this sector. In some cases, these tensions were reinforced by the different roles the two groups played in the labour process. The manufacturers often attempted to heighten these tensions, particularly by using anti-Semitic appeals to try to keep the non-Jews from uniting with more militant Jewish workers in the interwar years. Although the anti-Semitism of non-Jewish garment workers did not usually lead to assaults with knuckledusters, this prejudice was an important factor not only during the 1930s but during the earlier part of the twentieth century as well. The ethnocentrism of both the Jewish and the non-Jewish workers also constituted an important factor. Consequently, it was extremely difficult to overcome the deep ethnic divisions within the workforce.

Notes

[1] Kumove, *Words like Arrows*, 141. The translation from the Yiddish is Kumove's.

[2] H. D. Langer to D. Dubinsky, 12 Oct. 1936, box 74, file 4A, DDP. See also TG and TS, 9 Oct. 1936.

[3] D. Dubinsky to H. D. Langer, 15 Oct. 1936, box 74, file 4A, DDP. Several right-wing populist, anti-Semitic movements arose in the United States during the 1930s. One of the most notorious and influential was headed by Charles E. Coughlin, the Canadian-born "Radio Priest" who broadcast his sensationalist appeals from Detroit.

[4] Calculations based on unpublished disaggregated census data available from Statistics Canada.

[5] On anti-Semitism in Eastern Europe see, for example, Baron, *The Russian Jew under Tsars and Soviets*, 52–75; and Antonovsky, ed., *The Early Jewish Labor Movement*, 18–26. The interviews with Joe Salsberg are especially useful for providing information on anti-Semitism in Toronto.

[6] The interview with Ed Hammerstein, for example, provides useful information.

[7] See, for example, Stowell, *The Journeymen Tailors' Union of America*, 86; Hardy, *The Clothing Workers*, 75, 78–84; and Foner, *Women and the American Labor Movement*, 376–8.

[8] See, for example, Stowell, *The Journeymen Tailors' Union of America*, 38, 51–2, 113–30, 135; T, 15 June 1915. Useful information is also available in the interviews with Ida and Sol Abel and Ed Tannenbaum.

[9] T, 24 Aug. 1915.

[10] See, for example, Belkin, *Di Poale Zion Bavegung in Kanade*, 84.

[11] See, for example, Foner, *Women and the American Labor Movement*, 376–8.

[12] See, for example, GW, 7 Jan. and 19 May 1916.

[13] See, for example, *Western Clarion*, 27 Oct. 1906; GW, 10 Jan. 1919; and J. Watt to E. J. Brais, 7 March 1915, box 55, file 14, AC.

[14] H. Madanick to J. Schlossberg, 18 and 25 July, 18 Aug., and 13 Oct. 1917, box 12, file 34, AC. See also Ontario Department of Labour, *Vocational Opportunities*, 5.

[15] J. Blugerman to J. Schlossberg, 4 March 1918, box 9, file 1, and 6, 15, and 16 March 1918, box 55, file 16, AC. The quotation is from 6 March.

[16] The first quotation is from Charles A. Tovey to J. Schlossberg, 10 July 1920, and the second quotation is from H. D. Rosenbloom to J. Potofsky, 16 Sept. 1920, box 55, file 17, AC.

[17] ATJBM, 11 June 1925.

[18] The quotation is from ATJBM, 10 Feb. 1927. On this incident see also 22 Feb. 1927. For other examples of friction in this union, see 22 July and 17 Aug. 1926.

[19] ATJBM, 18 August [1927].

[20] AGEBM, 27–29 Nov. 1930, 9, box 165, file 14.

[21] The quotation is from H. D. Langer to D. Dubinsky, 6 July 1937, box 88, file 1b, DDP.

[22] For general information on the nationalist orientation of the ACCL see, for example, Abella, *Nationalism, Communism, and Canadian Labour*, 44.

[23] LG, Dec. 1933 and April 1934; ATJBM, 9 and 22 Nov. [1933].

24 M. Finch to W.T. Burford, 5 Feb. 1934, vol. 95, file: "Clothing Workers of Canada ..." CLCC. See also K, 9 March 1934.

25 CU, May 1935.

26 M. Finch to W.T. Burford, 5 Feb. 1934, vol. 95, file: "Clothing Workers of Canada ..." CLCC.

27 M. Finch to W.T. Burford, 5 Feb. 1934, and [W.T. Burford] to M. Finch, 7 Feb. 1934, vol. 95, file: "Clothing Workers of Canada ..." CLCC.

28 On Finch's ethnocentrism see M. Finch to N. S. Dowd, 9 Dec. 1937 and 6 Dec. 1939, vol. 95, file: "Clothing Workers of Canada ..." CLCC.

29 E. Smith to Ontario's attorney-general, 21 March 1933, box 9, file: "ILGWU, 1933," RDLO, Office of Deputy Minister, General Subject Files. On Smith's leading role in the ACCL's needle-trades activities in Toronto see, for example, ATJBM, 20 Aug. [1931].

30 M. Finch to N. S. Dowd, 1 April and 11 Nov. 1938, and 18 March 1939, vol. 95, file: "Clothing Workers of Canada ..." CLCC. ACCL records also document the NCWC's deep collusion with the employer at another of the few shops this union managed to organize. The actions of the NCWC at this shop were so unethical and so compromising that the ACCL's head office had to repudiate the actions of its own affiliate in this case. See W.T. Burford to W. J. Douglas, 14 Feb. 1935, vol. 159, file: "Toronto N.L. Council, 1935," CLCC. See also Minutes of the National Labour Council of Toronto (ACCL), 15 March 1936, reel M2294, Labour Council of Metropolitan Toronto Collection. Interference in other garment unions' strikes seems to have been the NCWC's main form of organizing.

31 A. McCormack to A. W. Miller, 27 Jan. 1915, box 20, file 44, IC.

32 A. McCormack to A. W. Miller, 2 March 1915, box 20, file 44, IC.

33 Interview with Ed Hammerstein.

34 IFWUGEBM, meeting of subcommittee of GEB, 12 Aug. 1931, box 3, file 15, 4. For further evidence of ethnic tensions within Toronto's IFWU, see IFWUGEBM, 25–28 Jan. 1937, box 3, file 22.

35 YZ, 21 July 1932.

36 YZ, 22 and 27 July 1932.

37 YZ, 29 Aug. 1932. See also YZ, 8 Aug. 1932, and W, 13 Aug. 1932.

38 YZ, 21 Aug. and 4 Sept. 1932; interview with Ed Hammerstein.

39 Interview with Ed Hammerstein.

40 Interview with Ed Hammerstein.

41 On the impact of key Canadian businessmen on immigration policy see, for example, Avery, "Dangerous Foreigners," 16–38.

42 YZ, 4 Jan. 1920.

43 YZ, 21 Aug. 1924.

44 YZ, 22 Jan. 1925. See also 5 Feb. 1925.

45 J, 12 Aug. 1927.

46 RCPSMPE, 4573.

47 Ibid., 4492. See also NC, 4 Aug. 1934. For an earlier incident of the same kind, see, for example, YZ, 27 Aug. 1919.

48 The quotation is from T, June 1913. See also Dec. 1912 and June 1914.

49 The quotation is from Cotton's Weekly, 17 Aug. 1911. See also 20 July 1911.

50 Ibid., 14 Sept. 1911.

51 Ibid., 17 Aug. 1911.

52 Ibid., 20 July 1911.

53 Ibid., 17 Aug. 1911.

54 IB, 1 Dec. 1916.

55 The quotation is from LGW, Feb. 1917. See also June 1917.

56 See, for example, Biss, "The Dressmakers' Strike," 367.

57 YZ, 3 Feb. 1925.

58 The quotations are from Charles A. Tovey to J. Schlossberg, 10 July 1920, box 55, file 17, AC. For details on the 1919–20 agreement see the copy of the agreement in PACM.

59 Biss, "The Dressmakers' Strike," 367. See also IGEBM, 10–16 Feb. 1931, 26.

60 A. Desser to Charles Zimmerman, 16 June 1935 (enclosure), box 4, file 3, CZP.

61 Interview with Ida and Sol Abel.

62 Fraser includes Toronto in his generalizations about the ACW, failing to notice Toronto's different ethnic composition in this sector and the different timing of Jewish immigration to Canada. Other problems with Fraser's analysis, even as it pertains to New York City, include his lack of understanding of the Jewish nature of the American Jewish labour movement. See Fraser, "Landslayt and Paesani."

Select Bibliography

Manuscript Collections

International Ladies' Garment Workers' Union Archives, New York
David Dubinsky Papers
ILGWU's general executive board minutes

National Archives of Canada, Ottawa
Canadian Labour Congress Collection
Labour Council of Metropolitan Toronto Collection

Interviews
(pseudonyms have been used for many of the key interviewees)
Ida and Sol Abel, Toronto, 1983
Jacob Black, Toronto, 1971 and 1984
Jim Blugerman, Toronto, 1971 and 1973
Ed Hammerstein, Toronto, 1977, 1983, and 1984

Newspapers
Garment Worker (New York)
Tailor (Bloomington, Illinois)
Western Clarion (Vancouver)
Der Yiddisher Zhurnal (Toronto)

Government Publications
Ontario, Department of Labour, *Vocational Opportunities in the Industries of Ontario: A Survey: Bulletin No. 4: Garment Making* (Toronto 1920)

Books, Pamphlets, Articles, and Theses
Abella, Irving Martin. *Nationalism, Communism, and Canadian Labour: The CIO, the Communist Party, and the Canadian Congress of Labour, 1935–1956.* Toronto 1973
Avery, Donald. *'Dangerous Foreigners': European Immigrant Workers and Labour Radicalism in Canada, 1896–1932.* Toronto 1979
Baron, Salo W. *The Russian Jew Under Tsars and Soviets.* New York 1964
Biss, I. M. 'The Dressmakers' Strike.' *Canadian Forum* 11, 130 (July 1931): 367–9
Fraser, Steven. "*Landslayt* and *Paesani*: Ethnic Conflict and Cooperation in the Amalgamated Clothing Workers of America," in Dirk Hoerder, ed., *"Struggle a Hard Battle": Essays on Working-Class Immigrants.* Dekald, Ill., 1986, 280–303
Kumove, Shirley. *Words like Arrows: A Collection of Yiddish Folk Sayings.* Toronto 1984

Glossary

Co-operative Commonwealth Federation (CCF). The CCF was formed in 1932 in the midst of the Great Depression. It was a coalition of farmers' organizations, labour unions, and labour-socialist parties and advocated political reform as expressed in the Regina Manifesto (1933). Committed to the nationalization of key industries and to the establishment of a social-welfare system, its electoral successes varied across the country, but flourished especially in Saskatchewan under Premier Tommy Douglas. Eventually, it merged with other groups to become the New Democratic Party in 1962.

Ethnocentrism. Judging other cultures and ethnicities according to one's own cultural attitudes, beliefs, and practices. Belief in the superiority of one's ethnic group or culture.

Industrial Standards Act. Beginning in the late nineteenth century, provinces across Canada passed legislation designed (at least in theory) to protect workers from exploitation. In 1935, the Ontario government introduced the Industrial Standards Act, which set industry-wide maximum hours of work. This specific act was part of an expanding body of legislation that sought to regulate worker-related issues, including minimum wages, hours of work, and minimum ages for factory workers.

Xenophobia. Fear or hatred of "foreigners" or strangers.

Further Reading

Abella, Irving, and Harold Troper. *None is Too Many: Canada and the Jews of Europe, 1933–1948.* Toronto: Lester and Orpen Dennys, 1982.

This ground-breaking study documents the anti-Semitism that existed in Canada before, during, and immediately after the Second World War.

Frager, Ruth. *Sweatshop Strife: Class, Ethnicity, and Gender in the Jewish Labour Movement of Toronto 1900–1939.* Toronto: University of Toronto Press, 1992.

This book details many of the issues raised in Frager's article reproduced in this collection. The author chronicles the history of the garment trades through the lens of class, ethnicity, and gender, and explores the factors that often divided the pre-Second World War labour movement.

McKay, Ian. *Rebels, Reds, Radicals: Rethinking Canada's Left History.* Toronto: Between the Lines, 2006.

This book is the introduction to McKay's forthcoming three-volume work on Canadian socialism, and is a broad synthesis of the history of Canada's left from the perspective of politics to culture.

Sangster, Joan. *Dreams of Equality: Women on the Canadian Left, 1920–1950.* Toronto: University of Toronto Press, 1989.

Sangster explores the ways in which Canadian women on the political left challenged both the capitalist order and gender inequality in the first half of the twentieth century.

Relevant Websites

Multicultural Canada
multiculturalcanada.ca/mcc_cjr

This website contains a digitized selection of the *Canadian Jewish Review* from 1921 to 1966. Founded in 1921 by George and Florence Freedlander, it provides insight into the experiences, views, and concerns of English-speaking Canadian Jews.

Canadian Committee on Labour History
www.cclh.ca

Provides a range of information, including publications, conferences, and prizes, pertaining to labour history in Canada.

Canadian Committee on Women's History
www.cha-shc.ca/ccwh-cchf/New%20Website/mainpage.htm

The website for the Canadian Committee on Women's History contains information on the field of women's history, including teaching, research, sources, and the status of women in the historical profession.

CHAPTER 8

THE RIGHT TO CONSENT?: EUGENICS IN ALBERTA, 1928–1972

JANA GREKUL

Introduction

In the late 1800s and well into the twentieth century, Canadians influenced by eugenic movements in Europe and the United States struggled with issues concerning heredity, population control, and race betterment. This chapter contributes to our understanding of eugenics and human rights in several ways. First, the genesis of one long-lived eugenics program, the Alberta program, is briefly discussed. Alberta's program, one of only two officially sanctioned Canadian provincial sterilization programs, kept pace with some of the most active eugenics programs in North America.[1] Second, the operation of the Alberta sterilization program and its outcomes are reviewed. It is suggested that the longevity of Alberta's program can be explained, in part, by two processes: 1) the political, economic, and social environment in Alberta, which created conditions that were ripe for this type of program and contributed to its continued existence; 2) the complicated ways in which the right to consent, which was officially eliminated for some categories of individuals, influenced the disproportionate sterilization of certain groups of people. The case of eugenics in Alberta illustrates how the rights of the marginalized were sacrificed by state and medical powers in the name of "progress."

A Brief History of Eugenics

Although this chapter focuses on the sterilization program in Alberta, eugenics movements sprung up in many European and American jurisdictions in response to historical, social, scientific, economic, and political processes occurring at the time. Francis Galton coined the term "eugenics" in 1883, building it from its Latin roots meaning "good in birth" or "noble in heredity." The science of eugenics was concerned with the improvement of the human stock and focused on the influence that would give "the more suitable races or strain of blood a better chance of prevailing speedily over the less suitable."[2] Eugenicists were concerned with controlling the direction human evolution would take: natural selection, about which Galton's cousin Charles Darwin wrote, was insufficient to deal with the needs of modern society. If left solely to nature, eugenicists argued, the dangerous classes who were thought to have a prolific reproductive rate would take over.

Illustrating the influence of genetic theory during this time, and reflective of the growing fear among many Canadians of "alien and inferior" immigrant classes, Canadian professor W. L. Lochhead applauded the application of the "new science" of eugenics to not only improve plant and animal breeding, but human reproduction as well:

> Many careful investigations of family records reveal the fact that both good and poor quali-
> ties are inherited according to Mendelian laws. Many defects such as feeble-mindedness,
> epilepsy, deaf-mutation, and disposition to tuber-culosis and other diseases are undoubt-
> edly inherited, and to put no hindrance to breeding of the unfit and degenerate persons
> exposes our country to the gravest risk of regression, especially when it is recognized that
> the population is being largely recruited from inferior stocks.[3]

Eugenicists showed through their population studies in the 1880s that the "unfit" were reproducing at a faster rate than the "fit"; these social planners believed that intervention was required if the race was to be saved from degeneration. Politicians, social scientists, and others, influenced by the science of eugenics and fears concerning immigration and the proliferation of the unfit (who were often also of lower class origins), were also encouraged by economic and technological trends. The coming of the Industrial Revolution had created greater class inequality than had formerly been the case; the lower classes were a source of anxiety for middle and upper classes. Informed by hereditary thinking, the popular belief among the middle and upper classes, the ranks from which eugenicists were drawn, was that "the poor were not demoralized; they were degenerate."[4] The Industrial Revolution played another role in the perpetuation of eugenic ideals: its attendant implication that man had control over progress contributed to the increasingly widespread belief that social engineering promised to solve the social problems of the day.

Perhaps the most well-known example of eugenics social engineering occurred in Nazi Germany, where thousands of people were sterilized in an effort to "cleanse" the German population.[5] Yet, around the world we find other examples, perhaps not as large-scale, of similar movements and policies.[6] Much has been written on American sterilization campaigns in the late nineteenth and early twentieth centuries, where groups referred to as "the dependent, defective, and delinquent classes" were targeted by government policies.[7] These *negative eugenics* policies, which targeted the "unfit," promoted marriage licences, segregation during childbearing years, and in the most exteme form, sexual sterilization. At the same time eugenicists, who observed that more "respectable" women were inclined to have fewer children, launched *positive eugenics* campaigns as well. Educational in emphasis, with the goal of encouraging reproduction of these "fit" members of society (and so too help stave off race degeneration), the targets were women in the middle and upper classes.

Eugenics ideas, promoted abroad, were quick to gain popularity in Canada in the early 1900s. Nova Scotia, in 1908, was home of the first "eugenics movement" in the country when the League for the Care and Protection of Feebleminded Persons was established in the province.[8] In Quebec, Ontario, and elsewhere, academics and physicians worked to recruit hereditarians to their ranks and publicly supported eugenics.

Further west, early twentieth-century milieu in Alberta fostered the promotion of eugenic ideals and policies. *Moral panic*, a widespread, intense public feeling that something is terribly wrong in society and that a particular group of "morally inferior" people are to blame for it, centred on the foreign (and therefore dangerous) "Other" in the form of immigrants. Eventually, labels such as "feeble-minded" and "mental defective" were used to encompass a wide range of deviant statuses, including mental disorder, mental illness, delinquency, criminal behaviour, alcoholism, promiscuity, and others. Drawing on the science of eugenics, notable public figures supported a variety of negative eugenic-based policies.

J. S. Woodsworth, a Social Gospeller, was particularly concerned about the change in "quality" of immigrants to Canada that occurred around 1882. He translated this fear into a public crisis, writing in his book *Strangers Within Our Gates* (1909) about the perils of unrestricted immigration that permitted "inferior stock" into the country. As time went on, he gravitated towards eugenic ideals, eventually serving as board member of the prairie-based Bureau of Social Research, which researched and reported on the problem of the "mental defective" in Western Canada. The Bureau actively campaigned for the segregation and sterilization of defectives.[9] The work of the Bureau and Woodsworth was complemented by the Canadian National Committee on Mental Hygiene, under the leadership of Dr. Clarence Hincks, which conducted a "Mental Hygiene Survey of the Province of Alberta" in 1921. The survey reported that mental abnormality and delinquency correlated with illegitimacy, prostitution, and dependency, thus setting the stage for increased activism towards eugenic legislation.[10]

Prominent citizens like Judge Emily Murphy added to the growing support for a eugenics program in Alberta. A vanguard of negative eugenics, Murphy promoted the cause through her writings and public speeches. Stating that "in Alberta alone, 70 percent of the patients in our mental hospitals were born outside Canada," and "every feeble-minded person is a potential criminal," Murphy contributed to the moral panic in the province. In what has been termed a "propagandistic masterpiece," Judge Murphy urged the adoption of a eugenics program by warning that

> ... the congenitally diseased are becoming vastly more populous than those we designate at "the upper crust." This is why it is altogether likely that the upper crust with its delicious plums and dash of cream is likely to become at any time a mere toothsome morsel for the hungry, the abnormal, the criminals and the posterity of insane paupers—in a word, of the neglected folk. [11]

Murphy, a suffragette, one of Canada's Famous Five, and therefore integral to the outcome of the 1929 *Persons* case in our country, had a good deal of clout and influence and regularly addressed women's groups in the province. The influence of one of these groups, the United Farm Women of Alberta (UFWA), on the passage of sterilization legislation cannot be overstated.

The UFWA was the Women's Auxiliary of the United Farmers of Alberta (UFA). The UFA began as a farmer lobby group reacting to provincial and federal politics of the time. However, it soon grew in influence, largely because of it revolutionary ideals. The UFWA had the "social sphere" as its primary focus, in particular the ambitious goal of remodelling society through social improvements in the home and schools. The group emphasized well-raised and genetically "superior" children as the hope for a future utopian society.

The UFWA vigilantly opposed anything that would threaten its plans; perhaps the greatest threat was children born of mentally deficient parents. Mrs. Parlby, leader in the organization, argued that "mental defectives are reproducing their kind at an alarming rate."[12] The UFWA actively supported sexual sterilization legislation; it was a focus of discussion at their annual conventions and meetings, and they encouraged the UFA to propose passage of the legislation. When faced with civil libertarian opposition, Margaret Gunn, in her 1924 presidential address to the UFWA, stated: "Democracy was never intended for Degenerates."[13]

As McLaren points out, the western provinces, particularly Alberta and British Columbia, provided a receptive and hospitable climate for this kind of thinking and programming. While a definitive answer explicating the "success" of the sterilization program in Alberta is beyond the scope of this chapter, it is likely a complex configuration of factors that made the province "ripe" for such a program and which contributed to its longevity. Included in these reasons are government leadership based in populist and grassroots ideology, which was linked to restrictionist policies and anti-immigrant sentiments, strong opposition to federalism, heavy government reliance on "experts" (including mental health experts), and a comparatively weak Catholic presence in the province. Although the Sexual Sterilization Act was passed by the United Farmers of Alberta, the Social Credit party came into power shortly after and maintained power until 1972, also the year the Act was repealed by the newly elected Conservative government. During its four-decade reign, the Social Credit government became complacent and stagnant; led by charismatic leaders who were also fundamentalist religious leaders, the populace also seemed to accept the status quo with little question. This cursory treatment of contributing factors to the passage and longevity of the sterilization legislation is not meant to be exhaustive, but provides a sense of the milieu within which the events occurred.

Within this setting, the Sexual Sterilization Act was passed by the provincial government on March 21, 1928. It allowed for sexual sterilization when an inmate was to be discharged from a mental health institution. Members of the Eugenics Board appointed by the provincial government were empowered to examine the person and direct sterilization if it was unanimously agreed that the patient could be safely discharged "if the danger of procreation with its attendant risk of multiplication of the evil by transmission of the disability to progeny were eliminated."[14] The operation could not be performed unless the inmate consented; if the inmate was not capable of providing consent, then a parent, guardian, or spouse was required to provide it. For those who could not consent, and who did not have a guardian or spouse to consent on their behalf, the Minister of Health was entitled to grant consent. The Act also provided for the protection from civil action of physicians performing sterilization operations under the legislation.

At one of its initial meetings the Eugenics Board established the procedure that would be followed during its quarterly meetings. Medical Superintendents from the mental health institutions that fell under the Board's jurisdiction would recommend and "present" cases to the Board. Documentation on each case would be provided to Board members; they would proceed with the case by examining it in terms of various criteria. Patients, it was decided, should be personally interviewed by the Board before any decision would be made. In cases where patients were unable to do so, the Board would visit them at their hospital ward.

The Eugenics Board of Alberta: Composition and Activities

The Eugenics Board comprised four individuals: the Chairman, two medical doctors, and a layperson. Over its 44-year existence the Board had two chairmen, Dr. J. M. MacEachran, who served from 1929 to 1965, and Dr. R. K. Thompson, who chaired from 1965 to 1972. A total of 19 individuals, most medical doctors, psychiatrists, and social workers, filled the other three Board positions between 1929 and 1972. Overall, there was relatively little turnover in the Board's composition, with the three original members (in addition to MacEachran) each serving approximately two decades.

While the details of the government-appointed Board's activities are documented elsewhere,[15] it is possible to summarize its actions by describing some of the pivotal points in its development, as well as by quantifying its accomplishments. The analyses presented in this chapter are based on three data sets built from the information contained in the Muir trial exhibits.[16] The first, a basic data file (N=4785), includes the name, gender, Eugenics Board number of each individual "presented" to the Eugenics Board between 1929 and 1972, presentation date, and sterilization date (if completed). The '1 in 5' database (N=861) is a representative sample (of the 4,785 cases) of one out of every five patient case files. This database includes information from the short, standardized "presentation summaries," which contain the information Board members saw for each case (e.g., gender, birthdate, ethnicity, place of residence, family and medical history, psychiatric diagnosis, IQ test information), as well as other standardized forms used by the mental health institutions and Eugenics Board. The third source of information is a database built from the 398 sets of Eugenics Board official meeting minutes for all meetings that occurred between 1929 and 1972. This information includes individuals in attendance at Board meetings, decisions made, topics discussed, additional information, correspondence, and other orders of business. This database was used to supplement the basic data file; Department of Health Annual Reports permitted the cross-check of some information in this database.

The Board passed 99 percent of the 4,785 cases it adjudicated. In other words, it approved the sterilization of almost all of the cases referred to it by the mental health institutions. The remaining 1 percent was made up of cases for which the Board "deferred" its decision, either requesting more information on the cases, or because it was uncertain whether the case fell under its jurisdiction. Essentially, the Board never said no to sterilization for patients.[17]

Of course approving sterilizations and actually performing them are two separate, though related, processes. Despite the Eugenics Board's near-perfect approval rate, 40 percent of approved sterilizations never took place. This is because of the complex nature of consent that appears to have plagued the Board almost since its inception.[18] In other words, while the Board ascertained that 99 percent of its patients fit the criteria for sterilization, conditions such as consent precluded the Board from "getting its way" in all 99 percent of cases. In some cases, patients (or their next of kin) exercised agency and refused to grant consent. In others, such agency was not an option. We turn now to an investigation of the ways in which consent interacted with personal characteristics such as diagnosis, age, gender, and ethnicity to influence whose fate was determined by the right (or not) to consent to sterilization.

Consent

At the Eugenics Board's first meeting, on January 29, 1929, the Board members unanimously agreed that "if at all possible, personal consent of the patient should be secured." Concern for obtaining consent was a common theme during the early meetings and through the early 1930s. One case, not unlike others during this time period, involves a father who consented to his daughter's sterilization. The Board, however, thought it best to obtain consent from the patient herself.

By June 1933, the Eugenics Board referred to the issue of consent in different terms. Consent by this time, approximately four years into implementation of the Sterilization Act, was a roadblock to the Board's efficiency. The Board dealt with the problem of obtaining consent in a manner that might be described as persuasive at best, heavy-handed at worst. In a case presented in March 1934, a patient's uncle refused consent for his nephew's sterilization. The decision of the Board was that "a further effort should be made to secure the consent of the uncle." Perhaps anticipating another similar incident in June of that year, the Board passed a case for sterilization contingent on consent of the father. However, added to this condition, "if the father refuses consent Dr. Baragar is authorized to investigate and consult the brother."

By fall of the same year, the Board began to move more concretely in the direction of bypassing patient consent as revealed by the case of a female patient whose husband's consent was obtained, but the patient herself refused consent. In this case, the Board "decided that the case should be passed subject to the approval of the legality of performing such an operation without the patient's consent" (minutes from September 13, 1934). At the Board's sitting the next day, a similar case was presented and an identical decision was made.

The Board's meeting minutes from February 23, 1935 provide insight into the debate surrounding consent. Appended to the minutes for this meeting is an excerpt from the article "Sterilization of Women," which appeared in the *British Medical Journal*. Emphasizing the legal position on sterilization without consent, the excerpt states:

> It had long been held that the person's consent was not a defence in a charge of maiming. Therefore … eugenics sterilization would probably be held to come under Section 20 of the [Offences Against the Person Act]: "Whosoever shall unlawfully and maliciously would or inflict any grievous bodily harm upon any other person, either with or without any weapon or instrument, shall be guilty of a misdemeanour, and being convicted thereof shall be liable … to be kept in penal servitude.

Important for our discussion, the article goes on to argue that "with regard to lunatics and mental defectives, if the sterilization of normal persons was a crime, the sterilization of persons who could not give consent and did not properly understand what was proposed would be so much more a crime." In conclusion, "the sterilization of a person for reasons of health was always lawful; for eugenics reasons, certainly unlawful; *and in the case of lunatics and mentally deficient persons, always unlawful unless undertaken for health reasons* [italics added]." Eventually the Act was amended to reflect changing constructions of sterilization and consent.

Bill No. 45 of 1937:
An Act to Amend the Sexual Sterilization Act

The 1937 Act to Amend the Sexual Sterilization Act was, at base, about the right to consent. Because it permitted the sterilization of diagnosed "mental defectives" without their consent, the amendment clearly influenced the direction and nature of the eugenics program post-1937, and is important as an indicator of changing sentiment regarding human rights among eugenicists and legislators at the time.

A careful reading of the 1937 provincial Act to Amend the Sexual Sterilization Act reveals the seriousness with which legislators took the *British Medical Journal* excerpt concerning conditions under which consent for sterilization is not required. The Act to Amend offers the following justification for sterilization:

> If, upon examination of any mentally defective person, the Board is unanimously of the opinion that the exercise of the power of procreation would result in the transmission to such person's progeny of any mental disability or deficiency, or that the exercise of the power of procreation by any such mentally defective person involved the risk of mental injury either to such person or to his progeny, the Board may direct, in writing....[19]

Recalling our earlier discussion of the Sexual Sterilization Act (1928), it permitted the Board to direct sterilization in cases where there was "a risk of multiplication of [the] evil by transmission of the disability to progeny...." Reflective of the moral panic that led to its passage, this discourse emphasizes the *danger and evil* of hereditary defect. The amendment, on the other hand, switches emphasis to the *risk of mental injury* should mental defectives be permitted to procreate. This change suggests movement away from moral panic and fear towards care and concern for the mental health of patients and their potential offspring. The excerpt from the *British Medical Journal* above indicated sterilization for this reason was legal and therefore acceptable. The assumption is that experts and professionals will naturally do what is best for their wards and naturally, being experts and professionals, will know what is best for them.[20] At the same time, the amendment expanded the reach of the Board by removing the consent requirement for mental defectives.[21]

Lingering caution concerning the legality of removing consent may in part explain why sterilizations did not immediately skyrocket following the amendment. Two mental health professionals involved in presenting patients to the Board explained the consent issues and celebrated the increasing ease with which the Board could conduct its business post-amendment.[22] However, as Grekul et al. illustrate, this jump in productivity did not occur immediately. There is a plausible explanation: it simply took time for the eugenic apparatus to process the increased number of patients who could be re-presented or presented under the new legislation, to schedule operations, and to perform them.

Sterilization Program Outcomes

The importance of consent and the legal and ethical challenges it posed for the Eugenics Board were briefly described above. How did the changes made at the level of decision-makers impact patients? Consent, or lack thereof, throughout the years interacted with a variety of personal and institutional factors that influenced the probability of sterilization for several groups: young people, women, mental defectives, and Aboriginals. We turn now to a discussion of the manner in which consent worked to facilitate the Eugenics Board's goals by discriminating against these groups.

Diagnosis, Institution, and Consent

Diagnosis, especially after 1937, affected a patient's right to consent. This in turn determined probability of sterilization. A high correlation existed between the absence of a consent requirement and eventual sterilization. As Grekul et al. report, 89 percent of individuals "presented and passed" without any consent requirements were sterilized, while in only 15 percent of cases where patient consent alone was a requirement did sterilizations take place.[23] The importance of "presenting institution" to this process is reflected in the composition of institutional populations during this time period.

Four "feeder" institutions presented patients to the Eugenics Board. These institutions differed somewhat in terms of the diagnosis and age of their respective populations, as well as their relative activity as presenters over the decades. Alberta Hospital (Ponoka) and Alberta Hospital (Oliver) both catered primarily to adults with conditions that would fall under the "mental illness" designation; they presented 60 percent and 14 percent of all cases ever presented to the Board, respectively. "Mentally defective" children and young people made up the population of the Provincial Training School in Red Deer; this institution presented 21 percent of all cases. Deerhome, also in Red Deer, was a home for mentally defective adults; often patients graduated from the PTS to Deerhome where they remained for their adult years. Deerhome was responsible for presenting 4 percent of cases. In addition to this, about 32 percent of cases were presented as a result of contact with a Mental Hygiene Clinic.[24]

The relevance of institutional populations hinges on the interaction of consent with age and diagnosis. Oliver and Ponoka, institutions dealing with mentally ill adults, who were unaffected by the amendment, were active presenters in the 1930s and into the 1940s. Following the 1937 amendment and the removal of the consent requirement, the sterilization of mentally ill adults gradually dropped. As Grekul et al. report, only about a third of the adults presented by Ponoka, the most active of the "feeder" institutions, had a mentally defective diagnosis. It was only when the PTS became the main feeder that the advantages of the 1937 amendment became most effective.

In other words, as time progressed, a shift towards the presentation of mentally defective PTS and Deerhome (younger) populations occurred. Part of this can be explained by the growing training school population in the 1950s and 1960s; in 1931, the PTS accounted for 11 percent of the 1,701 inhabitants of the four feeder institutions. By 1961, 37 percent of the 4,178 patients in the four institutions were from the PTS and Deerhome.[25] As the number of mentally defective children and teenagers residing in the PTS and Deerhome steadily increased, these institutions together became the primary "feeders" to the Eugenics Board. A large part of the shift is explained by the diagnosis characteristic of institutional residents. Oliver and Ponoka remained active presenting institutions, but their patients were more likely to avoid sterilization because of consent conditions. Patient consent was required for only about 1 percent of all cases presented and passed at the PTS compared to 59 percent of those from Ponoka.

Age

The combined effect of consent, diagnosis, and age is best illustrated in the activities of the Provincial Training School in Red Deer. As Figure 8.1 illustrates, children, teens, and young adults (and adults over 40) were most likely to be diagnosed as mentally defective. These individuals were housed in the PTS and Deerhome, institutions which became more active presenters in the late 1950s and into the 1960s and early 1970s (until the demise of the Board).

FIGURE 8.1: Percentage of "Mentally Defective" Diagnoses* by Gender, Age at Presentation, Decade of Presentation, and Presenting Institution ('1 in 5' sample)

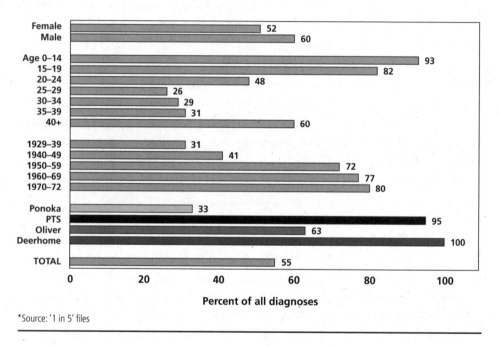

*Source: '1 in 5' files

Between 1921 and 1971, teenagers (ages 15 to 19) in Alberta made up 10 percent of the population but constituted 27 percent of cases presented to the Board, and young adults (ages 20 to 24), whose representation in the provincial population was less than 10 percent, made up 17 percent of cases that appeared before the Board.[26] Was this pattern deliberate or was it the unintentional result of the activities of legislators, medical staff, and Board members working independently? The pattern that resulted in the overrepresentation of teens and young adults in sterilization operations was certainly influenced by diagnosis and the amendment. However, it was also aided by the activity of individual superintendents, in particular Dr. L. J. LeVann, Medical Superintendent of the PTS from 1949 to 1974, when he resigned.

In the 1950s, the Eugenics Board granted individual Medical Superintendents of mental health institutions the freedom to decide whether to discuss sterilization with patients and/or their parents following a decision of "Passed Clear" (no consent required) by the Eugenics Board. The Board also granted them the discretion to decide "whether or not the operation itself should be performed if the patient and/or the parent objected to it."[27] This decision essentially shifted the decision-making power to individual Superintendents and explains to some extent the "overactivity" of certain institutions (e.g., the PTS) and the relative "underactivity" of others (e.g., Ponoka and Oliver).

At the September 23, 1955 meeting, it was decided that the Provincial Training School in Red Deer would require parents to sign "blanket" consent forms upon admitting their children to the institution. In fact, the Board debated the use of the form, which reads as follows:

> I understand that in accordance with the Alberta Statutes my child will be presented to the Provincial Eugenics Board, and that if they deem it advisable he will subsequently be sterilized.

The alternative was to speak with parents at an appropriate time following admission of their child regarding the sterilization and then make a "written note of their reactions to the whole subject" in the Trainee's file (minutes from September 23, 1955). Shortly after this meeting, the forms came into use.

Why the consent forms for mentally defective children whose consent or that of their parents was not legally required? At this point, speculation is all there is to offer; perhaps post-World War II reaction to revelations of the Nazi eugenics program caused Alberta eugenicists to exert caution. Awareness of the cessation of many European and American eugenics programs probably affected the Board as well, though clearly not enough to move in the same direction.

Patient and parent agency, as revealed in several controversial cases where parents threatened to, and in some cases did, consult lawyers in an attempt to thwart attempts to sterilize their children, may have caused mental health professionals to retrace their steps and exhibit caution. The influence of patient agency, however, was counteracted by the overrepresentation of women among the sterilized.

Gender

Sixty-four percent of all women ever presented to the Eugenics Board were sterilized, compared to 54 percent of men. There existed a two-stage gender bias within the Alberta eugenics apparatus: women experienced a greater probability of presentation by the feeder institutions and a resultant greater probability of sterilization as well. Their overrepresentation at both stages in the process was not a result of more female residents in the feeder institutions.[28] Fifty-eight percent of the 2,834 individuals sterilized were women (N=1651).

Overall, patient consent was required in 42 percent of male cases and 39 percent of female cases. Furthermore, almost all (91 percent) cases involving women who were presented and passed without a patient consent condition were sterilized, compared to 86 percent of men. These high percentages attest to the significance of consent to the process. A closer look at the data reveals two patterns worth examining in more detail. First, as discussed earlier, by the 1950s and 1960s fewer Eugenics Board decisions included patient consent as a condition for sterilization. This was the result of the interaction between age, diagnosis, and consent. However, a second interesting pattern is revealed by Figure 8.2: consent was more often required in the sterilization of men in the 1930s and 1940s; in the following decades this pattern was reversed.[29]

FIGURE 8.2: Percentage of Cases Passed by Eugenics Board in Which "Patient Consent" Was One of the Conditions for Sterilization* by Decade by Gender

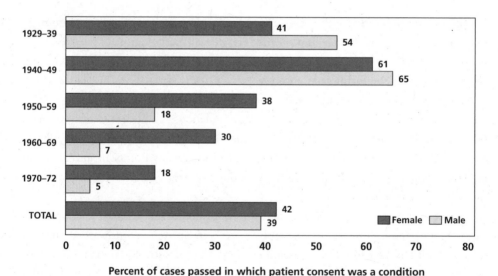

Percent of cases passed in which patient consent was a condition

*Source: Minutes of the Eugenics Board; 46 "deferrals" and 3 additional cases for which information was not available are excluded. "Patient Consent" and "consent of patient and other(s)" combined to calculate proportions.

In the 1950s, 1960s, and up to 1972 (the year the Sterilization Act was repealed), female patients were more likely to have a patient consent condition attached to the Board's approval of the case. Yet, sterilization occurred in 21 percent of women's cases where patient consent was a requirement, and in only 9 percent of men's cases where patient consent was a condition of sterilization.[30] If we assume that consent is a good thing to possess and sterilization a bad thing to undergo, we are left asking why women, who in the latter decades of the province's eugenics program were more likely to be granted consent, were more likely to be sterilized?

To answer this question, patient diagnosis must be considered. Fifty-one percent of females were diagnosed as mentally defective while 60 percent of males received the same diagnosis (see Figure 8.1). In other words, males were more likely to be diagnosed as mentally defective, thus making sterilization without patient consent possible. Yet, females, more often considered mentally normal (i.e., not diagnosed as "mentally defective" and therefore not under the jurisdiction of the 1937 amendment), were more likely to consent and therefore more likely to be sterilized. This pattern seems to contradict what we might expect. How can this contradiction be explained?

Perhaps the most obvious answer is reached by considering gender norms and reproductive roles of the time: women bear the children and they more often carry the responsibility of childrearing. Offered the opportunity for state-sponsored birth control, it is possible that some mentally capable women reasoned that sterilization was a viable option and conceded to the surgery. Eugenics and sexual sterilization, which in some instances overlap, are separate. On the other hand, given the previously discussed manoeuvres of the Eugenics Board and Medical Superintendents, it is possible that mentally normal women were coerced or convinced to consent to sterilization. Research conducted on eugenics during this time in Switzerland reports that 90 percent of sterilizations were carried out on women.[31] According to this research, psychiatrists report that it is much easier to persuade women to be "voluntarily" sterilized than men. Men "see in sterilization a proper castration in the psychological sense and it is hard to combat against this principle."[32] Two Alberta eugenicists similarly note the increased difficulty of convincing men to accept sterilization, speculating that "the operation would be a blow to (their) pride or vanity."[33] Ultimatums in the form of "consent or be institutionalized or imprisoned" occurred, as in the case of two women referred to the Board by Mental Hygiene Clinics, who did not show up to the Eugenics Board meeting where their cases were to be considered. At the October 29, 1959 meeting, "the Social Workers wished to find out if there might be any way to 'force' the women in question to come before the Board, and, if the Board should so direct, have the operation for sexual sterilization performed."

Did the method of persuasion change over time? Kline presents a convincing argument of a trend towards emphasizing "reproductive morality" among couples and especially women during the post–World War II era in the United States.[34] She provides evidence that American jurisdictions moved towards marital counselling for couples, which provided an air of voluntarism and choice, but upon closer examination was actually a thinly veiled modification of eugenic ideals and strategies. Did this also occur in Alberta during this time?

The question begs further research. Board meeting minutes do not explicitly refer to a switch in emphasis, but the higher percentage of mentally normal (i.e., not diagnosed as mentally defective) women who consented to sterilization may be indicative of such a trend. As Kline and others argue, among eugenicists there existed a continuum of problematic behaviour: men's deviance had to be more extreme (e.g., criminally deviant sexual behaviour) to warrant sterilization while women's deviance tended to fall on the less severe end of the continuum (e.g., promiscuity, illegitimate children, drinking and dancing).[35] This double standard may help explain the gender differences revealed in the Alberta case.

Ethnicity

In addition to age, gender, and diagnosis, ethnicity interacted with consent to affect probability of sterilization. Aboriginal patients were more likely to be diagnosed as mentally defective (77 percent), which also resulted in their overrepresentation in sterilizations. Seventy-four percent of Aboriginal patients were eventually sterilized compared to the overall sterilization rate of 60 percent. Consent was far less likely for Aboriginal patients (17 percent) compared to Eastern European cases (49 percent), Western European cases (44 percent), and Anglo-Saxon/Canadian cases (38 percent).[36]

Conclusions

The objective of this chapter was to explore how it was that one province in Canada, Alberta, succeeded in implementing a sterilization program in the early twentieth century that rivaled others in the world. The Sexual Sterilization Act was passed in 1928, but beginning in 1937 the Act was amended; "mental defectives" no longer possessed the right to consent to sterilization surgery. The province was one of only two provinces where such legislation existed. Certainly the province's unique political, economic, and social characteristics contributed to passage of the Act, its implementation, and the longevity of the sterilization program. In addition, the right to consent interacted with diagnosis, age, gender, and ethnicity in ways that ensured the continued existence of the province's program, by targeting different groups at different times, as well as its "success" in sterilizing 2,834 individuals between 1929 and 1972.

As revealed through glimpses into its meeting minutes, the Eugenics Board of Alberta initially expressed concern for the protection of patient rights, including the right to consent, but by the mid to late 1930s, was already moving in the direction of quashing that right for certain categories of people. Over the course of the next three decades, the Board and one of the Medical Superintendents in particular pushed for a loosening of controls over the types of people who could be sterilized, and the manner in which consent was obtained.

Documents appended to the Board meeting minutes suggest members were aware of the legal problems that could ensue with removal of patient consent. However, legislators managed to skirt the issue by permitting sterilization without consent for mentally defective individuals (or their children) who might experience mental injury as a result of procreating. Once the amendment passed, it seemed the doors opened for a variety of abuses of power. For example, the Board approved 18 testicular biopsies for men with Down Syndrome in the 1950s and 11 during the 1960s to facilitate the research of one of their members, despite the existence of an academic research journal article appended to the minutes that reported that men with Down Syndrome are infertile.[37] Similarly, under Le Vann's supervision, children in the PTS were used as subjects in his experiments with antipsychotic drugs, without the consent of parents or guardians.[38] Along the same lines, over two hundred women were told they were having appendectomies but were sterilized at the same time.[39]

Beyond these blatant abuses of power, we saw that there were subtleties in the operation of the sterilization machine that selected for certain groups of people. Age, gender, diagnosis, and institutional residence all interacted and contributed to the overrepresentation of teens and young adults, women, mental defectives, and Aboriginal patients in sterilization operations. The overrepresentation of these groups did not occur at once; rather, the selection occurred in phases over the forty-four years of operation of the Eugenics Board. Initially, residents from Ponoka and Oliver, institutions primarily for mentally ill adults, were dominant in presentations and sterilizations. During these early years men were more likely to receive consent conditions.

By the 1950s and 1960s, the Provincial Training School in Red Deer, and eventually Deerhome, became more active feeder institutions. As these institutions became more actively involved in referring patient to the Eugenics Board, the emphasis changed: their clientele comprised children, teens, and young adults diagnosed as mentally defective whose consent was not required. Throughout the four decades, however, women experienced a probability of presentation and sterilization that was consistently higher than that for men. Women, who were less likely to receive a mental defective diagnosis and who were therefore required to consent to sterilization, tended to do so.

The violation of the right to consent to actions that affect one's person contributed to the "success" of the Alberta eugenics program. Power and privilege—decision-makers were educated, middle and upper class professionals with political power—were used to control the behaviour of marginalized groups. Targeting the "Other," those different from themselves, eugenicists, who began with images of "misfits" propagating and spreading evil, switched their focus to helpful guidance for the unfortunate who, if permitted to reproduce, would inflict harm on themselves or their progeny. Regardless of motive or the discourse used to provide justification for the eugenics apparatus, the end result was a successful campaign that rolled on, long after eugenic theory was proven false, long after revelations of abuses promulgated by other eugenics programs were revealed. The Alberta program insulated itself from these outside occurrences and continued to discriminate against marginalized groups, causing irreparable damage to thousands of lives.

This dark chapter in our country's history is worth remembering. Let us not too hastily cast it aside as an example of a different time, a different period; a mistake we would never repeat today. In fact, it was only a few short years after the Alberta Sterilization Act was repealed that Canada passed the Canadian Human Rights Act (1976), considered by many to be the first important step for disability rights in the country. When the Canadian Charter of Rights and Freedoms was proposed in 1980, the disabled were excluded. However, by the time the Charter was passed, disability rights groups had achieved victory: the right to equality before the law and to the equal protection of the law without discrimination based on disability was established in section 15 of the Charter.

Yet, in 1998, when hundreds of former patients of the Eugenics Board came forward and launched a lawsuit against the Alberta government claiming wrongful sterilization and wrongful confinement, then-Premier Ralph Klein invoked the Charter's notwithstanding clause in an effort to limit the damages plaintiffs could claim. Klein apparently concurred with UFWA President Mrs. Gunn's 1924 proclamation that "democracy was never intended for degenerates." However, within 24 hours of publicly stating his position, and as a result of enraged public outcry, Klein backed down. The $80 million remuneration paid to survivors of Alberta's experiment in eugenics by Klein's Conservative government in an out-of-court settlement sends a strong message to victims of human rights violations in our country and to citizens generally: democracy is indeed intended for all.

Notes

[1] British Columbia passed sterilization legislation in 1933. About ten times as many people were sterilized in Alberta as in BC (Grekul et al., 2004: 358). During the 1930s Alberta's sterilization rate of 9.02 per 100,000 people outpaced the US rate of 2.05 per 100,000 (although several states had rates that were much higher than this). Alberta's sterilization rate dropped to 6.21 in the 1940s, but was still 3.7 times as high as the US rate of 1.68. By the 1960s, when many American jurisdictions halted sterilization programs, Alberta's rate reached 6.56. By the 1970s, Alberta and North Carolina were the only two North American jurisdictions with forced sterilization programs (Grekul et al., 2004: 376).

[2] Daniel J. Kevles, "Eugenics in North America," in Robert A. Peel, ed., *Essays in the History of Eugenics* (London: The Galton Institute, 1997).

[3] Lochhead, 1919, in Angus McLaren, *Our Own Master Race: Eugenics in Canada, 1885–1945* (Toronto: McClelland & Stewart Inc., 1990), 13.

[4] McLaren, 19.

[5] R. Proctor, *Racial Hygiene: Medicine Under the Nazis* (Cambridge, M.A.: Harvard University Press, 1988).

[6] E. S. Gosney and P. Popenoe, *Sterilization for Human Betterment* (New York: MacMillan, 1929); Philip Reilly, *The Surgical Solution: A History of Involuntary Sterilization In the United States* (Baltimore and London: The Johns Hopkins University Press, 1991).

[7] Nicole Hahn Rafter, "Claims-Making and Socio-Cultural Context in the First U.S. Eugenics Campaign," *Social Problems* 39 (1992): 17–34; Diane B. Paul, *Controlling Human Heredity: 1865 to the Present* (New Jersey: Humanities Press International, Inc., 1995).

[8] McLaren, 24.

9 Terry Chapman, "The Early Eugenics Movement in Western Canada," *Alberta History* 25 (1977): 9–17.

10 Timothy J. Christian, *The Mentally Ill and Human Rights in Alberta: A Study of the Alberta Sexual Sterilization Act* (Edmonton, Alberta: Faculty of Law, University of Alberta, unpublished research report, 1974).

11 Ibid., 12.

12 *Mental Deficiency: An Address Delivered by the Honorable Mrs. Parlby before the U.F.W.A.. January 1924* (Provincial Archives of Alberta, Ascension 1971.0420, File #19—Winnifred Ross Papers), 11.

13 Richard Cairney, "'Democracy Was Never Intended for Degenerates:' Alberta's Flirtation with Eugenics Comes Back to Haunt It," *Canadian Medical Association Journal* 155, 6 (September 15, 1996): 791.

14 *The Sexual Sterilization Act*, S.A. 1928, c. 37.

15 Jana Grekul, Harvey Krahn, and Dave Odynak, "Sterilizing the 'Feeble-minded': Eugenics in Alberta, Canada, 1929–1972," *Journal of Historical Sociology* 17, no. 4 (2004): 358–384.

16 We were allowed access to this information by the kind permission of Ms. Muir (*Muir v. Her Majesty the Queen*, 1995. Trial Exhibits).

17 Grekul et al.

18 Ibid.

19 *An Act to Amend the Sexual Sterilization Act*, 1937, Bill No. 45.

20 Kristen Ellard, "The Struggle for Identity: Issues and Debates in the Emerging Specialty of American Psychiatry from the Late 19th Century to Post-WWII," *Human Architecture: Journal of the Sociology of Self-Knowledge* IV, 1 & 2 (Fall/Spring, 2006): 227–264.

21 Meeting minutes reveal that in the years following the amendment, groups of patients were re-presented because of their change in status under the revised Act. Most of these patients were diagnosed as mentally defective and had refused consent prior to 1937.

22 R. R. MacLean and E. J. Kibblewhite, "Sexual Sterilization in Alberta: Eight Years' Experience, 1929 to May 31, 1937," *Canadian Public Health Journal* (1937): 587–590.

23 Grekul et al., 370.

24 Mental Hygiene Clinics (by 1939 they were referred to as Guidance Clinics) would travel to rural areas and small towns where they offered mental health services and referrals, and could recommend that individuals be presented to the Eugenics Board.

25 Deerhome opened in 1958.

26 Grekul et al., 374. These authors report that children under 15 and adults over 40 were underrepresented in Eugenics Board presentations. Twelve percent of all cases presented to the Eugenics Board were children under 15; this group's representation in the general population during 1921 and 1971 fluctuated between 29 percent and 36 percent. Adults over 40 made up five percent of presentations but between 22 percent and 31 percent of the general population.

27 Jana Grekul, "The Social Construction of the Feebleminded Threat: Implementation of the Sexual Sterilization Act in Alberta, 1929–1972," Ph.D. diss. (University of Alberta, 2002), 165.

28 Grekul et al., 372. These authors also note that while overall more women than men appeared before the Board, several years during the 1930s were exceptional in that they witnessed the reverse trend. These authors also report that the overall probability of presentation in any given year for both sexes over the entire span of time the Eugenics Board existed was 0.032 (each year, on average, three percent of the patients in the four presenting institutions were presented for sterilization), however, probability of presentation decreased gradually over the years. Overall, the probability of presentation for women was double that of men (0.048 versus 0.024), though the gender differences were smaller in the 1930s, but increased as the decades wore on.

29 Ibid., 367.

30 Ibid., 370.

31 Natalia Gerodetti, "From Science to Social Technology: Eugenics and Politics in Twentieth-Century Switzerland," *Social Politics* 13, no. 1 (Spring 2006): 59–88.

32 Grossenreiter (1995) as cited in Gerodetti, 237.

33 MacLean and Kibblewhite, 588.

34 Wendy Kline, *Building a Better Race: Gender, Sexuality, and Eugenics from the Turn of the Century to the Baby Boom* (Los Angeles: University of California Press, 2001).

35 Allison C. Carey, "Gender and Compulsory Sterilization Programs in America: 1907–1950," *Journal of Historical Sociology*, 11, no. 1 (March 1998): 74–105; Paul, 1995.

36 Grekul et al., 375.

37 Grekul, 2002.

38 Doug Wahlsten, "Airbrushing heritability," *Genes, Brain & Behavior* 2, no. 6 (2003): 327–329.

39 Grekul, 2002.

Glossary

Eugenics. A theory and a social movement based on the belief that "fit" members of society should be encouraged to reproduce and the "unfit" should be prevented from doing so.

Moral panic. A widespread, intense public feeling that something is terribly wrong in society and that a particular group of "morally inferior" people are to blame for it.

Negative eugenics. Refers to the targeting of "unfit" members of society for population control through marriage licences, segregation, or sterilization.

Positive eugenics. Refers to the targeting of "fit" members of society through educational campaigns encouraging reproduction.

Sexual Sterilization Act. Provincial legislation in Alberta, enacted in 1928 and repealed in 1972, permitting the Eugenics Board of Alberta, a government-appointed body, to direct sterilization operations for individuals who fell under its jurisdiction.

Further Reading

Caulfield, Timothy, and Gerald Robertson. "Eugenic Policies in Alberta: From the Systematic to the Systemic?" *Alberta Law Review* XXXV, no. 1 (1996): 59–79.

This article provides a detailed history of the eugenics movement in Alberta, including an examination of the relevance of autonomy, personal choice, health care reform, and medical legal issues as they relate to the danger of a "new eugenics" today.

Grekul, Jana. "Sterilization in Alberta, 1928–1972: Gender Matters." *Canadian Review of Sociology* 43, no. 3 (2008): 247–266.

This research is an investigation into the gendered nature of the eugenics movement in Alberta.

McLaren, Angus. *Our Own Master Race: Eugenics in Canada, 1885–1945.* Toronto: McClelland & Stewart Inc., 1990.

This book provides a detailed historical account of eugenics in Canada.

Park, Deborah C., and John P. Radford. "From the Case Files: Reconstructing a History of Involuntary Sterilisation." *Disability and Society* 13, no. 3 (1998): 317–342.

By analyzing the qualitative information contained in patient case files, these researchers show how social factors such as social class influenced the ways in which patients of the Eugenics Board were described and constructed.

Wahlsten, Douglas. "Leilani Muir versus the Philosopher King: Eugenics on Trial in Alberta." *Genetica* 99 (1997): 185–198.

Offering a case study of the life of one of the victims of the Alberta sterilization program, Wahlsten uses the events in this case to examine aspects of the sterilization program in detail.

Relevant Websites

Canadian Association for Community Living
www.cacl.ca

The Canadian Association for Community Living is a Canada-wide association of family members and others working for the benefit of person of all ages who have an intellectual disability.

Canadian Centre on Disability Studies
www.disabilitystudies.ca

The official website for the Canadian Centre on Disability Studies, which is dedicated to research, education, and information dissemination on disability issues.

Disability Rights in Canada
disabilityrights.freeculture.ca

This website offers a virtual museum of disability rights in Canada.

Eugenics Archive
www.eugenicsarchive.org

Provides information on the social origins, scientific origins, research methods, traits studies, research flaws, and other historical information on eugenics.

What Sorts
www.whatsorts.net

This is the website for "What Sorts of People Should There Be?", a broad interdisciplinary, collaborative project that is focused on human variation and normalcy.

PART III

Social, Political, and Legislative Change

TRANSNATIONAL MOVEMENTS FOR CHILDREN'S RIGHTS AND THE CANADIAN POLITICAL CULTURE:

A HISTORY

Dominique Marshall

Introduction

In 1924, the General Assembly of the League of Nations adopted the Declaration of Geneva, on the rights of children. The Canadians involved believed that there was a strong connection between child welfare, what they called "public opinion," and international affairs. Walter A. Riddell, for instance, the Canadian Advisory Officer at the League of Nations (LON), would report four years later that:

> There are, in fact, few questions with which the League deals which appear to a wider constituency or are more suitable for comparative study and research.... The results will be ... valuable for the prestige of the League and for the well-being of generations yet unborn.[1]

This study of the Canadian aspects of the history of the Declaration of 1924 and of its successors, the United Nations Declaration of the Rights of the Child of 1959, and the UN Convention on the Rights of the Child of 1989, shows that children's entitlements have often occupied a privileged place in transnational political cultures, and that the connections identified eighty years ago have remained. Children's rights play an important role in the history of democracy and citizenship in Canada, not only because they concern the prerogatives of a considerable portion of the population, but also because the history of their meanings and of their uses is a necessary counterpart to the history of the rights of adults. Indeed, debates and practices surrounding children's rights have provided at once a refuge, a relay, or even a testing ground for discussions about the rights of all.[2]

Conversely, phenomena that are far away from children themselves have often determined the major moments in the history of children's rights, the kinds of children involved, and the social facts that children symbolize at a given time. This article refers to a historiography that considers childhood both as an institution and as a language, and children as relatively autonomous members of society.[3] It is especially attentive to the ways in which children's lives have influenced the formation of children's universal rights and, in the opposite direction, to the ways in which lives might have changed because of the enactment of various declarations and conventions concerning younger citizens. This study also apprehends the history of rights at many levels of the political culture, from international relations to national, regional, local and intimate actions and convictions.[4] It identifies, within the Canadian "public opinion" evoked by children's rights advocates of all periods, the proponents and the opponents of "moral and humanistic principles," the "context [in which each] secured their legitimacy," and the traditions to which they belonged.[5] Finally, it contributes to the critical literature on current uses of children's rights by showing the origins of many current tensions, as well as the changing meaning of terms from their inception.

Before the First World War

In the nineteenth century, Canadian lawyers and reformists participated in an international movement in favour of the best interests of the child.[6] Part of this development was due to the political and intellectual advances of liberalism, which attributed, to various and debated degrees, a measure of individuality and freedom to immature citizens.[7] The idea of children's rights was born in close association with the equally liberal ethics of parents' responsibility for their children's education and protection.[8] The Enlightenment founded paternal authority on a social contract, in contrast with the older notion of a natural superiority of fathers (*patria potestas*). Only because they were to bring up vulnerable and "unfinished" beings were parents now entrusted with rights over their children.[9] When Canadian adults could not perform this role, the joint inheritance from British Common Law and from French Civil Law called the State to act as a parent (*parens patriae*). These notions regarding the respective places of child, parent, and State informed the creation of children's aid societies, from the 1880s, and the enactment of the Canadian Juvenile Delinquent Act of 1907.

Isolating children as an object of attention, from their family and community, was part of the intentions of several rising professionals who were themselves establishing the domains in which they could assert their exclusive competencies, from pediatricians to social workers and educators. As images of children offer a potent language to speak of unequal relations in a democratic society, they lent themselves especially well to experts' claims of authority on those they wanted to help. Such programs of subjection to professional authorities coexisted with liberal ideas about children's autonomy.[10]

The idea that the young had rights distinct from those of their parents informed a larger child-saving movement, whose origins can be traced to the rise of romantic notions of children as vulnerable objects of compassion.[11] Children's entitlements figured preeminently in Western states' efforts to correct the most scandalous abuses of capitalism, besides death and injury in the workplace and help to dependent mothers.

Local actions and beliefs on behalf of children were often related to transnational exchanges. Children's aid societies resulted from the collaboration with American reformists and social workers; the charitable institutions of Quebec devoted to children were built in reference to their French and Belgian counterparts, and Canadian pediatricians participated in international conferences.[12] New associations devoted to child-related issues of an obvious transnational nature were part of the flurry of international institutions born in the mid-nineteenth century onwards. In the 1910s, shared standards for programs of child migration, a domain in which Canada was especially involved, besides Australia and New Zealand, had brought Canadian social worker Charlotte Whitton to international meetings. In addition, international conferences had gathered since 1899 on the "traffic of children" across borders, resulting in an International Convention on the Traffic of Women and Children in 1910.[13] In Brussels, which reformists ambitioned to transform into the capital of the world for social and economic collaboration, an international association for the protection of children inaugurated a machinery of meetings and exchanges of information. They corresponded with Canadians such as Dr. Helen MacMurchy, the public health administrator of the Ontario—and later Canadian—governments.[14]

Children also figured in the preoccupations of international women's groups. The Women's International League for Peace and Freedom, the International Council of Women (ICW), and the International Union of Catholic Women's Leagues all addressed questions of childhood, which they saw as the special responsibility of their sex. In addition, in many countries, women's increasing authority in families was contributing to more attribution of rights of their own to children.[15] Using international activities as a means to surround impediments encountered at the national level, many such women's associations were fighting for a democratization of international relations.[16] These concerns were formulated in the language of universal rights and, in 1922, the ICW drafted its own "Children's Charter."[17] All in Canada did not agree with this attribution of debates over children to women's public life: Agnes Macphail, the first woman member of the Canadian House of Commons, refused to sit on the committee on Social Questions of the Assembly of the League, arguing that the reputation of the committee as a women's responsibility weakened its impact.[18]

Finally, the promotion of children's rights stemmed from a rise in the political leverage of workers. In general, the transformation of the economy, by creating a distance between fathers and children, and by calling for more school training, was contributing to the spread of the idea of children as having rights of their own.[19] More precisely, the regulation of child labour and the promotion of mass and compulsory schooling accompanied the enfranchisement and the unionization of the working class. The early proponent of child labour legislation in Quebec, Louis Guyon, and the pro-labour journalist Jules Helbronner both visited European social exhibitions. There also existed a tradition of child labourers demanding rights for themselves.[20] Workers' international actions converged towards a permanent international pole with the creation of the International Association for the Legal Protection of Workers in 1900, which placed the regulation of child labour amongst its priorities. The Association became part of the League of Nations in 1919, under the name International Labour Organization.[21]

The First World War, Emergencies, and Children's Rights

The Declaration of the Rights of the Child of 1924 was widely endorsed at a time when the international protection of universal human rights seemed impossible, since "even democratic governments were wary of the idea of an international status for human rights, an idea which as yet had no base of support among public opinion."[22] Historians generally agree that the Declaration was mainly a product of the war.[23] Moreover, to its creators there existed a direct development from the protection of soldiers inaugurated by the Red Cross half a century earlier to the protection of children: the sense of indignation that had made Henry Dunant's work in Solferino so popular had turned to children.[24] Faced with the ruthless nature of modern warfare, the unprecedented scale and depth of devastation amongst civilians, many chose to give children of other countries a pre-eminent significance, from anti-slavery campaigners, pacifists, or proponents of friendship with Germany to Churches and trade unions. They benefited from a wide support in the general population, which they sought in turn to encourage. Why did childhood now warrant intervention in others' national affairs?

There seems to be a strong correlation between the rise of children as objects of rights and the extension of political citizenship amongst adults in wartime. The unprecedented proportion of the population involved in the conflict seems to have made childhood into a central theme in discussions about the social dimension of the war. By 1919, Eglantyne and Dorothy Jebb, the British founders of the Save the Children Fund (SCF), a charity first aimed at feeding the children of former enemies across the blockade imposed just after the war by the allied forces, were acknowledging forces that surprised them as well. What they established, more than anyone before them, is the power of images of children to attract the sympathy of donors. Their use of images was indeed abundant, self-conscious, and professional, and the mass reproduction of photographic images helped reach less educated publics.[25]

Members of the working class contributed to the levies in unprecedented proportions, maybe as "an extension ... of the informal patterns of aid to neighbours in distress that had kept so many working-class families going for generations."[26] The very knowledge of the children's situation engaged the moral responsibility of adults from elsewhere. Raoul Dandurand, Canadian senator and a "chief supporter" of the Fund, evoked a "great obligation" one should honour in order to have "clear conscience."[27] The direct relation between the use of the rhetoric of children's entitlements and the amount of private donations a charitable organization was able to levy was repeatedly confirmed. The different funds administered by American philanthropist, and later President, Herbert Hoover, most of which included Canadian donations, offer a case in point, when he coordinated the neutral Committee for the Relief of Belgium (CRB) (1914–1921) and when he served as the Food Administrator of the United States (1917–1919). Hoover focused on children's suffering, especially when he had to increase his reliance on private donations in countries of donors, or when he attempted to diminish a commitment in countries of beneficiaries.[28] Most Canadian contributions to the CRB came as individual amounts of $1 to $2 or less. A total of 115,000 persons contributed to the "Tag Day" of July 1916, for instance, for a total of $9,393.[29]

The SCF also liked to emphasize the international nature of its support. In its publicity, Canada figured as the most generous country of the Commonwealth, as well as the origin of some of its most exotic donations. London and Geneva marvelled at the fact that, during the Greek campaign of the early 1920s, even the Eskimos helped, a story first related by the bishop of Mackenzie River. The group of Inuits who answered the fundraising campaigns appeared in many adverts, beside the equally impressive group of descendents of the mutinous crew of the Bounty, on the Cairn Island.[30]

It also seems that the First World War temporarily accelerated the movement between the advent of the image of the child as a subject of rights, mentioned earlier, and the "translation [of the principle] in institutions and educational practices."[31] The war multiplied circumstances that separated children from their families, and for which citizens were called to care for the children of others. The proliferation of stories and representations of European children left alone with Canadian soldiers is a witness to this situation (see Figure 9.1). Such is the story of a Belgian girl who sang "Tipperary" when Canadian soldiers liberated her village near Mons in 1918: she had waited four years for the return of the English soldier who had taught her the song when he stayed at her home in 1914 (Mons had been the first British battle). In such tales, children acted as the symbol of

FIGURE 9.1: In such images, often used in charitable campaigns after the war, children acted as the symbol of the civilian population, and Canadian soldiers' concern for orphaned children stood for the humanitarian concerns of the whole country.

Source: William Rider-Rider, Peter Robertson, "Gunner of the Canadian Field Artillery comforted a child whose mother has just been killed during a bombardment: Mons, November 1918." Relentless Verity. Canadian Military Photographers Since 1885. Ottawa, Public Archives of Canada, 1973, p. 81.

the civilian population, and Canadian soldiers' concern for orphaned children stood for the humanitarian concerns of the whole country.[32]

It is as if the scale of the social disruption occasioned by the war demanded not only a restatement of the nature of societies' and parents' responsibilities towards children, but also an extension of public responsibilities towards children to all adults. The preamble of the Declaration of 1924 was to point in this direction, which states that "Men and women of all nations, recognize that mankind owes to the Child the best that it has to give, declare and accept [the declaration] as their duty."

The fact that the war required a greater involvement of children in public life also explains the popularity of the rhetoric of the rights of children. Allowing citizens between the ages of eighteen and twenty-one to enlist blurred the line between adulthood and childhood (see Figure 9.2). The status of soldier gave to these otherwise disenfranchised minors a right to vote, and more leverage. Enlistment could thus divide parents and children: from 1915, some Canadian courts overruled parents' rights to withdraw their children from the army. Testimonies of young Canadians yearning to become soldiers abound. This confusion of generations, however, did not extend to representation of

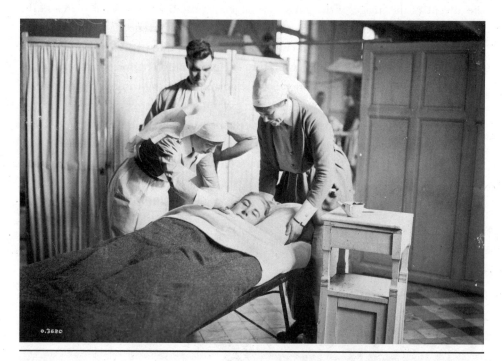

FIGURE 9.2: The enlistment of minor children in the army might have advanced the enactment of children's rights in the interwar years.

Source: "Private Lawrence, aged 17, who was wounded fifteen minutes before the declaration of the Armistice ending the First World War." William Rider-Rider / Canada, Dept. of National Defence / Library and Archives Canada / PA-003535. (Soldier identified as Pte. Lawrence of Brantford, Ont. by Alf. Sherman (1st Div. Engineers, C.E.F.), Barrie, Ont.)

children soldiers as heroes, a symbol that was popular in countries that had to cope with the memory of defeat.[33]

A second type of public engagement of youth increased with the war: calls for children to perform volunteer work became conspicuous (see Figure 9.3). Associations and institutions had long counted on children for fundraising and for work related to international endeavours. Religious missions abroad and anti-slavery societies, amongst them, had helped establish connections between children and communities outside of their own country. In addition, patriotic groups had created children's activities that would enhance children's loyalty to their country and their understanding of democracy. When the Ottawa Women's Canadian Club, founded in 1910 "to foster patriotism and encourage the study of Canadian life," "for the welfare and progress of the Dominion," became the "recognized agency for Belgian Relief in the Ottawa Valley," "children in schools joined the general effort." Thus, patriotic associations "encouraged sympathetic interest in the countries which were the first to suffer." In Montreal, levies mobilized not only "the local Belgian community [and] hosts of friends," but also "churches, commercial travelers, boy scouts and moving picture houses."[34]

Their success is partly explained by the fact that "children take images seriously for their capacity to haunt."[35] When a British Columbian mother of four boys, between ages

FIGURE 9.3: Scouts raising money for the Canadian Patriotic Fund in Ottawa, a semi-private charity that supplemented the salaries of soldiers depending on their family charges. Such voluntary work of a civic nature might have increased the political leverage of children in the interwar years.

Source: William James Topley, "Group in front of the Patriotic fund Headquarters." Library and Archives Canada / PA-042857.

four and nine, replied personally to the circular letter of the British president of the SCF, the Duke of Atholl, in a letter attached to her contribution to the relief of Greek refugee victims of the wars of the early twenties, she insisted that it was her children who had been moved by the description of the plight of children refugees.[36] By 1924, associations of Canadian children who were sending money for this cause included "members from our Finnish Sunday School in Copper Cliff, from Indian children on the Six Nations Reserve, from members of the Junior Red Cross societies, and from scores of Sunday schools as well as day schools."[37] Canadian SCF officials understood this sympathy as a kind of solidarity between members of the same generation: it was "most fitting that our highly favored children should be given a chance to help other children who are in direst of need."[38]

With the war, the sheer volume of children's voluntary work required on the home front gave young people a renewed public importance. Voluntary recruiters also believed that many young persons who were now left alone at home needed safe and social activities. We know from observations made during the Second World War that there existed amongst children themselves a "desire to be perceived as a valued member of the group" which they could use "as a lever." Some children also wished to see their fathers come back from the front, and wartime emergencies gave many a sense that voluntary work had become more meaningful.[39]

How did the children who received charitable help from abroad perceive these donations? Accounts of ceremonies, letters, and testimonies abound to document their thankfulness. In the archives of the Herbert Hoover Museum, most letters by Belgian children follow a set template, probably provided at school. At times, however, a measure of autonomous judgment seems to lead the author away from the prescribed deference. One boy, in a display of middle-class solidarity, explained that the goods sent from abroad were distributed in Belgium to poor children by better-off children like him: "How many children were happy because of the Christmas presents that you sent to them." Others were eager to tell foreign donors that they also were giving their own charitable money to poor children of their surroundings. In a display of egalitarian belief, another child described the relation between him and his North American reader not as the reception of benevolence, but rather as the entitlement of a people who fight "a just cause."[40] The French War Relief Committee of the Ottawa Women's Canadian Club received thanks from French adult correspondents written in a similar language of rights and collaboration. Writing during the last weeks of the conflict, the director of an association devoted to maternal help of Paris spoke of the "great and beautiful task that we have undertaken," of the "cause of the Right of man and of humanity in its entirety [that] was ultimately triumphing. Our work survives the war and more than ever we have to protect the child."[41]

Reconstruction and Children's Rights

As we have seen, children's rights were not only granted to them but, to some extent, earned by them as a consequence of their military and voluntary work. It is mainly this type of voluntary activity that the authors of the Declaration of the Rights of the Child of the LON had in mind when writing its fifth article: "The child must be brought up in the consciousness that its talents must be devoted to the service of fellow men." Given the role children had played in the war, and the meaning that such voluntary work had had for them, our findings may help qualify recent critics, for whom this type of children's involvement represented no more than a simulacrum of political action. Their opinion resembles that of a contemporary of the Declaration, the Polish educator Janus Korczak, who believed that children should have the right to be part of decisions that pertain to them. Similar criticisms come from historians of relief movements who show how the concentration on food was accompanied by a belief that science could solve most of the world problems, a stance that allowed many to surround the question of the political role of the population that was helped.[42]

Once the war was over, national jealousies compromised the implementation of universal humanitarian ideals. Patriotic elements present in the charitable campaigns were now threatening to compromise internationalist ones. Hostility towards former enemies caused the cancellation of a talk the American social worker and pacifist Jane Addams was to give to the Imperial Order Daughters of the Empire at the University of Toronto in 1920. Similarly, the four members of the Canadian National Council of Women, who returned from the ICW conference in Christiana (Oslo) in the Autumn of 1920 with a campaign to alleviate "the common suffering of mothers," had to face hostility towards Germans amongst their membership, together with pressures to expel former enemies from the international agency.[43]

Many attempted to rescue the international movement from this withdrawal. In the eyes of one optimistic member of the Buxton family, who counted amongst the prominent founders of the SCF in Britain, the Canadians he visited in the early twenties were especially charitable, and this was the promising sign of a universalism:

> Looked at from the Atlantic, the sack of Smyrna, a famine on the Volga, children starving in Vienna of Cologne might well seem matters too remote for personal concern. Yet, Ontario farmers, university students, town workers all over the Dominion, individuals in the most remote of lumber camps, have again and again pinched themselves in order to send help to suffering children thousand miles away. One has only to consult the records of the National Council of Women, of the Daughters of the Empire, of the Red Cross Society, of the SCF, etc., to find abundant proof of a generous international outlook. It speaks well of the government which encourages such action; it speaks well of the Churches and it speaks well for the Press.[44]

This, he maintained, was the fruit of a country's maturity, the "unfolding of the national consciousness along universal lines—a deep recognition that the hurt of one is the harm of all and that humanity contains no boundary line." This attitude, he continued, was in the country's self-interest, as Canada would be prepared to face disasters herself: "it is right and proper that she should ... have a sympathetic and practical attitude toward any world disaster because we have, more than once, received timely help from other nations. Whenever Canada has had a great catastrophe, like that of Halifax, she has been the recipient of generous help from far and near."[45]

Canadian voluntary organizations such as the British Empire War Relief Fund, the League of Red Cross Societies, and the Canadian Red Cross launched an "Armistice Week" and convened a meeting of "ladies and gentlemen" in Toronto, on October 16, 1920, for the relief from "the menace of typhus" and for the ten million children orphaned by war and for starving children in general. Herbert Hoover was the guest of honour. The man who "the Canadian people knew almost as well as he knew himself"[46] used praise, moral imperatives, and threats all at once:

> ... these children are the obligation of every man and woman in the Western hemisphere, for we have suffered less ... they are a charge on the heart of the entire world. This is the real flotsam, it is the real wastage, from the war. This mass of undernourished, underclad, mentally and morally and physically destitute children must twenty years from now furnish the foundation of civilization in Europe.[47]

Hoover congratulated Canadians for their exceptional generosity that, he trusted, would survive the war. In this way, the rhetoric of fight and sacrifice had survived the conflict in the face of new enemies: disease, poverty, and social unrest.

The renewed patriotism mentioned soldiers in their humane capacity:

> *Ils aiment beaucoup les enfants* (They love the children very much) was a remark frequently made by the people of France, among whom the soldiers of the Canadian Corps were billeted. It fitted the Canadian soldiers for, hard hitter though they were in the firing line, they liked nothing better when in their "rest billet" than to play with and amuse children. It was a very usual sight in the Canadian areas to see a heavy gunner with "Canada" on his shoulder straps, or a stalwart sergeant of infantry, or a sturdy sapper of the engineers, holding Madam's tiny *bébé* while she improved the time at her multifarious household duties or perhaps making *une tasse de café pour les soldats*. Nor do we think that the soldiers—big hearted and fair minded as they were—could have withheld their tenderness even had the tiny baby been a little Hun. [This] only typified the character of the nation to which he belongs.[48]

Like earlier calls for Belgium, the campaigns appealed to the pride in the advantages of the country: "Is it nothing to us in Canada, with our bountiful stores of food and with all about us that makes life happy—and luxurious compared to theirs—that millions of children should be crying for help?"[49]

Despite such efforts, interest for international humanitarian actions receded in favour of a renewed attention to domestic problems. The Canadian Council of Child Welfare (CCCW), for instance, was founded in 1919 to answer concerns for the health of the young brought by the war. But this "new enthusiasm" for the promotion of social well-being during peacetime was never to match the energy of wartime.[50]

The Interwar Years:
The League of Nations and the Rights of the Child

The rights of children were often presented as a way to carry over the energies of wartime into peace activity. In 1925, the Save the Children International Union (SCIU) held a Conference on Child Welfare to this avail. Here is how the journal of the Social Service Council of Canada (SSCC), *Social Welfare,* reported on the event:

> Although the great tragedy of the refugee children in Europe and their urgent and immediate need for food and clothing and shelter has up till now more than taxed all the efforts of international organizations for the welfare of children, as these conditions are ameliorated more and more, effort is being released for the comprehensive programme of Child welfare as defined in the Declaration of Geneva.[51]

To many, children offered the key to future peace. Their hopes turned to the LON where "national delegates would begin to look behind their strict national perspectives and act as members of a wider transnational community of citizens."[52] The mural painting devoted to "Peace" in the room of the Council of the League of the new "Palace of Nations" showed a mother standing on a gun and holding her baby high.[53] When the SCIU succeeded in having its Declaration of the Rights of the Child adopted by the LON in 1924, it became the first universal instrument of human rights of this international body. SCIU officials expected that, widely distributed, the Declaration would preside over a reform of society. By pressing for institutional changes, they were replicating at the international level what many had done for national legislatures: to help moral ideas about children to become part of legal codes.[54] The form of this charter, a shortlist of rights easily memorized, had also been devised with the mobilization of public opinion in mind.

Who, in Canada, shared this optimism and answered this call? The Declaration was adopted anonymously, but Canadian diplomats barely mentioned it in their report from

Geneva. We know that in November 1930, at the Imperial Conference in London, Prime Minister R. B. Bennett signed the document, together with Richard Squires of Newfoundland. But when the bureaucracy of foreign affairs was asked to contribute to the work of the Child Welfare Committee, also created by the League in 1924, it relied for its answer on Canadian agencies of social work, partly because matters of welfare were largely in private hands. In the absence of federal constitutional prerogatives over welfare, the Canadian Council of Child Welfare was the closest institution the country had to a Children's Bureau.[55] The Canadian branch of the SCIU had promoted children's rights as early as 1923. The SSCC publicized the Charter through its monthly publication, *Social Welfare,* and reported on the activities of the League. In Montreal, the Council of Social Agencies contributed to its distribution, and reminded its members "of our part in that Declaration and our consequent duty as Canadians in interpreting that Charter and translating its clauses into practical action in whatever our work may permit."[56]

Amongst other promoters of children's rights, we find the same agencies that had been involved in humanitarian campaigns for children in distress during the war: the Canadian Red Cross published the Declaration twice in 1924 and the United Church distributed copies to all its ministers. The support of churches is not surprising given that religious and human rights discourses contain a shared and "basic sense of fellow humanity, respect for human dignity, and mutual respect."[57]

"Social questions" soon became the most important dimension of a new internationalism within the Canadian population. Donald Page has found that there existed a widespread support for the LON amongst Canadians, "thousands [of whom] had learned to view this country as part of a world community rather than as an isolated North American entity." The League of Nations Society of Canada (LNSC), largely responsible for channeling the peace activities of "farmer, labour, church, and women's organizations," depicted the League as a "humanitarian service club." The Canadian delegate at the Child Welfare Committee of the League, Charlotte Whitton, together with the leaders of the LNSC, and Walter Riddell, the Canadian Permanent Delegate in Geneva mentioned earlier, all maintained that the social activities of the League was what caused its popularity in the country, especially those related to children. The Canadian delegate herself contributed substantially to the activities of the Child Welfare Committee, especially in the organization of international enquiries on child placement and the determination of standards of nutrition.[58]

Such institutionalization of the temporary arrangements of wartime provided, in turn, a new momentum. On his return from the SCIU conference of 1925, mentioned earlier, Frank Yeigh, the Canadian representative of the Save the Children Fund, commented:

> As session succeeded session, the effect was to enlarge the boundaries of one's interest in
> child welfare as a whole, and this without detracting from interest in the needy home or

national child, which indeed comes first. One became ashamed of a provincial point of view, and realized the universality of the child.[59]

Most discussions of the impact of the Declaration concerned the rights of children within the country where it was bringing concrete results. In 1931, following a speech of Rachel Crowdy, the head of the Social Question Section of the LON, to the Kiwanis Club at the Chateau Laurier, the *Ottawa Citizen* published an article entitled "Children Happier and Healthier by Work League Does."[60] From Geneva, the SCIU often quoted Canada as an example of successful implementation of the new principles: it welcomed efforts in Montreal towards outdoor leisure for children, it also reproduced an article of *Social Welfare* deploring rates of infant mortality in Montreal, and it published an article by Helen McGill on "Juvenile Courts and their Work in Canada."[61] Children's involvement in civic projects, such as the ones put together by the Junior Red Cross, were heralded as examples of the accomplishment of their responsibility towards fellow citizens enshrined in the fifth article. They "gave to children a part in the humanitarian work." The bulletin of the SCIU welcomed the example of a club of boys in a city of the Saskatchewan Prairies who gathered rags and papers in bundles to sell them to the garbage merchants. The *Bulletin international de protection de l'enfance* also listed some examples of Canadian welfare worth attention, such as the British Boys for the Dominion or the Manitoba Welfare Act of 1922.[62]

This concentration on domestic affairs was not new. From the very start, in the face of local critics, the British SCF had been eager to fund local initiatives. Similarly, on his return to the United States, Herbert Hoover undertook to "translate into service through the American Child Health Association the experience in organization and administration gathered in eight years' fight against famine in twenty-three European countries."[63] In 1922, now Secretary of Commerce for the Republican administration of Harding, he applied the "basic principles" of "child feeding work" he had written abroad to American children. It was later entitled "The Child's Bill of Rights," the first in a series of three authored by Hoover. From the mid-forties onwards, Hoover's charter was well known in Canada, as its wording seems to have had more influence in the making of the Canadian welfare state than the LON's Declaration.[64]

In one remarkable instance, the Declaration caused international embarrassment to Canadian authorities. In 1923, an Alberta rural schoolteacher, A. Josephine Dobbs, read the Declaration on the cover of the Christmas issue of *Social Welfare* and understood that it applied not only to regions of famine but also to the children around her. The international documents had, she wrote, opened her shrinking mind. Five months later, *Social Welfare* published her "impressions" on the state of children's rights in her district, an indictment of the "economic burden ... the majority of the people of the province placed on the youth of their country."[65] Familiar with this district of the lower mountains for five years, having the experience of teaching 100 children in three different schools, and of inspecting areas where there were no schools yet, Dobbs undertook to compare the existing rights of children in her district with those listed in the Declaration. Studying the right to education, for instance, she identified families deprived of any possibility of schooling, and others where adulthood started as soon as children could earn their keep. The situation may have been unavoidable in remote areas, but she deplored the suspicion of farmers towards education, which they did not see fit for vigorous pioneer work. Even if the availability of land was diminishing, boys were put to work as soon as they found employment.

SCF officials in London and Geneva welcomed her report as the very kind of reaction they hoped the Declaration would provoke: "No abstract analysis of the Declaration would better show its precision and its scope," and "this article ... showed the way to do enquiries to know to what extent the principles of the Declaration were put to practice."[66] They published the report in their periodical, but in the eyes of the Canadian government, the report became an undue exposure of local problems. An official of the new federal Department of Health now called the LON to stop the distribution of Dobbs' article. "The Department of Health [of] Canada knows fully well that this article does not in any way truly reflect school conditions in Canada as a whole—even the Author, in the article, admits this; and I am also firmly of the opinion that it does not truly reflect the school conditions in the Province of Alberta." Their letter suggested that "articles of this type should not be re-published and given such wide publicity as the League of Nations affords." The Assistant Deputy Minister suggested that writings of private citizens should not be published before authorization was given by the authorities of the country, in this case provincial and federal. The Chief of the Social Section answered by saying that the LON was not the SCIU but, judging by the large number of copies remaining on the shelves of the SCIU archives, the Canadian campaign succeeded otherwise.[67] The elitist conception of international relations the League was supposed to change had survived.

In the meantime, the rhetoric of children's rights continued to offer a means to speak about child welfare in the rest of the world, especially when the SCIU turned its energies to the organization of a conference on African children in 1931. The founders hoped to put the universalism of their Declaration into practice on the southern continent, whose preamble had promised rights "beyond and above all considerations of race, nationality, or creed." The gathering aroused the interest of colonial administrators, missionaries, doctors, and philanthropists.[68] At the conference, the rhetoric of children's rights often served as a way to avoid talking about the political rights of adults in European colonies. The depictions of African children published in the *Junior Bulletin* of the Canadian Red Cross conveyed this sense of irresponsibility.[69]

However, at a time when imperial governments increasingly spoke of their civilizing role in terms of welfare and education, but when the economic depression had them rely more on missions to bring these institutions to native populations, the gathering served as a forum to underline the discrepancies between colonial intentions and the lack of means given to Africans to accomplish them. In addition, the voluntary nature of the SCIU provided a space to discuss human rights, which was not available within the institutions of the League. The Chief of the Native Labour Section of the International Labour Office of the LON, for instance, participated in the organization of the conference as his attempts to conduct enquiries about labour in colonies, and to protect the rights of native workers, had met the jealous answers of imperial governments.[70]

The SCIU was now ready to "aid in accordance to public answer," but it took five years and the invasion of Ethiopia by Italians for the organization to be able to raise sufficient funds. Ethiopia was eager to adopt such a program to gain international recognition. The conjunction of this work on behalf of children's rights, and of the willingness of the only independent country of the continent, Ethiopia, to welcome a voluntary worker, made for a child welfare centre in Addis Ababa. This initiative represents one of the very first lay humanitarian institutions in Africa.[71]

The United Nations Declaration of Children's Rights of 1959

Later conflicts triggered a larger enthusiasm for questions of children's rights: in 1936–37, the Spanish Civil War helped reconstitute the fledging SCF in Canada. The Second World War saw the multiplication of quotes from the Declaration. When Charlotte Whitton left the Canadian Council, she toured the continent with lectures about war and social welfare, where she mentioned the Declaration.[72] This movement found echoes in Canada, where the government was promising, for the end of the war, a world where "social security and human welfare [would be] the main concern of men and nations."[73] Canadian leaders were participating in an international movement for human rights that had stemmed first from the commitment of masses of citizens to the defence of their nation. H. G. Wells and international academies of jurists in the interwar years are credited for the "rediscovery" of human rights during the Second World War.

Hoover attempted to repeat the Belgian experience in occupied territories, but his ideas met the opposition of Churchill and Roosevelt. They preferred to commit resources and money to a new international agency for relief and rehabilitation under the auspices of an international institution, the United Nations Relief and Rehabilitation Administration (UNRRA), which would only take charge of civilian populations once they were "liberated." The Canadian Mary McGeachy, a former employee of the LON's Secretariat, would chair the UNRRA's section on children's welfare. At the end of the conflict, Hoover conducted reviews of the resources of the post-war world for his country. Like the SCF a quarter of a century before, Hoover was to take the initiative to extend his mandate to the children of the developing world.

At home, many promises of universal social and economic rights were translated into programs directed at the next generation.[74] Public demands for equality by parents, truancy officers, social workers, and trade unionists often underlined the influence of wartime. In 1943, for instance, the same *Monde Ouvrier* that had promoted the Belgian Fund stated: "Why, in the light of the grave events where its fate is at stake, [is the government] wanting to persist to trim on what is owed to the people in matter of progress and security?"[75] The government was shy to speak the language of universal entitlements about children, but not about adults: the leaflet introducing family allowances, produced not long before the federal election of 1945, was entitled "A Children's Charter." Indirectly, perhaps, the rights of children might have acted as a relay: they helped to maintain an environment where questions of fairness remained important.

The public endorsement of the rhetoric of the rights of the young contributed to a certain equalization of the experiences between girls and boys, rural and urban children, Aboriginal children and children of European descent, and to a larger autonomy of children within and outside of their families.[76] They also provided a basis to ask for more justice, as one of the parents wrote, "Since we are under the control of a compulsory law, it seems to me that we should be able to demand the advantages necessary to follow it faithfully."[77] At the same time, the politics of children's rights contained tensions that would become important later: the tendency to equate freedom and consumption, the political expediency that had weakened the program's universalistic features at the time of their inception.

For a few years after the war, the United Nations continued discussions over the rights of all. At the founding Conference of San Francisco, "for some delegations, most notably the United States, the promotion and protection of human rights was an integral part of any attempt to secure lasting peace in the postwar world." Moreover, in the eyes of the delegates, the mention of "respect for human rights and for fundamental freedoms for all" was explicitly devised to ensure the assent of non-governmental organizations. The Canadian government, for its part, had generally been indifferent to American projects of human rights during the war, and continued to approach the issue reluctantly afterwards. The efforts of Canadian diplomats focused on the construction of an international bureaucracy in the image of their own, in order to ensure Canada an important place in the new international organization, and at the expense of a commitment to universal entitlements that threatened to inflame the Canadian public. Ironically, that very participation was helping to develop commitments to human rights at home.[78] In the longer term, a withdrawal from the question of the rights of all to the question of children's rights was about to occur.

As early as 1946, the same groups that had compelled the LON to act after the First World War asked the United Nations to update the Geneva Declaration of 1924. To the members of the Secretariat who answered them at the time, the Declaration was "harmless enough but rather a nuisance." Adopted in 1948, the Universal Declaration of Human Rights made the Declaration irrelevant, according to John Humphrey, the Canadian Secretary of the new Human Rights Commission.[79] Despite their reticence, the matter of children's rights would resurface in indirect ways, along logics that are now familiar.

After the war, agencies of the UN took the responsibility for children in distress, unlike the LON assembly a quarter of century before that had left the task to private agencies. When the time came to dissolve UNRRA, the UN allocated the remaining money to a temporary agency, the International Children's Emergency Fund (ICEF). Later, the agency became permanent and its scope international, following the initiative of Pakistan, in the name of the millions of children outside of the territory of ICEF who were still in need of assistance.[80] The Canadian delegates were ready to abandon the new UNICEF, but they had to change their position in light of what they perceived as a public opinion favourable to human rights.

In addition, when the time came to put the principles of the Universal Declaration of Human Rights into practice, the topic of children provided the only matter of possible agreement amongst the members of the Human Rights Committee (HRC). So it was then, during the harshest years of the Cold War, that the UN Declaration of the Rights of the Child was adopted, both as an excuse not to discuss the rights of all and as a way to keep the general discussion on human rights alive.

But the success of the notion of children's rights cannot be attributed only to a retrenchment. To its defenders, the notion called for a specific kind of rights, distinct from all those now stated in the Universal Declaration, because of their judicial minority. Accordingly, the Declaration of 1959 stated that children needed specific attention because of their "physical and mental immaturity."[81] The new declaration also acknowledged state responsibilities, following recent developments in national welfare states that guaranteed children a minimum of welfare and education.[82] In addition, the threatening climate of the Cold War enhanced the wish of Western leaders to value and educate children, not only to prepare their own countries, but also to predispose the non-aligned countries towards them.

Conclusion and Epilogue: The Convention on the Rights of the Child of 1989 in Historical Perspective

The Convention on the Rights of the Child of 1989 is in part the product of a child liberation movement of the 1970s promoting the freedom of the child, which, in turn, can be seen as a development of ideas present in the Enlightenment. The "linchpin" of the Convention was the idea that children are autonomous and capable of full participation in society, and this tendency had already influenced a series of UN treaties from the 1970s, such as the guidelines on refugee children of 1988 and the Declaration on Foster Placement and

Adoption in 1986. At the same time, the principle of the protection of children remained and with it the possibility of "radical disagreement concerning the appropriate interpretation of the Convention," a tension, as we have seen, that is as old as liberal ideas of childhood. The relation between children's entitlements and their duties also remained.[83]

The universal commitments of the Convention could have radical implications for claims by the South for a transfer of resources from the North, a question already present in the negotiations preceding the Declaration of 1959. But, at the same time, and in echo of contradictions present at the Conference on the African Child of 1931, critics see the notion children's rights as the new moral face of Western ambitions for the South, a movement strong enough, they argue, to serve as a replacement to anti-communism.[84]

Brian Mulroney played a pre-eminent role in the international meetings leading to the Convention, especially as the co-chair of the September 1990 World Summit for Children, held in New York, which helped gather support for the new document, and foreign minister Joe Clark had been the "most important" politician to offer support for the idea of a summit. Earlier, in 1979, Mulroney had been the vice chairman of the commission of the UN for the International Year of the Child, an outcome of NGO pressures to attract the attention of the world to children, after years of focus on "development," which, in their opinion, had had detrimental influences on childhood. In conjunction with his international endeavours, at home, a Canadian Commission for the International Year of the Child had presided over a large movement towards children's rights and away from an approach based on child saving.[85] Again, children's rights offered a topic on which a middle power such as Canada could exert more international influence than its military of demographic weight warranted. But analysts of Canada's role point, again, to "the growing public interest in the issue of children's rights," a movement that cannot be reduced to the pragmatic positioning of international relations.[86]

Finally, the impact of the Convention on the population is impeded by many problems: the federal nature of the country, for one; the importance of the bureaucracy required to ensure its implementation and the good functioning of the monitoring system; and the tendency of many conservative reformists and governments, like that of Hoover before, to use the topic of children to diminish their engagements towards the welfare of all.[87] The Senate committee charged with a review of the state of children's rights in the country has recently attracted most of the public attention to the fate of Aboriginal children, whose lives, they deplore, are those of third-world citizens.[88] This tension between the promotion of children's rights as a way to help people abroad and children's rights as a measure of Canada's own welfare, like most current problems mentioned above, are recurring features of the history of children's rights in the country.

Acknowledgements

Hugh Cunningham and Tom Buchanan have provided invaluable suggestions, and Langdon Pearson has helped with most aspects of recent history. Many archivists have facilitated this work: Paulette Dozois, Matthew T. Schaefer, and Marcus Eckhardt, Rodney Breen and Jennifer Sneddon, Catherine Santschi and Danielle Prost, Alfred Guindi and Remo Becci. Funds for this research have been granted by the SSHRC, Carleton University, the Institute of Commonwealth Studies, the Leverhulme Trust International Visiting Fellowship, and Oxford Brookes University.

Notes

1   W. A. Riddell, "Canada and International Affairs. II: Canada's Part in the Social and Humanitarian Work of the League," *Social Welfare* IX, 5 (February 1927): 354–355.

2   On the necessity to study conceptions of adults and children simultaneously, see Chris Jenks, *Childhood*, 2nd ed. (London and New York: Routledge, 2005), 5; Georges Vigarello, "Les paradigmes d'une Histoire de l'enfance," *Le Débat* 121 (September–October 2002): 153, 157.

3   Hugh Cunningham, *Children and Childhood in Western Society since 1500* (London and New York: Longman, 1995).

4   I use a theory of international history which sees "foreign policy as the cultural product of each country" and "international encounters [as] a reflection of domestic social conditions and ideologies." Patricia Clavin, Review of *The Lights that Failed*, *Reviews in History*, http://www.history.ac.uk/reviews/paper/clavin.html, accessed January 2006, 4. See also her "Defining Transnationalism," *Contemporary European History* 14, 4 (2005): 421–439.

5   Simeon Ilesanni, "Human Rights," in William Schweiker, ed., *The Blackwell Companion to Religious Ethics* (London: Blackwell, 2006), 506.

6   Neil Sutherland, *Children in English-Canadian Society: Framing the Twentieth-Century Consensus* (Waterloo: Wilfrid Laurier University Press, 2000); Katherine Covell and R. Brian Howe, *The Challenge of Children's Rights for Canada* (Waterloo: Wilfrid Laurier University Press, 2001), chapter 3. Canadian laws were already international by nature, as they were based on codes imported from Europe.

7   For a discussion of the uneven advent of children as subjects of rights, see Jean-Marie Fecteau, *La liberté du pauvre. Crime et pauvreté au XIXe siècle québécois* (Montreal: VLB Éditeur, 2004), 179–207.

8   Alain Renault, "L'enfant dans la dynamique de la modernité," *Le Débat, op. cit.*, 171.

9   Dominique Youf, "Construire un droit de l'enfance," *Le Débat*, 121, (September–October 2002): 160, 165.

10 Nicholas Thomas, "Colonial conversions: a difference, hierarchy, and history in early twentieth-century evangelical propaganda," in Catherine Hall, ed., *Cultures of Empire. A Reader. Colonizers and the Empire in the Nineteenth and Twentieth Centuries* (New York: Routledge, 2000), 298–328; Marcel Gauchet and Gladys Swain, *Madness and Democracy: The Modern Psychiatric Universe* (Princeton: Princeton University Press, 1999); Joseph M. Hawes, *The Children's Rights Movement. A History of Advocacy and Protection* (Boston: Twayne Publisher, 1991), 20–21.

11 Hugh Cunningham, "The Rights of the Child from the Mid-Eighteenth to the Early Twentieth Century," *Aspects of Education* 50 (1994): 2–16.

12 Tamara Hareven, "An Ambiguous Alliance: Some Aspects of American Influences on Canadian Social Welfare," *Histoire sociale/Social History* 3 (1969): 82–98. See also my article, "Tensions ethniques et religieuses autour des droits universels des enfants: la participation canadienne au Comité de protection de l'enfance de la Société des Nations, entre 1924 et 1945," *Lien social et politique* (Autumn 2000): 101–123.

13 The abolition of this traffic would be enshrined in the League of Nations' Covenant and, in 1921, the League adopted an International Convention for the Suppression of Traffic in Women and Children. In 1922, an Advisory Committee on the Traffic in Women and Children was inaugurated within the League to which, in 1924, a new Child Welfare Committee was attached.

14 Marie-Sylvie Dupont Bouchat, "La Belgique capitale internationale du patronage au XIXe siècle," in Commission Royale des Patronages (Belgium), *Justice et aide sociale. 100 ans d'évolution* (Brussels: Bruylant, 1994), 281–336, here 305; see also *Congrès international de la protection de l'enfance* (Bordeaux: Bourlange, 1895), and *Deuxième Congrès de la protection de l'enfance* (Bruxelles, 1921, Rapports, Bruxelles, Office de publicité, 3 tomes: 1. Questions; 2. Pays; 3. Débats). For the detail of these events, see my article, "The Formation of Childhood as an Object of International

Relations: the Child Welfare Committee and the Declaration of Children's Rights of the League of Nations," *International Journal of Children's Rights* 7, 2 (1999): 103–147.

15 Carol Miller, "'Geneva—the Key to Equality': Inter-War Feminists and the League of Nations," *Women's History Review* 3, 2 (1994): 219–245; "The Social Section and Advisory Committee on Social Questions of the League of Nations," in Paul Weindling, ed., *International Health Organisations and Movements 1918–1939* (Cambridge: Cambridge University Press, 1995), 154–175; Mary Ann Mason, "Children's Rights," in Paula Fass, ed., *Encyclopedia of Children and Childhood: in History and Society* (New York: Macmillan Reference USA, 2004).

16 For Canada, see Donald M. Page, "Canadians and the League of Nations before the Mandchurian Crisis," Ph.D. diss. in History (University of Toronto, 1972), 30.

17 Philip Veerman, *The Rights of the Child and the Changing Image of Childhood* (Dordrecht/Boston/London: Martinus Nijhoff Publishers, 1991), 325–328.

18 Terry Crowley, *Agnes Macphail and the Politics of Equality* (Toronto: J. Lorimer, 1990).

19 Mason, "Children's Rights."

20 Robert McIntosh, *Boys in the Pits: Child Labour in Coal Mines* (Kingston: McGill-Queen's Press, 2000), chapters 7 and 8. For an instance of school children asking for rights, see also "Some school children 'strike' to aid parents," *The Globe*, 13 November 1935, 1.

21 Jean-Pierre Després, *Le Canada et l'Organisation internationale du travail* (Montreal: Fides, 1946). On the constitutional problems in the implementation of such conventions, see Allan Gotlieb, "The Changing Canadian Attitude to the United Nations Role in Protecting and Developing Human Rights," in his *Human Rights, Federalism and Minorities* (Toronto: Canadian Institute of International Affairs, 1970), 16–53.

22 The Covenant of the League of Nations contained provisions on the rights of minorities and, later, the General Assembly would adopt a declaration concerning rights for women. Jan Herman Burgers, "The Road to San Francisco: The Revival of the Human Rights Idea in the Twentieth Century," *Human Rights Quarterly* 14 (1992): 459, 464. On the reluctance of colonial governments to envisage an infringement of their sovereignty, see Marika Sherwood, "'Diplomatic Platitudes': The Atlantic Charter, the League of Nations and Colonial Independence," *Immigrants and Minorities* 15 (1996): 135–150.

23 "Introduction," in Michael Freeman, ed., *Children's Rights. A Comparative Perspective* (Aldershot: Darthmouth Publishing Company, 1996), 1–6. I have explored the relationship between war and children's rights at length in "Peace, War and the Popularity of Children's Rights in Public Opinion, 1919–1959: The League of Nations, the United Nations and the Save the Children International Union," in James Marten, ed., *Children and War. An Anthology* (New York University Press, 2002), 184–199.

24 Archives of the Save the Children Fund, London, Suzanne Ferrière Papers, SF/22, letter to Ferrière, 27 June 1924. Hugo Slim and Patricia Sellick, eds., *The Save the Children Fund Archive*, London, Primary Source Microfilm, 2002, Western Aid and the Global Economy (hereafter ASCF). Series one. F. M. Wilson, *Rebel Daughter of a Country House: The Life of Eglantyne Jebb, Founder of the Save the Children Fund* (London: Allen & Unwin, 1967), 180.

25 Carolyn Moorehead, *Dunant's Dream. War, Switzerland and the History of the Red Cross* (London: Harper Collins, 1988), 280–281, 288; Douglas Keay, Interview with David Buxton, 22 June 1993, Save the Children Oral History, ASCF; Roland Cosandey, *Eloquence du Visible—la Famine en Russie 1921–1923 une Filmographie commentée*, Institut Jean Vigo, 1998, collection « Archives », nos. 75/76. Michèle Martin, *Images at War: Illustrated Periodicals and Constructed Nations* (Toronto: University of Toronto Press, 2006).

26 There has been an intimate connection, earlier, between the history of press photograph and the popularity of images of war, to the extent that, historians of photography tell us, one cannot be understood without the other. On the involvement of the working class in war charities in Britain and its causes, see Simon Fowler, "War Charity Begins at Home," *History Today* (September 1999): 18.

27 "Consul-General for Belgium Thanked Gothland Visitors for Canada's Assistance," *Pro Belgica*, 14 June 1916, 1. See also 28 June and 16 August 1916.

28 See my article, "Children's Rights and Children's Action in International Relief and Domestic Welfare: the Work of Herbert Hoover Between 1914 and 1950," *Journal of the History of Children and Youth* 1, 3 (Fall 2008).

29 *Pro Belgica*, 31 May 1916, 2; 14 June 1916, 4; 21 June 1916. Eric Leroux, *Gustave Francq, Figure marquante du syndicalisme et précurseur de la FTQ* (Montreal: VLB éditeur, 2001). Francq, who was President of the Comité de Secours Belge du Comité Central de l'Œuvre de Secours pour les victimes de la guerre en Belgique, also represented the Trades and Labour Congress of Canada at the Pre-Peace Conferences of Labor in Switzerland.

30 "How the Eskimos Helped," *The World's Children* (April 1924): 126. The story impressed the SCIU, which repeated it as a sign of the popularity of the campaign. Archives of the Union internationale de protection de l'enfance, Archives d'État de Genève (hereafter AUIPE), Memorandum concernant l'UISE, Geneva, not dated, 4. The AUIPE is the successor of the SCIU.

31 Renaut, "L'enfant dans la dynamique de la modernité," 173. To him, only the 1960s would match the pace of the Enlightenment.

32 H. A. Halliday, "Through Artists' Eyes: War Art in Canada," *Canada's Visual History*, Canadian Museum of Civilization & National Film Board of Canada, CD-ROM, 1996.

33 Tim Cook, "'He was determined to go': Underage Soldiers in the Canadian Expeditionary Force," unpublished manuscript, 2006. Cook adds that "with most adolescents out of school and working by sixteen, parts of Canadian society seems not to have viewed these adolescents as boys but as men." He also points out that reformists who had fought against teenage drinking were less likely to fight against their enlistment, in a climate of enhanced patriotism. Stéphane Audoin-Rousseau, "Quand les enfants font la guerre," *L'Histoire* 169 (Septembre 1993): 6–12. Soldiers who were Aboriginal Canadians living on Reservations were temporarily granted the franchise in the same fashion, as well as military women nurses.

34 *Le Monde ouvrier/Labour World*, 22 July 1916, 2. Report on the Work of the Ottawa Women's Canadian Club, August 4, 1914 to March 1915, Library and Archives Canada (hereafter LAC), Ottawa Women's Canadian Club Fonds, MG 28, I35, vol. 6, 2/2.

35 George Didi-Hubermann, *Annales E.S.C.*, 61, 5 (October 2006): 1041.

36 Testimony published in *The World Children*.

37 Frank Yeigh, "Saving the Child," *East and West* (August 2, 1924), 245, MG 28 I 42, vol. 7.

38 Frank, circular letter, 28 April 1925, LAC, MG 28-I42, vol. 7.

39 F. K. Prochaska, "Little Vessels: Children in the Nineteenth Century Missionary Movement," *Journal of Imperial and Commonwealth History* VI, 2 (January 1978): 103–118; Nancy M. Sheenan, "Philosophy, Pedagogy, and Practice: the IODE and the Schools in Canada, 1900–1945," *Historical Studies in Education* 2, 2 (1990): 307–321, mentions children raising money for Belgium.

40 These results are based on a preliminary study of letters to American children from Belgian children preserved by the Hoover Museum and listed in the Museum card drawer entitled: "1928 to baskets, Section entitled "Albums and scrapbooks." These cases are related to the Committee for the Relief of Belgian and bear the numbers 62-1-350 for the citation; 62.8.51(11), (12), (16), (19), and (32).

41 LAC, MG 28, I 35, R2834-0-7-E. Here, file 2/2, "W.W.1 Work of OWCC, 1916–18," 8 October 1918 and 1918 (date unreadable).

42 John F. Hutchinson, "The Junior Red Cross Goes to Healthland," *American Journal of Public Health* 87 (1997): 1816–1823; Veerman, *The Rights of the Child*, chapter VII; Nick Cullather, "American Pie: The Imperialism of the Calorie," *History Today* 57, 2 (February 2007): 34–40.

43 Newspapers quoted and paraphrased by James Weber Linn, *Jane Addams. A Biography* (New York, London: Appleton-Century Company, 1935), 338, 346; Jane Addams and Alice Hamilton, "After the Lean Years. Impressions of Food Conditions in Germany when Peace was Signed," *The Survey* 42, 23 (6 September 1919): 796.

44 Rev. Harold Buxton, "How Canada Saves the Children," *The World's Children* (April 1924): 125–126.

45 Article prepared for the *Canadian Press*, 30 January 1930, LAC, MG 28 I 42, vol. 8. Yeigh called this phenomenon the "golden rule." This idea became the central argument for the movement in favour of an international emergency fund, which failed. John F. Hutchinson, "Disasters and the International Order: Earthquakes, Humanitarians, and the Ciraolo Project," *The International History Review* XXII(1) (March 2000): 1–36, and "Disasters and the International Order—II," 23, 2 (2001): 253–298.

46 See note 47.

47 Mr. Balfour on the Typhus Outlook, *British Empire War Relief Fund* (To Combat Disease and Distress in War Stricken Areas in Europe and Asia), statements by Rt. Hon. Arthur Balfour, Mr. Herbert Hoover, Dr. John Todd, and Dr. Norman White, issued by the Canadian Red Cross Society, Toronto, 1920, distributed by the Provincial Division, 1–4. Mr. Hoover's Address, *idem*. The *Oxford Dictionary* defines "flotsam" as "Such part of the wreckage of a ship or its cargo as is found floating on the surface of the sea." http://dictionary.oed.com (accessed in July 2007).

48 "Appeal Culminates Armistice Week …" Amicus no. 8222247. *Souvenirs. New Exhibition of Canadian Official War Photographs in Colour*, under the direction of the Canadian War Records Office, [1914?], presented a picture of "A Canadian boy acts as a nurse to a wounded Belgian baby whose mother was killed by a shell near Mons."

49 British Empire War Relief Fund, 16.

50 Strong Boag, *The Parliament of Women*, 387–388; Page, "Canadians and the League of Nations," 164–165.

51 "The International Conference on Child Welfare," *Social Welfare* VIII, 2 (November 1925): 1.

52 Clavin's review, 3.

53 José Maria Sert, "Hope," in Arturo Colorado Castellari, The Murals by José Maria Sert in the "Francisco de Vitoria Room" (Council Chamber). The Cultural Legacy of the Palais des Nations, New York, United Nations, 1985, 12.

54 This idea comes from the work of David Rodogno on the history of humanitarianism. The various ILO conventions included entitlements, but they were not presented in terms of rights.

55 *The World's Children* (December 1930): 51. On the constitutional and rights, see Kwong-Long Tang, "Implementing the United Nations Convention on the Rights of the Child. The Canadian Experience," *International Social Work* 46, 3 (2003): 277–288.

56 Frank Yeigh, "Saving the Child," *East and West* (August 2, 1924): 245; LAC, Save the Children Fund, MG 28 I 42, vol. 7; Charlotte Whitton, "Child Welfare at the League—1928," *Social Welfare* X, 9 (June 1928): 197–200; "A Distinguished Visitor to Canada," *Social Welfare* VIII, 7 (May 1926): 1; MCSA, "Welfare Work in Montreal," *Women's Directory Montreal*, 1926, 81. I thank Sue Morton for the reference.

57 *Bulletin de l'Union internationale de secours aux enfants*, 5, 15 (15 August 1924): 338; "The Children's Charter in the Canadian West," *Child Welfare News* 2, 1 (February 1925): 51; Ilesanni, *op. cit.*, quoting Witte. The emblem of the SCIU, the child Christ and its motto, *"salvate parvulos,"* point at such a primordial belonging to the world.

58 Page, "Canadians and the League of Nations," 1. LAC, Canadian Council on Social Development, MG 28, I 10, vol. 15, 1927; Whitton to Skelton, 21 January 1937, RG 25, G-1, 1827, 154–part 1. P. T. Rooke and R. L. Schnell, "Internationalizing a Discourse: Children at Risk, the Child Welfare Committee, and the League of Nations," *New Education* 14 (1992): 61–72; "'Uncramping Child Life': International Children's Organizations, 1914–1939," in Paul Weindling, dir., *International Health Organisations and Movements, 1918–1939* (Cambridge: Cambridge University Press, 1995), 176–202.

59 Frank Yeigh, "World Congress Recognizes Need of Caring for Children," *Toronto Star*, September 1925, MG 28 I 42, vol. 7. Yeigh published a similar account in the Bulletin of the CCCW. Yeigh has been the author of books for people intending to immigrate to Canada, and was later known for his promotion of the work of the Aboriginal writer Pauline Johnson.

60 9 December 1931, in LAC, RG 29, vol. 31, 25-2-4 (2) to 25-3-1 (3).

61 "Récréation organisée," *Revue internationale de l'enfant (RIE)* 4, 22 (October 1927) : 672–673. It reproduced a picture from *Social Welfare*; *RIE* 6, 31 (August 1928): 536–7; *RIE* 6, 34 (October 1928): 678–683.

62 M. Lyman Brisson, "La civilisation sauvée par les enfants," *BUISE* 18 (30 April 1921): 225; 15 May 1923, 457 (from the *Times Education Supplement*); 30 June 1923, 569 (from the *Journal of Social Hygiene*).

63 Phillip Van Ingen, "Editorial, American Child Health Association," *Mother and Child* 4, 4 (February 1923): 77–81.

64 See my "Children's Rights and Children's Action …" Canadian Council of Child and Family Welfare, *The Protection of the Child. A Story Told in Pictures,* Ottawa, 1930, CCCFW Publication no. 51; LAC, MG30, vol. 20.

65 A. Josephine Dobbs, "The Children's Charter (Declaration of Geneva). An Alberta Teacher's Reaction," *Social Welfare* (May 1924): 150–155. Translated and published in *BUISE* (1924): 339–352. PVCE UISE, 124ᵉ séance, 5 August 1924, AUIPE.

66 *BUISE* 5, 12 (30 June 1924): 272; PVCE UISE, 124ᵉ séance, 5 August 1924, AUIPE.

67 For both quotations, see Dr. D. A. Clark, Assistant Deputy Minister, Department of Health, to the Secretary of the League of Nations, 25 September 1924, Archives of the League of Nations (ALON), 12, 39472. Crowdy to Clark, 15 October 1924, ALON, R 686, 12, 39472.

68 I have discussed these issues in "Children's Right and Imperial Political Cultures: Missionary and Humanitarian Contributions to the Conference on the African Child of 1931," *International Journal of Children's Rights* 12 (2004): 273–318.

69 "Our African Friend," *Canadian Red Cross Junior*, 1922.

70 "L'enfance non-européenne," unpublished document (Geneva, 1928), 5, AUIPE, M.8.1; Victor-Yves Ghébali, "Aux origines de l'ECOSOC: l'évolution des commissions et organisations techniques de la SDN," *Annuaire français de droit international* (1972): 499. The committee of experts set up in 1932 on the question of slavery, mainly thanks to the pressures of the Anti-slavery Society, were integra difficulty within the machinery of the League.

71 John Iliffe, *The African Poor* (Cambridge: Cambridge University Press, 1988), 198–199. The archives of the Canadian SCF, LAC, MG 28, I 42, show information about the conference and appeal for money to finance its sequel, but there is no account of any Canadian contribution to the Ethiopian campaign. The archives of the Canadian Red Cross show some interest.

72 "Save the Children Fund," *The Charlottetown*, 23 December 1940, reprinted the Declaration and the words by which the Queen, the Archbishop of Canterbury, and the novelist J. B. Priestly had pronounced on the BBC, Sunday, 29 September 1940, LAC, MG 28, I 42, vol. 7. "Problems of Childhood in Wartime Discussed Here," *Los Angeles Daily News*, 29 September 1942, MG 30, E 256, vol. 115, Clippings.

73 Cited in my article, "Reconstruction Politics, the Canadian Welfare State and the Ambiguity of Children's Rights, 1940–1950," in Greg Donaghy, ed., *Uncertain Horizons: Canadians and their World in 1945* (Ottawa: Canadian Committee for the History of the Second World War, 1996), 263.

74 See my article, "The Language of Children's Rights, the Formation of the Welfare State and the Democratic Experience of Poor Families, Quebec, 1940–1955," *Canadian Historical Review* 78, 3 (Fall 1997): 409–441.

75 "Fréquentation scolaire obligatoire?", *Le Monde ouvrier*, 20 March 1943: 1. My translation.

76 Magda Fahrni, Household Politics. Montreal Families and Postwar Reconstruction (Toronto: University of Toronto Press, 2005).

77 "Reconstruction Politics ..." 44.

78 Robert A. Spencer, Canada in World Affairs. From UN to NATO, 1946–1949 (Toronto: Oxford University Press), 162–4; Christopher MacLennan, Towards the Charter. Canadians and the Demand for a National Bill of Rights, 1929–1960 (Montreal and Kingston: McGill-Queen's University Press, 2003), 65–66, 192–195. Their reasons were mainly the "the looseness of the drafting," constitutional difficulties involved in the implementation of international treaties and, largely, the fear of governments that the Canadian public opinion would use the document to call for more policies, 78–79. The NCW, the United Church, and civil libertarians were part of the organizations that were pressuring the Special Joint Committee on Human Rights, 79.

79 Covell and Howe, 20; Michael Longford, "NGOs and the Rights of the Child," in Peter Willet, ed., "The Conscience of the World": The Influence of Non-Governmental Organisations in the UN System (Washington, DC: Brookings Institution, 1996), 216. The question of their relevance was still debated in the 1980s. Stephen J. Toope, "The Convention on the Rights of the Child: Implications for Canada," in Michael Freeman, ed., Children's Rights. A Comparative Perspective (Aldershot: Darthmouth Publishing Company, 1996), 33–35.

80 Maggie Black, Children First. The Story of UNICEF, Past and Present (New York: Oxford University Press, 1996), 7–8. In Canada, the government contributed additional money to UNICEF. A Canadian Council for Reconstruction through UNESCO, created in 1946, worked with the "Campaign Appeal for Children" to raise money for books and other school equipment and UNESCO fellowships. They received a grant from the Canadian government's post-UNRRA appropriations, together with 1,500 cases of "basic schoolroom supplies" coming from the "dimes and nickels of thousands of Canadian school children." Spencer, Canada in World Affairs, 1959, 73, 184–185, 190–191.

81 Youf, 161–162. This formulation had been developed by the IUCW. "Canada and Children's Rights," 198. On this period, see my article, "Canada and Children's Rights at the United Nations, 1945–1959," in Greg Donaghy, ed., Canada and the Early Cold War, 1943–1957 (Ottawa: Department of Foreign Affairs and International Trade, 1998), 183–214.

82 See my book, The Social Origins of the Welfare State. Québec Families, Compulsory Education, and Family Allowances, 1940–1955 (Waterloo: Wilfrid Laurier University Press, 2006), translated by Nicole Doone Danby; and "Canada and Children's Rights," 188–189. A specific list of agencies responsible for children's rights was included in the Declaration, a feature absent from 1924.

83 See the preamble of the Convention and Article 29. Toope, "The Convention" 47. "Introduction," in Freeman, ed., Children's Rights, 3; Sonja L. Taylor, "International Organizations," in Paula Fass, ed., Encyclopedia of Children and Childhood: In History and Society (New York: Macmillan Reference USA, 2004). The moral panic over child abuse seems to have been an important factor, and the trend, amongst psychologists, to favour the right of children to reach their own potential. Hawes, The Children's Rights Movement, 60. According to Landon Pearson, the notion of "child liberation" itself received little popularity in Canada, where it was often associated with pedophiles; on sexual exploitation, see R. Brian Howe and Katherine Covell, eds., Children's Rights in Canada. A Question of Commitment (Waterloo, Wilfrid Laurier University Press, 2007, 404.

84 Toope, "The Convention," 46–47, 56. In 1996, according to Landon Pearson, children's rights started to be mentioned in Canadian statements of foreign policy, and they became central to the action of the Canadian International Development Agency. V. Pupavac, "Without Borders: the International Children's Rights Regime," Disasters 25, 2 (2001): 95–112; see also Nancy Scheper-Hughes, "The Rites of the Child: Global Discourses of Youth and Reintegrating Child Soldiers in Sierra Leone," Journal of Human Rights 4, 2 (June 2005).

85 Black, Children First, 27, 29; Black, 13–14, 22. Foreign Affairs and International Trade Canada, "Senator Landon Pearson," http://www.dfait-maeci.gc.ca/department/skelton/pearson-bio-en.asp (consulted on February 22, 2008).

86 Andrew F. Cooper, "Good Global Governance or Political Opportunism? Mulroney and UN Social Conferences," in Nelson Michaud and Kim Richard Nossal, eds., Diplomatic Departures: The Conservative Era in Canadian Foreign Policy, 1984–93 (Vancouver: UBC Press, 2001), 160–172; On the current importance of "public interest," and of "Canadians devoting a large percentage of their charitable contributions to children's charities, especially those operating in the developing world," for the future the Convention, see also Toope, "The Convention," 51, 53. On the exceptional importance of NGOs in the drafting of the Convention, based on their "special experience and professionalism," and NGOs in the monitoring of the Convention, see Longford, "NGOs," 222, 231, 235.

87 Kathryn Morrell, "Passive, not Active: Prince Edward Island and the Implementation of the United Nations Convention on the Rights of the Child in Provincial Policy and Legislation on Children, 1989–1991," M.A. thesis in History (Carleton University, 1997); Howe and Covell, eds., Children's Rights in Canada, 13.

88 In 2003, the UN committee on the rights of the child expressed the same worry. Marlyn Bennett, "Aboriginal Children's Rights. Is Canada Keeping its Promises?", in Howe and Covell, eds., Children's Rights in Canada, 279.

Glossary

Childhood. "Childhood is made both by culture and biology. Even though children are physically different from adults, and through time the processes by which children's bodies become adults' bodies have changed only a little ... still it is misleading to think of childhood as founded in nature. Childhoods are shaped by historical processes and transformed by their economic and cultural contexts ..." Nancy Janovicek and Joy Parr, eds., *Histories of Canadian Children and Youth* (Don Mills and New York: Oxford University Press, 2003), 2.

League of Nations. "League of Nations, international organization established at the Paris Peace Conference (1919) at the end of WWI. It was founded on the principles of collective security and preservation of peace through arbitration of international disputes. ... Canada was a member throughout the league's existence, and served 1927–30 on the council.... The league provided opportunities for international discussion of political and legal questions, disarmament, economic relations, the protection of minorities, communications and transit, and health and social questions. Richard Veatch, League of Nations." *The Canadian Encyclopedia*, Historica Foundation of Canada, 2008, http://www.thecanadianencyclopedia.com.

Political culture. "A term meant to encompass political values and attitudes wider than intimated by the more formal political system, and to some extent upholding it.... A political culture can encourage participation and involvement by the majority of citizens, as tends to be the case in democratic politics ... or it can promote attitudes of passivity and acquiescence." Allan Bullock et al., eds., *The Fontana Dictionary of Modern Thought*, 2nd ed. (London: Fontana Press, 1988).

Transnationalism. An approach to international history which sees "foreign policy as the cultural product of each country" and "international encounters [as] a reflection of domestic social conditions and ideologies." Patricia Clavin, Review of *The Lights that Failed*, *Reviews in History*, http://www.history.ac.uk/reviews/paper/clavin.html (accessed January 2006).

Further Reading

Cunningham, Hugh. *Children and Childhood in Western Society since 1500*. London and New York: Longman, 1995.

An important review of the history of Western childhood, which informs much of Canadian developments, told at both the level of the experiences of children and the level of ideas about children.

Howe, Brian, and Katherine Covell, eds. *Children's Rights in Canada. A Question of Commitment.* Waterloo: Wilfrid Laurier University Press, 2007.

A recent introduction to the current challenges and impacts of the Convention of 1980.

Janovicek, Nancy, and Joy Parr, eds. *Histories of Canadian Children and Youth*. Don Mills and New York: Oxford University Press, 2003.

A good collection of recent articles on the history of Canadian children, including questions of rights.

Sutherland, Neil. *Children in English-Canadian Society: Framing the Twentieth-Century Consensus.* Waterloo: Wilfrid Laurier University Press, 2000.

The most comprehensive history of the period between 1870 and 1920, organized mainly around reformists projects concerning schools, delinquency, and public health. A 1978 book reprinted with a new Foreword.

Veerman, Philip. *The Rights of the Child and the Changing Image of Childhood.* Dordrecht/Boston/London: Martinus Nijhoff Publishers, 1991.

The most comprehensive survey of the many episodes in the history of the formulation of charters of universal children's rights, which addresses national and international efforts. The charters are reproduced, analyzed systematically, and replaced in their respective international contexts.

Relevant Websites

Canadian History of Children and Youth Group
edst.educ.ubc.ca/HCYG/
The rich website of the Canadian History of Children and Youth Group, which contains documents, essays, announcements, and other links.

Collections Canada
collectionscanada.gc.ca
Library and Archives Canada maintains a detailed catalogue of the archives of the Canadian Council of Child Welfare, now the Canadian Council of Social Development, which led many of the initiatives on children's rights since its creation in 1919.

Landon Pearson Resource Centre for the Study of Childhood and Children's Rights
www.crin.org/organisations/viewOrg.asp?ID=3151
Senator Pearson's archives and library form the core of this new Centre, located at Carleton University.

McCord Museum
www.mccord-museum.qc.ca/en/keys/webtours/tourID/VQ_P4_4_EN
The McCord Museum's "thematic tours" of their collection, documents pertaining to public health, and childhood.

UNICEF
www.cf-hst.net
The website of UNICEF's archives and publications. It contains many digitized books and essays about UNICEF, as well as many documents pertaining to the history of the organization and the catalogue of their archives.

CHAPTER 10

FROM REPRESSION TO RENAISSANCE:

FRENCH-LANGUAGE RIGHTS IN CANADA

BEFORE THE CHARTER

Matthew Hayday

Introduction: Language Rights, Human Rights, and the Canadian State

Language rights are somewhat difficult to classify within the pantheon of rights. Because language is integrally intertwined with interpersonal communication, these rights cannot be exercised in the absence of a community of other people who speak the same language. This places language rights at least partially within the realm of collective or group rights. And yet language rights, at least in the Canadian context, are primarily exercised by individuals interacting with public- or private-sector institutions. Consequently, they are perhaps best classified as hybrid rights.[1] There is also a vigorous debate over whether language rights can be considered fundamental human rights. Michael MacMillan uses the three major criteria for human rights established by Maurice Cranston to evaluate whether language rights meet the test of being classified as such: they must be of paramount importance, practicable, and universal. In his determination, MacMillan concludes that language rights partially meet these criteria, depending on the specific right in question. The test of paramount importance is subject to one's interpretation of whether community membership defined by language is crucial to a person's identity. This position is defended by political theorists such as Charles Taylor and Wil Kymlicka,[2] but contested by those who see language as simply a functional medium of interaction. Applying the test of practicability is equally complex, as the practicability of guaranteeing language rights depends on whether one is speaking of a tolerance-oriented right (such as the right to speak a language in the home) or a promotion-oriented right (such as the right to receive government services in one's maternal language), and the size of the minority language community. The test of universality is also complicated, as the size of a minority language community and its political positioning within a society will help determine whether this community is entitled to language rights. MacMillan thus concludes that while language rights meet many of the criteria associated with human rights, they do not do so extensively enough to be classified with the "'supremely sacred' nature of traditional civil liberties."[3]

An examination of how the Canadian state has dealt with the issue of language rights clearly demonstrates that these rights have not always been readily accepted. Debates over these rights have occupied a particularly important place in Canadian political discourse ever since the British Conquest of Quebec in 1760. Colonial authorities and then the Canadian government have long wrestled with the question of which language rights would be recognized by the state. In 1982, with the passage of the Canadian Charter of Rights and Freedoms, Canada's two official languages, English and French, became officially entrenched in the Constitution, along with a number of language rights related to use of the two official languages in the Parliament, the courts, and government offices of the federal government and the provincial government of New Brunswick. The entrenchment of these rights did not merely codify long-standing practice in Canada; many of these rights were brand-new or only recently recognized. Indeed, for French-speaking Canadians, particularly those living outside of Quebec, much of Canada's history since Confederation had been a tale of the progressive deprivation of their language rights, and the elimination of rights that had been recognized in the initial Confederation pact.

How do we account both for this progressive restriction of French-language rights and their subsequent reinstatement? Many European theorists, contemplating the state of minority language rights in Europe, have posited that the passage of legislation and enactment of human rights accords will lead to the extension of language rights, and they certainly believe that it is from this framework of laws and international agreements that language rights will flow.[4] However, as the following examination of the history of French-language rights in Canada from Confederation to the Charter will demonstrate, this argument does not necessarily stand up in practice. Not only did Canada's francophone minorities see their constitutionally protected language rights overturned or ignored, but these same rights were reinstated as the result of factors other than the niceties of legal frameworks and international human rights accords. Indeed, the Canadian experience demonstrates that the recognition (or lack thereof) of language rights in Canada can be explained through a combination of intensive lobbying efforts by the rights claimants, the receptivity of political and bureaucratic elites at certain junctures in Canadian history, and the cold financial calculations associated with the extension of these rights. An absence of these factors proved the undoing of French minority-language rights over the first fifty years following Confederation, and it would not be until these factors were positively combined in the late 1950s and into the 1960s that French-language rights began to be restored and expanded in Canada.

The Establishment of French-language Rights in British North America and Canada

When British forces conquered the French colony of New France in 1760, it appeared that the British government would not extend any recognition to pre-existing institutions in the colony, nor any French-language rights. The Royal Proclamation of 1763 prohibited Roman Catholics (the religion of most French-speaking colonists) from holding public offices, and economic ties with France were severed. Despite this inauspicious start, the political and military situation in North America soon led to the granting of certain rights to the French–Canadian Catholic population.

The first major step in expanding the rights of French Canadians came in 1774 with the passage of the Quebec Act, which was intended to win French–Canadian support for a British Crown facing upheaval in the Thirteen Colonies to the south. The seigneurial system, which had been abolished, was reinstated, and an appointed Legislative Council was created to aid the governor in administering the colony. Significantly, Roman Catholics could be members of this council. This indicated that Britain was pulling back from a full commitment to its goal of assimilating the local population into an English-speaking, Protestant mould. The question of Catholic religious rights was more important than language rights to the French–Canadian population at this point, and the re-establishment of these confessional rights was a major victory. A framework for establishing a political base for protecting French-language and Catholic rights was further established in 1791 by the Constitutional Act, which created the two separate jurisdictions of Upper and Lower Canada, with French-speaking Catholics forming the majority in the latter jurisdiction. Elected legislative assemblies were created for each jurisdiction, which could be used for the promotion of French–Canadian interests.

Indeed, the efforts of Louis-Joseph Papineau and his *Patriote* followers to use the Lower Canadian legislative assembly as a vehicle for French–Canadian protest against the actions of the appointed legislative council led to the failed rebellions of 1837–8 and the subsequent visit of Lord Durham. Durham's now-infamous report wrote of finding in the Canadas "two nations warring in the bosom of a single state." His solution to this conflict was to promote the wholesale assimilation of French Canadians into the English majority. With this goal in mind, the Act of Union of 1840 fused the two colonies together into the province of Canada, with a legislative assembly weighted towards English-speaking representatives. While the goal of this assembly was to assimilate the French Canadians, politics intervened. Divided between Reformers and Conservatives, English-Canadian politicians had to seek French–Canadian allies to form a viable government. Moreover, after the death of assimilationist governor Lord Sydenham, subsequent governors recognized that if the colony were to be governable, they would have to concede some status to the French language. In 1848, Robert Baldwin, leader of the Reformers in Canada West, came to power in a governing coalition with Louis-Hippolyte Lafontaine, leader of the Bleus (the Catholic Conservative party) in Canada East, with the understanding that he would support French-language rights in the colony and help put an end to the assimilationist project. Later that year, the British Parliament amended the Act of Union to permit the use of the French language in the colonial legislature.

The French-speaking Acadian community of the Maritimes faced an even more difficult uphill battle. Deported in 1755 by the British, who feared that they would be used as subversives in the war with the French, the Acadians were permitted to return to Nova Scotia in 1764, provided that they agree to take the oath of allegiance to the British Crown. Finding their original settlements around the Bay of Fundy occupied by English-speaking farmers, they had to resettle in more remote parts of the colony. No French-language rights were extended to these minorities. Moreover, as Catholics, the Acadians were denied political rights. They would not obtain the vote in Nova Scotia until 1789; those in New Brunswick and PEI would have to wait until 1810. It would not be until 1830 that Catholics could be members of the Maritime colonial legislatures.

In the Confederation debates, the central issue for the French-speaking delegates from Canada East (there were none to directly represent the Acadians or the francophones of Canada West) was the protection of Quebec's right to manage its educational and cultural institutions, and by extension, their French-language character. French-language rights, per se, were not a priority. There was also a desire to ensure that federal courts and Parliament would be accessible to French-speakers.[5] The main foundations of language rights in Canada for the first century of the post-Confederation era were laid out in section 133 of the British North America Act, 1867 (BNA Act), which reads:

> Either the English or the French language may be used by any Person in the Debates of the Houses of the Parliament of Canada and of the Houses of the Legislature of Quebec; and both those Languages shall be used in the respective Records and Journals of those Houses; and either of those Languages may be used by any Person or in any Pleading or Process in or issuing from any Court of Canada established under this Act, and or from all or from any of the Courts of Quebec.
>
> The Acts of the Parliament of Canada and of the Legislature of Quebec shall be printed and published in both those Languages.

Although this provision of the BNA Act made provisions for the official languages of the legislatures and courts of Quebec and the federal government, it did not impose any such requirements upon the other provincial legislatures or courts. Nor did this section make any guarantees as to the language of government services.

One other important note must be made concerning the provision of rights under the British North America Act, 1867. Education, considered a crucial sphere of jurisdiction for French-Canadian identity, was placed under provincial jurisdiction under section 93. As a result of lobbying from Catholic church leaders from outside Quebec and Protestant politicians from Quebec, confessional education rights in the Canadas were included; these provisions would protect Catholic schools in Ontario and Protestant schools in Quebec. These guarantees were on the basis of religion, *not* language. Although most Protestants in Quebec were anglophones, and a large proportion of the Catholics in Ontario were francophones, it was not deemed necessary to enshrine language rights in education into the BNA Act, as these rights were assumed to flow from the religious orientation of the schools. As for the other colonies, the legislation was silent, apart from guaranteeing that pre-existing confessional rights at the time of union would be protected.

In 1870, following the uprising organized by Métis leader Louis Riel in the Red River settlement, negotiations between representatives of the colony and the Canadian government led to the creation of Canada's fifth province, Manitoba. The population of this colony was approximately evenly split between English- and French-speakers, and many of Riel's key demands for the governance of the new province entailed the protection of both Catholic and French-language rights. These demands were met in the Manitoba Act, 1870, which provided protection for confessional schools in the province, and included the right to use either the English or the French language in either house of the legislature, in the records or journals of those houses, and in the courts of the province.[6] Language rights in the remainder of the Northwest would be covered by the North-West Territories Act, 1875, which provided for Catholic schools in the territory, and was amended in 1877 to include section 110, which provided the same status for the French language as in Quebec and Manitoba.[7]

While Riel's passionate political advocacy and the demographic weight of the francophone population in Western Canada led to certain protections being included in these Acts, this did not set precedents for the other new provinces. British Columbia and Prince Edward Island were admitted to Confederation with no mention of protection for confessional schools or language rights. The state of language rights was decided strictly on a province-by-province basis, with no thought of creating an officially bilingual country. Notably, there was little substantial interest in this from elites in Quebec, who were primarily concerned with protecting provincial jurisdiction from federal interference.

Eliminating French-language Rights in Canada

The first major blow against French-language rights in the newly minted country of Canada came indirectly. In 1871, New Brunswick passed a Common Schools Act that denied public funding to denominational schools. In practice, the "public" schools envisioned under this system would be Protestant, and thus it was the Catholic schools, serving the large French-speaking Acadian minority, that would be denied funding. After tensions escalated, culminating in riots in the Acadian community of Caraquet in northeastern New Brunswick in 1875 over the right to Catholic education, a compromise was struck, allowing for religious instruction outside of school hours and the use of French as a language of instruction in the primary schools.[8] However, the Department of Education provided little in the way of curricular support in French, which would ultimately result in a poor school participation rate for New Brunswick Acadians. Lacking clout in the government, and with the Catholic schools not protected by law prior to the passage of the British North America Act, there was little the Acadians could do to protect the French-language education system. Elsewhere in the Maritimes, there was little discussion of French-language education. In Nova Scotia, legislation was silent on the matter until 1902, at which point French was allowed for the first three years of school and then phased out. In Prince Edward Island, separate Acadian schools that taught in French were tolerated until 1862 and then progressively assaulted, first by legislation passed that year doubling the salary of Acadian teachers who taught in English, followed by an 1877 act establishing non-denominational public schools, both of which contributed to the anglicization of the system.

While no specific act of repression occurred in the Maritimes to restrict the other major traditional language rights claims—the rights to use French in the courts and in the legislature, and to receive government services in French—nor were these rights recognized. In Nova Scotia and Prince Edward Island, the right to use French in criminal proceedings would not be recognized until 1987. Greater progress in this respect was made in New Brunswick, but not until after the Second World War.

In Western Canada, the constitutionally protected language rights of the Manitoba Act and the North-West Territories Act were gradually chipped away. A major demographic shift occurred as large numbers of British Canadians from Ontario moved into the North West and sought to model the region after their province of origin. Led by Conservative MP D'Alton McCarthy and provincial Attorney General Joseph Martin, the Manitoba government abolished the official use of the French language in Manitoba legislature, courts, and civil service with the Manitoba Official Language Act, 1890.[9] That same year, Manitoba switched to a single, non-denominational education system under the Act Respecting the Department of Education and the Act Respecting Public Schools, eliminating the public funding of Catholic schools.[10]

Controversies over the education decision raged for the next six years, until Prime Minister Wilfrid Laurier reached a compromise with Manitoba Premier Thomas Greenway in 1897. Religious instruction would be permitted after regular school hours, and Roman Catholic teachers would be allowed to continue to teach. Bilingual instruction would also be permitted where ten pupils in a class spoke a minority language, a provision that applied not only to the French-Canadian population, but also to other immigrant groups such as the Ukrainians and Germans. These language regulations effectively stripped French Canadians in the province of their unique status, reducing them to having the same language rights as other ethnic minority groups. The Laurier-Greenway compromise allowed Catholic and French-language education to continue in Manitoba for the next two decades. It did not, however, completely resolve the issue. In 1916, the T. C. Norris government, in an effort to anglicize foreigners, eliminated the bilingual schools.[11] French Canadians were caught up in this sweep, as the Laurier-Greenway compromise was ended by the Manitoba government's unilateral action.

The rest of the Northwest followed Manitoba's lead. In 1890, the territories were given the authority to choose their language status and opted to have English as their sole official language in 1892. In 1901, English was made the obligatory language of instruction in schools after the first grade.[12] The unilingual status of Alberta and Saskatchewan was retained when they became provinces in 1905, with the use of French as a language of instruction strictly proscribed. Under Alberta regulations adopted in 1925, French could only be used as the language of instruction for grades 1 and 2. In Saskatchewan, French was only permitted for the first year of instruction under the Schools Act of 1920.[13] Thus, for most of the first half of the twentieth century, French-language rights in education were not officially recognized by the provincial governments in the West, although Manitoba's Department of Education did quietly tolerate the existence of a few rural French-language schools.[14] Otherwise, French-language education could only be obtained in privately run schools that were not recognized by the government.

Francophones in Manitoba attempted to challenge the constitutionality of the Official Language Act, 1890 in the courts. As Raymond Hébert notes, two judicial decisions, *Pellant v. Hébert* (1892) and *Bertrand v. Dussault and Lavoie* (1909), ruled that the Act was unconstitutional. However, the provincial government chose to simply ignore the rulings and did not bother to appeal them. Without an enforcement mechanism, or political clout, the French-Canadian population of Manitoba was unable to obtain justice and have their rights recognized.[15]

Ontario moved more subtly to eliminate French-language rights in education. In 1890, the government stated that English was to be the language of instruction in the province, "except insofar as this is impracticable by reason of the pupil not understanding English;" a regulation which did little to reduce the practice of French-language instruction.[16] As French Catholics and Irish Catholics came into increasing contact in Eastern Ontario schools, the French-Canadian elite was convinced that its "bilingual" schools were threatened by a movement to transform them into English-language schools. They formed the Association canadienne-française d'éducation de l'Ontario (ACFÉO) in 1910 to lobby the government to officially recognize French-language education rights.

ACFÉO was now on a collision course with opponents of French-language schooling.[17] In response to School Inspector F.W. Merchant's report that the province's "bilingual schools" were doing a poor job of teaching English, the Ontario government passed the controversial and provocative Regulation 17 in 1912. Regulation 17 made English the sole language of instruction for the province after grade two, and called for strict enforcement by school inspectors. These restrictions caused an uproar, and the quest to overturn Regulation 17 and officially recognize French-language education rights would be ACFÉO's raison d'être for the next fifty-six years. In 1927, the implementation of Regulation 17 was softened to permit the functioning of "bilingual" elementary schools in practice, but the Regulation was not completely taken off the books, and the province continued to refuse to recognize any right to French-language education.[18]

Thus, by the end of the First World War, French-language rights in education, provincial legislatures, courts, and government services outside of the province of Quebec and the federal government had been eliminated. Grossly outnumbered, the French-Canadian and Acadian minority communities had little clout in their provincial legislatures, limited financial resources, and few political allies. Even a sympathetic federal Prime Minister such as Sir Wilfrid Laurier was only willing to intervene in provincial jurisdiction or in court proceedings on a limited basis. The continued survival of these communities was largely the product of support from the Catholic church and fraternal institutions based in Quebec. Even legal and constitutional protections for language rights were worthless, it seemed, when Manitoba's legislature could run roughshod over its constitutional status as a bilingual province. Without recognition of their language rights, many French-speakers opted for assimilation into the anglophone majority. Yet, about forty years after the end of the First World War, advocates of French-language rights in Canada would have some cause for hope.

Political Will, Financial Resources, and Community Organization: The Resurgence of French-language Rights in Canada

It would not be until 1958 that the right to use either English or French in the federal House of Commons would be made meaningful by the introduction of simultaneous interpretation. It would be from this point forward, as the decolonization movement spread around the world, that language rights in Canada came to the forefront of public discourse. The neglect of French-Canadian interests in the federal civil service, which was overwhelmingly dominated by Anglo-Canadians, began to actively rankle French-speaking Quebecers, who increasingly felt that the federal government was not representing their interests. They also criticized the Quebec government for not adequately addressing the socio-economic needs of francophones. In 1960, the conservative Union Nationale government of Maurice Duplessis fell and was replaced by the interventionist Liberal government of Premier Jean Lesage. This kicked off a period of reform in Quebec known as the Quiet Revolution, which accelerated the reformist trends that had begun in the 1950s to modernize and secularize Quebec's economy and bureaucracy, with an eye to giving French-speaking Quebecers a much more prominent place in the running of their province.[19]

Facing the determination of francophone Quebecers to play an active role in the political and economic life of their province and country, Prime Minister Lester Pearson took the advice of the neo-nationalist editor of Le Devoir, André Laurendeau, and appointed the Royal Commission on Bilingualism and Biculturalism in 1963. Mandated to "inquire into and report upon the existing state of bilingualism and biculturalism in Canada and to recommend what steps should be taken to develop the Canadian Confederation on the basis of an equal partnership between the two founding races …" the formation of this commission marked the beginning of an active federal interest in the needs and rights of French Canadians. The timing was crucial, as Marcel Martel notes, since by the mid-1960s, the pan-Canadian institutional supports of French-Canadian and Acadian minority communities—the Catholic church and Quebec-based fraternal organizations—were in decline, as the church faced diminishing resources, and the identity of francophone Quebecers shifted from a pan-Canadian identity of *Canadiens-français* to a provincially bounded identity of *Québécois*.[20] The Commission undertook a massive study of bilingualism and biculturalism in Canada, producing a five-volume report filled with recommendations on how to promote and protect the English and French languages in Canada. Among the many groups testifying before the commission were the provincial associations representing Acadian and French-Canadian minorities, who rightly saw the Commission as a key opportunity to have their rights protected by the federal government.

Quebec was not the only province where francophones were beginning to exercise their influence. In 1960, New Brunswick, with an Acadian minority comprising over one-third of the population, elected the government of Liberal Premier Louis Robichaud. His government set about enacting an ambitious series of reforms to make the operation of government services more equitable in the province, including in terms of English-French relations. This included the appointment of a francophone Deputy Minister of Education, the creation of new second language requirements for students, and education reforms associated with the 1965 Equal Opportunities Program, which included a uniform provincial taxation system for education and the creation of language-based school districts.[21] In 1969, the Robichaud government passed the Official Languages of New Brunswick Act, legally enshrining English and French as the two official languages of the province, including the right to use either language in the legislature, in the courts, and in government services. The right to an education in either official language was also included.

The major strides made in French-language rights in New Brunswick in the 1960s are at least partly accountable to the political strength of the Acadian community. But one should not discount the political agency of Premier Robichaud, who had to convince anglophone members of his party (and those of the Conservative opposition) to pass these crucial pieces of legislation. Similarly, in Ontario, Conservative Premier John Robarts was beginning to take action to address Franco-Ontarian grievances. Robarts believed that improving the status of the Franco-Ontarians would demonstrate to Quebec's political class that English-Canada was serious about making an effort for the two dominant language communities to live together. As a preliminary step, his Department of Education authorized the teaching of history, geography, and Latin in the French language in the province's public secondary schools over the course of 1963 and 1964.[22] In July

1968, the Ontario government passed Bills 140 and 141, which guaranteed the right of Franco-Ontarians to publicly funded French-language secondary schools, if a minimum number of students could be reached.[23]

Less dramatic, but nonetheless important for the recognition of French-language rights in education, were the reforms introduced in the western Canadian provinces in response to the Royal Commission's calls for the extension of French-language education rights. In 1967, the Manitoba government passed Bill 59, which permitted the use of French as a language of instruction for up to fifty percent of the school day, a move adopted in Alberta and Saskatchewan the following year. The minimal nature of this permissive legislation, however, demonstrates the importance of political leadership and community organizational strength in winning language rights, as these latter gains were quite modest compared to New Brunswick and Ontario. However, this nevertheless reflected government attention to the question of French-language education rights, a topic on which British Columbia, Nova Scotia, Prince Edward Island, and Newfoundland's legislation remained silent.[24]

Aggressive Promotion of Language Rights: The Trudeau Period

The election of Pierre Elliott Trudeau as Prime Minister and head of the Liberal party had a decisive impact on language rights in Canada. A fierce opponent of Quebec neo-nationalism since the 1950s, Trudeau had entered federal politics in an effort to reassert a francophone presence in the national government. He was fiercely opposed to efforts made by the Quebec government to devolve federal powers to the provinces, believing that in order for Canadian federalism to function, both levels of government had to vigorously exercise the powers allotted to them under the Constitution, and both major language communities had to fully participate in the federal government.[24]

As Prime Minister, Trudeau passed the Official Languages Act, 1969, which declared English and French to be Canada's two official languages and included a number of provisions granting Canadians the right to access government services and communications in the official language of their choice at central offices and at regional offices where there was significant demand. The Act further established the office of the Commissioner of Official Languages to monitor infractions of the Act, and to recommend improvements to the government's language services. There was debate over how to determine which regional offices of government departments would offer services and operate in both languages. The proposal of the Royal Commission on Bilingualism and Biculturalism had been to establish criteria for the designation of bilingual districts, following the Finnish model. After six years of study and negotiation, however, it proved politically impossible to establish these criteria, and the bilingual districts scheme was abandoned.[25]

The federal government went even further in terms of fostering language rights. In 1969, it created the Official Language Minority Groups Program (OLMGP) under the Social Action Branch of the Secretary of State Department, which provided funding to provincial minority language organizations in support of their core activities.[26] In essence, the federal government provided funding to organizations that supported its objective of expanding language rights and services in Canada, and which would stimulate the demand for services called for under the Official Languages Act. This also provided a much-needed boost to the cash-starved minority language community associations to carry out their community development and lobbying work.

This program also helped support another federal language rights initiative. In September 1970, Ottawa and the provinces agreed to the creation of the *Federal-provincial programme of cooperation for the promotion of bilingualism in education,* officially renamed the Official Languages in Education Program (OLEP) in 1979. This program was designed to support provincial programs for official language minority education (English-language education in Quebec, French-language education in the rest of Canada) and second-language instructional programs. Ottawa agreed to pay for a percentage of the cost of educating students enrolled in these provincial programs, in the hopes that this would encourage the provinces to expand their program offerings in this sector. The B&B Commission had discussed the creation of a right to official language minority education. However, in 1970 there was a sense that this would be deemed unacceptable in many provinces, and so this route of encouraging the provinces to improve access to their programs was taken.

The OLEP would prove to be a very effective "carrot" in encouraging provinces to take steps to expand their official languages programs. For example, the Manitoba government passed Bill 113, which provided for the guaranteed creation of French-language classes if a minimum number of students were reached. If the number of students was fewer, the Minister could still decide to create these classes.[27] With its core funding largely provided by the OLMGP, the Société franco-manitobaine (SFM) published brochures on the details of Bill 113 and the federal OLEP grants, and organized community meetings to pressure school boards to implement the provisions of the amended School Act and to fulfill the objectives of the OLEP. The SFM also called on the Manitoba government to take an active role in preventing the further assimilation of Franco-Manitobans and to establish French-language units within the Department of Education.[28] In 1974, the province created a *Bureau de l'Éducation Française* to manage the province's French-language education programs.

Similar gains were made in the expansion of French-language education programs across the country. Many provinces created French Immersion programs to provide intensive second-language learning experiences for anglophone students. Other provinces lifted the caps on the maximum time spent on French-language instruction. In 1976, Alberta Minister of Education Julian Koziak announced that his province was raising the ceiling for French-language instruction to eighty percent of the school day, a response to a long-term demand of the Association canadienne-française de l'Alberta (ACFA).[29] In Ontario, francophone federations such as the Association canadienne-française de l'Ontario (ACFO) used the existence of the OLEP funds to pressure the provincial government to create separate facilities for French-language secondary schools in Sturgeon Falls, Essex, and Penetanguishene.

Quebec was a notable exception to this trend of expanding language rights. By the early 1970s, neo-nationalists had decided that the Quebec government needed to become actively involved in the promotion of the French language in both the public and the private sectors. The manner in which the government opted to do so entailed some rather strict restrictions on access to English-language rights. Quebec's Official Language Act (Bill 22), passed by the Liberal government of Robert Bourassa in 1974, declared French to be the only official language of the province. It introduced measures to encourage businesses to francize their daily operations, and restricted access to English-language schools to those students who could pass a test of their English-language skills. More coercive measures were introduced by the Parti Québécois government of René Lévesque elected in 1976. One of his government's first pieces of legislation in 1977, the Charte de la langue française (Bill 101) built on the foundations of the Official Language Act, but went much further with mandatory regulations on the use of French in the workplace and a ban on languages other than French on commercial signs. Access to the English-language minority education system was restricted to the children of parents resident in Quebec when the law was passed who had received their education in English, children already in the English system, and children whose parents or older siblings had been educated in English in Quebec.[30] In effect, any new migrant to the province of Quebec was barred from sending their children to publicly funded English schools, including those from other provinces of Canada.

There was a section of the Charter of the French Language that provided for the possibility for migrants from other provinces to send their children to Quebec's English-language schools. However, this required that their province of origin enter into a reciprocal agreement with Quebec which guaranteed the right to French-language education to migrants from the province of Quebec. Prime Minister Trudeau quickly urged the premiers to reject the Lévesque government's proposed reciprocal agreements, arguing that minority official language education should not be considered a bargaining chip, but a right that should be enshrined in the Constitution. To Lévesque's chagrin, the provinces who were leaders in the provision of minority language education were quick to reject these agreements. Ontario Premier William Davis declared that "an issue as fundamental as language rights in education … should be accepted as a matter of fundamental principle and not be the subject of quid pro quo arrangements."[31] New Brunswick Premier Richard Hatfield took a step further by supporting Ottawa's call for the constitutional entrenchment of minority language education rights.[32]

The expansion of minority language education, funded by the OLEP, had made many of the premiers more comfortable with the concept of minority language education rights, although some, like Manitoba Premier Sterling Lyon, opposed the constitutional entrenchment of these rights. All nine rejected the reciprocal agreements, not wanting to be seen as sympathetic to the sovereignty-association project being pushed by the Parti Québécois. Capitalizing on this crucial juncture for language rights, New Brunswick Premier Richard Hatfield, who was slated to hold a premiers' conference at St. Andrew's in August 1977, attempted to craft a joint provincial response to Lévesque's proposals, which while rejecting the Quebec plan would still indicate that the premiers were not hostile to French-language rights. The agreed-upon declaration stated that the provinces would "make their best efforts to provide instruction in English and French wherever numbers warrant."[33]

In agreeing to this declaration, the provinces were seeking to set the terms of the language education debate themselves, rather than simply agreeing to either Trudeau's or Lévesque's vision. This was a very significant step, as the St. Andrew's declaration was the first time that the nine premiers had come together to publicly declare support for some form of minority language education rights; this declaration would provide the basis for further progress towards constitutional recognition of these rights.[34] The following February, the ten provincial ministers of education agreed to another declaration in Montreal, which stated that: "Each child of the French-speaking and English-speaking minority is entitled to an education in his or her language in the primary or the secondary schools in each province wherever numbers warrant. The implementation of this principle will be as defined by each province."[35] The Montreal declaration was more restrictive than St. Andrew's, limiting language rights to the official language minority populations and leaving interpretation and implementation up to individual provinces. However, the use of "rights talk" was now clearly entering provincial discourse on the language issue.[36]

The Trudeau government's commitment to the expansion of language rights and the revitalization of francophone community associations had numerous impacts in other sectors over the course of the 1970s and early 1980s. In New Brunswick, federal programs provided funding to permit the provincial bureaucracy to hold language training courses that would foster functional bilingualism in the civil service. In Ontario, organizations such as the Conseil des affaires franco-ontariens and ACFO lobbied for the right to government services in French, including a major push for French-language health services.[37] In Manitoba, Georges Forest and Roger Bilodeau challenged the constitutionality of the Official Language Act, winning their cases in the Supreme Court of Canada.[38] At the national level, the Fédération des francophones hors-Québec, a new umbrella organization for French-Canadian and Acadian minority communities, was fighting for the recognition of French-language rights in the government, media, and education.[39]

In the aftermath of the 1980 Quebec referendum on sovereignty-association, Prime Minister Trudeau initiated the process of constitutional reform that would ultimately lead to the passage of the Constitution Act, 1982, which contained the Canadian Charter of Rights and Freedoms. The St. Andrew's and Montreal declarations would prove to be useful leverage for securing provincial consent for the inclusion of language rights in the Charter. Sections 16 to 22 of the Charter enshrined English and French as the official languages of the federal and New Brunswick governments, and the rights of Canadians to use either official language in their Parliaments, courts, and in communications with the head offices of their government departments. Section 23 went further, entrenching the right of Canadian citizens of either official language minority population to have their children receive elementary or secondary school instruction in that language, where numbers warranted. Acceptance of this right had been gradually built up over the course of the 1970s through federal funding programs, supportive bureaucracies, and parental lobbying efforts. By 1982, these programs already existed in most of the country. The constitutional entrenchment of a right to these programs was an important legal step to protect their continued existence, but recognition that this right existed in some form had already been extended by the provincial premiers, thanks to federal and community-based efforts to foster these programs.

Conclusions

The Canadian experience with French-language rights prior to the Canadian Charter of Rights and Freedoms suggests that the conditions for the recognition and exercise of language rights cannot be created by legal texts and conventions alone, although these do provide additional moral weight behind the demands of rights claimants. Several factors were crucial to the development of the Canadian language rights framework in the pre-Charter period. The first, and most obvious, is political power and will. The initial language rights that were created during the Confederation period for federal institutions, Quebec, Manitoba, and the North West and the converse lack of recognition of these rights in other provinces are attributable to the political clout and demographic weight of the francophone populations in these regions. The revitalization of federal government interest in bilingualism and language rights would likely not have been so vigorous in the 1960s and 1970s were it not for the challenge to the Canadian political order posed by Quebec neo-nationalism.

Blunt political power of groups alone cannot account entirely for either the decline or resurgence of language rights in Canada. Individual agency played a key role as well. The personal ideologies and political positioning of individuals such as Louis Riel, D'Alton McCarthy, Louis Robichaud, John Robarts, and Pierre Trudeau played a crucial role in determining the political responses to rights demands in their respective political spheres. Moreover, one should not dismiss the importance of key lobbying activities and community support associations, which first kept francophone communities alive in a period of political repression, and then fought for the expansion of their language rights when faced with opportunities in their political jurisdictions.

This leads us to the often neglected issue of funding and its relationship to the recognition and exploitation of language rights. When the cost of recognition of language rights vis-à-vis government services is perceived as an unsupportable burden on the taxpayer, it becomes easier to eliminate these rights. This clearly played a role in the Prairie provinces when the francophone population became vastly outnumbered by the anglophone majority, and the cost of maintaining French-language services was seen as an excessive expense. Conversely, the willingness of the federal government to shoulder the financial burden of minority language education made it possible for French-Canadian and Acadian community associations to overcome the reluctance of their provincial governments to providing these services, eventually leading to recognition of their right to education in their mother tongue.

So too does federalism occupy a crucial place in the dynamic of Canadian language rights recognition. Throughout Canadian history, the recognition of language rights in the political jurisdictions of the country has resembled a patchwork quilt of different degrees of legal recognition of rights, provision of government services in the minority language, and political approaches to the language question. At times, the divided jurisdictions under the Canadian system of federalism has been used to justify a decision by one government not to interfere when it believed language rights were being trampled upon by another, such as Quebec's response to the New Brunswick Schools Question of the 1870s, or Ottawa's response to Manitoba's Official Language Act. Moreover, an absence of political will to defend and respect codified language rights could render these rights meaningless, as it did in Manitoba for the better part of the twentieth century. Since the 1960s, however, the federal government has found ways to work within the federal system to influence the actions of other jurisdictions. Funding programs using the federal spending power, support of third-party organizations, and mobilization of personal networks at the bureaucratic level all proved to be effective strategies for building up institutional support for recognition of language rights, overcoming the reluctance of provincial governments to speak in terms of rights rather than privileges.

Thus, in order to understand the development and functioning of language rights in Canada, a host of bureaucratic, political, financial, and even personality-based factors must be considered, going beyond the legal and constitutional language that is often mistakenly viewed as the only source of language rights. In the absence of a clear-cut claim to status as fundamental human rights, language rights claimants in Canada have had to manoeuvre through a complicated political web to have these rights recognized, a process that is ongoing even now, almost a quarter-century after these rights were incorporated into the Charter.

Notes

1   C. Michael MacMillan, *The Practice of Language Rights in Canada* (Toronto: University of Toronto Press, 1998), 32–3.

2   Will Kymlicka, *Finding Our Way: Rethinking Ethnocultural Relations in Canada* (New York: Oxford University Press, 1998); Charles Taylor, *Reconciling the Solitudes: Essays on Canadian Federalism and Nationalism* (Montreal & Kingston: McGill-Queen's University Press, 1993).

3   MacMillan, *Practice of Language Rights*, 15–22.

4   Professor Fernand de Varennes, currently of Murdoch University, Australia, recently expanded upon this theme in his paper "Implementing International Language Rights Standards: Challenges, Difficulties and Possibilities," presented at the Language Law and Language Rights Conference, June 14–17, 2006 in Galway, Ireland, organized by the International Academy of Linguistic Law. Several other papers at this conference expressed a similar outlook.

5   Arthur I. Silver, *The French-Canadian Idea of Confederation*, 2nd Edition (Toronto: University of Toronto Press, 1997), 33–55.

6   Raymond Hébert, *Manitoba's French-Language Crisis: A Cautionary Tale* (Montreal: McGill-Queen's University Press, 2004), 7–9.

7   Silver, 105.

8   Gilberte Couturier LeBlanc, Alcide Godin, and Aldéo Renaud, "French Education in the Maritimes, 1604–1992," in Jean Daigle, ed., *Acadia of the Maritimes* (Moncton: Chaire d'études acadiennes, 1995), 532–3.

9   Official Language Act, S.M. 1890, c. 14.

10 Hébert, *Manitoba's French-Language Crisis*, 10–12; An Act Respecting the Department of Education, S.M. 1890, c. 37; An Act Respecting Public Schools, S.M. 1890, c. 38.

11 R. C. Brown and Ramsay Cook, *Canada 1896–1921* (Toronto: McClelland & Stewart, 1974), 259.

12 Gratien Allaire, "Le rapport à l'autre: l'évolution de la francophonie de l'Ouest," in Joseph-Yvon Thériault, ed., *Francophonies minoritaires au Canada: l'état des lieux.* (Moncton: Éditions d'Acadie, 1999), 172.

13 "Histoire des francophones de la Saskatchewan," *Revue de l'Association canadienne d'éducateurs de langue française* 6(2) (novembre 1977): 26.

14 Paul-Emile Leblanc, "L'enseignement français au Manitoba, 1916–1968," M.A. diss. (University of Ottawa, 1969).

15 Hébert, *Manitoba's French-Language Crisis*, 15–16.

16 Robert Choquette, *Language and Religion: A History of English-French Conflict in Ontario* (Ottawa: University of Ottawa Press, 1975), 57.

17 Choquette, 45–81.

18 Louis-Gabriel Bordeleau,, Roger Bernard, and Benoît Cazabon, "L'éducation en Ontario français," in Joseph Yvon Thériault, ed., *Francophonies minoritaires au Canada: l'état des lieux* (Moncton: Éditions d'Acadie, 1999), 444.

19 For a much more comprehensive account of these changes, see Michael Behiels, *Prelude to Quebec's Quiet Revolution* (Montreal: McGill-Queen's University Press, 1985) or Kenneth McRoberts, *Quebec: Social Change and Political Crisis* (Toronto: McClelland & Stewart, 1993).

20 Marcel Martel, *Le deuil d'un pays imagine* (Ottawa: Presses de l'Université d'Ottawa, 1997).

21 Della Stanley, *Louis Robichaud: A Decade of Power* (Halifax: Nimbus Publishing, 1984), 156.

22 Archives of Ontario (AO), RG 2-200, Council for Franco-Ontarian Education, Acc. 22309, Box 5, File: Federal-Provincial—CMEC—Éducation dans la langue de la minorité 1977, Part 1—Elementary and Secondary Levels—history and current status of language education.

23 Brigitte Bureau, *Mêlez-vous de vos affaires: 20 ans de luttes franco-ontariennes* (Ottawa: l'Association canadienne française de l'Ontario, 1989), 25.

24 Pierre Elliott Trudeau, "The New Treason of the Intellectuals," in *Federalism and the French Canadians* (Toronto: MacMillan, 1968), 151–181.

25 Daniel Bourgeois, *Canadian Bilingual Districts: From Cornerstone to Tombstone* (Montreal: McGill-Queen's University Press, 2006).

26 See Leslie Pal, *Interests of State: The Politics of Language, Multiculturalism and Feminism in Canada* (Montreal: McGill-Queen's University Press, 1993), for a detailed analysis of the impact of this program.

27 Raymond Hébert, "Historique de la législation scolaire au Manitoba," *Revue de l'Association canadienne d'éducation de langue française* 6(2) (1976): 11.

28 Centre du patrimoine Saint-Boniface (CP), S1 - SFM, 44/7 Education, Brief submitted to the Minister of Education, Saul Miller, by the SFM, February 1971.

29 Provincial Archives of Alberta (PAA), 85.360, Association canadienne-française de l'Alberta (ACFA), Box 1, File: Réunions et autres documents—Bureau de l'éducation— ACFA 1978 (1), Statement by Peter Lougheed and Education Minister Julian Koziak re: Minority Language Instruction, 24 February 1978.

30 Alison D'Anglejan, "Language Planning in Quebec: An Historical Overview and Future Trends," in Richard Bourhis, ed., *Conflict and Language Planning in Quebec* (Clevedon: Multilingual Matters, 1984), 41.

31 AO, RG 58-9-1, Ministry of Intergovernmental Affairs, TR 83-1499, Box 52, File: SD 7g—Bilingualism—Quebec Language Policy, Letter from Premier Davis to Premier Lévesque, 21 July 1977.

32 Provincial Archives of New Brunswick (PANB), RS 417 Richard Hatfield, Box 16-14-9-1, File 2320-2 Minority Language 1978, Letter from Premier Hatfield to Alex Morris, Quebec Federation of Home and School Associations, 13 March 1978.

33 William Johnson, Robert Williamson, and Jeffrey Simpson, "Leaders pledge school rights, but no pacts," *The Globe and Mail*, 20 August 1977, 1.

34 MacMillan, *Practice of Language Rights in Canada*, 78–82.

35 Provincial Archives of Alberta (PAA), 85.360, ACFA, Box 22, File: Dossier éducation et dossier constitutionnel ACFA 1981, Statement of Policy and Legislation for Providing instruction in languages other than English in Alberta, January 1981.

36 More details on the evolution of the OLEP and the St. Andrew's declaration can be found in Matthew Hayday, *Bilingual Today, United Tomorrow: Official Languages in Education and Canadian Federalism* (Montreal: McGill-Queen's University Press, 2005).

37 Matthew Hayday, "Pas de problème: The Development of French Language Health Services in Ontario, 1968–86," *Ontario History* 94(2) (Fall 2002): 183–200.

38 Hébert, *Manitoba's French-Language Crisis*.

39 In 1977, the Fédération and its constituent provincial associations published a manifesto and action plan of the changes they were seeking for language rights in Canada. Fédération des francophones hors Québec, *Les héritiers du Lord Durham* (Ottawa: FFHQ, 1977).

Glossary

Anglophone. An individual whose primary language of communication and/or mother tongue is English.

Confessional. A term used to refer to a religion-based system. In Canada, this normally refers to either Catholic or Protestant education rights.

Federalism. A political system in which most or all elements of the state—executive, legislative, judiciary, taxation mechanisms—are duplicated at two levels, which cover the same territory and population, and neither level of government or set of structures can abolish the other's jurisdiction. In Canada, this system divides authority between the federal government and the provincial governments.

Francization. The process whereby businesses and other institutions convert to French as the language of work.

Francophone. An individual whose primary language of communication and/or mother tongue is French.

Further Reading

Behiels, Michael. *Canada's Francophone Minority Communities: Constitutional Renewal and the Winning of School Governance.* Montreal & Kingston: McGill-Queen's University Press, 2004.

Behiels traces the development of French-Canadian rights in education from the adoption of the Charter of Rights and Freedoms to when these communities won the legal right to govern their own schools. He focuses on how this process was shaped by the constitutional battles of the 1980s and 1990s and the strategies employed by francophone minority communities.

Bourgeois, Daniel. *Canadian Bilingual Districts: From Cornerstone to Tombstone*. Montreal & Kingston: McGill-Queen's University Press, 2006.

Bourgeois traces the development of the "bilingual districts" concept of the Official Languages Act, which was intended to cover language rights for federal government employees. He demonstrates how internal governmental processes ultimately led to the abandonment of this concept by the mid-1970s, leaving language rights in the federal bureaucracy in a state of limbo.

Hayday, Matthew. *Bilingual Today, United Tomorrow: Official Languages in Education and Canadian Federalism*. Montreal & Kingston: McGill-Queen's University Press, 2005.

Hayday traces the development of language rights in education from the Official Languages Act through to the 1990s. He demonstrates how federal support for official languages programs in education, coupled with interest group activism and supportive bureaucracies, helped to solidify language rights in education prior to the adoption of the Charter of Rights and Freedoms, and then helped these programs to rapidly expand.

MacMillan, C. Michael. *The Practice of Language Rights in Canada*. Toronto: University of Toronto Press, 1998.

MacMillan examines how a number of different groups in Canada have made claims to language rights, and the extent to which these rights have been recognized in law and public policy. Through his comparative analysis of how these rights have been recognized, he attempts to suggest broad outlines for a consensus on a conception of language rights.

Silver, Arthur. *The French-Canadian Idea of Confederation, 1864–1900*. Toronto: University of Toronto Press, 1982.

Silver examines the manner by which French-Canadian rights were incorporated into the British North America Act, and how they were subsequently applied. He notes that the constitutional protections for minority language rights were actually quite weak, but that Quebec-based politicians were reluctant to call on the federal government to intervene when these rights were violated, for fear of federal intervention in Quebec's jurisdiction.

Relevant Websites

Canadian Heritage
www.pch.gc.ca

The Department of Canadian Heritage is the branch of the federal government responsible for implementing programs to promote and protect official language rights in Canada, including funding programs to promote minority language education and community supports.

Fédération des communautés francophones et acadiennes du Canada
www.fcfa.ca/home/index.cfm

This is the national umbrella organization for the major associations representing Canada's francophone and Acadian communities.

International Academy of Linguistic Law
www.iall-aidl.org

The International Academy of Linguistic Law is an international multidisciplinary organization that brings together jurists, linguists, social scientists, and all those worldwide who are interested, scientifically or professionally, in issues pertaining to linguistic diversity as well as to law and language.

Language Fairness
www.languagefairness.ca

Canadians for Language Fairness is a lobby group opposed to the implementation of official bilingualism in Canada. It is one of the most recent groups of its kind, which have included the Alliance for the Preservation of English in Canada and Canadians Against Bilingualism Injustice.

Official Languages
www.ocol.gc.ca

The Commissioner of Official Languages is Canada's independent commissioner responsible for overseeing the implementation of the Official Languages Act. At various points in its history, this office has also been an advocate for a more vigorous promotion of language rights.

CHAPTER 11

PIERRE ELLIOTT TRUDEAU'S LEGACY:

THE CANADIAN CHARTER OF RIGHTS AND FREEDOMS

MICHAEL D. BEHIELS

I have long believed that freedom is the most important value of a just society, and the exercise of freedom its principal characteristic. Without these, a human being could not hope for true fulfillment—an individual in society could not realize his or her full potential. And deprived of its freedom, a people could not pursue its own destiny—the destiny that best suits its collective will to live.[1]

—Pierre Elliott Trudeau

Introduction

The 1982 *Canadian Charter of Rights and Freedoms*[2] is the luminous diamond in Pierre Elliott Trudeau's legacy to Canadians and citizens of the world. The Charter is uniquely Canadian. Why? Because it is a hybrid document combining conventional fundamental freedoms with minority collective rights. How does one explain the distinctiveness of Canada's Charter? It was the product of interplay between character—Pierre Elliott Trudeau—and circumstance—Quebec's authoritarian politics of the 1930 to 1960 era and its subsequent neo-nationalist and secessionist "Quiet" and "Not-So-Quiet" revolutions. Trudeau's character was forged in this hothouse environment. Thanks to his informal and formal educations and the profound influence of his social democratic mentor, Frank Scott, Trudeau emerged a strong civil libertarian and anti-nationalist. The emergence of Québécois secessionist movements in the 1960s radicalized dramatically the political and constitutional agendas of Quebec's political and intellectual classes. By the late 1960s, these developments undermined Canadians' relatively weak sense of identity, threatened their fundamental freedoms, and attacked the legitimacy of the Canadian nation-state. Trudeau, the visionary Minister of Justice in 1967, responded to the crisis by conceiving a hybrid charter, one protecting fundamental rights and promoting a stronger sense of Canadian identity to counter Quebec's secessionist movement. He declared that:

… the adoption of a constitutional Bill of Rights is intimately related to the whole question of constitutional reform. Essentially, we will be testing—and, hopefully, establishing—the unity of Canada. If we reach agreement on the fundamental rights of the citizen, on their definition and protection in all parts of Canada, we shall have taken a major first step toward basic constitutional reform.[3]

Trudeau understood that public opinion had to be swayed to accept his hybrid charter. It was relatively easy to convince ordinary Canadians about the advantages of entrenching fundamental rights and freedoms in a renewed Constitution. It was far more challenging to persuade them that it was necessary to protect the rights of minority communities—official language minorities, Aboriginal peoples, and ethno-cultural communities. Fundamental freedoms and minority rights became partners in the same charter. The momentous achievement of the Charter, coming after 15 years of mega-constitutional negotiations, reflected the maturation of Canadian society, indeed, a long overdue democratization of its national and regional political cultures. Prior to Trudeau becoming Prime Minister in 1968, Canadians shared, and largely accepted, very elitist, deferential political cultures. The formulation of public policy, on small as well as significant matters, resided in the hands of their national and provincial political leaders. When it came to addressing and, ideally, resolving national unity conflicts—especially matters concerning the place of the French-Canadian minority within Confederation—a closed-door process of elite accommodation was the norm.[4]

Canada's founding Constitution, the *British North America Act, 1867*,[5] did not contain a ringing declaration of the sovereignty of the Canadian people but a rather narrow form of representative democracy. Its central clauses dealt with the distribution of powers between Ottawa and the provinces. Consequently, the vast majority of Canadians showed little interest in this British statute. Only when the distribution of powers affected them directly—provincial struggles for control over taxes and resources or Ottawa's desire to establish a social welfare state—did Canadians concern themselves with the flaws of Canadian federalism. The fact that Canada's political leaders failed for over a century to agree on an amending formula—enabling the patriation and Canadianization of the *BNA Act, 1867*—reinforced the accepted view that Canada's Constitution remained quasi-colonial. Canada was not fully independent and the Canadian people were not sovereign.[6] The *Constitution Act, 1982*[7] and the Charter, in sweeping away the last vestige of British colonialism, constitute a major watershed in Canada's political and constitutional development. Canadians now share a more democratic political culture and possess the constitutional tools to refashion their constitutional future.

The impact of the Charter has been far more comprehensive than either its supporters or critics could ever have imagined. The Charter, as a symbol of shared values and citizenship, has proven to be far more popular among Canadians than even its most optimistic supporters predicted. More importantly, the Charter's popularity has not been eroded by two decades of vociferous criticism from right- and left-wing Charterphobes. Early academic and political critics—contending that rights and federalism are incompatible in a liberal state—campaigned aggressively for a regime of dual charters, Canadian and Quebec. Later critics—focusing on how the Charter is transforming the executive, legislative, and judicial branches of government in ways that were largely unforeseen—have targeted

Canada's Supreme Court. In an attempt to delegitimize the Supreme Court, these critics denounce its neo-liberal, anti-democratic interpretation of the Charter. The Supreme Court justices are promoting the collective interests of Charter Canadians—a myriad of civil libertarian, Aboriginal, feminist, official language minority, and ethno-cultural organizations dubbed the Court Party by their critics—at the expense of Canadians' individual rights.[8] More significantly though, the Charter is profoundly altering the way Canadians and their organizations view their place in Canadian society as well as the way they relate to all three branches of government. This larger debate is just getting underway. The Charter will continue to transform Canadian society, its governance, and its national and regional political cultures. Most assuredly, it will continue to mould and strengthen Canadians' sense of identity for many decades to come. Canadians are just beginning to analyze and explain this remarkable metamorphosis. Indeed, no other Canadian politician has left such a unique, progressive, and enduring legacy as Pierre Elliott Trudeau. The profound influence of the *Canadian Charter of Rights and Freedoms* on Canadians and their society will reverberate far beyond Canada's shores for decades to come.

★★★★★

The Charter of Rights as an Instrument of Minority Rights and National Unity, 1960–1980

Trudeau hoped to use the emerging crisis—created by the election of a separatist government in Quebec and the incessant demands of western premiers for greater decentralization of the federation—to convince Canadians to support his approach to national unity. He believed he could convince them that freedom and equality, the core values of any just society, were being systematically denied to Canadian citizens thereby weakening national unity. Beginning in 1976, he repeatedly invited the premiers to join him in a new round of mega-constitutional negotiations.[9] In a document entitled *A Time for Action: Toward the Renewal of the Canadian Federation*, Trudeau presented a convincing range of arguments for a comprehensive charter of rights and freedoms entrenching citizens' fundamental civil liberties as well as language and education rights for Canada's official language minority communities. "The unity of Canada," Trudeau argued persuasively, "must transcend the identification Canadians have with provinces, regions and linguistic or other differences. But for Canada to be deserving of the transcendant [sic] loyalty that such unity involves, there must be a sense that it does serve, as a country, the vital needs of all its citizens and communities."[10] Trudeau was convinced that a hybrid charter—in transferring sovereignty to the people by limiting the power of the state, federal and provincial—would foster the development of national identity so crucial to undermining the ever-dangerous secessionist Quebec government.

Prime Minister Trudeau, it seemed, would never get the opportunity to achieve his goal. The premiers' lists of demands, in exchange for a charter, grew longer year by year. Trudeau refused to trade Charter rights for more provincial powers. In the 1979 election, Joe Clark's Progressive Conservatives defeated the Trudeau government. Trudeau gave notice that he intended to retire from politics. In a strange twist of fate, Clark's minority Conservative government was defeated on its poorly managed budget. By offering Trudeau a final opportunity to defeat the Quebec secessionists and bring in his charter, loyal supporters convinced him to return. The task was not too difficult since Trudeau was stung by George Radwanski's biography, which portrayed Trudeau as an unfulfilled prime minister.[11] Few politicians ever get a second opportunity to leave a lasting legacy. Having been handed that chance, Trudeau was convinced that for the sake of national unity he would not, could not, fail. Winning the 1980 national election in great style—taking 74 out of 75 seats in Quebec—Trudeau declared on election night, "Welcome to the 1980s!" He promised Canadians that he intended to fight the Quebec secessionists and then move quickly on constitutional renewal.[12]

Trudeau's Successful Campaign for a Dual-purpose *Canadian Charter of Rights and Freedoms*

Determined to win the Quebec referendum, the Trudeau government did everything in its power to convince francophone Quebecers that it was not in their political or economic interests to vote for secession. When it became clear that Claude Ryan, leader of the Quebec Liberal Party, was no match for René Lévesque and the Parti Québécois, Trudeau sent in his most trusted and experienced Minister, Jean Chrétien, to head up the NO campaign. Quebec Liberal and Conservative politicians and senators campaigned vigorously for the NO Committee. Trudeau weighed in with four timely and very powerful speeches in which he warned that voting Yes to secession would create a major political crisis. He reminded everyone that neither he nor the premiers had a mandate to negotiate the breakup of the country. On the contrary, under the Constitution it was his responsibility to maintain the territorial integrity of Canada. In a calculated move to bind the premiers to his agenda, Trudeau promised that if a majority of Quebecers voted No to secession his government would proceed immediately with constitutional renewal. Despite a shaky start, the NO forces won a resounding victory, 60 to 40 per cent. Trudeau was overjoyed that the NO forces had triumphed over the Parti Québécois's ambiguous and misleading question on sovereignty-association.[13]

As promised, Trudeau proceeded quickly and decisively. He surrounded himself with a team of tough-minded advisors, including Michael Kirby, his executive assistant, and Michael Pitfield, Clerk of the Privy Council. Over the summer, his Minister of Justice, Jean Chrétien, visited the premiers to tell them that Ottawa would move unilaterally if

they were unwilling to cooperate in a limited package of constitutional reforms comprising the Victoria Charter's amending formula, patriation, and a basic charter of rights and
freedoms. True to form, the premiers demanded additional powers in exchange for a
charter. Trudeau restated his position: Ottawa would not swap the charter, his "people's
package," for more powers to the provinces. The breakup of the September 1980 federal/
provincial conference was a foregone conclusion. Encouraged by his cabinet and caucus,
Trudeau decided to proceed with a comprehensive "people's package" charter, including
a full range of rights and freedoms as well as linguistic and education rights for Canada's
official language minorities. Initially, the government tried to limit the scope of the tele-
vised parliamentary hearings on its constitutional resolution. But once it realized that
most of the witnesses favoured the charter and wanted substantial improvements, the
government decided to use the Joint House and Senate Committee proceedings to give
its "people's package" much greater visibility and political legitimacy.[14]

Given the political and judicial counterattack launched by the "Gang of Eight"
premiers, Trudeau required all the public support his "people's package" could muster.
The premiers, except Bill Davis of Ontario and Richard Hatfield of New Brunswick,
were determined to derail Trudeau's constitutional package. First, they argued that the
Charter undermined legislative sovereignty and that the region-based amending formula
undermined the equality of the provinces. René Lévesque rejected Trudeau's "people's
package" because, if passed, it would end his party's struggle for any form of sovereignty-
association. The premiers lobbied in London to convince the Thatcher Conservative
government not to consider a patriation bill that was not supported by all the provinces.
Second, they challenged the constitutional validity of Ottawa's patriation bill in the courts
of Quebec, Newfoundland, and Manitoba. The Manitoba[15] and Quebec[16] courts ruled
that the patriation bill was constitutional. The Newfoundland court[17] ruled that it was
illegal. Meanwhile, Joe Clark's Conservative party prevented the passage of the constitutional resolution by refusing to allow it to come to a vote. Trudeau agreed to put off a
final vote on the patriation bill until after the Supreme Court's ruling on his government's
patriation reference. The eight opposing premiers proposed a limited patriation package
comprising a 7/50 amending formula; that is, 7 provinces comprising 50 per cent of the
Canadian population, the right of fiscal compensation for any province opting out of a
constitutional amendment, and the right of Parliament to delegate legislative authority to
any province. There was no mention of a charter. Surprisingly, Lévesque agreed to relin-
quish Quebec's alleged constitutional veto. Apparently, he was convinced that the "Gang
of Eight" alliance guaranteed the defeat of the Trudeau government's patriation bill.[18]

Much to Trudeau's shock and dismay, the Supreme Court justices produced an unexpected and unorthodox two-part ruling on the patriation reference.[19] First, they ruled,
seven judges to two, that the Liberal government's unilateral patriation bill was legal.
Second, by a majority of six to three, they ruled that, although legal, the unilateral

patriation bill did not accord with what they considered was a constitutional convention requiring that Ottawa obtain the support of a "substantial number" of provinces before proceeding with its patriation bill. The Trudeau government won the legal battle but lost the political battle.[20] Trudeau disagreed fundamentally with the Supreme Court's ruling but waited for his retirement before expressing his incisive criticism of the Court's confusing and unsubstantiated patriation decision.[21] Prime Minister Trudeau was disappointed because the questionable decision, requiring that he consult the premiers once again, invariably would force him to accept unwanted amendments to bring several provinces on side.

The November 1981 federal-provincial conference was Trudeau's most dramatic and most crucial. All of his tremendous efforts on behalf of national unity hung in the balance. He knew that he had to break the "Gang of Eight" if there was any hope of obtaining the "substantial number" of provinces called for by the Supreme Court. Ready to make strategic but not substantive concessions to achieve his goal, Trudeau set out to isolate René Lévesque by proposing a referendum on the amending formula and Charter within two years of patriation. Lévesque jumped at the offer, convinced that he could defeat Trudeau the second time around. When he realized his terrible tactical mistake, it was too late. His decision confirmed growing doubts among his provincial allies about his loyalty to the "Gang." The premiers were conscious that a large majority of Canadians favoured patriation, an amending formula, and a charter of rights and freedoms. Neither would Canadians countenance any further obstructionism and delay. Two premiers, Allan Blakeney of Saskatchewan and Bill Davis of Ontario, appointed their Attorneys General, Roy Romanow and Roy McMurtry, to hammer out a deal with the federal Minister of Justice, Jean Chrétien. In the kitchen of Ottawa's National Congress Centre, the three cobbled together a deal. The premiers would accept Trudeau's charter if they obtained a "notwithstanding" legislative override clause in it. Trudeau would have to give up his region-based amending formula (giving Quebec a veto) for the Alberta 7/50 amending formula based on the equality of the provinces. And, there would be no deadlock-breaking referendum mechanism.

Initially, Trudeau rejected the deal because it weakened the Charter. "I saw the Charter," he recalled in his memoirs, "as an expression of my long-held view that the subject of law must be the individual human being; the law must permit the individual to fulfil himself or herself to the utmost. Therefore the individual has certain basic rights that cannot be taken away by any government. So, maintaining a strong Charter was important to me in this basic philosophical sense. Besides, in another dimension, the Charter was defining a system of values such as liberty, equality, and the rights of association that Canadians from coast to coast could share."[22] Since Trudeau conceived of the Charter as Ottawa's primary instrument in the enhancement of Canadian identity and national unity, it was very painful for him to make compromises. He agreed with the "notwithstanding" clause on the condition that it did not apply to sections 16 to 23 protecting the rights of Canada's official language minorities. But compromise he must. Why? Because Premier Davis of Ontario, who had been his staunch ally from the outset, informed Trudeau that both he and Premier Hatfield supported the "kitchen" deal. Neither would remain allied with the Canadian government if Trudeau proceeded to London with an unamended patriation bill. Trudeau had his back against the wall. It was too risky for his government to proceed unilaterally since UK Prime Minister Margaret Thatcher's Conservative government did not support the Charter. A reluctant Trudeau agreed to the deal and took it to the premiers. To his surprise, nine premiers agreed with the "kitchen" deal, leaving the very bitter and angry separatist premier of Quebec on the sidelines. No premier wanted to be seen as opposing the popular Charter by siding inadvertently with René Lévesque.[23] While Trudeau complained bitterly that he did not get his ideal charter, he was wise enough to appreciate that it was far better than no charter. Furthermore, it was premier Lévesque, not he, who was responsible for giving up Quebec's historic veto. It was the separatist premier of Quebec who had put himself and his government in the untenable situation of not being able to participate constructively in the renewal of Canada's Constitution. Trudeau was firmly convinced that Canadians had found, in their Charter, a new and very powerful instrument of shared citizenship and national unity.

Implementing, Challenging, and Defending the *Canadian Charter of Rights and Freedoms*

Queen Elizabeth II proclaimed the *Constitution Act, 1982*[24] with its Charter on April 17, 1982, in a brief ceremony on Parliament Hill. The sky was overcast and the ceremony was cut short by a downpour, perhaps an omen of the controversy that would swirl around the Charter over the next two decades. Since then, left- and right-wing opponents continue to challenge the Charter's legitimacy and to charge that an overly activist, non-deferential Supreme Court is undermining parliamentary sovereignty. The battle over the interpretation and scope of Charter rights and its impact upon Canadian institutions and society has occurred in three intertwined and overlapping phases. In phase one, Charter Canadians lobbied politicians, bureaucrats, and eventually the courts to ensure a liberal interpretation and a timely implementation of their mandated rights and freedoms. Several important victories for holders of section 15, equality rights, and section 23, official language minority education rights, sparked heated debates between Charter advocates and opponents. In phase two, Charter critics—arguing that true federalism and rights are incompatible in a liberal state—lobbied for dual charters, Quebec and Canadian. Indeed, the re-opening of mega-constitutional negotiations by Prime Minister Brian Mulroney and Premier Bourassa gave some ambitious and determined anti-Charter premiers and their governments the opportunity to attempt to limit the scope of the Charter. In the third and most recent phase, further victories by Charter federalists fuelled a heated "jurocracy versus democracy" debate among academics, constitutional experts, and political leaders. Over the past decade, Supreme Court justices have become the focus of a political firestorm over their interpretation of the Charter. Vocal Charter critics, mostly located in western Canada and backed by the right-wing, populist Reform/Canadian Alliance party, allege that an overly activist, non-deferential Supreme Court threatens both individual rights and parliamentary supremacy. This vociferous debate has extended into the inner sanctum of the Supreme Court as individual justices have felt compelled to side with either the school of judicial activism or the school of judicial deference.

In phase one, Charter Canadians championed a broad and liberal interpretation of their rights followed by the federal and provincial governments' quick and comprehensive implementation of these mandated rights. The literature on the Charter groups, including corporations, who have made successful use of the Charter, is quite extensive and will expand as scholars continue to analyze the impact of the Charter on these groups and Canadian society in general.[25] My current research focuses on Canada's Francophone minority communities and the role played by their national and provincial organizations in securing constitutional recognition for, and then implementation of, their linguistic education rights.[26] Throughout the 1970s, Francophone organizations lobbied successfully for the entrenchment of the *Official Languages Act, 1969* with the addition of education rights for Canada's official language minorities in any new charter. Premier Lévesque and his Parti Québécois government fought the addition of education rights to the bitter end since these would render unconstitutional Bill 101's Quebec clause, which compelled Canadian citizens moving to Quebec to enroll their children in French-language schools. With the Charter's section 23 education rights Canadian citizens won the right to move to Quebec and enroll their children in English-language schools.[27] Furthermore, thanks to the Supreme Court's liberal and remedial interpretation of section 23 rights, Francophone Canadian parents won the right to manage and control minority Francophone schools and school boards in every Canadian province.[28]

Interestingly, the framers of section 23 rights, the Prime Minister and the premiers, had never intended that section 23 rights include full school governance by the official language minority communities. Nevertheless, national and provincial Francophone leaders and their organizations were determined that section 23 education rights had to be interpreted as collective rights; that is, the right of the Francophone minority communities to control and manage their own system of French-language, public and Catholic, schools and school boards. Their lengthy and expensive political and judicial battles with several provincial governments led them through the provincial courts all the way to the Supreme Court. In three landmark decisions—*Mahé*,[29] *Reference re Public Schools Act (Manitoba)*,[30] and *Arsenault-Cameron*,[31] the Supreme Court ruled that section 23 rights entailed, where numbers warranted, a sliding-scale of school governance rights beginning with power-sharing within majority English-language boards and extending all the way to fully autonomous French-language boards. Reluctant provincial governments eventually complied with the Supreme Court ruling by amending their education acts to facilitate the creation of publicly funded, French-language classes, schools, and school boards. Even the Parti Québécois government, when Lucien Bouchard was still Premier, obtained Ottawa's cooperation for a bilateral constitutional amendment abolishing subsections 93(1) to 93(4) of the *Constitution Act, 1867*, which mandated Quebec's dual denominational school systems.[32] Premier Bouchard replaced the denominational school systems with two linguistic systems, one French and the other English. The English-language system is demographically limited because Quebec's Anglophone community is declining through out-migration and because it cannot recruit immigrants into its schools. Nevertheless, the Charter prevents any Quebec government from abolishing the education rights of its dwindling English-language minority.[33]

While the various battles over the interpretation and implementation of Charter rights was underway, two dramatic but ultimately unsuccessful political attempts were made to limit the scope of the Charter. Fuelling this anti-Charter political movement was the unsubstantiated assertion, advanced by academics and politicians, that the Charter and federalism are incompatible. They perceive the Charter as a powerful centralizing and homogenizing force destroying two fundamental components of Canadian federalism, that is, provincial autonomy and the two-nations territorial conception of duality, Quebec and Canada.[34] No one, least of all former Prime Minister Trudeau, expected the very integrity of the Charter to be challenged so directly and forcefully within the first few years of its existence. What was even more surprising was that it was Trudeau's successor, Prime Minister Brian Mulroney, working in tandem with a highly nationalistic Quebec Premier, Robert Bourassa, who led the unexpected attack on the Charter. It was unexpected because Mulroney had publicly supported the *Constitution Act, 1982* with its Charter.[35] The highly ambitious and short-sighted Mulroney, encouraged by his secessionist friend and political supporter, Lucien Bouchard, made a political deal with Québécois nationalists and secessionists to obtain their votes in the 1984 federal election. Falling prey to the Parti Québécois's fabricated myth that Quebec had been deliberately excluded from the *Constitution Act, 1982*, Mulroney promised to reintegrate Quebec into the Canadian Constitution family. Consequently, Canadians found themselves once again thrust into the vortex of mega-constitutional politics.

The controversial Meech Lake Constitutional Accord of 1987 was Mulroney's first ill-fated attempt to fulfill his promise. Bourassa's first, and most important, of five conditions for accepting the *Constitution Act, 1982* was the Accord's amendments redefining Canada as two nations, a French-speaking Canada and an English-speaking Canada, and instructing the courts to interpret the entire Constitution, including the Charter, in a way that recognized Quebec as a "distinct society" within Canada. The Accord then mandated the legislature and government of Quebec to "preserve and promote" its "distinct society." The Quebec government was empowered, in Trudeau's words, "to subordinate the rights of every individual Canadian living within its borders to the rights of a chosen community, presumably the French-speaking majority."[36] Quebec would no longer have to use section 33, the notwithstanding clause, to shield discriminatory legislation against the Charter. All it had to do was invoke the powerful "distinct society" interpretative clause to justify any legislation that restricted its citizens' democratic, mobility, and linguistic rights. Other provincial governments, as they insisted, had a very limited responsibility to "preserving" their French-language minority communities. This narrowly defined role, they hoped, would enable them to fend off pressures to declare their governments officially bilingual while allowing them to deny Francophone-minority communities school governance.[37]

The Quebec "distinct society" clause, when combined with the wholesale decentralist thrust of the Meech Lake Accord's four other elements granted to every province, created a groundswell of opposition from Canadians in every region. Indeed, Québécois nationalists and separatists denounced the deal as being far too little far too late.[38] Speaking before the Joint Committee of the House of Commons and the Senate, Trudeau articulated a scathing critique of every aspect of the Meech Lake Accord.[39] "It was revolutionary," Trudeau informed the Special Joint Committee, "because its provisions would quickly transform Canada from a genuinely balanced federation, one in which the Canadian nation-state was greater than the sum of its provinces and territories, into a decentralized confederation dominated by provincial potentates intent on serving their own agendas."[40] Concerned Canadians, who intuitively trusted Trudeau on constitutional matters, paid close attention.

Newly elected New Brunswick, Newfoundland, and Manitoba premiers, responding to pressure from the Accord's growing legion of critics, insisted that the Meech Lake Accord be amended before they proceeded with ratification. Mulroney and Bourassa chanted that the Accord was a "seamless web" not to be reopened. Their intransigence produced a classical political standoff until the very last week before the Accord's ratification deadline on June 22, 1990. Fearing a political firestorm from Quebec's nationalists and secessionists, the recalcitrant premiers bowed to Mulroney's and Bourassa's pressure tactics. They agreed to pass an unamended Meech Lake Accord on the condition that their constitutional concerns be dealt with in a second round. And yet, Prime Minister Mulroney's premeditated roll of the political dice backfired. He failed to pay attention to the Assembly of First Nations' (AFN) vehement opposition to the Meech Lake Accord. Making good use of the opportunity handed to him in Manitoba, AFN leader Ovide Mercredi convinced Elijah Harper, a Cree New Democratic Party member of Manitoba's Legislative Assembly, to deny the necessary unanimous agreement required to bring the Accord to a vote before the deadline. Premier Clyde Wells, realizing that Manitoba would not hold a vote, decided not to put the defeated Accord through another humiliating defeat in Newfoundland's House of Assembly. Indeed, Trudeau's devastating interventions played a decisive role in galvanizing widespread public opposition to the Accord. Canadians, expressing their new-found political sovereignty, forced two premiers, who might otherwise have given their approval to the Accord, to deny ratification. Trudeau, of course, had a personal as well as a professional motive for intervening in the Meech Lake Accord debate. He was defending the principle of a charter of fundamental rights and freedoms. He was also defending his legacy; that is, a uniquely *Canadian Charter of Rights and Freedoms*, one incorporating official language minority, gender, ethno-cultural, and Aboriginal rights, as an instrument of shared citizenship and national unity.[41]

Paradoxically, the Meech Lake Accord's defeat persuaded Mulroney and Bourassa to pursue and promote an even more controversial and divisive constitutional deal. They hoped to capitalize on the nationalist and separatist backlash in Quebec, a development that they fuelled by blaming Canada's English-speaking majority for the failure of their Meech Lake Accord. Bourassa, backed by Mulroney and actively supported by the Parti Québécois, orchestrated a high stakes political gamble culminating in a referendum by late October 1992. Quebecers would be asked to vote on either an acceptable constitutional package from the rest of Canada or political independence for Quebec. Ottawa and the provinces, joined by representatives from Canada's four national Aboriginal organizations, negotiated a complex and ambitious, but highly ambiguous, constitutional deal comprising the Meech Lake Accord, an omnibus Canada clause defining Canada's fundamental characteristics, a qualified Triple-E Senate, more powers to the provinces, and an elaborate Aboriginal constitution recognizing the Aboriginal peoples' right to a third order of government within the federation.[42]

Premiers, Aboriginal leaders, corporate leaders, and Charter groups felt reasonably satisfied with the complex constitutional package that offered something for each of them. Yet, a majority of Canadians, left outside the bargaining process, were bewildered, confused, and angered by the radical nature of the 60 constitutional amendments and the 25 political accords remaining to be negotiated. During the referendum campaign, a wide variety of poorly funded, diverse NO organizations criticized various aspects of the deal. Their persistence managed to convince Canadians in every region that the Charlottetown Consensus Report, as the deal was called, was even more flawed than the Meech Lake Accord. In an increasingly polarized political environment, Mulroney found himself alone defending a constitutional deal, one that had no chance of approval in Quebec where the NO forces included not only the Québécois nationalists and secessionists but most Canadian nationalists and Charter supporters. Western Canadians disliked the Meech Lake Accord aspects of the new deal and the creation of a third order of government for Canada's Aboriginal peoples, and they felt badly cheated by the powerless Triple-E Senate that was obtained at the cost of giving Quebec a perpetual guarantee of 25 per cent of the seats in the House of Commons. Ontarians, fearful of what impact Quebec's secession would have on their economy, yet strong defenders of Trudeau's vision of Canada and the Charter, were torn as to what they should do. Atlantic Canadians, realizing that their region would be cut off from the rest of Canada if Quebec seceded, reluctantly decided to support the Charlottetown deal.

Initially, Trudeau simply chose to advise Jean Chrétien, the new leader of the Liberal party, that he should demand and get from Mulroney a national referendum on any constitutional deal. In return, Trudeau promised Chrétien that he would remain silent. It was a promise that he could not keep. Once he analyzed the complicated and confusing legal text of the deal, Trudeau felt compelled to speak out. Realizing in late September 1992 that the government YES forces had far more financial and organizational resources than the NO forces, Trudeau decided to intervene in the referendum debate. He pronounced a devastating critique of the corrupt, anti-democratic political process that had produced a second egregiously flawed constitutional deal. Entitled "Quebec's Blackmail," Trudeau's article fingered Bourassa as the master blackmailer who orchestrated the "political knife" to Canada's throat in order to obtain unlimited constitutional powers from the rest of Canada, except that is, the power to grant Quebec lots of money.[43] In his now-famous October 1, 1992 speech at the Maison du Egg Roll in Montreal, Trudeau addressed the substance of the Charlottetown Report. Following his trenchant and perceptive analysis of the Canada clause, whose elaborate hierarchy of rights turned the Charter on its head, and his warning that the highly damaging decentralist thrust of the deal imperiled Canada's future, Trudeau concluded that the Charlottetown deal was "A Mess that deserves a big NO."[44]

Trudeau argued that the counter-revolutionary Charlottetown constitutional deal overturned the gains of 1982 by replacing the Charter's shared values, which enhanced Canadian identity and national unity, with a decentralized, tri-national, territorial-based conception of a segregated and hierarchical Canada in which the Quebec and Aboriginal communities functioned almost entirely as sovereign nation-states. Much to Mulroney's dismay—his political future lay in the balance—the Charlottetown deal was defeated in the October 26, 1992 referendum by a margin of 54 to 45 per cent. As expected, a slight majority of Quebecers rejected the deal. Western Canadians voted 60 per cent against the deal, the YES side carried weak majorities in the Atlantic provinces and the northern territories, while Ontarians, whom Mulroney and the pundits fully expected to support the YES side by a healthy margin, voted 50-50.

★★★★★

On a positive note, the 1992 referendum was an important moment in the evolution of Canada's political culture. It was Canadians' first collective opportunity to express their belief, despite the lack of a referendum mechanism in the 1982 amending procedures, that they constituted a sovereign people capable of deciding for themselves the constitutional evolution of Canada.[45] It is highly unlikely that in the near future Canada's political leaders will attempt, through mega-constitutional negotiations, to weaken the Charter, especially given that recent analysis demonstrates conclusively that proponents of the centralization thesis are wrong. Supreme Court Charter decisions have not undermined Canadian federalism by undercutting provincial autonomy.[46]

Just as this mega-constitutional politics phase came to an abrupt, unsuccessful conclusion, the battle against "Charter Canadians," dubbed the "Court Party" by their critics, and the role of the Supreme Court entered a new and potentially more damaging phase.[47] The Supreme Court's broad and liberal interpretation of most Charter rights, including section 23 official language minority education rights, coupled with the failure of the premiers to limit the nature and scope of the Charter, prompted Charter critics to attack the court's activist role in defining and promoting Charter rights. Left-wing and right-wing Charterphobes, ranging from respectable academics to highly partisan and self-serving critics bent on preserving the social, economic, and political *status quo*, denounced the Supreme Court's unwarranted activism, particularly on sensitive social and moral issues such as abortion and sexual orientation.[48] The critics' assertion that "jurocracy threatens democracy" has turned into an unrelenting tirade. Supreme Court critics, led by F. L. Morton, a University of Calgary political scientist, contend that the courts are usurping the role of the legislatures; that is, they are making the law rather than enunciating the law.[49] Western Canada's Reform Party, now the Canadian Alliance Party, joined the attack on the Supreme Court. Its former leader, Preston Manning, demanded a parliamentary committee to "review the decisions of the Supreme Court and advise the House when any decision appears to violate the purpose for which Parliament passed legislation or the original intent of the Charter of Rights and Freedoms."[50] The Reform Party adopted a policy calling for all federally appointed judges, including Supreme Court Justices, to be nominated by the provincial governments and ratified by a Triple-E Senate. The critics' goal is to delegitimize the Supreme Court's role in the interpretation and application of the Charter. They hope to pressure the Supreme Court justices to abandon judicial "activism" in favour of a policy of complete judicial "deference" toward the legislatures. In his defence, one critic argues that "'Charter democracy' has come to mean two different forms of politics with two different agendas. The collectivist, judicially driven equality-of-results program of the Court Party is on a collision course with the individualistic, equality-of-opportunity, participatory politics of the Reform Party."[51]

This increasingly strident and radical response of the Charter's and the Supreme Court's critics stems from the transforming power of the Charter on Canadian society and its legislative, executive, and judicial institutions in ways unforeseen by both its advocates and opponents. "When the *Canadian Charter of Rights and Freedoms* became part of the Canadian legal and political landscape in 1982," notes Janet Hiebert, "it changed fundamentally the role and responsibilities of the Canadian Courts."[52] Just as importantly, Hiebert convincingly demonstrates that the Charter had a tremendous unrecognized impact on governance in Canada. It changed "the political environment and climate of legislating and is influencing legislative choices at all stages of the policy process."[53] Articulate and progressive Charter advocates, such as Lorraine Weinrib, demonstrate that the *Charter of Rights and Freedoms* was deliberately "designed to transform the Canadian legal system."[54] The Charter is more progressive than the U.S. Bill of Rights in that it rejects a paternalistic and patriarchal model of society—it guarantees freedom of conscience as well as freedom of religion, does not entrench property rights, permits affirmative action, and requires interpretation that respects gender equality and multiculturalism.

★★★★★

The Charter facilitates a "dialogue" between the judges and the legislatures via two mechanisms. First, the general limitation clause (section 1), which stipulates that the guaranteed rights are subject to "such reasonable limits prescribed by law as can be demonstrably justified in a free and democratic society." Second, the override power of section 33, applicable to all sections except 3, 6, and 16 to 23, allows a legislature to pass a law, valid for up to five years, contravening the Charter. Their review of Supreme Court Charter decisions reveals that in 46 of the 66 cases in which the Court struck down legislation, legislators passed new laws conforming to the Charter, in seven cases legislatures repealed the offending laws, while in 13 cases there was no legislative response. "A critique of the Charter of Rights," they conclude, "based on its supposed usurpation of democratic legitimacy simply cannot be sustained."[55] Of course, the Charter's critics reject this notion of a dialogue, preferring, instead, the term "monologue" to describe the Supreme Court's role. Legislators' freedom or willingness, Morton maintains, to respond to Supreme Court decisions is determined by the specific issue and the political context. When the issue is too controversial and politically unrewarding, legislators will invariably abdicate responsibility to the courts, putting in jeopardy the Canadian tradition of responsible government.[56] The survival of Trudeau's legacy, the Charter, will not depend on the outcome of the ideological debate—as important and useful as it is—between its opponents and supporters. The Charter will remain a prominent fixture of Canada's constitutional framework as long as it remains popular among Canadians. Paradoxically, Charter critics who claim to be defending democracy, or Charter supporters who are fearful for its survival, refuse to acknowledge that an overwhelming majority of Canadians—82 per cent—from all regions including Quebec, continue to support the Charter while nearly two-thirds agree that the Supreme Court should have the final say on the constitutionality of legislation.[57] The debate about the impact of the Charter, no doubt, will become a mainstay of Canadian political life but the Charter will survive because it is essential for the stable development of postmodern, pluralistic societies.

Conclusions

Trudeau's long struggle for the *Canadian Charter of Rights and Freedoms* was successful for several reasons. First, Trudeau's classical and legal education, his early travel and work experiences, and his close friendship with Frank Scott ensured that he became, emotionally and intellectually, a committed civil libertarian and anti-nationalist. Second, Canadian society and its governance changed tremendously after World War II thanks to massive urbanization, immigration, higher levels of education, and the advent of television. Canadians were also witness to, and supporters of, the development of an international human rights culture in the wake of the fascist and communist movements that expanded tremendously following the atrocities of World War I. Third, Prime Minister Trudeau was able to link the "liberal" imperative for a *Canadian Charter of Rights and Freedoms* to all these developments. More importantly, he shrewdly linked the need for a charter to Canada's growing crisis of national unity caused by the rise of Quebec's secession movement. He used this crisis to convince a majority of Canadians that a hybrid charter—protecting fundamental freedoms and the rights of Canada's official language minorities, its Aboriginal peoples, and its expanding multicultural communities—could serve as an effective unifying counterforce against the Québécois secessionist movement. Quebec's "Quiet" and "Not-So-Quiet" revolutions of the 1950s and 1960s undermined Canadians' fragile sense of identity and seriously threatened the very fabric of the nation-state. Trudeau set out to fashion a Canadian civic nationalism, one based on both liberal and communitarian values inscribed in a uniquely Canadian *Charter of Rights and Freedoms*, hoping thereby to defend the integrity of the Canadian nation-state and promote national unity.

When the secessionist Parti Québécois came to power in 1976 and proceeded with a referendum on independence for Quebec, Trudeau skillfully exploited the crisis to achieve his goal. Following the Parti Québécois's defeat in the referendum, Trudeau first sought the support of the provinces, which was not forthcoming, and then set out to reform Canada's constitution unilaterally. His political opponents forced a reference to the Supreme Court where the justices ruled that his patriation bill was legal but unconstitutional in a conventional sense. He required the support of a substantial number of provinces. Fortunately, the government's decision to strengthen the Charter ensured widespread support for patriation with an entrenched Charter. During a crucial last negotiating session, Trudeau's political experience, his formidable intellect, and his tactical and strategic planning enabled him to best the premiers. He obtained the Canadian Charter by accepting an amending formula based on provinces, not regions, and a "notwithstanding" clause for some but not all aspects of the Charter. These important concessions won the support of all of the premiers, except Premier Lévesque of Quebec. A 15-year struggle had come to a successful conclusion.

Much has transpired on the Charter front since 1982, most of it positive but some of it negative. Charter Canadians—civil libertarians, women, the official language minority and ethno-cultural communities, and Canada's Aboriginal peoples—have been able to acquire, for the first time since 1867, a respect for and recognition of their rights. The impact on the Canadian legal and political systems has been comprehensive. All legislators have amended or rescinded offending legislation while keeping the Charter in view when formulating new legislation. At the judicial level, a majority of Canada's Supreme Court cases pertain to disputes based upon the rights outlined in the Charter. Trudeau's hybrid Charter has and, no doubt, will continue to transform Canadian society and its institutions in ways that few are able to predict. The social, political, and intellectual controversies surrounding this ongoing transformation will ensure that Trudeau's legacy will endure well into and perhaps even beyond the twenty-first century. Just as importantly, Canada's Charter has evoked interest from every part of the globe. The values of justice, freedom, and equality are goals that citizens everywhere aspire to as they struggle to confront the homogenizing, dehumanizing forces of a globalizing economy. Indeed, Trudeau, the cosmopolitan world traveller, has made an enduring contribution not only to Canadians, but to citizens everywhere who cherish freedom. Trudeau defined the Charter as the "people's package" and Canadians are determined to use it to their full advantage. In so doing, Canadians will become a fully mature sovereign nation while ensuring that the Charter will remain Trudeau's most enduring legacy to the nation and the world.

Notes

1 P. E. Trudeau, "The Values of a Just Society," in T. S. Axworthy & P. E. Trudeau, eds., *Towards a Just Society* (Toronto: Viking, 1990), at 357.

2 *Canadian Charter of Rights and Freedoms*, Part I of the *Constitution Act, 1982*, being Schedule B to the *Canada Act, 1982* (U.K.), 1982, c. 11.

3 P. E. Trudeau, "A Constitutional Declaration of Rights," in *Federalism and the French Canadians* (Toronto: Macmillan, 1968), at 52–53.

4 For a discussion of the democratization of Canada's political culture consult N. Nevitte, *The Decline of Deference* (Toronto: Broadview Press, 1996).

5 *British North America Act, 1867* (U.K.), 30 & 31 Vict., c. 3.

6 P. H. Russell, *Constitutional Odyssey. Can Canadians Become a Sovereign People?* 2nd ed. (Toronto: University of Toronto Press, 1993), at 3–6.

7 *Supra*, note 2.

8 The term "Charter Canadians" was coined by A. C. Cairns, "Citizens (Outsiders) and Governments (Insiders) in Constitution Making: The Case of Meech Lake" (1988) 14 Can. Pub. Pol'y, at 121–45.

9 P. E. Trudeau, *A Time for Action Toward the Renewal of the Canadian Federation* (Ottawa: Government of Canada, 1978); see also *Sessional Papers*, No. 303-4/2 (1978).

10 *Id.*, at 12.

11 G. Radwanski, *Trudeau* (Toronto: Macmillan, 1978).

12 P. E. Trudeau, *Memoirs* (Toronto: McClelland & Stewart, 1993), at 264–72.

13 *Id.*, at 273–84.

14 S. Clarkson & C. McCall, *Trudeau and Our Times. Volume I: The Magnificent Obsession* (Toronto: McClelland & Stewart, 1990), at 274–97.

15 *Reference re Amendment of the Constitution of Canada* (1981), 117 D.L.R. (3d) 1 (Man. C.A.).

16 *Reference re Amendment of the Constitution of Canada (No. 3)* (1981), 120 D.L.R. (3d) 385 (Que. C.A.).

17 *Reference re Amendment of the Constitution of Canada* (1981), 29 Nfld. & P.E.I.R. 503 (Nfld. C.A.).

18 P. E. Trudeau, *Memoirs*, at 310–14; S. Clarkson & C. McCall, *Trudeau and Our Times. Volume I*, at 328–48.

19 *Re Resolution to Amend the Constitution*, [1981] 1 S.C.R. 753.

20 S. Clarkson and C. McCall, *Trudeau and Our Times. Volume I*, 352–56.

21 P. E. Trudeau, "Patriation and the Supreme Court," in Gérard Pelletier, ed., *Against the Current. Selected Writings 1939–1996* (Toronto: McClelland & Stewart, 1996) , at 246–61. Trudeau outlines the contrary position of the dissenting judges who included Chief Justice Bora Laskin. They could find no evidence whatsoever in Canada's constitutional history for any sort of constitutional convention. Trudeau contended that the "Supreme Court allowed itself—in Professor P. W. Hogg's words—'to be manipulated into a purely political role,' going beyond the lawmaking functions that modern jurisprudence agrees the Court must necessarily exercise." (at 252).

22 P. E. Trudeau, *Memoirs*, at 322.

23 *Id.*, at 323–25; S. Clarkson & C. McCall, *Trudeau and Our Times. Volume I*, at 376–86.

24 *Supra*, note 2.

25 G. Hein, "Interest Group Litigation and Canadian Democracy," in P. Howe & P. H. Russell, eds., *Judicial Power and Canadian Democracy* (Montreal & Kingston: McGill-Queen's University Press, 2001), at 214–54; I. Brodie, "Interest Group Litigation and the Embedded State: Canada's Court Challenges Program" (2001) 34 Can. J. Pol. Sc., at 357–76.

26 M. D. Behiels, *Canada's Francophone Minority Communities, Constitutional Renewal, and the Winning of School Governance* (Montreal & Kingston: McGill-Queen's University Press [forthcoming in 2003]).

27 *Quebec Assn. of Protestant School Boards v. Quebec (Attorney General), supra*, note [12].

28 *Quebec Assn. of Protestant School Boards v. Quebec (Attorney General), supra*, note [12]; *Mahé v. Alberta*, [1990] 1 S.C.R. 342; *Reference re Public Schools Act (Manitoba) (sub nom. Reference re s. 79(3), (4) & (7) of the Public Schools Act (Manitoba))*, [1993] 1 S.C.R. 839; *Arsenault-Cameron v. Prince Edward Island*, [2000] 1 S.C.R. 3.

29 *Supra*, note [28].

30 *Supra*, note [28].

31 *Supra*, note [28].

32 *Constitution Amendment, 1997 (Quebec)*, SI/97-141.

33 For an excellent overview consult Office of the Commissioner of Official Languages, *School Governance: The Implementation of Section 23 of the Charter* (Ottawa: Minister of Public Works and Government Services Canada, 1998).

34 J. B. Kelly, "Reconciling Rights and Federalism during Review of the Charter of Rights and Freedoms: The Supreme Court of Canada and the Centralization Thesis, 1982–1999" (2001) 34 Can. J. Pol. Sc., at 321–55.

35 P. E. Trudeau, "The Meech Lake Accord (1)," in *Against the Current, supra*, note 2[1], at 229–36.

36 Cited in L. E. Weinrib, "Trudeau and the Canadian Charter of Rights and Freedoms: A Question of Political Maturation," in A. Coyne & J. L. Granatstein, eds., *Trudeau's Shadow: The Life and Legacy of Pierre Elliott Trudeau* (Toronto: Random House of Canada, 1998), at 278.

37 M. D. Behiels, *The Meech Lake Primer. Conflicting Views of the 1987 Constitutional Accord* (Ottawa: University of Ottawa Press, 1989), at 139–46.

38 A. Cohen, *A Deal Undone. The Making and Breaking of the Meech Lake Accord* (Vancouver/Toronto: Douglas & McIntyre, 1990). This did not stop the nationalists and secessionists from blaming anglophone Canadians for the defeat of the Meech Lake Accord!

39 D. Johnson, ed., *With a Bang, Not a Whimper. Pierre Trudeau Speaks Out* (Toronto: Stoddart, 1988), at 23–105.

40 M. D. Behiels, "Who Speaks for Canada? Trudeau and the Constitutional Crisis," in A. Coyne & J. L. Granatstein, eds., *Trudeau's Shadow, supra*, note [36], at 335.

41 M. D. Behiels, *id.*, at 331–43.

42 A. C. Cairns, "The Charlottetown Accord: Multinational Canada v. Federalism," in C. Cook, ed., *Constitutional Predicament. Canada after the Referendum of 1992* (Montreal/Kingston: McGill-Queen's University Press, 1994), at 40.

43 P. E. Trudeau, "Quebec's Blackmail," in *Against the Current, supra*, note 2[1], at 262–74.

44 P. E. Trudeau, *Trudeau: "A Mess that deserves a big NO"* (Montreal: Robert Davies Publishing, 1992).

45 M. D. Behiels, "Who Speaks for Canada?" *supra*, note [40], at 347–49.

46 J. B. Kelly, "Reconciling Rights and Federalism," *supra*, note [34], at 354–55.

47 See F. L. Morton & R. Knopff, "The Supreme Court as the Vanguard of the Intelligentsia: The Charter Movement as Post-Materialist Politics," in J. Ajzenstat, ed., *Canadian Constitutionalism, 1791–1991* (Ottawa: Canadian Study of Parliament Group, 1992). Their most recent book is *The Charter Revolution and the Court Party* (Peterborough, Ont.: Broadview Press, 2000).

48 R. Sigurdson, "Left- and Right-Wing Charterphobia in Canada: A Critique of the Critics" (1993) 7-8 International Journal of Canadian Studies, at 95–115.

49 F. L. Morton, "The Charter of Rights: Myth and Reality," in W. D. Gairdner, ed., *After Liberalism: Essays in Search of Freedom, Virtue, and Order* (Toronto: Stoddart, 1998), at 33.

[50] P. Manning, "Parliament, Not Judges, Must Make the Laws of the Land," *The Globe and Mail* (June 16, 1998), A23. See also, P. R. Russell, "Reform's Judicial Agenda," with a reply by P. Manning, "A 'B' for Prof. Russell," in P. Howe & P. R. Russell, eds., *Judicial Power and Canadian Democracy*, at 118–28.

[51] F. L. Morton, "The Charter and Canada Outside Quebec," in Kenneth McRoberts, ed., *Beyond Quebec. Taking Stock of Canada* (Montreal & Kingston: McGill-Queen's University Press, 1995), at 111.

[52] J. L. Hiebert, "Wrestling with Rights: Judges, Parliament and the Making of Social Policy," in P. Howe & P. H. Russell, eds., *Judicial Power and Canadian Democracy* (Montreal & Kingston: McGill-Queen's University Press, 2001), at 165–66. She recommends that governments recognize the Charter's impact on governance and legislators take a more proactive role in ensuring that legislation meets the test of the Charter.

[53] *Id.*

[54] L. E. Weinrib, "The Activist Constitution," in P. Howe & P. H. Russell, eds., *Judicial Power and Canadian Democracy*, *supra*, note 79, at 81; See also L. Weinrib, "Canada's Charter of Rights: Paradigm Lost," unpublished paper given by the author in August 2001.

[55] P. W. Hogg and A. A. Thornton, "The Charter Dialogue between Courts and Legislatures," in P. Howe & P. H. Russell, eds., *Judicial Power and Canadian Democracy*, *supra*, note [52], at 106–10; See also Hogg & Bushell, "The Charter Dialogue between Courts and Legislatures: Or Perhaps the Charter of Rights Isn't Such a Bad Thing After All" (1997) 35 Osgoode Hall L. J., at 75–124.

[56] F. L. Morton, "Dialogue or Monologue," in P. Howe and P. H. Russell, eds., *Judicial Power and Canadian Democracy*, *supra*, note [52], at 111–17.

[57] J. F. Fletcher & P. Howe, "Public Opinion and Canada's Courts," in P. Howe & P. H. Russell, eds., *Judicial Power and Canadian Democracy*, *supra*, note [52], at 255–61.

Glossary

British North America Act. In 1867, the Dominion of Canada was created and united the British colonies of New Brunswick, Nova Scotia, and the Province of Canada (the latter would be divided into the provinces of Ontario and Quebec). The colonies were governed by the British North America Act (BNA Act), legislation that was drafted by the "Fathers of Confederation" and passed by the British Parliament. The BNA Act divided power between the federal and provincial governments, created a federal nation, and established a British-style Parliament with a House of Commons and Senate.

Parti Québécois. This political party was established in 1968 and dedicated to political sovereignty for Quebec. Its first leader was René Lévesque. It first became the government of Quebec in 1976.

Quiet Revolution. This term refers to the period of Quebec history following the death of Premier Maurice Duplessis and election of a Liberal government under Jean Lesage (1960–66). Quebec underwent a transformative process of modernization that saw the secularization of education, the expansion of state bureaucracy, the creation of many public institutions, and a rise in French-Canadian nationalism.

Further Reading

Karaian, Lara. "Troubling the Definition of Pornography: Little Sisters, a New Defining Moment in Feminists' Engagement with the Law?" *Canadian Journal of Women and the Law* 17, no. 1 (2005): 117–133.

Karaian examines feminism's relationship to the legal regulation of pornography. The author concentrates on a Supreme Court of Canada decision regarding Canada Customs violations of the free expression and equality rights of a Vancouver-based gay and lesbian bookstore.

Kelly, James B. *Governing with the Charter: Legislative and Judicial Activism and Framer's Intent.* Vancouver: UBC Press, 2005.

This book examines the Charter's impact on the relationship between the judiciary and Parliament. Addressing critics of the Charter, Kelly challenges the notion that the courts undermine federalism and democracy.

Leane, G. W. G. "Enacting Bills of Rights: Canada and the Curious Case of New Zealand's 'Thin' Democracy." *Human Rights Quarterly* 26, no. 1 (February 2004): 152–188.

This article compares the legal and political contexts of New Zealand and Canada and their Bills of Rights.

Relevant Websites

Canadiana
www.canadiana.org/citm/themes/constitution/constitution16_e.html
This website contains an array of material concerning the history of Canada. Built around the government documents collection of the Early Canadiana Online collection, it provides secondary and primary information on Canada's constitutional history.

Canadian Heritage
www.canadianheritage.gc.ca/progs/pdp-hrp/canada/guide/index_e.cfm
This website is maintained by the Human Rights Program of the Department of Canadian Heritage. It reproduces and provides explanatory notes for the Canadian Charter of Rights and Freedoms.

Charter Information
faculty.marianopolis.edu/c.belanger/QuebecHistory/federal/parl.htm
Created by a faculty member of Marianopolis College in Quebec, this website provides a brief analysis of the implications of the Canadian Charter of Rights and Freedoms on the supremacy of Parliament.

Trudeau Archives
archives.cbc.ca/politics/prime_ministers/topics/2192/
Details about the life and career of Pierre Elliott Trudeau are contained in this CBC archival website. The text is accompanied by many video clips of Trudeau.

CHAPTER 12

SOCIAL MOVEMENTS AND JUDICIAL EMPOWERMENT:
COURTS, PUBLIC POLICY, AND LESBIAN AND GAY ORGANIZING IN CANADA

MIRIAM SMITH

Introduction

Public attitudes towards homosexuality have been transformed over the last generation throughout the Anglo-American democracies and beyond. The rise of the lesbian and gay movement from the early 1970s challenged the existing structure of public policy on issues ranging from the recognition of same-sex relationships, adoption, and parenting rights to the regulation of queer sexuality. Same-sex marriage is the latest chapter in an ongoing process of recognition of lesbian and gay rights. Yet there is substantial cross-national variation in the recognition of lesbian and gay rights, even among similar systems such as Canada, the United States, and Britain. This article presents a case study of lesbian and gay organizing and public policy change in Canada, a country at the forefront in lesbian and gay rights recognition. I argue that Canada provides such extensive recognition of lesbian and gay citizens because of the impact of judicial empowerment on social movement politics and public policy in the lesbian and gay area. In Canada, the entrenchment of a constitutional bill of rights in 1982 intersected with the rise of the modern lesbian and gay movement. The process of judicial empowerment shaped the emerging lesbian and gay movement, which was drawn into the process of litigation and into a rights-based legalized politics that is not found to the same extent in other countries. In turn, the legalized networks of lesbian and gay activism were successful in pushing the courts toward the recognition of rights claims.

Canada's human rights protections for lesbian and gay citizens are among the most extensive in the world. In June 2003, the Ontario Court of Appeal ruled in favour of same-sex marriage in the *Halpern*[1] case, ordering Toronto City Hall to issue marriage licences to same-sex couples.[2] Courts have ruled in favour of same-sex marriage in six other Canadian provinces and one of the three northern Canadian territories. Only two other countries—Belgium and the Netherlands—recognize same-sex marriage.[3] In addition, Canada offers broad and deep human rights protections for lesbians and gay men, including measures that still do not exist in many parts of the developed world, such as enforceable protection from employment and housing discrimination; employment benefits for same-sex partners in the public and private sectors; adoption rights for lesbians and gays in many provinces; family rights with respect to health care decision-making and wills; special sentencing provisions in criminal law for crimes motivated by hate on the grounds of sexual orientation; and protection from hate speech. The impact of these public policy changes has reached beyond Canadian borders as same-sex couples (including non-citizens) married under Canadian law have sought recognition of their marriages in the United States and the European Union.[4] While efforts by Canadian-married couples to challenge US laws may fail, the proximity of Canada to the United States and the migration between the two countries, especially important in regions such as the US Northeast, means that Canadian developments have brought pressure to bear on US courts and lawmakers.

Why does Canadian public policy on lesbian and gay rights recognition differ so markedly from that of other similar systems such as the United States and Britain? This article suggests that policy change in Canada must be read in the light of the extensive political-institutional changes entailed by the process of judicial empowerment beginning in 1982. The constitutional entrenchment of the Canadian Charter of Rights and Freedoms (Charter) gave the courts a new political importance in Canada. Before the Charter, judicial review was largely confined to enforcing the division of powers between levels of government in the federal system. On the rare occasions in which courts considered individual rights, such issues were decided in terms of constitutional and political debates over federalism. In contrast, in the wake of the Charter, the Supreme Court of Canada—the country's highest court—has adjudicated important public policy issues such as the rights of accused criminals and prisoners, tobacco advertising, DNA collection and use, language rights, corporate "freedoms," gun control, abortion, sexual assault laws, pornography, and lesbian and gay rights. In one generation, the Supreme Court of Canada has become central to Canadian political life, and Canadians have increasingly become accustomed to American-style debates over judicial activism.[5] This makes Canada another case in the growth of global judicial empowerment, that is, the enhancement of the role of the judiciary in the political system and the extension of the jurisdiction of courts and legal adjudication into new areas of public policy.[6]

Strong courts alone, however, are not enough to produce human rights protections for vulnerable minority groups. The US case shows that strong courts are not always friendly to lesbian and gay rights claims. Drawing on social movement and historical institutionalist perspectives,[7] this article suggests that judicial empowerment is a long-term historical process and that its effects must be explored through longitudinal study of the impact of courts and justiciable human rights protections. Furthermore, the process of judicial empowerment is not simply a political-institutional rearrangement. As scholars of legal mobilization have demonstrated,[8] courts also influence the process of social movement mobilization. In Canada, the process of legal mobilization in the lesbian and gay rights case was critically shaped by the *timing* of judicial empowerment, relative to the emergence of the post-Stonewall lesbian and gay movement.

In the first section of the article, I explore the case of lesbian and gay organizing in comparative perspective, in order to emphasize the ways in which the role of courts relative to social movement organizing in the lesbian and gay area differs across similar systems such as the United States and Britain. In the middle sections, I present the study of the Canadian lesbian and gay rights movement before and after the Charter, demonstrating how a movement that, like the US movement today,[9] was reluctant to use law as a political strategy, has become dominated by legal mobilization. The case study was conducted using qualitative research methods including interviewing lesbian and gay activists, lawyers, and litigants and surveying the lesbian, gay and mainstream press as well as the major lesbian and gay rights legal cases.[10] The analysis shows how the entrenchment of the Charter opened up new political opportunities for litigation by the Canadian lesbian and gay rights movement—litigation that, in turn, translated into concrete policy gains for lesbian and gay equality. The legal mobilization of the lesbian and gay movement pushed the envelope of public policy on equality rights, anti-discrimination, relationship recognizing, and same-sex marriage. In the conclusion, I place the case study in the wider context of comparative research on courts and human rights. Many of the key debates on courts and social change have centred on the impact of courts on the actual implementation of public policy.[11] This case study demonstrates the impact of rights-based litigation on the evolution of public policy in the lesbian and gay area; however, it also emphasizes the ways in which judicial empowerment moulds the process of social movement mobilization. While litigation has produced positive results for the lesbian and gay movement in Canada, such results have been achieved via the creation of legalized forms of social movement politics.

Comparative Considerations

The process of judicial empowerment has sparked a lively political debate in Canada over the meaning and limits of rights. The Charter has been criticized on the left, especially by Canadian scholars of critical legal studies, as a danger to progressive movements in that engagement with law and litigation may depoliticize grassroots mobilization.[12] There is a well-developed legal literature on queer politics, much of which is skeptical or critical of the ways in which the legalized rights agenda may lead to the reinforcement and replication of social and economic inequality.[13] While critical legal studies scholars are skeptical of rights politics, the political left in Canada, as represented by political parties such as the social democratic New Democratic Party, has long supported strong civil rights protections in Canadian law and policy and welcomed the Charter as an important step in the development of Canadian human rights policies. The Liberal Party of Canada, the party that championed the Charter, is strongly identified with the document and uses the social liberalism of the Charter as a distinctive badge of party identification.

The Conservative Party of Canada (newly reformed following a merger of two older right-wing parties) is home to partisan right-wing critics of rights politics, who have often opposed the Supreme Court's decisions on abortion and lesbian and gay rights. The positions of right-wing Charter critics would be quite familiar to American students of public law. In fact, in many cases, right-wing Charter critics in Canada have imported American arguments wholesale, arguing, for example, that unelected judges should not dictate public policy to legislators or that judges should not engage in "politics."[14]

At the same time, however, in the twenty years since the entrenchment of the Charter, rights claims have taken on a symbolic potency in Canadian society. The process of political mobilization around the courts and the decisions of the Supreme Court of Canada have established the discursive construction of "equality-seeking," "equality rights," and "Charter values," all of which are increasingly seen as tied to national identity for English-speaking Canadians. Although francophone Quebecers may not name such values as "Canadian," they are no less supportive of the rights claims of lesbians and gay men (more so, in most public opinion studies, than English-speaking Canadians). Like Canada's Medicare system, gay rights and same-sex marriage have become wedded to Canada's claims of distinctiveness, especially its distinctiveness compared to the US. This is true even for Canadians who *oppose* same-sex marriage.[15] Such claims of distinctiveness have become even more potent in Canada, as American politics veered right during the presidency of George W. Bush.

★★★★★

Policy differences on lesbian and gay rights are rapidly accelerating in the first decade of the new millennium. Neither Britain nor the United States has taken the extensive measures in recognition of lesbian and gay equality that have been taken in Canada. In Britain, same-sex marriage is not even on the policy agenda.[16] Rather, civil unions have been proposed for same-sex partners along the lines of the policies that have been undertaken in Scandinavian countries, which, despite their much-vaunted social liberalism, still reserve a different set of symbolic and substantive legal rights and obligations for legally married opposite-sex partners.[17] The United States is even further behind than Britain, leading one analyst to label the US position on lesbian and gay rights as yet another form of American exceptionalism.[18] In the United States, sodomy was still illegal in many states in 2003, when the Supreme Court's *Lawrence*[19] decision struck down the Texas sodomy statute. Most US states do not allow adoption (or partnership adoption) by same-sex couples, and employment discrimination against lesbian and gay citizens is legal in thirty-seven states.[20] Although litigants have taken same-sex marriage challenges to US courts, the politics of such challenges is completely different from in Canada. In Canada, same-sex marriage is the culmination of a decade of thoroughgoing legal and political change that has placed lesbian and gay citizens on an equal footing with heterosexuals in almost every sphere of life that is touched by law. In contrast, in the United States, same-sex marriage challenges are much more likely to be defeated, they are more likely to face organized and well-financed opposition and, even where successful in court, they cannot be used to leverage change across other states or jurisdictions as they were in Canada.[21] Perhaps most importantly, while same-sex marriage represents the culmination of broad-ranging policy and political change in this area in Canada, in the United States, the same-sex marriage issue is used to obtain changes in the other key areas such as adoption, parenting rights, health care, wills, and employment discrimination.[22] The United States does not lack social movement organizing in the lesbian and gay field. However, in the United States, same-sex marriage is the *means* to legal protections that already exist in Canadian jurisdictions.

★ ★ ★ ★ ★

The social movement politics surrounding lesbian and gay rights also differs cross-nationally. Canada's lesbian and gay movement is entirely focused on litigation at the national level; in contrast, in the US case, lesbian and gay groups have undertaken a broad range of political strategies. Litigation funds are only one of the organizational types found in the US lesbian and gay movement.[23] This reflects the timing of judicial empowerment in the US compared to Canada. In the US, courts were empowered prior to the rise of modern social movements, and they have blocked lesbian and gay rights at least as often as they have supported them. In contrast, judicial empowerment in Canada has been a product of the post-sixties universe of social movement politics. Both the content and politics of the Charter have reflected the impact of historical timing on the process of legal mobilization. Until very recently, litigation has been a marginal strategy in British lesbian and gay rights organizing. Litigation is not even mentioned as a political strategy by major lesbian and gay groups such as Stonewall and Outrage in their self-descriptions, despite the increasing importance of courts for human rights in Britain.[24] In the next twenty years, courts and legally focused politics will play a more important role in British queer organizing. As the process of judicial empowerment occurs in Britain (through the 1998 *Human Rights Act*, the proposed supreme court, and the impact of European Union courts), existing British social movement organizations in the lesbian and gay area will become drawn into the legally centred human rights template.

Differences in the associational sector or the pattern of social movement politics across similar systems reflect and reinforce the policy differences among the cases. The lesbian and gay movement in Canada, a weak and fractured network of activists at the time of the entrenchment of the Charter, has come of age alongside the growth of strong courts. Judicial empowerment shaped the movement at a formative stage of its development, sparked the creation of certain types of advocacy organizations and certain specific patterns of movement organization, and produced legally dominated advocacy organization. In other words, the timing of judicial empowerment has not only encouraged social movement politics, it has encouraged a certain *type* of social movement politics in the lesbian and gay "sector." Organizationally, judicial empowerment has provided incentives for litigation organizations and for the privileging of legal expertise within such organizations and strengthened the appeal of human rights as the dominant public demand of the movement. The movement was able to shape the interpretation of the equality rights guarantees of the Charter ("equality rights" in Canadian legal parlance) from the ground up. The movement's active role in litigation helped produce the positive legal decisions that laid the groundwork for changing public policy. The Canadian culture of rights has its origins in the social movement politics of the sixties, while the US debates on the legal protection of minority rights through judicial review originate with the US constitution itself. In the British case, most similar to Canada in its parliamentary institutions, the process of judicial empowerment in the human rights area is very recent, dating from the expansion and deepening of European Union integration. In each case, litigation has played a different role in the lesbian and gay movement, with different results for human rights policy.

The Canadian Lesbian and Gay Rights Movement: The Politics of Rights before the Charter

In order to evaluate the effects of the entrenchment of the Charter on the evolution of lesbian and gay politics, this section presents a picture of the character of the lesbian and gay movement in the period before the Charter. The rise of the modern lesbian and gay rights movement in Canada can be traced to the 1960s, when small homophile groups were established. These groups and their allies helped to create the climate for legal change, which occurred in 1969 when the Liberal government of Pierre Trudeau decriminalized homosexual acts between consenting adults as part of a sweeping reform of Canada's divorce and family law. These amendments were modelled on changes made in Britain during the same period and rested on the concept of the right to privacy, summarized by Trudeau in his statement that "the state has no business in the bedrooms of the nation."[25]

Cross-nationally, early gay liberation organizing tended to focus on the same set of issues in Western countries: legalization of homosexual behaviour; an end to state regulation and repression of lesbian and gay life; and the passage and enforcement of anti-discrimination measures, most importantly in the area of employment.[26]

★★★★★

In order for the movement to succeed, it needed to have members and political support from the lesbian and gay community. The publicly expressed claims of the movement, then, were aimed not only at influencing policy debates but also at creating, reinforcing, and politically mobilizing the lesbian and gay community. Therefore, the public statements and expressions of the activist leadership of the movement were strategically framed to build the movement as well as to influence society and public policy.

Litigation as a political strategy played an important role within this framework. Activist leaders of the period believed that the "civil rights strategy," as they called it in reference to the rights claims and political strategies of the US civil rights movement, was a means to the fulfillment of the ideology of gay liberation.[27] Rights claims were political resources, used to politicize grievances and to create a sense of political identity.[28] Although the legal opportunity for lesbian and gay rights claims prior to the Charter was not very promising, gay liberation activists in the three major cities of movement activism—Montreal, Toronto, and Vancouver—pursued litigation as a political strategy during the seventies. A Toronto gay liberation group supported a racing steward, John Damien, who had been fired from his job for being gay.[29] In the case known as *Gay Tide*, the first gay rights challenge ever put before the Supreme Court of Canada, a Vancouver gay liberation group unsuccessfully contested a Vancouver newspaper's refusal to publish an ad for their newspaper.[30] In Montreal, a gay liberation group challenged a school's refusal to rent meeting space to the group. This litigation, undertaken in a context in which there were few legal resources for the defence of lesbian and gay rights, was used to raise consciousness and to create lesbian and gay organizations such as the Canadian Lesbian and Gay Rights Coalition, which took on the role of representing the lesbian and gay community in federal politics, the first time this had occurred.[31]

The "civil rights strategy" was not successful in changing public policy, however. With the exception of Quebec,[32] neither the provinces nor the federal government sought to include sexual orientation as a prohibited ground of discrimination in human rights legislation during the pre-Charter period.[33] State regulation and repression of lesbian and (especially) gay sexuality continued unabated during this period, with a series of raids on gay bathhouses in 1981 and a host of obscenity charges being laid against the gay liberation newspaper *The Body Politic*.[34]

This was the context in which the process of judicial empowerment occurred. In the late seventies and early eighties, debates occurred over the amendment of Canada's constitution, itself sparked by the election of a sovereignist government in Quebec in 1976 and its unsuccessful referendum on separation in 1980. The clash of nationalisms between the Canadian and Quebec governments over this period, and the regional backlash in Western Canada against the federal government, were the main factors driving the constitutional changes that led to the entrenchment of the Charter.

★★★★★

The Politics of Rights after the Charter, 1985–1993

In the initial phase of judicial empowerment, during the first three years of the Charter from 1982 to 1985, the lesbian and gay rights movement was strongly focused on AIDS organizing.[35] The effects of the Charter appeared gradually and incrementally over a long time period, finally accelerating with moves towards relationship recognition and same-sex marriage in the late nineties and early 2000.

The first effects of the Charter were felt in the establishment of informal legal networks surrounding the Charter. Lawyers, especially young lesbian and gay lawyers, were in the vanguard of the move to deploy the Charter on behalf of lesbian and gay rights.[36] Lawyers networked through a series of legal conferences in the early nineties as well as through their organizations such as the Canadian Bar Association, the National Association of Women and the Law, and the Women's Legal Education and Action Fund. Over time, this network has been formalized into the Sexual Orientation and Gender Identity Conference of the Canadian Bar Association. [...] Lawyers were the initial "meaning makers" of the Charter in the lesbian and gay area. They were the first to see the opportunity provided by the Charter and to think through the possibilities of Charter litigation and judicial empowerment for lesbian and gay citizens.

A second effect occurred during the process of implementing the Charter. As part of the coming into force of the equality rights section of the new Charter in 1985, the Progressive Conservative government of Brian Mulroney appointed a parliamentary committee to consider the implications of these provisions. The parliamentary committee hearings drew a large number of submissions from local lesbian and gay groups[37] and galvanized a group of lawyers and trade union activists to form an Ottawa-based group which would keep up the pressure on the federal government with regard to lesbian and gay equality rights.[38] The Equality Writes Ad Hoc Committee was formed to conduct a letter-writing campaign, to network with other human rights groups, and to lobby MPs and the Mulroney government on its response to the parliamentary committee report.[39] In the wake of some small successes in wrenching policy promises from the Mulroney government, the Equality Writes Ad-Hoc Committee transformed itself into *Egale*[40] at its first meeting in May 1986.[41]

In this way, the implementation of the Charter through the process of the parliamentary committee hearings sparked the establishment of a pan-Canadian lesbian and gay litigation and advocacy group and marked the formal beginnings of Charter-centred political activism by gay and lesbian groups. These first effects of the Charter—the establishment of formal legal networks and the establishment of Egale—were closely linked, as it was mainly the members of the legal network who founded Egale.

★★★★★

While the early gay and lesbian groups were rooted in part in the youth counterculture of the period, Egale was based on the emerging middle-class communities of visible ("out") lesbians and gays who potentially stood to benefit from the recognition of lesbian and gay relationships in law. Its leadership, especially in its early period, was provided mainly, although not exclusively, by white male professionals, especially lawyers and trade unionists from Ottawa's powerful public sector unions.[42] Unlike earlier lesbian and gay organizations, which had been based on group membership, Egale was based on individual membership, and it did not draw on the resources of provincial groups. Egale did not share the gay liberation meaning frame and discourse that had informed the groups of the seventies; it lacked a broader analysis of heterosexism and patriarchy and did not share the early groups' emphasis on sexual liberation in general. Especially in its early period, Egale did not take on issues concerning state regulation of sexuality such as age of consent laws, anal sex laws, censorship, and pornography.

Therefore, not only did institutional change produce new social movement organizations and informal legal networks, it also produced a certain *type* of social movement politics, namely one in which human rights recognition, codified in law, was defined as an end in itself rather than as a rights template for the tactical mobilization of a social movement.

In the wake of these new forms of social movement organization, from 1985–1993, there were several important cases that began to generate legal pressure for relationship recognition and for the inclusion of sexual orientation in section 15 of the Charter and in federal human rights legislation. These cases were neither planned nor financially supported by Egale, which did not have the resources to fund litigation, although Egale acted as a third party intervener in several of them. Many of those who undertook Charter litigation were social movement activists with histories in the women's movement, trade union movement, or gay liberation movement.[43] Two of the key cases in the late eighties and early nineties were *Veysey*[44] and *Haig & Birch*.[45] In these two cases, courts ruled that the exclusion of sexual orientation from federal human rights legislation violated the rights guarantees of the Charter.[46] Because of these decisions, it was widely understood in the legal community that sexual orientation had been "read into" the Charter of Rights and into federal human rights legislation through court decisions, despite the lack of a formal federal legislative amendment and despite the lack of a ruling from the Supreme Court of Canada. The Canadian Human Rights Commission, the enforcer of the federal human rights code, was itself a strong supporter of the inclusion of sexual orientation within its ambit and immediately recognized the implications of the *Veysey* and *Haig & Birch* decisions by accepting over two hundred complaints based on sexual orientation after 1992.[47] This change enabled lesbian and gay rights claimants to challenge discriminatory laws in federal jurisdiction. Throughout these cases, intervener coalitions between equality-seeking groups in the women's movement, ethnocultural communities, and Egale constituted a new form of group politics in advocacy litigation.[48]

The *Egan*[49] case was a turning point in lesbian and gay litigation. In this case, the court ruled that sexual orientation was included within the ambit of the equality rights clause of the Charter. At the time of this landmark case in 1995, there had been fourteen cases concerning sexual orientation under the Charter.[50] Of these fourteen cases, the majority were brought by those who had either been lesbian and gay activists before bringing their cases or who became activists as a result of their cases.[51] Cases concerning the inclusion of sexual orientation as a prohibited ground of discrimination in the federal human rights act—*Veysey* and *Haig & Birch*—had been successful, while cases concerning relationship recognition had not. In addition, cases that concerned discrimination in the Armed Forces (*Douglas*)[52] and immigration (*Morrissey & Coll*)[53]—the right of lesbians and gay men to sponsor their partners for immigration to Canada—had been settled out of court by the federal government. The Progressive Conservative government had staved off some of the direct lesbian and gay rights challenges by settling issues out of court and incrementally adjusting policies on the Armed Forces and immigration, although these policy changes fell short of the clear and enforceable policy directives favoured by Egale and other lesbian and gay rights activists.

The initial effects of the Charter, then, included the establishment of informal legal networks, the founding of a new litigation group with a positivist, rights-based legal ideology, and a growing set of Charter litigants drawn from the grassroots of lesbian and gay activism. During this initial phase, the policy effects of the Charter on lesbian and gay rights were relatively limited. This was to change in the second phase, after 1993.

The Politics of Rights after the Charter, 1993–2003

The second phase of judicial empowerment may be dated from the election of a series of majority Liberal governments starting in 1993. During the mid-nineties, Egale was reorganized and strengthened, and the pace of favourable court decisions on lesbian and gay rights issues accelerated. At the national level, the movement was dominated by Egale, and in turn Egale began to play an important role in the process of Charter litigation, strengthening the hand of Charter litigants in the lesbian and gay area by providing legal resources and third party intervention. In turn, as courts increasingly rule in favour of lesbian and gay rights, the movement is provided with enhanced policy resources.

Throughout this ten-year period, partisan politics on the lesbian and gay issue can be read as a stalemate between supporters and opponents. The election of the Liberals signalled some openness to lesbian and gay rights claims. As the party that had brought Canada the Charter, the Liberals prided themselves on their commitment to human rights, which provided a lever for lesbian and gay activists to hold the government accountable for its actions. The 1993 election also signalled the transition from a three-party Parliament to a five-party Parliament with the fracturing of the Progressive Conservative Party and the rise of the Western right-populist Reform Party (later Canadian Alliance) and the Quebec-based nationalist Bloc Québécois.[54] Reform in particular was a consistent opponent of lesbian and gay rights claims and was backed by evangelical Christian supporters from Western Canada. The Bloc was largely supportive, although the issue was peripheral for the party. Within the Liberal caucus, there was some opposition to lesbian and gay rights from a small group of pro-family MPs. Liberal governments were highly sensitive to the opposition to lesbian and gay rights from within their own party and from the right-wing Reform/Canadian Alliance party.

In this sense, the Liberal government would have stalemated on the issue and ignored it had it not been for the impact of judicial empowerment. Court rulings provided the lesbian and gay movement with the policy resources to force policy change on reluctant legislators. The establishment of legal networks and the formation and strengthening of Egale increasingly assisted litigants in bringing successful Charter challenges. Judicial empowerment served the interests of legislators who were sensitive to the relatively strong opposition to lesbian and gay rights who had a strong voice in Parliament in the Reform Party[55] and, to a lesser extent, within the Liberal caucus. The government preferred to deflect pressure from lesbian and gay rights opponents by shifting responsibility for the issue to the courts. At the same time, the government continued the Trudeau-era policies of supporting litigation for disadvantaged groups in the equality rights and language rights areas. Lawyers working in favour of lesbian and gay rights, as well as Egale itself as an organization, undertook legal research funded by these programs.[56] Thus, while the government was reluctant to legislate in favour of lesbian and gay rights unless forced into it by the courts, its policies continued to provide part of the support structure for lesbian and gay rights litigation.[57]

Over this time, Egale strengthened its organizational base, developed its membership and finances, and hired a full-time employee (a lawyer) for the first time. The organization began to reach out to provincial organizations across Canada and started to act as a clearinghouse for the legal networks that were solidifying around Charter issues. Increasingly, Egale coordinated litigation and sought to act as a US-style litigation fund in directing the course of the rights campaign through the courts, while using the media and lobbying the government, especially the Department of Justice and the Prime Minister's Office.[58]

★★★★★

Over this period, a series of key decisions expanded the definition of discrimination from the individual to the same-sex couple. Table 12.1 outlines these cases. Starting with the *Egan* decision in 1995, there are eleven major decisions that raise sexual orientation as a constitutional issue under section 15 of the Charter, based on Canadian law reports. They show the progression from the Supreme Court's clear recognition of sexual orientation as a prohibited ground of discrimination under the Charter in the *Egan* decision of 1995 through the trio of decisions on same-sex marriage in Quebec, British Columbia, and Ontario in 2002–04. Two of the eleven cases—*Egan* and *Vriend*[59]—concern the constitutional question of including sexual orientation as a prohibited ground of discrimination in the Charter itself and in human rights legislation. Six of the cases (including *Egan* again) deal with issues of same-sex relationship recognition, including adoption, pensions, spousal support upon relationship breakdown, and legal marriage. Three of the cases concern education and culture: the banning of books in a British Columbia school district (*Surrey*),[60] the certification of teacher-training programs (*Trinity Western*),[61] and the seizure of lesbian and gay reading material by Canada Customs (*Little Sisters*).[62] Egale was an active intervener in nine of the eleven cases and the litigant in one case. Thus, of the eleven cases, Egale was actively involved as an intervener or litigant in all but one. In *Hendricks*,[63] Egale was informally involved and close communication occurred at the later stages of the case between the legal team and the pan-Canadian lesbian and gay legal network. This marks a substantial increase from the earlier period of Charter litigation in which Egale was involved in only five of fourteen Charter cases.

Examining the policy evolution represented by these cases, Charter jurisprudence has moved from discrimination against individuals to discrimination against same-sex couples. In *Egan*, the Supreme Court of Canada ruled that sexual orientation was analogous to the other grounds of discrimination enumerated in section 15 of the Charter and that hence it was included de facto or "read in" to the Charter, thus confirming the implications of the earlier judgments in *Haig & Birch* and *Veysey*. In response to this, the Liberals came under increasing pressure to amend the *Canadian Human Rights Act*, the legislation covering private discrimination in federal jurisdiction, to include sexual orientation, a change that had already been informally included because of the *Haig & Birch* judgment. Led by Egale, the lesbian and gay legal networks, and the Canadian Human Rights Commission itself, the Liberals acted to amend the Act in 1996. In the same year, the government also included sexual orientation in a criminal code amendment on sentencing for hate crimes, providing for harsher sentences for offences motivated by hate. The few remaining provinces that had not included sexual orientation in their provincial human rights legislation were forced to change their policies because of the Supreme Court's decision in *Vriend*, which concerned the case of a gay man in Alberta who alleged he had been fired from his teaching job for being gay.

The more dramatic policy changes concerned the question of same-sex relationship recognition as an extension of anti-discrimination law. The evolution of policy in this area began with the *Egan* decision on same-sex spousal support under the federal *Old Age Security* pension legislation. This case failed but subsequent cases succeeded, including

TABLE 12.1: Select Cases in Lesbian and Gay Rights in Canada, 1995–2003

Case	Venue and Year	Litigant Activists?	Egale's Role	Issue	Legal Outcome	Policy Consequences
Egan & Nesbitt v. Canada	Supreme Court of Canada, 1995	Yes	Intervener	Same-sex spousal support under federal Old Age Security.	Unsuccessful, but the Court recognized that sexual orientation was analogous to the other grounds of discrimination in the equality rights* provision of the Charter.	Sexual orientation is considered to be included de facto in the Charter, thus opening the way for other Charter challenges on sexual orientation.
Re K. & B.	Ontario Provincial Court, 1995	No	None	Constitutionality of opposite-sex definition of spouse in provincial adoption legislation.	Successful.	Despite the fact that this decision was legally binding in Ontario only, some other provinces began to change their adoption rules in its wake.
Rosenberg v. Canada	Supreme Court of Canada, 1998	No	Intervener	Constitutionality of opposite-sex definition of spouse in federal tax code for the purpose of registering an employer pension plan.	Successful. Employers and workers could receive tax benefits in private employer pension plans even if the plans offered pension benefits to same-sex couples.	This was an important case, indicating that same-sex relationship recognition in federal and provincial legislation would likely be constitutionally required under the Charter. Note the change in the Court's direction from Egan.
Vriend v. Alberta	Supreme Court of Canada, 1998	No	Intervener	Alberta's refusal to include sexual orientation in its human rights legislation.	Successful. Provincial human rights legislation must provide for complaints based on sexual orientation discrimination.	The Alberta government chooses not to use the notwithstanding clause to circumvent the court's decision. Thus, sexual orientation is "read in" or included in Alberta's human rights legislation.

Case	Venue and Year	Litigant Activists?	Egale's Role	Issue	Legal Outcome	Policy Consequences
M v. H	Supreme Court of Canada, 1999	No	Intervener	Spousal support on breakup of a long-term lesbian relationship.	"M" is successful. Support awarded.	Comprehensive legislation on relationship recognition, federally (2000) and in most provinces.
Little Sisters Book and Art Emporium v. Canada	Supreme Court of Canada, 2000	Yes	Intervener	Constitutionality of Canada Customs' actions in stopping the Little Sisters bookstore's imports of lesbian and gay materials at the US border.	The burden of proof is on Canada Customs to show that the materials are "obscene." Canada Customs' right to stop "obscene" materials is upheld.	A draw. Little Sisters, as well as lesbian and gay bookstores in Toronto, Montreal, and Ottawa continue to have their imports seized by Canada Customs.
*Barbeau et al. v. British Columbia** *	British Columbia Supreme Court, 2001	No/yes	Litigant	Constitutionality of common law bar on same-sex marriage.	Unsuccessful. Appealed (see Barbeau 2003, below).	The first court to rule on same-sex marriage. The decision does not have a big impact because of the weakness of the constitutional arguments provided in the judgment.
Halpern v. Canada	Ontario Divisional Court, July 12, 2002	No	Intervener	Constitutionality of common law bar on same-sex marriage.	Successful. The common law bar is unconstitutional. Appealed (see Halpern, 2003, below).	The first court to rule in favour of same-sex marriage.
Hendricks v. Québec	Superior Court of Québec, Sept. 6, 2002	Yes	None	Constitutionality of legislative and civil code ban on same-sex marriage.	Successful. The bans are unconstitutional. Remedy suspended for two years. Under appeal.	The second case in favour of same-sex marriage builds further policy pressure on federal government.

Case	Venue and Year	Litigant Activists?	Egale's Role	Issue	Legal Outcome	Policy Consequences
Chamberlain v. Surrey School Board	Supreme Court of Canada, December 2002	Yes	Intervener	The banning of books depicting same-sex families from the elementary school classroom in Surrey, BC.	Successful. The book ban is unconstitutional.	The school board voted to continue the ban on the original books, but voted to allow two other books that depict same-sex relationships. A major setback for the evangelical movement in British Columbia.
Barbeau et al. v. British Columbia	British Columbia Court of Appeal, May 1, 2003	No/yes	Litigant	Constitutionality of common law bar on same-sex marriage.	Successful. The common law bar is unconstitutional. Remedy is suspended until July 2004. Outdated by subsequent request by Barbeau et al.	The third court to agree with same-sex marriage, overturning a lower British Columbia court ruling against same-sex marriage. Adds to policy pressure for action from federal government.
Halpern et al. v. Canada	Ontario Court of Appeal, June 10, 2003	No/yes	Intervener	Constitutionality of common law bar on same-sex marriage. Appeal from Barbeau et al. 2001.	Successful. The remedy is to take effect immediately. The litigants' marriages (which took place in 2001) are to be immediately recognized by the province. Unlike the other successful decisions, the court did not give the provincial government time to devise a legislative solution.	On June 18, 2003, the federal government announced it would not appeal the Ontario decision and would draft legislation recognizing same-sex marriage. The legislation would be referred to the Supreme Court of Canada and then put to a free vote in the legislature.

Case	Venue and Year	Litigant Activists?	Egale's Role	Issue	Legal Outcome	Policy Consequences
Barbeau et al. v. British Columbia	British Columbia Court of Appeal, July 2003	No/yes	Litigant	Constitutionality of common law bar on same-sex marriage.	Request for immediate lifting of British Columbia suspension in light of Ontario remedy.	Suspension lifted on July 8, 2003. Marriage licences issued for same-sex couples in British Columbia.

* The equality rights section of the Charter states that "15 (1) Every individual is equal before and under the law and has the right to the equal protection and equal benefit of the law without discrimination and, in particular, without discrimination based on race, national or ethnic origin, colour, religion, sex, age, or mental or physical disability." This clause can be overridden using the "notwithstanding clause," section 33 of the Charter which enables legislatures, federal or provincial, to override certain sections of the Charter for a renewable period of five years. See Schedule B, Canada Act (UK), 1982.

** *Halpern v. Canada* (A.G.) (2002), 60 O.R. (3d) 321 (Div. Ct.); *Barbeau v. British Columbia* (A.G.), 2003 BCCA 406; *Re K. & B.* (1995) 125 D.L.R. (4th) 653; and *M. v. H.* [1999] 2 S.C.R. 3. *Barbeau* and *Halpern* appear multiple times in the table in order to show the detailed progress of the "marriage cases" through the various levels of litigation and the policy interactions among the various decisions. However, in the discussion of case totals in the text, *Barbeau* and *Halpern* are each counted once. This standardizes the method of counting the cases across the board, as the other cases have been listed by their Supreme Court appearances and not by their lower court rulings.

Source: Canadian law reports.

Note: Litigant information is drawn from interviews conducted by the author or by publicly available information about litigants' identities.

Rosenberg on the constitutionality of the exclusion of same-sex couples from the federal *Income Tax Act*, and most important, *M v. H*,[64] in which spousal support was awarded on the breakup of a lesbian relationship. Organizing, intervention, and advocacy created political pressures on the court and on the government's reaction to court decisions. Egale, along with trade unions and other allies, were closely involved in *Egan, Rosenberg*,[65] and *M v. H*. The legal networks that had formed in the mid-nineties contributed the lawyers who represented the parties (including interveners) in these cases, and Egale kept up the pressure on the federal government to amend federal laws in anticipation of and in reaction to Charter decisions.[66] Egale acted to bring pressure to bear on provincial governments such as Nova Scotia in cases in which lesbian and gay organizing at the provincial level was weak, and, in other cases such as Quebec worked with provincial lesbian and gay groups to effect policy change at the provincial level.

As the legal direction from the Court in the wake of *M v. H* seemed clear, the federal government forestalled this omnibus case by passing the *Modernization of Benefits and Obligations Act* (2000). This legislation extended the benefits and obligations of common law status to same-sex couples, amending sixty-nine federal laws and regulations affecting spousal benefits and obligations. These included conflict-of-interest regulations under many statutes such as the *Bank Act* and the *Elections Act*, family support claims under the *Bankruptcy Act*, the right to survivor benefits under the Canadian Pension Plan, and the right to benefits for a broad range of federal government appointees and employees including members of Parliament and judges. The bill equated same-sex and opposite-sex common law partners as equal in benefits and obligations to married couples, while maintaining a separate status in law for married and non-married couples.[67] Because of fears of opposition from within the federal caucus, the Department of Justice drafted the legislation so that it would not affect the legal definition of the term "spouse," which would continue to be reserved for heterosexual couples.[68] Egale supported the legislation but argued that the "separate but equal" provision of equating same-sex couples with common-law heterosexual couples would not survive constitutional scrutiny. The Charter decisions also shaped public policy at the provincial level as most provinces, including the three most populous provinces of Ontario, Quebec, and British Columbia, moved to forestall litigation by amending their own legislation in reaction to these rulings.

Throughout the period from 1995–2002, changes in public policy had occurred on the assumption that same-sex couples would not be accorded the right to legal marriage. Yet the potential for a challenge to opposite-sex marriage laws arose almost immediately in the wake of the *M v. H* decision. The Supreme Court of Canada had accepted that same-sex relationships were worthy of legal protection and support and that they were no different from common-law heterosexual relationships which are relatively well protected in Canadian law. Just a few years earlier, in *Layland*[69] in 1993, the Ontario Court of Appeal ruled against a gay couple that wished to marry. After an extensive consultation on the issue of marriage within the lesbian and gay legal and political communities, led and coordinated by Egale, it was decided that no appeal would be launched against the *Layland* decision for fear that the Supreme Court would set a precedent against same-sex marriage.[70] But, *M v. H* changed the legal calculus, and, even before Egale could organize marriage claimants, litigants came forward from Quebec and British Columbia. Lesbian and gay-positive churches also became involved in order to defuse the challenge to religious rights posed by the ban on same-sex marriage. The Metropolitan Community Church (MCC) in Toronto issued banns (a public announcement of a pending marriage) for the marriage of a gay and a lesbian couple (subsequently married in the MCC church in January 2001) in an attempt to circumvent legally the ban on same-sex marriage by using the traditional concept of banns. The church itself became a litigant in the Ontario marriage cases by arguing that its religious freedom under the Charter was violated by preventing its clergy from performing same-sex marriages.[71] Two sets of British Columbia litigants (whose cases were joined), two sets of Ontario litigants (MCC couples and another set of couples), and the Quebec couple (Hendricks-Laboeuf) came before British Columbia, Ontario, and Quebec courts. These cases resulted in legal successes in the three provinces, most notably in Ontario on June 10, 2003 when the Ontario Court of Appeal not only ruled that barring same-sex marriage was unconstitutional but made its decision immediately effective. The British Columbia Court of Appeal, which had earlier ruled in favour of same-sex marriage but had delayed the legal remedy until 2004, lifted its suspension to permit same-sex marriages in British Columbia. Given that same-sex marriages were occurring in two provinces, the federal government, which had begun parliamentary committee hearings on the issue of same-sex marriage in late 2002, decided to undertake another omnibus response to the courts, promising legislation that would legalize same-sex marriage across Canada, subject to a constitutional reference from the Supreme Court of Canada in late 2003 or early 2004.[72]

By the late nineties and the first years of the new millennium, the Charter had remade Canadian public policy on lesbian and gay rights in general and same-sex relationships in particular. The survey of the movement before and after the Charter demonstrates that the place of legally based rights-claiming within the overall ideology and frame of the lesbian and gay movement had changed fundamentally. Where once rights-claiming through litigation had been seen as means to the end of building the gay liberation movement and of fundamentally challenging heteronormative social codes, in the post-Charter period law and litigation were increasingly taken literally as the measure of political and social change. The desire for human rights recognition was no longer placed in the broader context of social and political inequality but rather was defined solely as a question of law and public policy change.

This shift in the ideological framing of the human rights issue can be plausibly linked to the entrenchment of the Charter, which is broadly seen as having given a new legalized rights consciousness to English Canadian political culture. With regard to the effects of the Charter on the mobilizing structure of the movement, it is clear that over a twenty-five-year period the organization of the lesbian and gay movement was transformed from locally based urban groups into a pan-Canadian legal network, dominated by lawyers and by one litigation and advocacy organization—Egale. The emergence of a national advocacy group so strongly focused on litigation and legal strategies and in which informal legal networks play such a critical role would not have occurred without the Charter. Without courts, the most likely route of change in the Canadian political system would have been through organizing within the political parties in order to influence one of the (potentially) governing parties, federally and provincially, or a broader based lobbying and grassroots mobilization effort connecting local organization to provincial and federal organizing. Yet, as lesbian and gay organizing was focused on the courts, other forms of organizing did not occur.

With regard to the effect of institutional change on the policy resources of the movement, the Charter opened up a political opportunity for the lesbian and gay movement that would not have existed otherwise. Institutional change sparked organization around litigation. The organization of activist legal networks and of Egale in turn spurred and supported the litigation. The political opening provided by the Charter galvanized lesbian and gay organizing through legal networks, initially based within the legal profession. The establishment of Egale as a Charter-focused, equality-seeking organization developed into a stable mobilizing structure for the lesbian and gay movement that by the late nineties played a key role in deploying the Charter as a political resource to mount lesbian and gay equality rights claims.

★★★★★

The broad application of the Charter and the positive rulings for lesbian and gay rights from the Supreme Court of Canada can in part be attributed to the influence of Egale and its allies who have acted as the transmission belt bringing social change to the courts. As attitudes toward homosexuality and same-sex relationships have occurred over this period, forming the backdrop for the story presented here, the interveners and supporters of litigation under the Charter have provided a link between the institutional change and policy change through the pressures they have brought to bear on the Court.

Conclusions

Over a twenty-year period, judicial empowerment in Canada has encouraged and reinforced a certain type of social movement politics, one that is dedicated to liberal rights-claiming using litigation as its greatest strategic asset. The enhanced role of the courts in the political system as a result of the entrenchment of the Charter intersected with the rise of the lesbian and gay movement. In the subsequent time period, successful lesbian and gay rights claims before the courts and rapidly, radically changing public policies on sexual orientation pushed the movement toward an ever-deepening material, organizational, strategic, and symbolic commitment to litigation as the means and measure of the changed status of lesbian and gay people in society. This had the effect of centering human rights as the dominant frame and ideology of the movement at the expense of the liberatory goals of the original gay liberation and lesbian feminist movements, of generating a mobilizing structure for lesbian and gay organizing that privileges legal networks and litigation-dominated organizations such as Egale, and of furnishing the movement with policy resources through legal victory. Without the mobilizing structure for litigation and without the pattern of legal victory under the Charter, elected politicians would have avoided the hot button of gay rights. The impact of judicial empowerment thus has been to force lesbian and gay rights onto the political agenda in a way that defines the issue as falling within the ambit of Charter-protected human rights, rights that are increasingly sacrosanct in Canadian political culture.

Critics of Charter politics in Canada from both left and right have pointed to this legalized form of social movement politics as one of the downsides of judicial empowerment. Left critics worry that legal engagement is depoliticizing for social movements while right-wing critics have criticized the Charter for empowering judges to enter a terrain of politics and policy-making that supersedes their legal role. These debates, which often rehash the well-worn ground of the controversy over judicial review, do not capture the political complexities of the current movement toward the recognition of lesbian and gay rights in Canada. Judicial empowerment has privileged the lesbian and gay movement in Canada, relative to movements in countries without strong courts such as Britain. The movement has been able to exercise an important influence on the definition of equality in the Canadian case, an opportunity that was closed to the modern American lesbian and gay movement, which faced the complex historical burdens of the US Bill of Rights.

The deployment of legal strategies by progressive political actors has long been questioned by critics who point to these legalized forms of politics as the downside of legal engagement. Yet, as "law and politics" scholars have noted, the call of human rights is an extraordinarily powerful political resource, especially for marginalized groups.[73] Rights on paper are given force and effect through the political mobilization of group actors. The clarion call of Charter-based equality rights has served to mobilize the lesbian and gay movement in Canada. While the movement has been successful in securing the recognition of legal equality, it has done so through the creation and reinforcement of a legalized form of social movement politics that has focused on rights issues as the major goal of mobilization and litigation as the central political strategy. Charter-based equality has been used to mobilize the lesbian and gay movement in Canada, demonstrating that legally based appeals are not always demobilizing, although they may produce social movement politics that replicate the limits of the liberal rights paradigm.

Notes

1   *Halpern et al. v. Canada* [2003] O.A.C. 405.

2   Tracey Tyler and Tracy Huffman, "Gay Couple Married after Ruling," *Toronto Star*, (June 11, 2003), A1.

3   Robert Wintemute and Mads Andenas, *Legal Recognition of Same-Sex Partnerships: A Study of National, European, and International Law* (Oxford: Hart, 2001), 12–78.

4   Douglas Saunders, "Quiet BC Wedding Reverberates in Europe," *Globe and Mail*, (November 10, 2004), A11.

5   Janet Hiebert, *Charter Conflicts: What is Parliament's Role?* (Montreal and Kingston: McGill-Queen's University Press, 2002).

6   Ran Hirschl, "The Struggle for Hegemony: Understanding Judicial Empowerment Through Constitutionalization in Culturally Divided Polities," *Stanford Journal of International Law* 73 (2000), 93–118; and Neal C. Tate, "Why the Expansion of Judicial Power?" in C. Neal Tate and Torbjörn Vallinder, eds., *The Global Expansion of Judicial Power* (New York: New York University Press, 1995), 1–32.

7   On social movements and political opportunity, the article draws especially from Tarrow's discussion of political opportunity. See Sidney Tarrow, *Power in Movement: Social Movements and Contentious Politics* (Cambridge: Cambridge University Press, 2nd ed., 1998). On historical institutionalism, the article draws on the macro-sociological perspective presented in Paul Pierson and Theda Skocpol, "Historical Institutionalism in Contemporary Political Science," in I. Katznelson and H.V. Milner, eds., *Political Science: The State of the Discipline* (New York and London: W.W. Norton, 2002), 693–721.

8   Stuart A. Scheingold, "Constitutional Rights and Social Change: Civil Rights in Perspective," in Michael W. McCann and Gerald L. Houseman, eds., *Judging the Constitution: Critical Essays on Judicial Lawmaking* (Glenview, IL: Scott, Forseman, 1989), 73–91; Gerald Rosenberg, *The Hollow Hope: Can Courts Bring About Social Change?* (Chicago: University of Chicago Press, 1991); and Michael McCann, *Rights at Work: Pay Equity Reform and the Politics of Legal Mobilization* (Chicago: University of Chicago Press, 1994).

9   Rebecca Mae Salokar, "Beyond Gay Rights Litigation: Using a Systemic Strategy to Effect Political Change in the United States," in Mark Blasius, ed., *Sexual Identities, Queer Politics* (Princeton: Princeton University Press, 2001), 256–85. The US Supreme Court ruling in *Lawrence v. Texas* (2003) on the constitutionality of sodomy laws may lead to some reassessment of the role of litigation in the US lesbian and gay rights movement.

10   Lesbian and gay activists and lawyers were identified through reading the lesbian and gay media and through their public participation in the main organizations of the movement or as lawyers in Charter cases involving lesbian and gay issues, as well as by using the "snowball" method. Two rounds of semi-structured interviews were conducted in 1995–96 and 2001–02. A small number of federal government policymakers were interviewed as well in 1995–96. Over fifty interviews were conducted over the two rounds, and particular insights from interviews are identified by source in the references. All of the interview subjects, except for one federal policymaker, gave permission for their words to be quoted and their identity to be revealed.

11   For example, Rosenberg, *Hollow Hope*; and McCann, *Rights at Work*.

12   Michael Mandel, *The Charter of Rights and the Legalization of Politics in Canada*. Revised, updated, and expanded edition (Toronto: Thomson Educational Publishing, 1994).

13   Susan B. Boyd, S. B. and Claire F. L. Young, "From Same-Sex to No Sex? Trends Towards Recognition of (Same-sex) Relationships in Canada," *Seattle Journal for Social Justice* 3 (2003), 757–93; and Didi Herman, "Are We Family? Lesbian Rights and Women's Liberation," *Osgoode Hall Law Journal*, 28(4), 789–815.

14   F. L. Morton and Rainer Knopff, *The Charter Revolution and the Court Party* (Peterborough, Ontario: Broadview Press, 2000); and Christopher P. Manfredi, *Judicial Power and the Charter: Canada and the Paradox of Liberal Constitutionalism*, 2nd ed. (Don Mills: Oxford University Press, 2001).

15   Michael Adams, *Fire and Ice: The United States, Canada and the Myth of Converging Values* (Toronto: Penguin Canada, 2003).

16   Kamal Ahmed and Gaby Hinsliff, "UK: Gay Couples Win Full Rights to 'Marriage'," *Guardian Online* (March 28, 2004).

17 Christel Stormhøj, "The Queer-Friendly Danish Welfare State? On Heteronormativity and Restricted Recognition." Presented at Gender and Power in the New Europe, the 5th European Feminist Research Conference, August 20–24, 2003 Lund University, Sweden.

18 Barry D. Adam, "The Defense of Marriage Act and American exceptionalism: The 'gay marriage' panic in the United States," *Journal of the History of Sexuality* 12: 2(2003), 259–76.

19 *Lawrence & Garner v. Texas*, 2003 WL 21467086.

20 Lambda Legal, Summary of States Which Prohibit Discrimination Based on Sexual Orientation. http://www.lambdalegal.org/cgi-in/iowa/documents/record?record=185 (2003).

21 David Moats, *Civil Wars: A Battle for Gay Marriage* (Orlando: Harcourt, 2004); and Evan Gerstmann, *Same Sex Marriage and the Constitution* (Cambridge: Cambridge University Press, 2003).

22 Lambda Legal, Marriage Project. http://www.lambdalegal.org/cgi-bin/iowa/documents/record?record=782 (2001).

23 Craig A. Rimmerman, *From Identity to Politics: The Lesbian and Gay Movement in the United States* (Philadelphia: Temple University Press, 2002); and Patricia A. Cain, *Rainbow Rights: The Role of Lawyers and Courts in the Lesbian and Gay Civil Rights Movement* (Boulder: Westview, 2000), 12–22.

24 Alkarim Jivani, *It's Not Unusual: A History of Lesbian and Gay Britain in the Twentieth Century* (Bloomington: Indiana University Press, 1997).

25 Cited in Tom Warner, *Never Going Back: A History of Queer Activism in Canada* (Toronto: University of Toronto Press, 2002), 44.

26 Barry D. Adam, *The Rise of a Gay and Lesbian Movement*, rev. ed. (Boston: Twayne, 1995); and David Rayside, *On the Fringe: Lesbians and Gays in Politics* (Ithaca: Cornell University Press, 1998).

27 Ken Popert, "Gay Rights Now!" *The Body Politic* 19 (August, 1975), 16; and Brian Waite, "Strategy for Gay Liberation," *The Body Politic* 3 (May 1972), 4.

28 Stuart A. Scheingold, *The Politics of Rights: Lawyers, Public Policy and Political Change*, 2nd ed. (Ann Arbor: University of Michigan Press, 2004), 131–45.

29 Warner, *Never Going Back*, 144–49.

30 W. W. Black, "Gay Alliance Toward Equality v. *Vancouver Sun*," *Osgoode Hall Law Journal* 17 (1979), 15–31; and J. Richstone and J. Stuart Russell, "Shutting the Gate: Gay Civil Rights in the Supreme Court of Canada," *McGill Law Journal*, 97:1 (1981), 92–117.

31 Warner, *Never Going Back*, 154–60.

32 Ross Higgins, *De la clandestiné à l'affirmation: pour une histoire de la communauté gaie montréalaise* (Montreal: Comeau & Nadeau, 1999).

33 Didi Herman, *Rights of Passage: Struggles for Lesbian and Gay Legal Equality* (Toronto: University of Toronto Press, 1994), 1–34.

34 Ed Jackson and Stan Persky, *Flaunting It! A Decade of Journalism from the Body Politic* (Vancouver and Toronto: New Star Books and Pink Triangle Press, 1982); and Tim McCaskell, "The Bath Raids and Gay Politics," in Frank Cunningham et al., eds., *Social Movements, Social Change: The Politics and Practice of Organizing* (Toronto: Between the Lines, 1982), 54–72.

35 David Rayside and Evert Lindquist, "AIDS Activism and the State in Canada," *Studies in Political Economy* 39 (1992), 37–76.

36 Barbara Findlay (lawyer), personal interview (Vancouver, 1996).

37 Blair Johnston, "Equality Hearings Delayed," *Goinfo* [Ottawa] 79 (July/August, 1985), 1.

38 Roger Roome, "Parliamentary Committee Recommends Equal Rights for Gays and Lesbians," *Goinfo* 82 (November), 3.

39 *Goinfo* [Ottawa] (1986a). News. [no author]. No. 85 (March), 6.

40 Egale's original name was Equality for Gays and Lesbians Everywhere/Égalité pour les gais et les lesbiennes. The acronym EGALE means "equality" in French. In 2001, Egale changed its name from the long form to simply Egale Canada Inc. Egale also has a spin-off group called Egale Canada Human Rights Trust, which conducts human rights education work. The latter has charitable status in Canadian tax laws and limits its political activities accordingly.

41 *Goinfo* [Ottawa], "Tory Government Will Offer Gays Protection," 2: No. 86 (April 1986), 2; and Christine Jean-François, "New Gay Rights Group Pushing for Government Action," *Goinfo* 90 (September 1986), 1.

42 Diane Kilby (Egale and trade union activist), personal interview (Ottawa, 1996); and LeBlanc interview.

43 Miriam Smith, "Political Activism, Litigation and Public Policy: The Charter Revolution and Lesbian and Gay Rights in Canada, 1985–1999," *International Journal of Canadian Studies* 21 (Spring 2000), 81–110.

44 *Correctional Services of Canada v. Veysey* (1990) 109 N.R. 300.

45 *Haig & Birch v. Canada* (1992), 9 O.R. (3d) 495, 94 D.L.R. (4th) 1, 16 C.H.R.R. D/226, 57 O.A.C. 272, 10 C.R.R. (2d) 287.

[46] Geoffrey York, "Ottawa Accepts Court Ruling on Gay Rights," *Globe and Mail*, (October 1, 1992), A10.

[47] Nitya Iyer, "Categorical Denials: Equality Rights and the Shaping of Social Identity," *Queen's Law Journal* 19: 1 (Fall 1993), 179–207; Douglas Sanders, "Constructing Lesbian and Gay Rights," *Canadian Journal of Law and Society* 9: 2 (Fall 1994), 350–79; and Karn Patrick, "Spousal Benefits," *Capital Xtra* 37 (September 20, 1994), 7.

[48] Avvy Go and John Fisher, *Working Together Across Our Differences: A Discussion Paper on Coalition-Building, Participatory Litigation and Strategic Litigation* (Ottawa: Court Challenges Program, 1998).

[49] *Egan & Nesbitt v. Canada* 124 D.L.R. (4th) 609 SCC.

[50] Deborah McIntosh, "Court Cases in Which Sexual Orientation Arguments under Section 15 of the Charter Were Raised," in Smith, *Lesbian and Gay Rights*, 157–63.

[51] This is based on personal interviews with some of the litigants and on publicly available information about their activist careers.

[52] *Michelle Douglas v. The Queen* [1992] 58 F.T.R. 147 Federal Court (Trial Division).

[53] *Morrissey & Coll v. The Queen* (filed, settled out of court).

[54] R. K. Carty, William Cross, and Lisa Young, *Rebuilding Canadian Party Politics* (Vancouver: University of British Columbia Press, 2000), 32–65.

[55] The Western-based right-populist Reform Party was renamed the Canadian Alliance in 2000. Officially, the party's name is Canadian Reform Conservative Alliance, but in everyday practice, the party uses the name Canadian Alliance. In 2003, the party merged with the Progressive Conservative Party to form the Conservative Party of Canada.

[56] Egale, *Annual Report* (Ottawa, 1998), 1–2.

[57] On the support structure for litigation in Canada, see Charles Epp, *The Rights Revolution: Lawyers, Activists, and Supreme Courts in Comparative Perspective* (Chicago: University of Chicago Press, 1998), 178–220.

[58] John Fisher (executive director, Egale), personal interview (Ottawa, 2001).

[59] *Vriend v. Alberta* [1998] 1 S.C.R. 493.

[60] *Chamberlain v. Surrey School Board No. 26*, 2002 SCC 86. File No. 28654.

[61] *Trinity Western University v. British Columbia College of Teachers* [2001] S.C.J. No. 32.

[62] *Little Sisters Book and Art Emporium v. Canada (Minister of Justice)*, 2000 SCC 69. File No. 26858.

[63] *Hendricks v. Québec (Attorney General)* [2002] J.Q. No. 3816.

[64] *M v. H* [1999] S.C.J. No. 23.

[65] *Rosenberg v. Canada (Attorney General)* [1998] 38 O.R. (3d) 577.

[66] Fisher interview; and Elliott interview.

[67] Egale, "Omnibus Federal Law Recognizes Same-Sex Couples," *InfoEGALE* [Ottawa] (Summer 2000), 1.

[68] Valerie Lawton, "Same Sex Legislation Due this Week," *Toronto Star*, (February 8, 2000), A3.

[69] *Layland v. Ontario* (1993), 14 O.R. (3d) 658, 104 D.L.R. (4th) 214 (Ont. Ct. of Justice, Gen. Div.).

[70] Fisher interview.

[71] Elliott interview; and Kevin Bourassa, and Joe Varnell, *Just Married: Gay Marriage and the Expansion of Human Rights* (Toronto: Doubleday Canada, 2002).

[72] Kim Luman, "Ottawa Backs Gay Marriage," *Globe and Mail* (June 18, 2003), A1.

[73] McCann, *Rights at Work*, 203–21.

Glossary

Egale. This is a national litigation and advocacy group originally formed in 1986 to pressure the Conservative government of Brian Mulroney to uphold lesbian and gay equality rights. The organization would eventually play an important role in the process of Charter litigation.

Judicial empowerment. This term is used to refer to an enhanced use of the courts to implement change, especially in regard to the political system and public policy. The legal mobilization of the human rights movement (including gay and lesbian activism) and its use of law as a political strategy became especially prominent after the entrenchment of the Canadian Charter of Rights and Freedoms in 1982.

Further Reading

Rayside, David M. *On the Fringe: Gays and Lesbians in Politics.* Cornell University Press, 1998.

Rayside's book explores the political activism of gays and lesbians in Britain, Canada, and the US.

Warner, Tom. *Never Going Back: A History of Queer Activism in Canada.* Toronto: University of Toronto Press, 2002.

Written by a gay activist and founding member of Ontario's Coalition for Lesbian and Gay Rights, this book examines the history of lesbian and gay activism as political movement and cultural ideology.

Relevant Websites

Canadian Lesbian and Gay Archives
www.clga.ca
This is the website for a rich archive located in Toronto that is dedicated to preserving lesbian and gay history in Canada. Its mandate is to collect and maintain information related to gay and lesbian life in Canada, including film, material artifacts, and interviews dealing with people, organizations, issues, and events.

UNIVERSAL DECLARATION OF HUMAN RIGHTS (1948)

On December 10, 1948, the General Assembly of the United Nations adopted and proclaimed the Universal Declaration of Human Rights, the full text of which appears in the following pages. Following this historic act the Assembly called upon all Member countries to publicize the text of the Declaration and "to cause it to be disseminated, displayed, read and expounded principally in schools and other educational institutions, without distinction based on the political status of countries or territories."

PREAMBLE

Whereas recognition of the inherent dignity and of the equal and inalienable rights of all members of the human family is the foundation of freedom, justice and peace in the world,

Whereas disregard and contempt for human rights have resulted in barbarous acts which have outraged the conscience of mankind, and the advent of a world in which human beings shall enjoy freedom of speech and belief and freedom from fear and want has been proclaimed as the highest aspiration of the common people,

Whereas it is essential, if man is not to be compelled to have recourse, as a last resort, to rebellion against tyranny and oppression, that human rights should be protected by the rule of law,

Whereas it is essential to promote the development of friendly relations between nations,

Whereas the peoples of the United Nations have in the Charter reaffirmed their faith in fundamental human rights, in the dignity and worth of the human person and in the equal rights of men and women and have determined to promote social progress and better standards of life in larger freedom,

Whereas Member States have pledged themselves to achieve, in co-operation with the United Nations, the promotion of universal respect for and observance of human rights and fundamental freedoms,

Whereas a common understanding of these rights and freedoms is of the greatest importance for the full realization of this pledge,

Now, Therefore THE GENERAL ASSEMBLY proclaims THIS UNIVERSAL DECLARATION OF HUMAN RIGHTS as a common standard of achievement for all peoples and all nations, to the end that every individual and every organ of society, keeping this Declaration constantly in mind, shall strive by teaching and education to promote respect for these rights and freedoms and by progressive measures, national and international, to secure their universal and effective recognition and observance, both among the peoples of Member States themselves and among the peoples of territories under their jurisdiction.

Article 1.

All human beings are born free and equal in dignity and rights. They are endowed with reason and conscience and should act towards one another in a spirit of brotherhood.

Article 2.

Everyone is entitled to all the rights and freedoms set forth in this Declaration, without distinction of any kind, such as race, colour, sex, language, religion, political or other opinion, national or social origin, property, birth or other status. Furthermore, no distinction shall be made on the basis of the political, jurisdictional or international status of the country or territory to which a person belongs, whether it be independent, trust, non-self-governing or under any other limitation of sovereignty.

Article 3.

Everyone has the right to life, liberty and security of person.

Article 4.

No one shall be held in slavery or servitude; slavery and the slave trade shall be prohibited in all their forms.

Article 5.

No one shall be subjected to torture or to cruel, inhuman or degrading treatment or punishment.

Article 6.

Everyone has the right to recognition everywhere as a person before the law.

Article 7.

All are equal before the law and are entitled without any discrimination to equal protection of the law. All are entitled to equal protection against any discrimination in violation of this Declaration and against any incitement to such discrimination.

Article 8.

Everyone has the right to an effective remedy by the competent national tribunals for acts violating the fundamental rights granted him by the constitution or by law.

Article 9.

No one shall be subjected to arbitrary arrest, detention or exile.

Article 10.

Everyone is entitled in full equality to a fair and public hearing by an independent and impartial tribunal, in the determination of his rights and obligations and of any criminal charge against him.

Article 11.

(1) Everyone charged with a penal offence has the right to be presumed innocent until proved guilty according to law in a public trial at which he has had all the guarantees necessary for his defence.

(2) No one shall be held guilty of any penal offence on account of any act or omission which did not constitute a penal offence, under national or international law, at the time when it was committed. Nor shall a heavier penalty be imposed than the one that was applicable at the time the penal offence was committed.

Article 12.

No one shall be subjected to arbitrary interference with his privacy, family, home or correspondence, nor to attacks upon his honour and reputation. Everyone has the right to the protection of the law against such interference or attacks.

Article 13.

(1) Everyone has the right to freedom of movement and residence within the borders of each state.

(2) Everyone has the right to leave any country, including his own, and to return to his country.

Article 14.

(1) Everyone has the right to seek and to enjoy in other countries asylum from persecution.

(2) This right may not be invoked in the case of prosecutions genuinely arising from non-political crimes or from acts contrary to the purposes and principles of the United Nations.

Article 15.

(1) Everyone has the right to a nationality.

(2) No one shall be arbitrarily deprived of his nationality nor denied the right to change his nationality.

Article 16.

(1) Men and women of full age, without any limitation due to race, nationality or religion, have the right to marry and to found a family. They are entitled to equal rights as to marriage, during marriage and at its dissolution.

(2) Marriage shall be entered into only with the free and full consent of the intending spouses.

(3) The family is the natural and fundamental group unit of society and is entitled to protection by society and the State.

Article 17.

(1) Everyone has the right to own property alone as well as in association with others.

(2) No one shall be arbitrarily deprived of his property.

Article 18.

Everyone has the right to freedom of thought, conscience and religion; this right includes freedom to change his religion or belief, and freedom, either alone or in community with others and in public or private, to manifest his religion or belief in teaching, practice, worship and observance.

Article 19.

Everyone has the right to freedom of opinion and expression; this right includes freedom to hold opinions without interference and to seek, receive and impart information and ideas through any media and regardless of frontiers.

Article 20.

(1) Everyone has the right to freedom of peaceful assembly and association.

(2) No one may be compelled to belong to an association.

Article 21.

(1) Everyone has the right to take part in the government of his country, directly or through freely chosen representatives.

(2) Everyone has the right of equal access to public service in his country.

(3) The will of the people shall be the basis of the authority of government; this will shall be expressed in periodic and genuine elections which shall be by universal and equal suffrage and shall be held by secret vote or by equivalent free voting procedures.

Article 22.

Everyone, as a member of society, has the right to social security and is entitled to realization, through national effort and international co-operation and in accordance with the organization and resources of each State, of the economic, social and cultural rights indispensable for his dignity and the free development of his personality.

Article 23.

(1) Everyone has the right to work, to free choice of employment, to just and favourable conditions of work and to protection against unemployment.

(2) Everyone, without any discrimination, has the right to equal pay for equal work.

(3) Everyone who works has the right to just and favourable remuneration ensuring for himself and his family an existence worthy of human dignity, and supplemented, if necessary, by other means of social protection.

(4) Everyone has the right to form and to join trade unions for the protection of his interests.

Article 24.

Everyone has the right to rest and leisure, including reasonable limitation of working hours and periodic holidays with pay.

Article 25.

(1) Everyone has the right to a standard of living adequate for the health and well-being of himself and of his family, including food, clothing, housing and medical care and necessary social services, and the right to security in the event of unemployment, sickness, disability, widowhood, old age or other lack of livelihood in circumstances beyond his control.

(2) Motherhood and childhood are entitled to special care and assistance. All children, whether born in or out of wedlock, shall enjoy the same social protection.

Article 26.

(1) Everyone has the right to education. Education shall be free, at least in the elementary and fundamental stages. Elementary education shall be compulsory. Technical and professional education shall be made generally available and higher education shall be equally accessible to all on the basis of merit.

(2) Education shall be directed to the full development of the human personality and to the strengthening of respect for human rights and fundamental freedoms. It shall promote under-standing, tolerance and friendship among all nations, racial or religious groups, and shall further the activities of the United Nations for the maintenance of peace.

(3) Parents have a prior right to choose the kind of education that shall be given to their children.

Article 27.

(1) Everyone has the right freely to participate in the cultural life of the community, to enjoy the arts and to share in scientific advancement and its benefits.

(2) Everyone has the right to the protection of the moral and material interests resulting from any scientific, literary or artistic production of which he is the author.

Article 28.

Everyone is entitled to a social and international order in which the rights and freedoms set forth in this Declaration can be fully realized.

Article 29.

(1) Everyone has duties to the community in which alone the free and full development of his personality is possible.

(2) In the exercise of his rights and freedoms, everyone shall be subject only to such limitations as are determined by law solely for the purpose of securing due recognition and respect for the rights and freedoms of others and of meeting the just requirements of morality, public order and the general welfare in a democratic society.

(3) These rights and freedoms may in no case be exercised contrary to the purposes and principles of the United Nations.

Article 30.

Nothing in this Declaration may be interpreted as implying for any State, group or person any right to engage in any activity or to perform any act aimed at the destruction of any of the rights and freedoms set forth herein.

CANADIAN CHARTER OF RIGHTS AND FREEDOMS (1982)

Being Part I of the *Constitution Act*, 1982

[Enacted by the Canada Act 1982 [U.K.] c. 11; proclaimed in force April 17, 1982. Amended by the Constitution Amendment Proclamation, 1983, SI/84-102, effective June 21, 1984. Amended by the Constitution Amendment, 1993 [New Brunswick], SI/93-54, *Can. Gaz. Part II*, April 7, 1993, effective March 12, 1993.]

Whereas Canada is founded upon principles that recognize the supremacy of God and the rule of law:

Guarantee of Rights and Freedoms

1. The *Canadian Charter of Rights and Freedoms* guarantees the rights and freedoms set out in it subject only to such reasonable limits prescribed by law as can be demonstrably justified in a free and democratic society.

Fundamental Freedoms

2. Everyone has the following fundamental freedoms:
    (a) freedom of conscience and religion;
    (b) freedom of thought, belief, opinion and expression, including freedom of the press and other media of communication;
    (c) freedom of peaceful assembly; and
    (d) freedom of association.

Democratic Rights

3. Every citizen of Canada has the right to vote in an election of members of the House of Commons or of a legislative assembly and to be qualified for membership therein.

4. (1) No House of Commons and no legislative assembly shall continue for longer than five years from the date fixed for the return of the writs at a general election of its members.

    (2) In time of real or apprehended war, invasion or insurrection, a House of Commons may be continued by Parliament and a legislative assembly may be continued by the

legislature beyond five years if such continuation is not opposed by the votes of more than one-third of the members of the House of Commons or the legislative assembly, as the case may be.

5. There shall be a sitting of Parliament and of each legislature at least once every twelve months.

Mobility Rights

6. (1) Every citizen of Canada has the right to enter, remain in and leave Canada.
    (2) Every citizen of Canada and every person who has the status of a permanent resident of Canada has the right
    (a) to move to and take up residence in any province; and
    (b) to pursue the gaining of a livelihood in any province.
    (3) The rights specified in subsection (2) are subject to
    (a) any laws or practices of general application in force in a province other than those that discriminate among persons primarily on the basis of province of present or previous residence; and
    (b) any laws providing for reasonable residency requirements as a qualification for the receipt of publicly provided social services.
    (4) Subsections (2) and (3) do not preclude any law, program or activity that has as its object the amelioration in a province of conditions of individuals in that province who were socially or economically disadvantaged if the rate of employment in that province is below the rate of employment in Canada.

Legal Rights

7. Everyone has the right to life, liberty and security of the person and the right not to be deprived thereof except in accordance with the principles of fundamental justice.

8. Everyone has the right to be secure against unreasonable search or seizure.

9. Everyone has the right not to be arbitrarily detained or imprisoned.

10. Everyone has the right on arrest or detention
    (a) to be informed promptly of the reasons therefor;
    (b) to retain and instruct counsel without delay and to be informed of that right; and
    (c) to have the validity of the detention determined by way of *habeas corpus* and to be released if the detention is not lawful.

11. Any person charged with an offence has the right
    (a) to be informed without unreasonable delay of the specific offence;
    (b) to be tried within a reasonable time;
    (c) not to be compelled to be a witness in proceedings against that person in respect of the offence;
    (d) to be presumed innocent until proven guilty according to law in a fair and public hearing by an independent and impartial tribunal;
    (e) not to be denied reasonable bail without just cause;
    (f) except in the case of an offence under military law tried before a military tribunal, to the benefit of trial by jury where the maximum punishment for the offence is imprisonment for five years or a more severe punishment;
    (g) not to be found guilty on account of any act or omission unless, at the time of the act or omission, it constituted an offence under Canadian or international law or was criminal according to the general principles of law recognized by the community of nations;
    (h) if finally acquitted of the offence, not to be tried for it again and, if finally found guilty and punished for the offence, not to be tried or punished for it again; and
    (i) if found guilty of the offence and if the punishment for the offence has been varied between the time of commission and the time of sentencing, to the benefit of the lesser punishment.

12. Everyone has the right not to be subjected to any cruel and unusual treatment or punishment.

13. A witness who testifies in any proceedings has the right not to have any incriminating evidence so given used to incriminate that witness in any other proceedings, except in a prosecution for perjury or for the giving of contradictory evidence.

14. A party or witness in any proceedings who does not understand or speak the language in which the proceedings are conducted or who is deaf has the right to the assistance of an interpreter.

Equality Rights

15. (1) Every individual is equal before and under the law and has the right to the equal protection and equal benefit of the law without discrimination and, in particular, without discrimination based on race, national or ethnic origin, colour, religion, sex, age or mental or physical disability.

(2) Subsection (1) does not preclude any law, program or activity that has as its object the amelioration of conditions of disadvantaged individuals or groups including those that are disadvantaged because of race, national or ethnic origin, colour, religion, sex, age or mental or physical disability.

Official Languages of Canada

16. (1) English and French are the official languages of Canada and have equality of status and equal rights and privileges as to their use in all institutions of the Parliament and government of Canada.

(2) English and French are the official languages of New Brunswick and have equality of status and equal rights and privileges as to their use in all institutions of the legislature and government of New Brunswick.

(3) Nothing in this Charter limits the authority of Parliament or a legislature to advance the equality of status or use of English and French.

16.1 (1) The English linguistic community and the French linguistic community in New Brunswick have equality of status and equal rights and privileges, including the right to distinct educational institutions and such distinct cultural institutions as are necessary for the preservation and promotion of those communities.

(2) The role of the legislature and government of New Brunswick to preserve and promote the status, rights and privileges referred to in subsection (1) is affirmed.

17. (1) Everyone has the right to use English or French in any debates and other proceedings of Parliament.

(2) Everyone has the right to use English or French in any debates and other proceedings of the legislature of New Brunswick.

18. (1) The statutes, records and journals of Parliament shall be printed and published in English and French and both language versions are equally authoritative.

(2) The statutes, records and journals of the legislature of New Brunswick shall be printed and published in English and French and both language versions are equally authoritative.

19. (1) Either English or French may be used by any person in, or any pleading in or process issuing from, any court established by Parliament.

(2) Either English or French may be used by any person in, or any pleading in or process issuing from, any court of New Brunswick.

20. (1) Any member of the public in Canada has the right to communicate with, and to receive available services from, any head or central office of an institution of the Parliament or government of Canada in English or French, and has the same right with respect to any other office of any such institution where
>   (a) there is a significant demand for communications with and services from that office in such language; or
>   (b) due to the nature of the office, it is reasonable that communications with and services from that office be available in both English and French.

(2) Any member of the public in New Brunswick has the right to communicate with, and to receive available services from, any office of an institution of the legislature or government of New Brunswick in English or French.

21. Nothing in sections 16 to 20 abrogates or derogates from any right, privilege or obligation with respect to the English and French languages, or either of them, that exists or is continued by virtue of any other provision of the Constitution of Canada.

22. Nothing in sections 16 to 20 abrogates or derogates from any legal or customary right or privilege acquired or enjoyed either before or after the coming into force of this Charter with respect to any language that is not English or French.

Minority Language Educational Rights

23. (1) Citizens of Canada
>   (a) whose first language learned and still understood is that of the English or French linguistic minority of the province in which they reside, or
>   (b) who have received their primary school instruction in Canada in English or French and reside in a province where the language in which they received that instruction is the language of the English or French linguistic minority population of the province, have the right to have their children receive primary and secondary school instruction in that language in that province.

(2) Citizens of Canada of whom any child has received or is receiving primary or secondary school instruction in English or French in Canada, have the right to have all their children receive primary and secondary language instruction in the same language.

(3) The right of citizens of Canada under subsections (1) and (2) to have their children receive primary and secondary school instruction in the language of the English or French linguistic minority population of a province
>   (a) applies wherever in the province the number of children of citizens who have such a right is sufficient to warrant the provision to them out of public funds of minority language instruction; and

(b) includes, where the number of those children so warrants, the right to have them receive that instruction in minority language educational facilities provided out of public funds.

Enforcement

24. (1) Anyone whose rights or freedoms, as guaranteed by this Charter, have been infringed or denied may apply to a court of competent jurisdiction to obtain such remedy as the court considers appropriate and just in the circumstances.

(2) Where, in proceedings under subsection (1), a court concludes that evidence was obtained in a manner that infringed or denied any rights or freedoms guaranteed by this Charter, the evidence shall be excluded if it is established that, having regard to all the circumstances, the admission of it in the proceedings would bring the administration of justice into disrepute.

General

25. The guarantee in this Charter of certain rights and freedoms shall not be construed so as to abrogate or derogate from any aboriginal, treaty or other rights or freedoms that pertain to the aboriginal people of Canada including

(a) any rights or freedoms that have been recognized by the Royal Proclamation of October 7, 1763; and

(b) any rights or freedoms that now exist by way of land claims agreements or may be so acquired.

26. The guarantee in this Charter of certain rights and freedoms shall not be construed as denying the existence of any other rights or freedoms that exist in Canada.

27. This Charter shall be interpreted in a manner consistent with the preservation and enhancement of the multicultural heritage of Canadians.

28. Notwithstanding anything in this Charter, the rights and freedoms referred to in it are guaranteed equally to male and female persons.

29. Nothing in this Charter abrogates or derogates from any rights or privileges guaranteed by or under the Constitution of Canada in respect of denominational, separate or dissentient schools.

30. A reference in this Charter to a province or to the legislative assembly or legislature of a province shall be deemed to include a reference to the Yukon Territory and the Northwest Territories, or to the appropriate legislative authority thereof, as the case may be.

31. Nothing in this Charter extends the legislative powers of any body or authority.

Application of Charter

32. (1) This Charter applies

    (a) to the Parliament and government of Canada in respect of all matters within the authority of Parliament including all matters relating to the Yukon Territory and Northwest Territories; and

    (b) to the legislature and government of each province in respect of all matters within the authority of the legislature of each province.

(2) Notwithstanding subsection (1), section 15 shall not have effect until three years after this section comes into force. [Section 32 came into force on April 17, 1982; therefore, section 15 had effect on April 17, 1985.]

33. (1) Parliament or the legislature of a province may expressly declare in an Act of Parliament or of the legislature, as the case may be, that the Act or a provision thereof shall operate notwithstanding a provision included in section 2 or sections 7 to 15 of this Charter.

(2) An Act or a provision of an Act in respect of which a declaration made under this section is in effect shall have such operation as it would have but for the provision of this Charter referred to in the declaration.

(3) A declaration made under subsection (1) shall cease to have effect five years after it comes into force or on such earlier date as may be specified in the declaration.

(4) Parliament or the legislature of a province may re-enact a declaration made under subsection (1).

(5) Subsection (3) applies in respect of a re-enactment made under subsection (4).

Citation

34. This Part may be cited as the Canadian Charter of Rights and Freedoms.

COPYRIGHT ACKNOWLEDGEMENTS

CHAPTER 7: 'Mixing With People on Spadina': The Tense Relations between Non-Jewish Workers and Jewish Workers, Ruth A. Frager. Source: Chapter 4 from Ruth A. Frager's *Sweatshop Strife: Class, Ethnicity, and Gender in the Jewish Labour Movement of Toronto, 1900–1939* (U of T Press, 1992).

FIGURE 9.1: William Rider-Rider/Canada. Dept of National Defence. William Rider-Rider, Peter Robertson "Gunner of the Cdn Field Artillery comforted a child whose mother has just been killed during a bombardment: Mons, November 1918," *Relentless Verity: Canadian Military Photographers Since 1885*. Ottawa: Public Archives of Canada, 1973, p.81.

FIGURE 9.2: William Rider-Rider / Canada Dept. of National Defence / Library and Archives Cnaada / PA-003535: "Private Lawrence, aged 17, who was wounded fifteen minutes before the declaration of the Armistice ending the First World War."

FIGURE 9.3: William James Topley / Library and Archives Canada / PA-042857: "Group in front of the Patriotic fund Headquarters."

CHAPTER 11: Reproduced with the permission of the publisher Lexis Nexis Canada Inc.: Behiels, Michael D. "Pierre Elliot Trudeau's Legacy: The Canadian Charter of Rights and Freedoms." Supreme Court Law Review Second Series, Vol. 19: August 2003.

CHAPTER 12: Miriam Smith: 'Social Movements and Judicial Empowerment: Courts, Public Policy, and Lesbian and Gay Organizing in Canada,' Politics and Society, vol. 33, no. 2 (June 2005): 327–353.

APPENDIX A: "Universal Declaration of Human Rights", 1948. United Nations. Reprinted with the permission of the United Nations.

INDEX

egalitarian rights, 24, 27–37, 40, 61;
    violations of, 13–16
Egan & Nesbitt v. Canada, 229, 230–31, 232, 236
egocentrism, 12
elderly, rights of, 56
Elections Act, 236
Elgin/Buxton Mission, 88
Elizabeth II, Queen, 207
emancipation, 84
Emergency Committee on Civil Rights, 32
employment:
    discrimination in, 52, 55, 220, 223–24, 225;
    equity in, 3, 14, 35;
    as human right, 50
employment benefits, same-sex couples and, 220
English-language rights, 193, 209
enlistment, 162
"equal citizenship," 50
Equality for Gays and Lesbians Everywhere. *See* Egale.
equality rights, 11–21, 36, 45, 61, 203, 207, 223, 225, 229, 230, 239
Equality Writes Ad Hoc Committee, 227
equal protection under the law, right to, 61
Equal Rights Association, 16
Ethiopia, 171
ethnic groups:
    discrimination against, 13, 52;
    language rights of, 187
    ethnicity, 3, 62;
    eugenics and, 148;
    gender and, 127;
    tension in, 117–22, 124–25, 130
"ethnic solitudes," multiplicity of, 19
ethnocentrism, 121, 130, 133
ethno-cultural communities, 202, 216, 229
eugenics, 135–50, 152;
    age and, 144–45;
    consent and, 140–46;
    diagnosis and, 143–44, 146–49;
    gender and, 145–48;
    history of, 135–39;
    Nazi, 145;
    negative vs. positive, 136
Eugenics Board of Alberta, 138–50
European Convention of Human Rights, 52
European Union, 224–25
evolution, 135
evolutionary racial ideas, 88–89
exceptionalism, American, 223
Exclusion Act. *See* Chinese Immigration Act.
expatriation, of Japanese Canadians, 62–64
extinguishment, of Indigenous land, 103, 109, 113

Fair Accommodation Practices acts, 35, 58n19.
    See also Ontario.
Fair Employment Practices (FEP) legislation, 74.
    See also Ontario.
"false consciousness," 12

family allowances, 172
family life, traditional, 14
family rights, 220–21
Famous Five, 137
Fascism, 117, 128
federalism, 191, 198, 213, 221;
    flaws of, 202;
    incompatibility of with rights, 202, 209;
    opposition to, 138
Federal-provincial programme of cooperation for the promotion of bilingualism in education, 191.
    See also Official Languages in Education Program.
Fédération des francophones hors-Québec, 194
feeblemindedness, 137
Feinberg, Abraham, 70
Female Employees Fair Remuneration acts, 47
feminism. *See* women's liberation movement.
Finch, Mezza, 121–22
Finlay, James, 63
First Nations. *See* Aboriginal peoples.
Forest, Georges, 194
Foucault, Michel, 95n6
franchise, 47, 50, 85–86, 87, 88;
    for Acadians, 185;
    for enlisted Aboriginal Canadians, 177n33;
    for enlisted minors, 162;
    for military women nurses, 177n33;
    for working class, 159
francization, 193, 198
francophone identity, 1, 6
francophone rights, 16, 183, 208.
    See also French-language rights.
Francq, Gustave, 176n29
Franklin v. Evans, 92
Fraser, Steven, 129
Fred Christie Defence Committee, 18
freedom of assembly, 44
freedom of association, 44, 48, 53, 57n11
freedom of conscience, 214
freedom of religion, 214
free press, 44
free speech, 28, 44, 45, 48, 57n11, 61
French Civil Law, 158
French Empire, 100, 101
French immersion programs, 192
French-language rights, 182–96
    elimination of, 186–89;
    establishment of, 183–86;
    resurgence of, 189–91
Front de libération du Québec, 1
Frost, Leslie, 47
fur industry, 122–24

Galton, Francis, 135
"Gang of Eight," 205–6
garment industry, Toronto, 116–30
gay liberation movement. *See* homosexuality; lesbian and gay.